# LIFE OF
# HEBER C. KIMBALL

# LIFE OF
# HEBER C. KIMBALL

## AN APOSTLE

THE FATHER AND FOUNDER OF THE BRITISH MISSION

---

BY

## ORSON F. WHITNEY

---

It is easy in the world to live after the world's opinion; it is easy in solitude to live after our own; but the great man is he who, in the midst of the crowd, keeps with perfect sweetness the independence of his character.—*Emerson.*

---

PUBLISHED BY THE KIMBALL FAMILY,
SALT LAKE CITY, UTAH.

Printed At The Juvenile Instructor Office.
1888

Copyright 2017

ISBN-13: 978-1540792716
ISBN-10: 1540792714

A re-typeset of the original 1888 first edition. This edition restores the original text, even keeping the spelling errors. The original page numbers are in [].

TO THE MEMORY OF

## My GRANDFATHER

AND TO THE GREAT

## Cause of Truth,

*For which he lived and died; and to all who love that
Memory and that Cause,
This Volume is reverently Dedicated by*
THE AUTHOR.

---

Who was Orson F. Whitney's grandfathers?

His grandfathers were Heber C. Kimball, First Counselor in the First Presidency, and Newel K. Whitney, Presiding Bishop of the Church. His father, Horace, was a writer and musician of some talent, and his mother, Emma Mar Kimball Whitney, was also an eloquent writer and advocate for the restored gospel.

# CONTENTS

## PREFACE
1888 PREFACE BY ORSON F. WHITNEY. . . . . . . . . . . . . . . . . . . . . . . . . . . . . . . . . . . . . . . 15

## CHAPTER 1
A PRE-EXISTENT GLIMPSE—GOD'S NOBLE AND GREAT ONES—HEBER C. KIMBALL A PREDESTINED PROPHET—OPENING OF THE LAST DISPENSATION—HEBER'S BIRTH AND PARENTAGE—EARLY INCIDENTS OF HIS LIFE—CLOUDS AND SUNSHINE. . . . . . . . . . . . . . . . 19

## CHAPTER 2
A ROMANTIC EPISODE—HEBER'S MARRIAGE WITH VILATE MURRAY—A SOLDIER AND A FREE MASON—HIS STERN ARRAIGNMENT OF THE ANCIENT ORDER—DEATH OF HEBER'S FATHER AND MOTHER. . . . . . . . . . . . . . . . . . . . . . . . . . . . . . . . . . . . . . . . . . . . . . . . . . . . . . . 22

## CHAPTER 3
HEBER'S POETIC NATURE—A ROUGH DIAMOND—EARLY RELIGIOUS EXPERIENCE—JOINS THE BAPTIST CHURCH—"SIGNS IN THE HEAVENS ABOVE"—HEBER C. KIMBALL AND BRIGHAM YOUNG—THE EVERLASTING GOSPEL. . . . . . . . . . . . . . . . . . . . . . . . . . . . . . . . . . . . . . . 26

## CHAPTER 4
HEBER EMBRACES MORMONISM—A BAPTISM OF FIRE—DEATH OF MIRIAM YOUNG—VILATE KIMBALL A MOTHER TO THE ORPHANS—HEBER ORDAINED AN ELDER—RESOLVES TO VISIT KIRTLAND. . . . . . . . . . . . . . . . . . . . . . . . . . . . . . . . . . . . . . . . . . . . . . . . . . . . . . . . . 30

## CHAPTER 5
THE LAND OF SHINEHAH—ARRIVAL OF HEBER AND BRIGHAM IN KIRTLAND—THEIR FIRST MEETING WITH THE PROPHET—THE KIMBALLS AND YOUNGS REMOVE TO OHIO—VEXATIOUS SUITS AND MOB VIOLENCE—FALLEN ON PERILOUS TIMES. . . . . . . . . . . 33

## CHAPTER 6
THE GATHERING OF THE TITANS—HEBER'S TESTIMONY OF JOSEPH AND THE TWELVE—THEIR MIGHTY MISSION—THE TEST OF FAITH—ZION'S CAMP. . . . . . . . . . . . . . 36

## CHAPTER 7
THE REDEMPTION OF ZION—ENOCH'S CITY TO RETURN—OBJECT OF THE UNITED ORDER—CAUSE OF THE JACKSON COUNTY EXPULSION—THE WHEAT FROM THE CHAFF . . . . . . . . . . . . . . . . . . . . . . . . . . . . . . . . . . . . . . . . . . . . . . . . . . . . . . . . . . . . . . . . 37

## CHAPTER 8
THE ZION'S CAMP EXPEDITION—JOSEPH AS A PROPHET-GENERAL—FINDING OF THE BONES OF ZELPH, THE ANCIENT—REBELLION IN THE CAMP—JOSEPH PREDICTS A SCOURGE—HEBER'S FAILURE AS A LAUNDERER—ZION'S CAMP SAVED BY A STORM. . . . . . 39

## CHAPTER 9
THE FISHING RIVER REVELATION—WHY ZION WAS NOT REDEEMED—THE CHOLERA IN CAMP—THE TEST OF FAITH COMPLETE—THE SHADOW OF A COMING EVENT. . . . . . . . . 48

## CHAPTER 10
BUILDING THE TEMPLE—JOSEPH AND HEBER WORKING IN THE QUARRY—THE THEOLOGICAL SCHOOL—A LESSON ON FAITH—CALL OF THE TWELVE—HEBER C. KIMBALL ORDAINED AN APOSTLE. . . . . . . . . . . . . . . . . . . . . . . . . . . . . . . . . . . . . . . . . . . . . . . 54

## CHAPTER 11

FIRST MISSION OF THE TWELVE—HEBER REVISITS THE SCENES OF HIS CHILDHOOD—MOBBING AN ABOLITIONIST—"THE ACCUSER OF THE BRETHREN"—DAYS OF REPENTANCE AND REFORMATION. .................................................. 61

## CHAPTER 12

HEBER'S DESCRIPTION OF THE TEMPLE—ITS DEDICATION—ANGELS ADMINISTER—THE "BELOVED DISCIPLE" JOHN SEEN—THE SOLEMN ASSEMBLY—THE ELDERS ENDOWED WITH POWER FROM ON HIGH—HEBER'S LONE MISSION. ................................. 65

## CHAPTER 13

THE WORSHIP OF MAMMON—THE TEMPORAL ABOVE THE SPIRITUAL—THE KIRTLAND BANK—FINANCIAL DISASTERS—APOSTASY—HEBER SORROWS OVER THE DEGENERACY OF THE TIMES. ............................................................................ 71

## CHAPTER 14

ZION'S SHIP AMONG THE BREAKERS—"SOMETHING NEW MUST BE DONE TO SAVE THE CHURCH"—HEBER C. KIMBALL APPOINTED TO OPEN THE BRITISH MISSION—SPIRITUAL THINGS TO THE FRONT—RIGHTING THE SHIP—HEBER'S PROPHECY TO WILLARD RICHARDS—"YEA, IN THE NAME OF THE LORD, THOU SHALT GO WITH ME"—THE DEPARTURE FOR ENGLAND. ....................................................................... 73

## CHAPTER 15

FAREWELL TO NATIVE LAND—"UPON THE WIDE, WIDE SEA"—HEBER'S DREAM OF JOSEPH—A SHIP OUT OF HER RECKONING—A DYING CHILD HEALED—APOSTLE HYDE PREACHES ON BOARD—ARRIVAL AT LIVERPOOL—THE ELDERS LEAP ASHORE. ...................... 79

## CHAPTER 16

STRANGERS IN A STRANGE LAND—THE ELDERS LED BY THE SPIRIT TO PRESTON—"TRUTH WILL PREVAIL"—THE REVEREND JAMES FIELDING—WONDERFUL FULFILLMENT OF HEBER'S PROPHECIES—A PEOPLE PREPARED FOR THE GOSPEL—THE ELDERS PREACH IN PRESTON ........................................................................................ 83

## CHAPTER 17

SATAN ALARMED—THE POWERS OF EVIL CONSPIRE AGAINST THE ELDERS—CHAPELS AND CHURCHES CLOSED AGAINST THEM—THE REVEREND MR. FIELDING IN HIS REAL COLORS—THE WORK CONTINUES TO SPREAD—AN ARMY OF DEMONS ATTACK THE ELDERS—THE DAWN AND VICTORY. ............................................... 87

## CHAPTER 18

THE REVEREND MR. FIELDING FORBIDS THE ELDERS TO BAPTIZE THEIR CONVERTS—APOSTLE KIMBALL'S ANSWER: "THEY ARE OF AGE AND CAN ACT FOR THEMSELVES"—PREMIER GLADSTONE AND SECRETARY EVARTS—FREE AGENCY AND UNRIGHTEOUS DOMINION—HEBER C. KIMBALL BAPTIZES IN THE RIVER RIBBLE—A MIRACLE ........................................................................................ 91

## CHAPTER 19

THE ELDERS SEPARATE FOR THE BETTER PROSECUTION OF THEIR WORK—JENNETTA RICHARDS—THE PRESTON BRANCH ORGANIZED—HEBER GOES TO WALKERFOLD—ANOTHER MINISTER'S "CRAFT IN DANGER"—MORE OF HEBER'S PROPHECIES—"WILLARD, I BAPTIZED YOUR WIFE TO-DAY". ..................................................................... 93

## CHAPTER 20

THE MISSION OF ELIAS—THE SYMBOLISM OF THE UNIVERSE—THE PAST PREPARATORY TO THE PRESENT AND FUTURE—THE WAY PREPARED FOR THE FULNESS OF THE GOSPEL—THE "LESSER LIGHTS" OF ENGLAND—FIELDING, MATTHEWS AND AITKEN—THE STARS PALING BEFORE THE SUN. ..................................................................... 97

## CHAPTER 21

THE TEMPERANCE REFORM IN PRESTON—A WORK PREPARATORY TO THE GOSPEL—PREACHING IN THE "COCK PIT"—HEBER WRITES HOME AN ACCOUNT OF HIS MISSION—THE WORK IN CUMBERLAND—EPISODE OF MARY SMITHIES—"SHE SHALL LIVE TO BECOME A MOTHER IN ISRAEL". .... 101

## CHAPTER 22

HEBER WRITES TO WILLARD IN BEDFORD—THE ELDERS BECOME LICENSED PREACHERS—THE "MILK" AND "MEAT OF THE WORD"—RAPID SPREAD OF THE WORK—MIRACLES—HEBER'S DREAM OF THE BULL AND FIELD OF GRAIN—A DISAPPOINTED MOB. .... 104

## CHAPTER 23

THE VOICE OF THE GOOD SHEPHERD—HEBER CONVERTS WHOLE VILLAGES—THE SPIRIT OF THE MASTER UPON HIS SERVANT—THE CHRISTMAS CONFERENCE IN PRESTON. .... 110

## CHAPTER 24

THE WORK OF GOD NOT DEPENDENT UPON MAN—HUMILITY A SOURCE OF POWER—EVERY MAN CHOSEN AND FITTED FOR HIS SPHERE—EXAMPLE OF PAUL THE APOSTLE—HEBER "HITS THE ROCK" IN LONGTON—THE APOSTLES VISIT THE BRANCHES PRIOR TO RETURNING TO AMERICA.. .... 113

## CHAPTER 25

CONDITION OF THE CHURCH AT HOME—PRUNING OFF THE DEAD BRANCHES—A DAY OF CHOOSING—APOSTATES CONSPIRE TO OVERTHROW THE CHURCH—FLIGHT OF THE PROPHET FROM KIRTLAND—FALL OF OLIVER COWDERY AND OTHER APOSTLES—"SHOW UNTO US THY WILL, O LORD, CONCERNING THE TWELVE!". .... 116

## CHAPTER 26

HEBER'S FAREWELL TO CHATBURN—AN AFFECTING SCENE—HIS SYMPATHY FOR THE POOR OF ENGLAND—THE APRIL CONFERENCE IN PRESTON—TWO THOUSAND SAINTS ASSEMBLE—JOSEPH FIELDING APPOINTED TO PRESIDE OVER THE BRITISH MISSION. .... 120

## CHAPTER 27

DEPARTURE FOR LIVERPOOL—HEBER'S LETTER TO THE SAINTS IN CHATBURN AND DOWNHAM—HIS PREDICTION CONCERNING THOMAS WEBSTER—ITS STRICT FULFILLMENT .... 123

## CHAPTER 28

THE ELDERS SAIL FOR HOME—A STORM AT SEA—HOW HEBER FOUND FAVOR WITH THE STEWARD—ARRIVAL AT NEW YORK—THE "GARRICK" AGAIN VICTORIOUS—JOURNEY TO KIRTLAND—ON TO FAR WEST—HAPPY MEETING WITH JOSEPH AND THE BRETHREN. .... 126

## CHAPTER 29

THE LAND WHERE ADAM DWELT—THE SAINTS IMPELLED TOWARD THEIR DESTINY—PERSECUTION REVIVES—ADAM-ONDI-AHMAN—THE ALTAR OF THE ANCIENT OF DAYS. .... 129

## CHAPTER 30

TIMES THAT TRIED MEN'S SOULS—THE MOB GATHERING AGAINST FAR WEST—BATTLE OF CROOKED RIVER—DEATH OF DAVID W. PATTEN—DAYS OF DARKNESS AND DISASTER .... 132

## CHAPTER 31

THE FALL OF FAR WEST—JOSEPH AND HIS BRETHREN BETRAYED TO THE ENEMY—HEBER FACING THE TRAITORS—HIS FEARLESS DENUNCIATION AND FIRM TESTIMONY—ATROCITIES OF THE MOB—HEBER'S PROPHECY OF RETRIBUTION—HE VISITS THE PROPHET IN RICHMOND JAIL. .... 135

## CHAPTER 32

MEMORIAL TO THE MISSOURI LEGISLATURE—A CHAPTER OF INFAMY—HOW MISSOURI REDRESSED THE WRONGS OF THE SUFFERING SAINTS—BRIGHAM AND HEBER SETTING IN ORDER THE CHURCH—ARRANGING FOR THE EXODUS. .............................. 140

## CHAPTER 33

THE FIRST PRESIDENCY INSTRUCT THE APOSTLES—BRIGHAM YOUNG CHOSEN PRESIDENT OF THE TWELVE—THE EXODUS BEGUN—HEBER TARRIES IN MISSOURI TO MINISTER TO HIS IMPRISONED BRETHREN—HIS FAITHFUL BUT FRUITLESS EFFORTS FOR THEIR RELEASE—THE LORD SPEAKS TO HEBER. .................................................... 147

## CHAPTER 34

A WORD FOR THE FALLEN—ONLY GOD KNOWETH THE WHEREFORE AND WHY—ORSON HYDE'S REPENTANCE AND RETURN TO THE CHURCH—HEBER C. KIMBALL AND HYRUM SMITH HIS CHAMPIONS—ISAAC RUSSELL'S APOSTASY—HEBER WRITES TO THE CHURCH IN ENGLAND.......................................................................... 151

## CHAPTER 35

THE BRETHREN IN LIBERTY JAIL—JUDGE KING'S COUP D'ETAT—THE MOB AGAIN THREATEN FAR WEST—FIENDS IN HUMAN FORM—THE PROPHET REGAINS HIS FREEDOM—THE APOSTLES FULFILL REVELATION—FIRST CONFERENCE OF THE CHURCH IN ILLINOIS... 153

## CHAPTER 36

NAUVOO THE BEAUTIFUL—HEBER'S PREDICTION OVER THE FATED CITY—ELDER RIGDON'S ALARM—HEBER'S SECOND ENCOUNTER WITH EVIL SPIRITS—PARLEY P. PRATT ESCAPES FROM PRISON, FULFILLING HEBER'S PROPHECY. ................................. 158

## CHAPTER 37

AN EPIDEMIC OF DISEASE—JOSEPH HEALS THE MULTITUDE—BRIGHAM AND HEBER START ON THEIR MISSION TO ENGLAND—SICKNESS BY THE WAY—HEBER POISONED—HIS LIFE SAVED BY BRIGHAM............................................................. 160

## CHAPTER 38

ON TO KIRTLAND—MIRACULOUSLY SUPPLIED WITH MONEY—CONDITION OF AFFAIRS AT THE OLD CHURCH HEADQUARTERS. .................................................. 167

## CHAPTER 39

THE APOSTLES SAIL FOR ENGLAND—GROWTH OF THE BRITISH MISSION DURING HEBER'S ABSENCE—LABORS OF ELDERS WOODRUFF AND TAYLOR—FIRST COUNCIL OF THE TWELVE AMONG THE NATIONS—WILLARD RICHARDS ORDAINED AN APOSTLE. ................. 169

## CHAPTER 40

HEBER VISITS THE BRANCHES RAISED UP DURING HIS FORMER MISSION—HIS REPORT OF THEIR CONDITION AND STANDING—FIRST GENERAL CONFERENCE AT MANCHESTER ............................................................................. 172

## CHAPTER 41

FOUNDING THE LONDON CONFERENCE—APOSTLES KIMBALL, WOODRUFF AND SMITH CHOSEN FOR THE WORK—SEEKING FOR A MAN WITH THE SPIRIT OF GOD—THE FIRST CONVERT—THE ELDERS HOLD OPEN-AIR MEETINGS IN TABERNACLE SQUARE. ....... 175

## CHAPTER 42

FATHER CORNER BAPTIZED—THE APOSTLES VISIT THE REVEREND ROBERT AITKEN—HEBER ATTACKED WITH CHOLERA—THE WORK IN OTHER PARTS—SECOND CONFERENCE AT MANCHESTER—BRIGHAM ACCOMPANIES HEBER TO LONDON—CONVERSION OF THE REV. JAMES ALBION................................................................. 178

## CHAPTER 43

OPENING OF THE YEAR 1841 IN LONDON—ENCOURAGING SUCCESS OF THE ELDERS—HEBER C. KIMBALL BLESSES THE QUEEN OF ENGLAND—THE WOOLWICH BRANCH ORGANIZED—ORGANIZATION OF THE LONDON CONFERENCE—THE PROSPECT OF WAR BETWEEN GREAT BRITAIN AND THE UNITED STATES HASTENS THE RETURN OF THE APOSTLES TO AMERICA. . . . . . . . . . . . . . . . . . . . . . . . . . . . . . . . . . . . . . . . . . . . . . . . . . . . . . . 184

## CHAPTER 44

HEBER ORGANIZES THE BIRMINGHAM CONFERENCE—MEETING OF THE APOSTLES IN MANCHESTER PRIOR TO RETURNING TO AMERICA—ORSON HYDE PRESENT ON HIS WAY TO PALESTINE—THE EXTENSIVE WORK OF ONE YEAR. . . . . . . . . . . . . . . . . . . . . . . . . . . . . 187

## CHAPTER 45

THE APOSTLES SAIL FOR HOME—ARRIVAL AT NEW YORK—HEBER'S LETTER TO THE "MILLENNIAL STAR"—HAPPY MEETING WITH THE PROPHET AND THE SAINTS AT NAUVOO—LABORS SPIRITUAL AND TEMPORAL—HEBER'S PHRENOLOGICAL CHART. . . . 189

## CHAPTER 46

REVELATION OF CELESTIAL MARRIAGE—SECRECY THE PRICE OF SAFETY—JOSEPH TESTS HEBER AND MAKES HIM HIS CONFIDANT—HOW VILATE KIMBALL WAS CONVERTED—HEBER AND VILATE GIVE THEIR DAUGHTER HELEN TO THE PROPHET IN CELESTIAL MARRIAGE
. . . . . . . . . . . . . . . . . . . . . . . . . . . . . . . . . . . . . . . . . . . . . . . . . . . . . . . . . . . . . . . . . . . . . . 194

## CHAPTER 47

JOHN C. BENNETT'S APOSTASY—HEBER AND THE TWELVE SENT OUT TO REFUTE HIS SLANDERS—HEBER'S FAMOUS SERMON: "THE CLAY IN THE HANDS OF THE POTTER"—INCEPTION OF THE RELIEF SOCIETY—VILATE'S VOW AND HEBER'S PRAYER
. . . . . . . . . . . . . . . . . . . . . . . . . . . . . . . . . . . . . . . . . . . . . . . . . . . . . . . . . . . . . . . . . . . . . . 199

## CHAPTER 48

HEBER'S LAST MISSION TO THE GENTILES—JOSEPH SMITH A CANDIDATE FOR THE PRESIDENCY OF THE UNITED STATES—THE APOSTLES HIS ELECTIONEERERS—THE MARTYRDOM—RETURN OF THE TWELVE TO NAUVOO. . . . . . . . . . . . . . . . . . . . . . . . . . . 204

## CHAPTER 49

CHOICE OF JOSEPH'S SUCCESSOR—A MIRACLE—THE MANTLE OF JOSEPH FALLS UPON BRIGHAM YOUNG—HEBER C. KIMBALL HIS RIGHT HAND MAN. . . . . . . . . . . . . . . . . . . 207

## CHAPTER 50

THE WORK MOVES ON IN SPITE OF PERSECUTION AND APOSTASY—THE NAUVOO TEMPLE FINISHED AND DEDICATED—THE SAINTS PREPARE FOR THEIR REMOVAL TO THE ROCKY MOUNTAINS. . . . . . . . . . . . . . . . . . . . . . . . . . . . . . . . . . . . . . . . . . . . . . . . . . . . . . . . . . . . 209

## CHAPTER 51

THE EXODUS—HEBER'S PROPHECY FULFILLED—EVACUATION OF NAUVOO—THE CAMP OF ISRAEL ON SUGAR CREEK—BRIGHAM AND HEBER LEAD THE CHURCH WESTWARD—ARRIVAL AT THE MISSOURI RIVER. . . . . . . . . . . . . . . . . . . . . . . . . . . . . . . . . . . . . . . . . . . . . . . . . 212

## CHAPTER 52

DESTINATION OF THE SAINTS—THE CALL FOR THE MORMON BATTALION—HEROIC RESPONSE OF THE EXILES—BRIGHAM, HEBER AND WILLARD AS RECRUITING SERGEANTS—DEPARTURE OF THE BATTALION—THE CAMP OF ISRAEL GOES INTO WINTER QUARTERS—THE FALL OF NAUVOO. . . . . . . . . . . . . . . . . . . . . . . . . . . . . . . . . . . . . . . . . 215

## CHAPTER 53

THE WORD AND WILL OF THE LORD CONCERNING THE CAMP OF ISRAEL—THE PIONEERS START FOR THE ROCKY MOUNTAINS—NAMES OF THE HEROES—INCIDENTS OF THE JOURNEY WEST. . . . . . . . . . . . . . . . . . . . . . . . . . . . . . . . . . . . . . . . . . . . . . . . . . . . . . . . . . . . . . . . . 218

## CHAPTER 54

ARRIVAL AT GRAND ISLAND—THE PIONEER BUFFALO HUNT—HEBER KILLS HIS FIRST BISON—THE SPIRIT OF LEVITY REBUKED—THE PIONEERS REACH FORT LARAMIE...... 224

## CHAPTER 55

THE PIONEERS CROSS THE PLATTE—GOVERNOR BOGGS AND THE MISSOURIANS—COL. BRIDGER "A THOUSAND DOLLARS FOR A BUSHEL OF WHEAT"—THE PIONEERS' FIRST GLIMPSE OF THE VALLEY OF THE GREAT SALT LAKE.................................................... 226

## CHAPTER 56

THE PIONEERS ENTER THE VALLEY—EXPLORING AND COLONIZING—A RENEWAL OF COVENANTS—SELECTION OF INHERITANCES—RETURN OF THE LEADERS TO WINTER QUARTERS............................................................................. 227

## CHAPTER 57

THE FIRST PRESIDENCY REORGANIZED—HEBER ATTAINS TO "THE HONOR OF THE THREE"—SECOND JOURNEY TO THE MOUNTAINS—SICKNESS AND DISTRESS—HEBER'S CHARACTER AS A COLONIZER.................................................... 231

## CHAPTER 58

THE CRICKET PLAGUE—SAVED BY THE GULLS—HEBER'S FAMOUS PROPHECY "STATES GOODS" SOLD IN GREAT SALT LAKE CITY CHEAPER THAN IN NEW YORK..................... 233

## CHAPTER 59

HEBER C. KIMBALL CHIEF JUSTICE AND LIEUTENANT GOVERNOR OF DESERET—IN THE LEGISLATURE—LAYING THE CORNER STONES OF THE SALT LAKE TEMPLE—HEBER'S CONSECRATION PRAYER—HIS PROPHECY IN RELATION TO THE TEMPLE—HE PREDICTS ANOTHER FAMINE............................................................. 237

## CHAPTER 60

THE FAMINE OF '56—HEBER A SECOND JOSEPH—A SAVIOR TO HIS PEOPLE—VILATE A MINISTERING ANGEL—A STRANGE PIECE OF COUNSEL—PRESIDENT KIMBALL'S LETTERS, DESCRIPTIVE OF THE FAMINE, TO HIS SON WILLIAM, IN ENGLAND................... 241

## CHAPTER 61

THE HAND-CART EMIGRATION—PERISHING IN THE SNOW—HEROIC CONDUCT OF WILLIAM H. AND DAVID P. KIMBALL—PRESIDENT KIMBALL'S PLEA AND EXERTIONS IN BEHALF OF THE SUFFERERS—THE UTAH WAR—THE GREAT REBELLION.............................. 248

## CHAPTER 62

SOME OF HEBER'S FAMILY HISTORY—A PATRIARCHAL HOUSEHOLD—NAMES OF HIS WIVES AND CHILDREN—EPISODE OF ABRAM A. KIMBALL—PETER, THE CHILD OF PROMISE—HEBER AT FAMILY PRAYERS—DAVID H. KIMBALL'S STORY—HEBER P. AND SOLOMON F. KIMBALL IN THE BLACK HAWK WAR................................................................ 250

## CHAPTER 63

ANECDOTES AND REMINISCENCES OF HEBER C. KIMBALL—THE MAN AS OTHERS KNEW HIM—GOLDEN GRAINS FROM THE SANDS OF MEMORY.................................. 258

## CHAPTER 64

GEMS FROM THE WORDS OF HEBER—SPIRIT RAPPINGS—ADDRESS AT THE FUNERAL OF MARY FIELDING SMITH—LOVE, UNITY AND THE COURAGE OF THE RIGHTEOUS—JOSEPH AND THE KEYS OF THE KINGDOM—CULTIVATION OF SPIRITS—HEAVEN AND HELL—ADMINISTRATION OF ANGELS AND THE SPIRITS OF THE ANCIENTS—THE RESURRECTION—THE SPIRIT WORLD—THE CLAY AND THE POTTER—A CAUSE OF APOSTASY—A MIRACULOUS CANE—THE CHURCH IN HEAVEN..................................................................... 271

## CHAPTER 65

GEMS FROM HEBER'S WORDS CONTINUED—HIS STRIKING VIEW OF TIME AND ETERNITY—HIS WORDS AND WORKS AT THE LAST CONFERENCE PRECEDING HIS DEATH—HIS LAST SERMON. . . . . . . . . . . . . . . . . . . . . . . . . . . . . . . . . . . . . . . . . . . . . . . . . . . . . . . . . . . . 277

## CHAPTER 66

DEATH OF VILATE, THE WIFE OF HEBER'S YOUTH—PRESIDENT BRIGHAM YOUNG PREACHES HER FUNERAL SERMON—HIS FEELING TRIBUTE TO HER MEMORY—HEBER PROPHESIES OF HIS OWN DEATH. . . . . . . . . . . . . . . . . . . . . . . . . . . . . . . . . . . . . . . . . . . . . . . . . . . . . . . . . . . . 280

## CHAPTER 67

DEATH OF APOSTLE KIMBALL—ALL ISRAEL MOURNS—EXPRESSIONS IN HONOR OF THE ILLUSTRIOUS DEAD. . . . . . . . . . . . . . . . . . . . . . . . . . . . . . . . . . . . . . . . . . . . . . . . . . . . . . . . . 282

## CHAPTER 68

OBSEQUIES OF PRESIDENT KIMBALL—TRIBUTES AND TESTIMONIES OF HIS BROTHER APOSTLES—"HE WAS A MAN OF AS MUCH INTEGRITY AS ANY MAN WHO EVER LIVED"—EARTH RETURNS TO EARTH AND THE SPIRIT UNTO GOD WHO GAVE IT. . . . . . . . . . . . . . . . . . . . 285

## APPENDIX

A GLIMPSE OF THE GREAT BEYOND—THRILLING EXPERIENCE OF DAVID PATTEN KIMBALL LOST IN THE DESERT—COMMUNING WITH THE SPIRITS OF THE DEPARTED—DAVID PREDICTS HIS OWN DEATH AND THE DEATH OF FOUR OTHERS—THE FULFILLMENT. . . 298

## INDEX. . . . . . . . . . . . . . . . . . . . . . . . . . . . . . . . . . . . . . . . . . . . . . . . . . . . . . . . . . . . . . . . . . . . 307

# PREFACE

IN presenting this work to the public, I not only fulfill the desires of my own heart and those of my kindred who have undertaken to publish what is here written and compiled, but likewise, I am persuaded, the wish of our departed ancestor. Laying the foundation for such a work while living (as the copious selections from his own writings will testify), he left its bringing forth as a sacred legacy to his posterity.

For many years this duty, unenjoined in words, but accepted by all in the light of a behest, was permitted to lie dormant. The death of President Kimball, on the 22nd of June, 1868, was a calamity so sudden and heavy in its effect upon his family, as to almost paralyze thought and effort. Though trained to independence and self-reliance, under his wise government, and never pampered in ease and luxury, they had ever looked to him for guidance and support, and had never known the weight of responsibility resting upon him as their parent and provider, only as from time to time he had taken certain ones into his confidence and permitted them to share his burdens.

In his absence they were as sheep that had lost their [iv] shepherd. "Who will provide for us now, and what shall we do to earn a livelihood?" Such were the thoughts presented to their minds, and the questions asked of their secret souls, as they looked around upon their temporal situation. The division of the parental estate had left them comfortable, though far from rich. None of his sons had trades, but all had been brought up to work. Realizing that a city life was no longer their lot, they resolved to separate, and, following the example of their ancestors for generations, go forth and colonize new regions. Some moved north, and others south, but few remaining in the city of their birth, and, at the expiration of fifteen years, many had become almost as strangers to each other.

About the year 1883 a spirit of inquiry commenced to manifest itself among the members of the Kimball family, causing them to "feel after" and evince more interest in each other's welfare. This sentiment increasing, some of the elder members at length opened a correspondence on the subject of a family reunion. By many this was deemed impracticable, owing to their scattered condition; some living in Idaho, some in southern Arizona, and others in California; and nearly all in circumstances which, it was thought, would hardly justify the necessary outlay. But the desire to meet and mingle with each other finally grew so urgent and so general among them—as though some unseen power were at work in their midst, with this object in view—that it was determined to hold the reunion, no matter what sacrifice it entailed. [v]

During the summer of 1886, a number of the family met and appointed a Committee on Reunion, selecting for the day, June 14th, 1887, (the eighty-sixth anniversary of their father's birth) and as the place of meeting, Fuller's Hill Gardens, Salt Lake City. There came together on that memorable occasion, fully three hundred members and relatives of the Kimball family, with others who had been invited to take part in the celebration. A programme, previously arranged, consisting of speeches, recitations, readings, vocal and instrumental music, etc., was carried out to the satisfaction and enjoyment of all, and the remainder of the time spent in amusement, festivity and recreation. A spirit of peace and union, powerful and indescribable, pervaded the assembly and permeated the whole occasion, causing every heart to swell with love, and many an eye to glisten with tears of gratitude and joy. As though, indeed, the spirits of the departed were there, bringing with them the sweet influences of the celestial world, to weld anew, as links of a broken chain, the souls of those so long separated. It was, in truth, a day never to be forgotten.

There were present, of the family of President Kimball, nineteen sons, six daughters, and several of his widows, besides grand-children, and many other relatives, near and remote.

One of the features of the programme was a sketch of the life of Heber C. Kimball, written for the occasion and read by his grandson, the author of this work. This incident determined and united the family on a project mooted by its members and partly executed several years [vi] before. It was the publication of the life of Heber C. Kimball. On the evening of the day of reunion the male members of the family met and appointed a committee of five on publication. Several thousand dollars of undivided property, still in the estate, was devoted to the purpose, and the author hereof solicited, and by unanimous voice chosen and engaged to write the history.

Such, in brief, were the immediate causes of the coming forth of this volume.

In the execution of my task, I have felt strongly moved upon by the spirit of my grandsire, and verily believe that his presence, though unseen, has hovered near me.

This book is written from the standpoint of a Latter-day Saint. It makes no apology for the honest expression of views, which, however false or fanatical they may seem to others, are in the opinion of the author only such as ought to be entertained by every sincere believer and defender of the faith. It is issued with the humble and earnest hope that it may go forth as a messenger of Truth to help prepare the way for greater things that shall glorify God and redeem Zion. The life of a man like Heber C. Kimball, with its lessons of faith and humility, of virtue, courage and devotion, cannot fail, if prayerfully read, to do something in this direction.

Wherever possible, I have allowed the subject to speak for himself. In lieu of converting facts found of record in his Journal into "original matter," I have presented them mostly in all their freshness and simplicity; [vii] as flowers of the field, with the dew and fragrance of their native meadow yet clinging to them. This has been done, not only out of deference to the wishes of his relatives, who desired that much of what their father had written should be incorporated in the book of his life, but because I have deemed it best to thus project upon the reader's mental vision, by means of the most superior process, the portrait of the man and his mission as painted by himself.

I cannot close this introductory without expressing my deep sense of indebtedness to the kind friends who have aided and encouraged me in the bringing forth of this, my first book. Their name is legion, but limited space will only permit the mention of a few. To President Wilford Woodruff and others of the Apostles I am indebted for kind words and encouragement, and for the appointment of a committee, at my request, to read the manuscript and pass upon it critically, as to doctrinal and historical points, before placing it in the hands of the printer; to Elder George Reynolds, for his intelligent advice and labors as one of said committee; and to Edward W. Tullidge Esq., the veteran author, for a collection of facts relating to my subject, gathered during his extensive experience as historian and biographer. Last, but not least, in this limited reference, I am under obligations of gratitude to my uncle, Solomon F. Kimball, the chief promoter of this work, who first approached me on the subject of writing his father's life, and who, in all the toils incident to such an undertaking, has proved my staunch and faithful friend. **[viii]**

My labor, I need hardly say, in conclusion, has been one of love and duty. I have fulfilled, imperfectly I know, conscientiously I am as certain, what I considered a sacred trust; the result of which I now lay at the feet of an indulgent public.

ORSON F. WHITNEY.

NOVEMBER, 1888. **[ix-17]**

# CHAPTER 1

A PRE-EXISTENT GLIMPSE—GOD'S NOBLE AND GREAT ONES—HEBER C. KIMBALL A PREDESTINED PROPHET—OPENING OF THE LAST DISPENSATION—HEBER'S BIRTH AND PARENTAGE—EARLY INCIDENTS OF HIS LIFE—CLOUDS AND SUNSHINE

MEN like Heber C. Kimball are not accidents. They are emphatically and in the truest sense, children of destiny. If we seek their origin, and would know their truth, we must not halt beside the humble cradle which "lulled their infant cares to rest." We must rise on spirit wings above the mists and vapors of mortality, and survey them in the light of an eternal existence, a life without beginning or end. Says one of old:

"Now the Lord had shown unto me, Abraham, the intelligences that were organized before the world was; and among all these there were many of the noble and great ones; and God saw these souls that they were good, and he stood in the midst of them, and he said, 'These I will make my rulers'; for he stood among those that were spirits, and he saw that they were good, and he said unto me, Abraham, thou art one of them, thou wast chosen before thou wast born."

Again, unto Jeremiah:

"Before I formed thee in the belly I knew thee; and before thou earnest forth out of the womb I sanctified thee, and I ordained thee a prophet unto the nations."

What is true in this respect of ancient prophets, is true also of modern prophets, for verily are their origin, their mission and their destiny the same. [18]

It devolved upon the subject of this writing to come forth at a time which has no parallel in all the ages of the past. The day of God's power and of Zion's glory was about to dawn. The Sun that set in blood behind Judea's hills was soon to rise o'er Zion's mountain-tops and flood the world with light. The latter-day dispensation was opening. All things in Christ were to be gathered in one. The curtain of history had risen on the last act of the tragedy of Time.

Would God leave the world without "great and noble ones" at such an hour?

---

Heber Chase Kimball was born into this life June 14th, 1801. The same soil produced him that in colonial times brought forth an Ethan Allen, the hero of Ticonderoga, and in later years the wondrous twain of spirits known to the world as Joseph Smith and Brigham Young.

A far greater work than the capture of a British fortress was in the future of this Mormon triad of "Green Mountain boys," who went forth "in the name of the great Jehovah" to invade the strongholds of Satan, and plant the banner of gospel truth above the ramparts of his conquered citadels.

Heber's birthplace was the town of Sheldon, Franklin County, Vermont, ten miles from the shores of Lake Champlain. He was the fourth child and second son in a family of seven, the order of whose birth was as follows: Charles Spaulding, Eliza, Abigail, Heber Chase, Melvina, Solomon and Daniel Spaulding, the last named of whom died in infancy. These were all born in Sheldon.

His father's name was Solomon Farnham Kimball, a [19] native of Massachusetts, where he was born in the year 1770. He was "a man of good moral character," and, though he professed no religion, taught his children correct principles. His mother's maiden name was Anna Spaulding; she was a strict Presbyterian, lived a virtuous life, and, according to her best knowledge, reared her family in the ways of righteousness. She was the daughter of Daniel and Speedy Spaulding, and was born in Plainfield, New Hampshire, on the banks of the Connecticut river.

The Kimballs were of Scotch descent, their ancient name, it is believed, being Campbell. Heber's grandfather and a brother came from England, in time to assist in gaining the independence of the colonies. In America his ancestors and those of the Prophet Joseph Smith were related by marriage.

Heber derived his given name from a Judge Chase, of Massachusetts, by whom his father was reared from a boy, and who chanced to visit his former protege soon after his son was born. The judge himself proposed the christening, and the parents being nothing loth, Heber Chase Kimball became the infant's name.

This Judge Chase, though presumably "learned in the law," like many of his class in those primitive, common sense days was not above following the humbler pursuits of life. He was a blacksmith, and taught Heber's father that trade, and when he had married, helped him to establish his smithy in the town of Sheldon.

"At the close of the Revolutionary War," says Heber, "my father was thirteen years old, and I can remember his rehearsing to me some of the scenes of the war.

"He was captain of a company of militia in Sheldon, and wore a cocked hat of the old English style, a straight-[20]bodied coat, and short breeches with a knee buckle, long stockings, and Suwarrow boots with a pair of tassels.

"He was partly bald, had dark-brown hair, blue eyes, sandy whiskers and light complexion; he was five feet, eleven inches high, and weighed two hundred pounds and upwards.

"He engaged in farming and clearing land, burning the wood into coal and ashes; he had also a forge and trip-hammer, in the manufacture of wrought iron.

"About the time of the embargo, before the last war with England, my father lost his property, as it was invested in salts, potash and pearlash; the embargo, having shut down the gate of commerce between the United States and England, left his property in his hands without much value."

In February, 1811, the Kimballs migrated from Vermont, and settled in West Bloomfield, Ontario County, New York, five hundred miles from their former home, where the head of the family reengaged in his occupations of farmer and blacksmith, to which he now added that of builder. He was aided in his new venture by Judge Towsley, of Scipio, Cayuga County, who had employed him for several months as foreman in a blacksmith shop.

Heber thus describes the journey from Sheldon to West Bloomfield, with incidents of their subsequent experience in that then new country:

"My father took my mother and six children in a sleigh, with one span of horses, a change of clothing for each of us, and some blankets to wrap us in; when we reached St. Albans, my father bought each of his boys a hat, which was the first hat I ever had on my head. We traveled on Lake Champlain, on the ice, and the wind being very high, my hat was blown off and lost. [21]

"We traveled on the ice up to Whitehall, a distance of one hundred and ten miles, where, spring being open, he traded his sleigh for a wagon and proceeded to West Bloomfield.

"He built an academy in West Bloomfield, also two tavern stands and several private dwellings; he made nearly all of the edge tools, such as scythes, augers, axes, knives, etc., also plow-shares and agricultural implements, for the country around, to a distance of fifty or sixty miles; and sometimes he had eight forges employed at once.

"He continued living in West Bloomfield during the 'last war' with England, which place was on the thorough-fare between Albany and Buffalo, on what was called 'the public turnpike,' and on which the soldiery passed during the war (1812-15). It was flourishing times, there being plenty of business and money, and most men in business became involved, so that when the war closed bankruptcy became common, as every merchant, tavern-keeper and grog-shop had a banking establishment, and issued 'shin-plasters' from one cent up to five dollars.

"My father lost the greater portion of his property, which broke him up in that place. He then moved two and one-half miles east, half way between East and West Bloomfield, where he bought a farm of a Mr. Stewart, near a small lake called Stewart's Pond; on this farm there was a little improvement. Here he established blacksmithing, built a large tavern stand, barns and other out-houses, and once more set out an orchard of various kinds of fruit trees.

"This was in the year 1816, which was called the cold season; the same year that the black spot was seen on the sun. The following year we had little to subsist [22] upon; for some three weeks we gathered milk weeds, and boiled and ate them, not having salt to put on them. It was with difficulty that bread could be procured."

Evidently the elder Kimball was a man of force and energy, qualities which his son Heber inherited, and in turn transmitted to his posterity. The Kimballs, with scarcely an exception, are, in this respect, of just such sterling stuff as their sire and grandsire, and invariably "show the mettle of their pasture," as colonizers, wherever their lot is cast.

The limited amount of schooling that Heber received in these days of his childhood and early youth, extended from his fifth to his fourteenth year, and was of the quality usually found in the primitive village schools of the day. He was not an ardent lover of books, but drew his lessons from life and nature in all their multiplied and varied phases. It was "about the time of the great eclipse in 1806" that he commenced going to school. The eclipse he "remembered well," as his father was about starting on a journey, but was obliged to wait on account of the darkness.

At the age of fourteen he was put to work in his father's blacksmith shop, and acquired a knowledge of that useful trade. When he was nineteen, his father having met with further reverses, he was thrown entirely upon his own resources, and now began to taste the first bitter experience of his life.

He was a singular compound, in his nature, of courage and timidity, of weakness and strength; uniting a penchant for mirth with a proneness to melancholy, and blending the lion-like qualities of a leader among men, with the bashfulness and lamb-like simplicity of a child.

He was not a coward; a braver man probably never [23] lived than Heber C. Kimball. His courage, however, was not of that questionable kind which "knows no fear." Rather was it of that superior order, that Christ-like bravery, which feels danger and yet dares to face it. He had all the sensitiveness of the poet—for he was both a poet and a prophet from his mother's womb—and inherited by birthright the power to feel pleasure or suffer pain, in all its exquisiteness and intensity.

Hear his own pathetic story of his early hardships:

"At this time, I saw some days of sorrow; my heart was troubled, and I suffered much in consequence of fear, bashfulness and timidity. I found myself cast abroad upon the world, without a friend to console my grief. In these heart-aching hours I suffered much for want of food and the comforts of life, and many times went two or three days without food to eat, being bashful and not daring to ask for it.

"After I had spent several weeks in the manner before stated, my oldest brother, Charles, hearing of my condition, offered to teach me the potter's trade. I immediately accepted the offer, and continued with him until I was twenty-one.

"While living with my brother, he moved into the town of Mendon, Monroe County, New York, six miles north of Bloomfield, towards the city of Rochester, where he again established the potter's business."

Here Heber finished learning his trade and commenced working for wages. Six months later he purchased his brother's business and set up in the same line for himself, in which he prospered for upwards of ten years. [24]

## CHAPTER 2

A ROMANTIC EPISODE—HEBER'S MARRIAGE WITH VILATE MURRAY—A SOLDIER AND A FREE MASON—HIS STERN ARRAIGNMENT OF THE ANCIENT ORDER—DEATH OF HEBER'S FATHER AND MOTHER.

MEANWHILE, the sun of love dawned on his horizon. In one of his rides he chanced to pass, one warm summer day, through the little town of Victor, in the neighboring County of Ontario. Being thirsty, he drew rein near a house where a gentleman was at work in the yard, whom he asked for a drink of water. As the one addressed went to the well for a fresh bucketful of the cooling liquid, he called to his daughter Vilate, to fetch a glass from the house, which he filled and sent by her to the young stranger.

Heber was deeply impressed with the beauty and refined modesty of the young girl, whose name he understood to be "Milaty," and who was the flower and pet of her father's family. Lingering as long as propriety would permit, or the glass of water would hold out, he murmured his thanks and rode reluctantly away.

How suggestive this incident, of Whittier's pretty tale, "Maud Muller:"

"Thanks!" said the Judge, "a sweeter draught
From a fairer hand was never quaffed."

It was not long before he again had "business" in Victor, and again became thirsty (?) just opposite the house where the young lady lived. Seeing the same [25] gentleman in the yard whom he had accosted before, he hailed him and asked him for a cup of water. This time the owner of the premises offered to wait upon him in person, but Heber, with the blunt candor for which he was noted, nearly took the old gentleman's breath by saying: "If you please, sir, I'd rather My-Laty would bring it to me."

"Laty," as she was called in the household, accordingly appeared and did the honors as before, and returned blushing to meet the merriment and good-natured badinage of her sister and brothers.

She, however, was quite as favorably impressed with the handsome young stranger, as he with her. More visits followed, acquaintance ripened into love, and on the 7th of November, 1822, they were married.

Vilate Murray—for that was her name—was the youngest child of Roswell and Susannah Murray. She was born June 1st, 1806, in Florida, Montgomery County, New York. At the time of her marriage she was only in her seventeenth year.

The Murrays, like the Kimballs, were of Scotch descent, and came to America during the Seven Years' War. As a race they were gentle, kind-hearted, intelligent and refined. Through many of them ran a vein of poetry. Vilate herself wrote tender and beautiful verses. She was an ideal wife for a man like Heber C. Kimball, by whom she was ever cherished as the treasure that she was.

Heber was now past twenty-one, and fast developing into as fine a specimen of manhood as one might wish to behold. Tall and powerful of frame, with piercing black eyes that seemed to read one through, and before whose searching gaze the guilty could not choose but quail, he moved with a stateliness and majesty all his own, as far [26] removed from haughtiness and vain pride, as he from the sphere of the upstart who mistakes scorn for dignity, and an overbearing manner as an evidence of gentle blood. Heber C. Kimball was a humble man, and in his humility, no less than his kingly stature, consisted his dignity, and no small share of his greatness. It was his intelligence, earnestness, simplicity, sublime faith and unwavering integrity to principle that made him great, not the apparel he wore, nor the mortal clay in which his spirit was clothed. Nevertheless, nature had given him a noble presence in the flesh, worthy the godlike stature of his spirit.

Vilate Kimball

## CHAPTER 2

"A combination and a form, indeed,
Where every God did seem to set his seal
To give the world assurance of a man."

The son and grandson of a soldier, he had early enrolled in an independent horse company of the New York State militia. Under Captain Sawyer, of East Bloomfield, and his successor in command, he trained fourteen years; one year more would have exempted him from further military service. He remarks, with honest pride, that he was never brought before a court martial or found delinquent in his duty.

Heber was also a Free Mason. In 1823 he received the first three degrees of masonry in the lodge at Victor. The year following, himself and five others petitioned the chapter at Canandaigua, the county seat of Ontario County, for the degrees up to the Royal Arch. The petition was favorably considered, but before it could be acted upon the Morgan anti-mason riot broke out, and the Masonic Hall, where the chapter met, was burned by the mob and all the records consumed.

Says Heber, "There are thousands of Masons who lived in those days, who are well aware of the persecution [27] and unjust proceedings which were heaped upon them by the anti-Masons; not as many as three of us could meet together, unless in secret, without being mobbed.

"I have been as true as an angel from the heavens to the covenants I made in the lodge at Victor.

"No man was admitted into a lodge in those days except he bore a good moral character, and was a man of steady habits; and a man would be suspended for getting drunk, or any other immoral conduct. I wish that all men were masons and would live up to their profession; then the world would be in a much better state than it is now."

Commenting on the degeneracy of the Ancient Order—the old, old story of the persecuted becoming persecutors—he continues:

"I have been driven from my houses and possessions, with many of my brethren belonging to that fraternity, five times, by mobs led by some of their leading men. Hyrum Smith received the first three degrees of masonry in Ontario County, New York. Joseph and Hyrum Smith were Master Masons, yet they were massacred through the instrumentality of some of the leading men of that fraternity, and not one soul of them has ever stepped forth to administer help to me or my brethren belonging to the Masonic Institution, or to render us assistance, although bound under the strongest obligations to be true and faithful to each other in every case and under every circumstance, the commission of crime excepted."

Yes, Masons, it is said, were even among the mob that murdered Joseph and Hyrum in Carthage Jail. Joseph, leaping the fatal window, gave the masonic signal of distress. The answer was the roar of his murderers' muskets and the deadly balls that pierced his heart. [28]

Heber continued to prosper in business, working in his pottery in summer, and at his forge in winter. He purchased land, built houses, planted orchards, and otherwise "situated himself to live comfortably."

In the spring of 1825, he gave his father a home with him in Mendon. The old gentleman was now a widower, his wife, Heber's mother, having died in February, 1824, at West Bloomfield, of consumption. Her husband survived her a little over a twelve-month, when he, too, fell a victim to the same malady.

It is a coincidence worthy of note that the deaths of Heber and Vilate were also about one year apart, she passing away first, and he, like his father, following soon the footsteps of his beloved partner to the spirit land.

We have traced his life's record through its initial stages. He was now fairly on the threshold of his remarkable career. [29]

## CHAPTER 3

HEBER'S POETIC NATURE—A ROUGH DIAMOND—EARLY RELIGIOUS EXPERIENCE—JOINS THE BAPTIST CHURCH—"SIGNS IN THE HEAVENS ABOVE"—HEBER C. KIMBALL AND BRIGHAM YOUNG—THE EVERLASTING GOSPEL

HEBER'S temperament was religious and poetical. Sociable as he was, and even bubbling over with mirth, at times, his soul was essentially of a solemn cast. He loved solitude, not with the selfish spirit of the misanthrope, but for the opportunities it gave of communing with his own thoughts—a pleasure that only poet minds truly feel—and of listening to the voice of God and nature, expressed in all the countless and varied forms of life.

He was capable of sensing fully—though probably he had never seen or heard—those sublime words of the poet:

> "There is a pleasure in the pathless woods;
> There is a rapture on the lonely shore;
> There is society, where none intrudes,
> By the deep sea, and music in its roar.
> I love not man the less, but nature more,
> From these our interviews; in which I steal
> From all I may be, or have been before,
> To mingle with the universe and feel
> What I can ne'er express, yet cannot all conceal."

True, he was a diamond in the rough, but a diamond, nevertheless, for all of its incrustations. Unlettered and untaught, save in nature's school, the university of experience, where he was an apt and profound scholar, he [30] was possessed of marvelous intuition, a genius God-given, which needed no kindling at a college shrine to prepare it for the work which providence had designed.

Not but that education would have polished the gem, causing it to shine with what the natural eye would deem a brighter lustre; but the fact remains that Heber

C. Kimball, as he was, not as he might have been, was best adapted for the divine purpose, the career marked out for him by the finger of Deity.

It is not strange that a nature of this kind, solemn, thoughtful and inspirational, should have been led early to seek "an anchor for the soul," a knowledge of the truth as it is in Christ Jesus. But his search for many years was in vain; he found not among the sects of Christendom the precious pearl which an honest soul will sell all that it hath to obtain.

"From the time I was twelve years old," says he, "I had many serious thoughts and strong desires to obtain a knowledge of salvation, but not finding anyone who could teach me the things of God, I did not embrace any principles of doctrine, but endeavored to live a moral life. The priests would tell me to believe in the Lord Jesus Christ, but never would tell me what to do to be saved, and thus left me almost in despair.

"During the time I lived in Mendon, I mostly attended the meetings of the Baptist church, and was often invited to unite myself with them. I received many pressing invitations to unite with different sects, but did not see fit to comply with their desires, until a revival took place in our neighborhood. I had passed through several of their protracted meetings and had been many times upon the anxious bench to seek relief from the 'bands of sin and death.' But no relief could I find until the meetings were passed by. [31]

"At this time I concluded to put myself under the watch-care of the Baptist church and unite myself to them; as soon as I had concluded to do this, the Lord administered peace to my mind, and accordingly, the next day I went, in company with my wife, and we were baptized by Elder Elijah Weaver; and we partook of the sacrament on that day for the first and also the last time with them."

Such was his initiation into religion, as pertaining to a Christian sectarian church. Though not in accord with the Baptist faith in all its teachings, it seemed to him to be nearest right according to the Bible; probably from the stress laid upon baptism by immersion, manifestly the Bible mode, and the only true way of being "born of the water." Besides, he deemed it wise to put a "guard" upon himself, to "keep him from running into evils."

The peace of mind that he experienced, as the sanction of the Holy One upon a prudent and conscientious act, was but the prelude and prophecy of far greater things to follow. The heavens were bestirring themselves. The invisible world was up in arms. Truth and Error were taking the field. The latter-day conflict had begun. The signs of the coming of the Son of Man were showing themselves in the heavens.

It was the eventful night of September 22nd, 1827. Says Heber C. Kimball:

"I had retired to bed, when John P. Greene, who was living within a hundred steps of my house, came and waked me up, calling upon me to come out and behold the scenery in the heavens. I woke up and called my wife and Sister Fanny Young (sister to Brigham Young), who was living with us, and we went out-of-doors.

"It was one of the most beautiful starlight nights, [32] so clear that we could see to pick up a pin. We looked to the eastern horizon, and beheld a white smoke arise toward the heavens; as it ascended it formed itself into a belt, and made a noise like the sound of a mighty wind, and continued southwest, forming a regular bow dipping in the western horizon. After the bow had formed, it began to widen out and grow clear and transparent, of a bluish cast; it grew wide enough to contain twelve men abreast.

"In this bow an army moved, commencing from the east and marching to the west; they continued marching until they reached the western horizon. They moved in platoons, and walked so close that the rear ranks trod in the steps of their file leaders, until the whole bow was literally crowded with soldiers. We could distinctly see the muskets, bayonets and knapsacks of the men, who wore caps and feathers like those used by the American soldiers in the last war with Britain; and also saw their officers with their swords and equipage, and the clashing and jingling of their implements of war, and could discover the forms and features of the men. The most profound order existed throughout the entire army; when the foremost man stepped, every man stepped at the same time; I could hear the steps. When the front rank reached the western horizon a battle ensued, as we could distinctly hear the report of arms and the rush.

"No man could judge of my feelings when I beheld that army of men, as plainly as ever I saw armies of men in the flesh; it seemed as though every hair of my head was alive. This scenery we gazed upon for hours, until it began to disappear.

"After I became acquainted with Mormonism, I learned that this took place the same evening that Joseph Smith received the records of the Book of Mormon from [33] the angel Moroni, who had held those records in his possession.

"John Young, sen., and John P. Greene's wife, Rhoda, were also witnesses.

"My wife, being frightened at what she saw, said, 'Father Young, what does all this mean?'

"'Why, it's one of the signs of the coming of the Son of Man,' he replied, in a lively, pleased manner.

"The next night similar scenery was beheld in the west by the neighbors, representing armies of men who were engaged in battle."

A wonderful foreshadowing, truly, of the warfare to be waged between the powers of good and evil, from the time Truth sprang from earth and Righteousness looked down from heaven upon the boy Joseph, predestined to bring to light the buried records of the past.

In Mendon began the intimacy and friendship of Heber C. Kimball with his life-long colleague, Brigham Young. The Youngs and Greenes, like the Kimballs, were from Vermont, and had moved into Mendon a few months prior to the event just related. In religion they were Reformed Methodists, but, being in lowly circumstances, were looked down upon by the proud members of the flourishing church to which they belonged. They had suffered greatly from sickness, and had seen much sorrow and affliction.

Heber's generous heart and that of his noble wife were touched with sympathy and compassion for their situation. Says he: "To them my heart was united, because a principle had existed in my breast from earliest childhood, to plead the cause of suffering innocence, to go on the side of the oppressed at all times; neither do I remember to have ever varied from this fixed principle at any time in my life; I have many times turned aside [34] from the company of those who were highly esteemed in the world, and sought the society of the poor and humble, those who loved the ways of the Lord better than the praise of the world."

He found in these families, which were related, congenial associates, for they too were seekers after truth, and truth they were all destined, ere many days, to find.

Sometime in the fall or winter of 1831, about three weeks after Heber and his wife had joined the Baptist church, five Elders of the Church of Jesus Christ of Latter-day Saints came from Pennsylvania to Victor, five miles from Mendon, and tarried at the house of Phineas H. Young. They were Eleazer Miller, Elial Strong, Alpheus Gifford, Enos Curtis and Daniel Bowen. Hearing of these men, Heber was prompted by curiosity to visit them, "when," says he, "for the first time I heard the fullness of the everlasting gospel."

The glorious news of a restored gospel and a living priesthood, commissioned of and communicating with the heavens; the promise of the Holy Ghost with signs following the believer, as in days of old; the wondrous declaration of angels revisiting the earth, breaking the silence of ages, bringing messages from another world;—all this fell upon the heart of this God-fearing man, and on the hearts of his friends and companions, like dew upon thirsty ground. As the voice of a familiar spirit, it seemed an echo from the far past—something they had known before.

To hear, with Heber, was to believe. He was convinced that they taught the truth, and was constrained to receive their testimony. He saw, more clearly than ever, that he had embraced but a portion of the truth in the Baptist faith; that the creeds of Christendom, the religions of the world, were but remnants of the everlasting [35] gospel, broken off fragments of that grand Rock of Ages, the same in all generations; mixtures of truth and error; lesser lights at best in the broad firmament of human faith; and that now, when the Sun had once more arisen, the stars that lit the night must pale away.

Both Heber and Brigham received the word gladly, and were impelled to testify of its divinity. Then the power of God fell upon them.

"On one occasion," says Heber, "Father John Young, Brigham Young, Joseph Young and myself had come together to get up some wood for Phineas H. Young. While we were thus engaged we were pondering upon those things which had been told us by the Elders, and upon the saints gathering to Zion, when the glory of God shone upon us, and we saw the gathering of the saints to Zion, and the glory that would rest upon them; and many more things connected with that great event, such as the sufferings and persecutions that would come upon the people of God, and the calamities and judgments that would come upon the world.

"These things caused such great joy to spring up in our bosoms that we were hardly able to contain ourselves, and we did shout aloud 'Hosannah to God and the Lamb.'"

This heavenly vision, vouchsafed as the reward of faith and pure desires, only made them eager to know more of the "marvelous work and wonder" which the God of Israel had set His hand to perform, in fulfillment of the words of His ancient prophets. The Holy Ghost had fallen upon them, as on Cornelius of old, before baptism. They had plucked from the Tree of Life, from branches overhanging the wall, luscious fruit, whose sweetness and flavor made them long to enter the garden and more fully satisfy the desire of their souls. [36]

Heber, accordingly, proposed a journey to Pennsylvania, the state from whence the Elders came, where several branches of the Church were established. It was winter; January, 1832. Putting his horses to the sleigh, he and his companions set off upon the journey, a distance of one hundred and twenty-five miles. The party consisted of Heber C. Kimball, Brigham Young, Phineas Young and the wives of the two latter. The branch they visited was in Columbia, Bradford County; that from which the Elders came, in Rutland, Tioga County.

They tarried about six days, attending the meetings of the Church, witnessing the manifestations of the gifts of the spirit, such as speaking in tongues, interpretations and prophecy, and learning more of the nature and mission of the great latter-day work. They returned home rejoicing, praising God, and bearing testimony by the way. [37]

## CHAPTER 4

HEBER EMBRACES MORMONISM—A BAPTISM OF FIRE—DEATH OF MIRIAM YOUNG—VILATE KIMBALL A MOTHER TO THE ORPHANS—HEBER ORDAINED AN ELDER—RESOLVES TO VISIT KIRTLAND

HEBER, be it remembered, was a potter, and, though fairly well-to-do in the world, continued to labor at his trade for a livelihood.

One day in April, of the spring following his visit to Pennsylvania, as he was working in his shop, in the act of forming a vessel on the wheel, Alpheus Gifford entered. This Elder was then on his second mission to those parts, in company with others of his brethren. The conversation turning on the subject of the gospel, Heber said: "Brother Alpheus, I am ready to go forward and be baptized."

What followed is thus graphically told. Says Heber: "I arose, pulled off my apron, washed my hands and started with him, with my sleeves rolled up to my shoulders, and went a distance of one mile, where he baptized me in a small stream in the woods. After I was baptized I kneeled down and he laid his hands upon my head and confirmed me a member of the Church of Jesus Christ, and said unto me, 'In the name of Jesus Christ, and by the authority of the holy Priesthood, receive ye the Holy Ghost;' and before I got up off my knees he wanted to ordain me an

Elder; but I plead with him not to do it, for I felt myself unworthy of such a calling, and such an office." [38]

This event, so important to Heber C. Kimball and his posterity, took place on Monday, the fifteenth of April, 1832. Brigham Young had been baptized the day before, by Elder Eleazer Miller. Two weeks later, Heber's wife, Vilate, was baptized by Joseph Young.

A branch was raised up in Mendon numbering over thirty souls; its members were as follows:

John Young, sen., and Mary his wife,
Brigham Young and Miriam his wife,
Phineas H. Young and Clarissa his wife,
Joseph Young,
Lorenzo D. Young and Persis his wife,
John P. Greene and Rhoda his wife and their children,
Joel Sanford and Louisa his wife,
William Stillson and Susan his wife,
Fanny Young,
Isaac Flummerfelt, wife and children,
Ira Bond and his wife Charlotte,
Heber C. Kimball and Vilate his wife,
Rufus Parks,
John Morton and Betsey his wife,
Nathan Tomlinson and his wife,
Israel Barlow with his mother, brothers and sisters.

The reception of the Holy Ghost was to Heber a veritable "baptism of fire." He thus describes his remarkable experience;

"Under the ordinances of baptism and the laying on of hands, I received the Holy Ghost, as the disciples did in ancient days, which was like a consuming fire. I felt as though I sat at the feet of Jesus, and was clothed in my right mind, although the people called me crazy.

"I continued in this way for many months, and it seemed as though my body would consume away; at the same time the scriptures were unfolded to my mind in [39] such a wonderful manner that it appeared to me, at times, as if I had formerly been familiar with them."

Thus did the Comforter, the spirit of truth, bringing things past to remembrance and showing things to come, move upon the heart of this "mighty man of valor," whom the Lord was raising up for a marvelous future work. One of the weak things of earth, through whom the Omnipotent would yet thresh the nations by the power of His Spirit.

The branch in Mendon began to flourish, and the gifts of the spirit were poured out upon its members. This branch is reputed to have been the second in the Church to receive the gift of tongues; one of the branches in Pennsylvania being the first in which that gift was manifested.

Such a pentecostal renewal could scarcely take place without a corresponding movement of opposition on the part of the powers of darkness. The inevitable was at hand. Satan commenced to rage, and the Saints were annoyed and persecuted. Heber's former friends turned against him. His creditors combined to push him to the wall. During one week five or six executions were taken out against him. His brother Solomon was the only one outside the Church, willing to lend him a helping hand in his financial troubles, resulting from the inimical actions of his neighbors and old-time associates. His brother Charles, who had formerly befriended him, was dead. But the Lord opened his way, much to the chagrin of his persecutors, and he obtained money to meet his liabilities, so that none of his property was sold at auction.

In September following the organization of the branch in Mendon, Brigham Young's wife, Miriam, died. She had been feeble for months, but in her expiring **[40]** moments, filled with a supernatural vitality, she clapped her hands and praised God, calling upon all around to join her in so doing. She continued in this happy state until she breathed her last, moving her lips in prayer when her voice could no longer be heard. Heber remarks that the death-bed scene of this zealous and devoted Saint was to him another testimony of the truth and power of the everlasting gospel. Vilate Kimball took charge of Miriam's two little daughters, and, thenceforth, until after they removed from Mendon, the families of Brigham and Heber were as one.

In the meantime, the latter had been ordained an Elder, under the hands of Joseph Young, and labored with him and Brigham in the ministry. They visited Genesee, Avon and Lyonstown, baptizing many and building up branches of the Church. The following incident, related by Heber, shows how powerfully the Holy Ghost wrought through him in his ministrations:

"Brother Ezra Landon preached in Avon and Genesee, baptized eighteen or twenty, and being afraid to confirm them and promise the Holy Ghost, he requested me to confirm them, which I did according to the best of my knowledge, pronouncing but a few words on the head of each one, and invariably saying, 'receive ye the Holy Ghost in the name of Jesus Christ.' Immediately the Holy Ghost fell upon them, and several commenced speaking in tongues before they arose from their knees, and we had a joyful time. Some ten or twelve spoke in tongues, neither of whom had ever heard any person speak in tongues before, they being the first baptized in that place."

The region in which he was laboring is thus interestingly described:

"From the time Father Bosley located near Avon, **[41]** he found and plowed up axes and irons, and had sufficient to make his mill irons, and had always abundance of iron on hand without purchasing.

"In the towns of Bloomfield, Victor, Manchester, and in the regions round about, there were hills upon the tops of which were entrenchments and fortifications, and in them were human bones, axes, tomahawks, points of arrows, beads and pipes, which were frequently found; and it was a common occurrence in the country to plow up axes, which I have done many times myself.

"I have visited the fortifications on the tops of those hills frequently, and the one near Bloomfield I have crossed hundreds of times, which is on the bluff of Honeyoye River, at the outlet of Honeyoye Lake.

"In that region there are many small deep lakes, and in some of them the bottom has never been found. Fish abound in them.

"The hill Cumorah is a high hill for that country, and had the appearance of a fortification or entrenchment around it. In the State of New York, probably there are hundreds of these fortifications which are now visible, and I have seen them in many other parts of the United States."

Readers of the Book of Mormon will remember that in this very region, according to that sacred record, the final battles were fought between the Nephites and Lamanites. At the hill Cumorah, the Nephites made their last stand prior to their utter extermination, A.D., 385.

Thus was Heber preaching the Gospel to the Gentiles, above the graves of the ancients of Israel, whose records with the fullness of that Gospel, and the relics of their prowess and civilization, were now "whispering from the dust." [42]

But another scene was about to shift in his life's drama. He had planned to visit Kirtland, the bosom of the Church, and home of Joseph the Prophet.

## CHAPTER 5

THE LAND OF SHINEHAH—ARRIVAL OF HEBER AND BRIGHAM IN KIRTLAND—THEIR FIRST MEETING WITH THE PROPHET—THE KIMBALLS AND YOUNGS REMOVE TO OHIO—VEXATIOUS SUITS AND MOB VIOLENCE—FALLEN ON PERILOUS TIMES.

KIRTLAND, at the time arrived at in our narrative, was the head-quarters of the Church of Jesus Christ of Latterday Saints. The home of the Prophet of God and many of the leading Elders of Israel, it was also the spot designated by revelation where the first temple was to be built in this dispensation.

The Church, organized at Fayette, Seneca County, New York, on the 6th of April, 1830, had entered on the third year of its existence, and the Saints throughout the eastern parts had been commanded to gather westward. Kirtland and its vicinity, or "the land of Shinehah," as it is named in revelation, had been settled as a stake of Zion since early in 1831, and from there, in the summer of the same year, had gone forth a colony of Saints to purchase and occupy "the land of Zion," in the western confines of Missouri. That region was then the nation's frontier, bordering on a wilderness inhabited by wild [43] beasts and savages, and but sparsely peopled itself by whites scarcely less ignorant and cruel.

The Gospel, preached by the first missionaries sent westward from New York, in October, 1830, had taken a firm hold among the honest-in-heart of Northern Ohio. Among those who had embraced the new faith—new, indeed, and wonderful to that generation—were Sidney Rigdon, Edward Partridge and Newel K. Whitney.

The Pratts, the Whitmers, and other noted families were already numbered among the followers of the "Mormon" Prophet, and it was Parley P. Pratt, Oliver Cowdery and other Elders who had first brought the Gospel to Kirtland.

The new branch throve so rapidly as to soon eclipse in importance all others; an event no doubt divinely ordered, as the Saints at large, in December, 1830, were commanded to "assemble together at the Ohio."

Late in October, or early in November, 1832, Heber C. Kimball, in company with Brigham and Joseph Young, arrived in Kirtland. They had traveled by team a distance of three hundred miles. Their first meeting with the Prophet, whom they had come so far to see, was on the 8th day of November. Joseph was felling trees in the forest when the party approached. It is related that, on seeing Brigham, he said; "There is a man who will yet preside over this Church."

As to Heber, the heart of Joseph was at once knit with his, in friendship like unto that of David and Jonathan; and this feeling of brotherly love, like a golden chain, uniting these two noble souls, was destined to endure unbroken through time and eternity.

Says Heber: "We saw brother Joseph Smith and had a glorious time; during which Brother Brigham spoke in tongues before Joseph, this being the first time he had heard anyone speak in tongues. He rose up and testi[44]fied that the gift was from God, and then the gift fell upon him and he spoke in tongues himself. He afterwards declared it was the pure, or Adamic language that he spoke. Soon after this the gift of tongues commenced in the Church at Kirtland generally. We had a precious season and returned with a blessing in our souls."

In the fall of 1833, Elder Kimball disposed of his possessions in Mendon, and settled his affairs preparatory to gathering to the bosom of the Church. He had borne faithful testimony to the inhabitants of the place which had been his home for so many years, but, with few exceptions, they had turned a deaf ear to his warning words. Heber was the only one of his father's household to embrace the Gospel. His brother Solomon, though friendly, and at one time, like Agrippa, "almost persuaded," did not come within the fold.

No sooner was Heber ready to start Zionward, than he was again beset by petty persecutions. This time they were not only malicious, but of an out and out dishonest character. Notwithstanding he had settled all his accounts, and paid every penny that he owed—"unless it was two cents to one man, in a case where change could not be procured"—and left debts owing to him, uncollected, to the amount of "some hundred dollars," attachments were issued at the instance of some of his neighbors, and his goods seized by officers of the law.

Rather than be delayed by a law-suit, in which, owing to religious prejudice, he had little hope of receiving fair treatment, he settled the unjust claims and departed.

His family at this time consisted of himself and wife, and their two children, William Henry and Helen Mar. Judith Marvin, an elder daughter, and Roswell Heber, a younger son—the first and latest born of the household[45]—had died. Brigham Young and his two little daughters went in the same wagon with the

Kimball family to Kirtland. They reached their destination about the last of October, or early in November. They first occupied a house belonging to Elijah Smith, uncle to the wife of Bishop N. K. Whitney; but Heber soon had a home of his own, which he continued to share with his friend and brother Brigham, until the latter procured a separate domicile.

It is an interesting fact that Brigham was the builder of Heber's house in Kirtland, he being a carpenter and joiner, as well as a painter and glazier.

"When I got to Kirtland," says Elder Kimball, "the brethren were engaged in building the House of the Lord. The commandment to build the House and also the pattern of it, were given in a revelation to Joseph Smith, jun., Sidney Rigdon, and Frederick G. Williams, and it was to be erected by a stated time. The Church was in a state of poverty and distress, in conseqence of which it appeared almost impossible that the commandment could be fulfilled. Soon after our arrival, there was a contribution called for to finish the school-house and printing office; I contributed the glass for the house, and I gave Brother Hyrum Smith two hundred dollars for the building of the temple."

The newly arrived pilgrims had fallen on perilous times. Mobocracy was rife and rampant; persecution was raging against the Church, both in Ohio and in Missouri. The infernal regions seemed stirred to their depths at the prospect of a temple, whose walls, now climbing heavenward, gave promise of salvation and deliverance for the living and the dead; the unlocking of prison doors, the bursting of spirit dungeons, the smiting off of fetters from the limbs of the slave of sin, and the [46] ushering forth of the penitent captive into the life and light of gospel liberty. Keys were about to be restored whereby the heavens would be brought nearer to the earth, the prophets of the past would minister in holy places to the prophets of the present, and the cause of human redemption receive such an impetus as would shake the throne of Satan to its foundations. No wonder the dominions of Sheol were agitated.

"Our enemies," says Heber, "were raging and threatening destruction upon us. We had to guard night after night, and for weeks were not permitted to take off our clothes, and were obliged to lie with our fire-locks in our arms, to preserve Brother Joseph's life and our own. Joseph was sued before a magistrate's court in Painesville, on a vexatious suit. I carried him from Kirtland to Painesville, with four or five others, in my wagon, every morning for five days, and brought them back in the evening. We were often waylaid, but managed to elude our enemies by rapid driving and taking different roads. Esquire Bissell defended the Prophet and he came off victorious.

"At this time our brethren in Jackson County, Missouri, were also suffering great persecution; about twelve hundred were driven, plundered and robbed, their houses burned, and some of the brethren were killed.

"Mobs were organized around Kirtland, who were enraged against us, ready to destroy us."

Such was the state of affairs with the Church of the living God, at the close of the year 1833. Such was the nature of the action upon which the hero of this history had entered. But he was of the gold, not the dross of the earth, and passed through the fire, purified, yet not consumed. [47]

## CHAPTER 6

THE GATHERING OF THE TITANS—HEBER'S TESTIMONY OF JOSEPH AND THE TWELVE—THEIR MIGHTY MISSION—THE TEST OF FAITH—ZION'S CAMP.

JOSEPH, Brigham and Heber together in Kirtland! By what strange fatality were these mighty lives thus interwoven? We have seen how Brigham and Heber came together, and how, from thenceforth, the currents of their lives and fortunes ran parallel. Now they were joined with Joseph, their prophet chief, like streams that swell a river.

Interesting is it also, if only as a coincidence, that so many of the leading spirits of the latter-day work should have been natives of Vermont—a diadem for thee, proud State, and one which thou wilt prize in coming time!—from whence scattered, ere acquaintance with the Gospel or with each other began, to meet as co-laborers in the same great cause, among the hills and dales of Northern Ohio. As though the heavens had decreed their lives should thus commingle.

And the heavens had so decreed. It was not chance, it was destiny "shaping their ends," and fulfilling her mission in their behalf. And though from the ends of the earth—what matter names or nativity?—it had been the same. "He that scattered Israel will gather him." From all nations that fated blood, when goes Jehovah's fiat forth, like the rain-drops sprinkled upon the hills, must trickle back to the Ocean whence it came. [48]

It was a coalescing of divine affinities, the relinking of a spirit chain, which, though it often part, is never broken, and though seemingly divided, forever inseparable.

"Are you ever going to be prepared to see God, Jesus Christ, His angels, or comprehend His servants, unless you take a faithful and prayerful course?"

"Did you actually know Joseph Smith?"

The questions are Heber C. Kimball's, addressed in later years to a congregation of the Saints.

"No," he answers for them, and continues:

"Do you know Brother Brigham? No."

"Do you know Brother Heber? No; you do not."

"Do you know the Twelve? You do not; if you did you would begin to know God, and learn that those men who are chosen to direct and counsel you, are near kindred to God and to Jesus Christ, for the keys, power and authority of the kingdom of God are in that lineage,"

This, then, was the purpose, the divine intending, for which they were now in conjunction; "noble and great ones," great in the heavens and great upon the earth, ordained as "rulers" ere morning stars sang gladsome greeting, or Sons of God shouted for joy around the cradle of the infant world. This, the object of their descent from celestial empires; to build up a Kingdom unto God, and prepare the world for the coming of Him "whose right it is to reign." Jewels from Jehovah's diadem, diamonds in the dust, unseen of saint or sinner in all their lustre, concealed from a world unworthy of the light it could not comprehend.

Had Heber's inspired mind probed the secret of Joseph's thought, expressed in his own oft-quoted words: "Would to God, brethren, I could tell you who I am!"

As Prophet, Seer, and Revelator to the Church of **[49]** Jesus Christ, its president and earthly head, and holder of the keys of the last dispensation, Joseph was already in the high and holy office for which he was predestined and fore-ordained. Not so, Brigham; not so, Heber; not so their apostolic compeers. A trial of their faith was first necessary, a trial now near at hand, to prove them worthy in the flesh of the great calling whereunto they were called in the eternal councils.

In the month of February, 1834, came a commandment from the Almighty unto His prophet, to "gather up the strength of His house," and "go up and redeem Zion;" in other words, to recover from the hands of a fierce and merciless mob the lands in Jackson County, Missouri, from which the Saints had been driven.

Such were the origin and object of Zion's Camp. Such, the nature of the perilous duty laid upon them.

---

## CHAPTER 7

THE REDEMPTION OF ZION—ENOCH'S CITY TO RETURN—OBJECT OF THE UNITED ORDER—CAUSE OF THE JACKSON COUNTY EXPULSION—THE WHEAT FROM THE CHAFF

THE redemption of Zion! The building of the New Jerusalem!
Theme of the ancient prophets and glory of the latter days!
Such was the sublime mission given to the Saints of the Most High. Thus came the word of the Lord concerning it, March, 1831: **[50]**

"Wherefore, I, the Lord, have said, gather ye out from the eastern lands, assemble ye yourselves together ye elders of my Church; go ye forth into the western countries; ...

"And with one heart and with one mind, gather up your riches that ye may purchase an inheritance which shall hereafter be appointed unto you,

"And it shall be called the New Jerusalem, a land of peace, a city of refuge, a place of safety for the Saints of the Most High God;

"And the glory of the Lord shall be there, and the terror of the Lord also shall be there, insomuch that the wicked will not come unto it, and it shall be called Zion.

"And it shall come to pass, among the wicked, that every man that will not take his sword against his neighbor, must needs flee unto Zion for safety.

"And there shall be gathered unto it out of every nation under heaven; and it shall be the only people that shall not be at war one with another.

"And it shall be said among the wicked, let us not go up to battle against Zion, for the inhabitants of Zion are terrible; wherefore we cannot stand.

"And it shall come to pass that the righteous shall be gathered out from among all nations, and shall come to Zion, singing with songs of everlasting joy."

With this glorious object in view, this sublime motive firing their souls and filling their hearts with holy zeal, the Saints, in the summer of 1831, had commenced gathering upon the land of Zion—Jackson County, Missouri, the chosen site of the great city and temple of God. Their purpose, to fulfil prophecy, to found the modern Zion, New Jerusalem, capital city of the kingdom of God. A counterpart of the Zion of Enoch, sanctified of old and taken into the heavens, to return in latter times as a leaven of righteousness, to leaven this lump of clay, the mother earth of our mortality, and make it like unto itself, and in due time a glori[51]fied planet, purified, redeemed, and from sin forever free.

To prepare the world for that supreme hour "when the Lord shall bring again Zion," was and is the mission of the Saints of latter days. And this that the scripture might be fulfilled, which says:

"The Lord hath brought down Zion from above.
"The Lord hath brought up Zion from beneath.
"The earth hath travailed and brought forth her strength:
"And truth is established in her bowels:
"And the heavens have smiled upon her:
"And she is clothed with the glory of her God:
"For he stands in the midst of his people."

The meeting of the Zions! The marriage of the worlds! Zion from beneath, the type of truth from earth, embracing Zion from above, the symbol of righteousness from heaven.

"And they twain shall be one!"

Preparatory to this miraculous event, and indeed to render it possible, the order of Enoch, the system of divine economy whereby the Zion of the ancients was redeemed and sanctified, had been newly revealed to the Zion-builders of the last days.

What says Moses of Enoch and his city?

"And the Lord called his people Zion, because they were of one heart and one mind, and dwelt in righteousness; and there was no poor among them."

Oh, the sweetness of those simple words! Oh, the sublimity of the picture they portray! Liberty, equality, fraternity! This is Zion—The Pure in Heart!

But the Saints in Jackson County, Missouri, were not all that the Lord requires of a people chosen to execute a purpose so sacred, so sublime. "There were jarrings, **[52]** and contentions, and envyings, and strifes, and lustful and covetous desires among them; therefore by these things they polluted their inheritances." Then was the lash of the Philistine applied, and they were driven forth from the goodly land. Satan hath his mission, as well as Christ.

Be it not inferred, however, that these hapless victims of mobocratic tyranny were utterly wicked and depraved, or that all were equally culpable in the eyes of Him, who, to punish the transgressors, permitted their enemies to come against them. With all their faults they were better far than their oppressors, more than the peers, in every Christian virtue, of the people of the world around them. Yet, judged by the higher law, the Gospel standard, which the world had not received, and were not under the same obligation to obey, these "children of the Light" were found remiss in many things.

The Kingdom of heaven is likened unto a field of grain, gathered unto the threshing-floor. The purpose of divine punishment is to purify. Upon the wheat and the chaff, alike, fell the iron flail of persecution. **[53]**

## CHAPTER 8

THE ZION'S CAMP EXPEDITION—JOSEPH AS A PROPHET-GENERAL—FINDING OF THE BONES OF ZELPH, THE ANCIENT—REBELLION IN THE CAMP—JOSEPH PREDICTS A SCOURGE—HEBER'S FAILURE AS A LAUNDERER—ZION'S CAMP SAVED BY A STORM

"GATHER up the strength of my house, and go up and redeem Zion!" Such was the burden of God's command to Joseph and his brethren in Kirtland. Such was their interpretation of the divine message and call.

Bidding farewell to his family and friends, whom he hardly dared hope he would ever meet again in the flesh, Heber enrolled himself in the little band of heroes who set out from Kirtland early in May, 1834. They were about one hundred strong, well armed and equipped, and were led by the Prophet Joseph in person. Subsequently their number increased to two hundred and five souls. But Heber will tell his own story of that eventful pilgrimage. Says he:

"Brother Joseph received a revelation concerning the redemption of Zion, part of which remains to be fulfilled. He sent messengers to the east and to the west and to the north and to the south, to gather up the Elders, and he gathered together as many of the brethren as he conveniently could, with what means they could spare, to go up to Zion, to render all the assistance that we could to our afflicted brethren. We gathered clothing and other necessaries to carry up to our brethren and sisters who had been plundered; and putting our horses to the wagons, and taking our firelocks and **[54]** ammunition, we started on our journey; leaving only Oliver Cowdery, Sidney Rigdon and a few aged workmen who were engaged on the temple; so that there were very few men left in Kirtland. Our wagons were about full with baggage, etc., consequently we had to travel on foot.

"We started on the 5th of May, and truly this was a solemn morning to me. I took leave of my wife and children and friends, not knowing whether I would see them again in the flesh, as myself and brethren were threatened both in that country and in Missouri by enemies, that they would destroy us and exterminate us from the land.

"There were about one hundred brethren in our company who started for Zion. These brethren were nearly all young men, and nearly all Elders, Priests, Teachers and Deacons. The second day we arrived at New Portage, being about forty miles, at which place on the 7th we made regulations for traveling, and appointed a paymaster, whose name was Frederick G. Williams, and put all our moneys into a general fund. Some of the brethren had considerable, and others had little or none, yet all became equal. While here one of my horses received a kick from another horse, which obliged me to trade away my span, and get another span of older horses, from Jonathan Taylor. We then proceeded on our journey twelve miles to the Chippeway River. Here we pitched our tents under a fine grove.

"The next day we were divided into companies of twelve each, and captains were appointed over each company. I organized my company in the following manner, appointing two to attend to cooking, two to see that fires were made, two to prepare the tent at night and likewise the bedding, and also to strike the [55] tent each morning, two to fetch and provide water, one to do the running, two to attend the horses, see that the wagon was greased and everything prepared for starting. My business was to see that the company was provided for, and that all things were done in order. Our living generally was very good, being able to buy bread from the bakers or inhabitants on the way through the settled part of the country. After this we purchased flour and had to bake our own bread. We sometimes had to live on Johnny cake and corn dodger, and sometimes our living was scant. Every night before we went to bed we united in our tent and offered up our prayers before the Lord for protection. This was done by all the companies, at the sound of a trumpet; and at the sound of a trumpet in the morning, every man was upon his knees, each one being called upon in his turn to be mouth in prayer. The same order was attended to in each tent. There were general officers appointed over the company, viz: Joseph Smith, commander; Dr. F. G. Williams, quartermaster and historian of the camp; Zerubbabel Snow and Nathan Tanner, commissaries of subsistence; Sylvester Smith, adjutant; and Roger Orton, captain of the guard.

"On the 8th we started on our journey, and on Saturday the 10th we passed through Mansfield, and camped for the Sabbath in Richfield. On Sunday the 11th Brother Sylvester Smith preached and the sacrament of bread and wine was administered to the company. On Monday the 12th we crossed over the Sandusky plains, and through the Indian settlements. We then passed through a long range of beech woods where the roads were very bad. In many instances we had to fasten ropes to the wagons to haul them out of the sloughs and mud holes by hand. While passing through the woods [56] the brethren scattered on each side of the road and went to hunting for wild game. We came to Belle Fontaine, where we first discovered refractory feelings in Sylvester Smith.

"We passed through a very pleasant country to Dayton, Ohio, where we crossed the Miami river, which is a very beautiful stream; the water being only about two and a half feet deep, most of the brethren waded it. We arrived at this place on Friday the 16th. The brethren were in good spirits, and the Lord was with us. On Saturday the 17th we passed into Indiana, just over the line betwixt the States of Ohio and Indiana, where we camped for the Sabbath, having traveled forty miles that day; our feet were very sore and blistered, and our stockings were wet with blood, the weather being very warm. I walked most of the journey, letting the lame and footsore ride in my stead. I frequently invited the Prophet to ride, seeing him lame and footsore. On such occasions he would bless me and my team with a hearty good will. My team performed the journey very well.

"During the night a spy from the enemy attempted to get into our camp, but was stopped by the guard. We had our sentinels or guards appointed every night, on account of spies continually harrassing us. This evening there was quite a difficulty between some of the brethren and Sylvester Smith, on occasion of which Brother Joseph was called to decide the matter. Finding quite a rebellious spirit in Sylvester Smith, and to some extent in others, he said they would meet with misfortunes, difficulties and hindrances, 'and you will know it before you leave this place;' exhorting them to humble themselves before the Lord, and become united, that they might not be scourged. A very singular occurrence took place that night and the next day, concerning [57] our teams. On the following morning when we arose we found almost every horse in the camp so badly foundered that we could scarcely lead them a few rods to the water. The brethren then deeply realized the effects of discord. When Brother Joseph learned the fact he exclaimed to the brethren that for a witness that God overruled and had His eye upon them, that all those who would humble themselves before the Lord should know that the hand of God was in this misfortune, and their horses should be restored to health immediately; and by twelve o'clock the same day the horses were as nimble as ever, with the exception of one of Sylvester Smith's which soon afterwards died.

"May 21st we passed through Indianapolis, the capital of Indiana, where we crossed White River. The teams forded the river, and most of the brethren crossed over the new bridge which was unfinished. We had been threatened by our enemies that we should not go through the town, but we passed through unmolested. Everything appeared to be in perfect silence as we went through, although the people looked aghast as if fear had come upon them. At night we camped on an open spot, the top of an eminence. Here we lost one horse.

"On Sunday, the 25th, we arrived at the edge of Illinois; we had no meeting, but attended to washing and baking to prepare for our journey. On the 26th we resumed our march. At night we were alarmed by the continual threatening of our enemies. I would here remark that notwithstanding so many threats were thrown out against us, we did not fear, nor hesitate to proceed on our journey, for God was with us, and angels went before us, and we had no fear of either men or devils. This we know because they (the angels) were seen. On Tuesday we came to the Okaw, a fork of the Kas[58]kaskia River, where we found two canoes; we lashed them together and they served as a kind of ferry boat. We took our baggage out of our wagons, put it on board and ferried it across; then took our wagons and horses, and swam them across, and when they got to the opposite shore the brethren fastened ropes into the tongues of the wagons and helped the horses and wagons out of the river. Others felled trees and laid them across the river, and thus helped themselves over. In this way we all crossed in safety. Wednesday, the 28th, we reached the township of Decatur, where we lost another horse. Saturday the 31st, at night, we camped one mile from Jacksonville and prepared for the Sabbath.

"On Sunday, June 1st, we had preaching all day, and many of the inhabitants of the town came out to hear. Brother John S. Carter preached in the morning. By this time the inhabitants began to flock down in companies to hear the preaching, as they understood we were professors of religion and had a meeting in the morning. Brother Joseph then proposed that some of the brethren should set forth different portions of the Gospel in their discourses. He called upon Brother Joseph Young to preach upon the principles of free salvation. He then called upon Brother Brigham Young to speak, who set forth baptism as essential to salvation. He was followed by Brother Orson Hyde, who proved by the scriptures that baptism was for the remission of sins. Lyman E. Johnson spoke at some length upon the necessity of men being upright in their walk, and keeping the Sabbath day holy. Brother Orson Pratt delivered an excellent discourse on the principles of the final restoration of all things. The services of the day were concluded by a powerful exhortation from Eleazer Miller. His voice was said to be heard a mile and a half. I would [59] here remark concerning Brother Eleazer Miller, who was one of the first that brought the Gospel to us at Mendon, New York: when he used to retire to a little grove near my house for secret prayer, he would get so filled with the Spirit and the power of the Holy Ghost that he would burst out in a loud voice so that he was heard by the surrounding inhabitants for more than a mile. After the services were over, many strangers were in our camp making remarks upon the preaching which they had heard. They said that Brother Joseph Young, by his preaching, they should judge was a Methodist. They thought Brother Brigham Young was a close communion Baptist. Brother Orson Hyde they supposed was a Campbellite or reformed Baptist. Brother Lyman E. Johnson they supposed was a Presbyterian, and Brother Orson Pratt a Restorationer. They enquired if we all belonged to one denomination. The answer was, we *were* some of us Baptists, some Methodists, some Presbyterians, some Cambellites, some Restorationers, etc.

"On Monday morning when we passed through Jacksonville, they undertook to count us; and I heard one man say, who stood in the door of a cabinet shop, that he had counted a little rising of five hundred, but he could not tell how many there were. This thing was attempted many times in villages and towns as we passed through, but the people were never able to ascertain our number.

"While traveling in Indiana some spies came into our camp. While we were eating dinner on the 21st of May, three gentlemen came riding up on very fine looking horses and commenced their enquiries of various ones concerning our traveling in so large a body, asking where we were from, and where we were going. The reply was as usual, some from Maine, some from New [60] York, some from Massachusetts, some from Ohio, and some replied, we are from the east, and as soon as we have done eating we shall be going to the west again. They then addressed themselves to Dr. Williams, to see if they could find out who the leader of the camp was. The doctor replied, we have no one in particular. They asked if we had not a general to take lead of the company. The reply was, no one in particular. But, said they, is there not some one among you whom you call your captain, or leader, or superior to the rest? He answered, sometimes one, and sometimes another, takes charge of the company so as to not throw the burden upon any one in particular. These same spies, who had come from the west, passed us that same day, and the next.

"On Monday, June 2nd, we crossed the Illinois River. The enemy had threatened that we should not pass over, but we were ferried across without any difficulty. Here we were counted by the ferryman and he declared we were five hundred in number, although there were only about one hundred and fifty of us. Our company had increased since we started from Kirtland in consequence of many having volunteered and joined us from the different branches of the Church through which we had passed on our journey. We camped on the west bank of the river until the next day.

"On Tuesday, the 3d, several of us went up with the Prophet to the top of a mound on the bank of the Illinois River, which was several hundred feet above the river, and from the summit we had a pleasant view of the surrounding country. We could overlook the tops of the trees and the meadow or prairie on each side the river as far as our eyes could extend, which was one of the most pleasant scenes I ever beheld. On the top of [61] this mound there was the appearance of three altars, which had been built of stone, one above the other, according to the ancient order; and the ground was strewn with human bones. This caused in us very peculiar feelings, to see the bones of our fellow creatures scattered in this manner,—fellow creatures who had been slain in ages past. We felt prompted to dig down into the mound, and sending for a shovel and hoe, we proceeded to move away the earth. At about one foot in depth we discovered the skeleton of a man, almost entire; and between two of his ribs we found an Indian arrow, which had evidently been the cause of his death. We took the leg and thigh bones and carried them to Clay County. All four appeared sound. Brother Brigham Young has yet the arrow in his possession. It was a common thing to find bones thus bleaching upon the earth in that country.

"The same day we pursued our journey. While on our way we felt anxious to know who the person was who had been killed by that arrow. It was made known to Joseph that he had been an officer who fell in battle, in the last destruction among the Lamanites, and his name was Zelph. This caused us to rejoice much, to think that God was so mindful of us as to show these things to His servant. Brother Joseph had enquired of the Lord and it was made known to him in a vision.

"While we were refreshing ourselves and teams, about the middle of the day, Brother Joseph got up in a wagon and said he would deliver a prophecy. After giving the brethren much good advice, he exhorted them to faithfulness and humility, and said the Lord had told him that there would be a scourge come upon the camp in consequence of the fractious and unruly spirits that appeared among them, and they would die like sheep **[62]** with the rot; still if they would repent and humble themselves before the Lord, the scourge in a great measure might be turned away; 'but, as the Lord lives, this camp will suffer for giving way to their unruly temper;' which afterwards actually did take place to the sorrow of the brethren.

"The same day when we had got within one mile of the Snye, we came to a very beautiful little town called Atlas. Here we found honey, for the first time on our journey, that we could buy. We purchased about two-thirds of a barrel. We went down to the Snye and crossed over that night in a ferry boat and camped for the night on the west bank. There was a great excitement in the country through which we had passed, and also ahead of us; the mob threatened to stop us; guns were fired in almost every direction through the night.

"We pursued our journey on the 4th and camped on the bank of the Mississippi River. Here we were somewhat afflicted, and the enemy threatened much that we should not cross over the river out of Illinois into Missouri. It took us two days to cross the river, as we had but one ferry boat, and the river was one mile and a half wide. While some were crossing others spent their time in hunting, fishing, etc. When we had all got over we camped about one mile from the little town of Louisiana, in a beautiful oak grove, immediately on the bank of the river.

"At this place there were some feelings of hostility again manifested by Sylvester Smith, in consequence of a dog growling at him while he was marching his company up to the camp, he being the last that came over the river. The next morning Brother Joseph said that he would descend to the spirit that was manifested by some of the brethren to show them the folly of their **[63]** wickedness. He rose up and commenced by saying, 'If any man insults me, or abuses me, I will stand in my own defence at the expense of my life; and if a dog growl at me, I will let him know that I am his master.' At this moment Sylvester Smith, who had just returned from where he had turned out his horses to feed, came up, and hearing Brother Joseph make those remarks said, 'If that dog bites me I'll kill him.' Brother Joseph turned to Sylvester and said, 'If you kill that dog I'll whip you;' and then went on to show the brethren how wicked and unchristian-like such conduct appeared before the eyes of truth and justice.

"On Friday, the 6th, we resumed our journey. On Saturday night we camped among our brethren at Salt River, in the Allred settlement, in a piece of woods by a beautiful spring of water, and prepared for the Sabbath. On the Sabbath we had preaching. We remained here several days, washing our clothes and preparing to resume our journey. Here we were joined by Hyrum Smith and Lyman Wight, with another company. The camp now numbered two hundred and five men, all armed and equipped. It was delightful to see the company, for they were all young men, with one or two exceptions, and all in good spirits.

"We were now reorganized in the following order: Joseph Smith was acknowledged commander-in-chief; Lyman Wight was chosen general of the camp; then Brother Joseph chose twenty men for his life guard, I being one of them; Brother George A. Smith was Brother Joseph's armor-bearer; Hyrum Smith was chosen captain of the life guard; the remainder of the camp was organized into companies as before stated. We had twenty-five wagons, two horses on each, and on some three. One day while we remained here our general **[64]** marched us out on a large prairie. He then proceeded to inspect us, examine our firelocks, etc. Afterwards we were marched in platoons, and, an object being placed, we discharged our pieces in order to try them. We were drilled about half a day, and then returned to the camp.

"My first attempt at washing my clothes took place at Salt River. My shirts being extremely dirty, I put them into a kettle of water and boiled them for about two hours, having observed that women who washed boiled their clothes, and I supposed by so doing they boiled out the dirt; I then took them and washed them, endeavoring to imitate a woman washing as near as I could. I rubbed the clothes with my knuckles instead of the palm of my hand, and rubbed the skin off so that my hands were very sore for several days. My attempts were vain in trying to get the dirt out of the clothes. I wondered at this considerably, and scolded and fretted because I could not get the dirt out, and finally gave it up, and wrung them and hung them out to dry. Having no flat-irons to iron them, I took them to Sisters Hollbrook and Ripley to get them ironed. When they saw them they said I had not washed my clothes. I told them I had done my best, and although I had boiled them two hours before washing, and had washed them so faithfully that I had taken the skin off my knuckles, still I had not been successful in getting the dirt out. They laughed heartily, and informed me that by boiling before washing I had boiled the dirt into them.

"On the 12th we again resumed our march; many of the inhabitants went with us several miles; they seemed to have much respect for us. We traveled about fourteen miles and camped on a large prairie.

"We tarried in the middle of this prairie, which was about twenty-eight miles across, on account of a rupture **[65]** which took place in the camp. Here F. G. Williams and Roger Orton received a very severe chastisement from Brother Joseph for not obeying orders. In this place further regulations were made in regard to the organization of the camp.

"A day or two after this, Bishop Partridge met us, direct from Clay County, as we were camping on the bank of the Wacondah River, in the woods. We received much information from Brother Partridge concerning the hostile feelings and prejudices that existed against us in all quarters of Missouri. It gave us great satisfaction to receive intelligence from him, as we were in peril and threatened all the time. I will here mention one circumstance that transpired during our stay at this place, which was that of Brother Lyman Wight baptizing Dean Gould, as he was not previously a member of the Church, yet had accompanied us all the way from Kirtland.

"We pursued our journey, following the bank of the river, for several miles. As we left the river and came into a very beautiful prairie, Brother William Smith killed a very large deer, which made us some very nourishing soup, and added to our comfort considerably.

"On Wednesday, the 18th, at night, we camped one mile from the town of Richmond, Ray County. On Thursday, the 19th, we arose as soon as it was light and passed through the town before the inhabitants were up. As Luke Johnson and others were passing through before the teams came along, Brother Luke observed a black woman in a gentleman's garden near the road. She beckoned to him and said, 'come here massa.' She was evidently much agitated in her feelings. He went up to the fence and she said to him, 'there is a company of men lying in wait here who are calculating to kill you this morning as you pass through.' This was **[66]** nothing new to us as we had been continually threatened through the whole journey, and death and destruction seemed to await us daily. This day we only traveled about fifteen miles. One wagon broke down and the wheels ran off from another, and there seemed to be many things to hinder our progress, although we strove with all diligence to speed our way forward. Our intentions were when we started to go through to Clay County that day; but all in vain.

"This night we camped on an elevated piece of land between two branches of the Fishing River. Just as we halted and were making preparations for the night, five men rode into the camp and told us we should see hell before morning, and such horrible oaths as came from their lips I never heard before. They told us that sixty men were coming from Richmond, who had sworn to destroy us, also seventy more were coming from Clay County, to assist in our destruction. These men were black with passion, and armed with guns, and the whole country was in a rage against us, and nothing but the power of God could save us. All this time the weather was pleasant. Soon after these men left us we discovered a small black cloud rising in the west, and not more than twenty minutes passed away before it began to rain and hail; but we had very little hail in our camp. All around us the hail was heavy; some of the hailstones, or rather lumps of ice, were as large as hens' eggs. The thunder rolled with awful majesty, and the red lightnings flashed through the horizon, making it so light that I could see to pick up a pin almost any time through the night. The earth quaked and trembled, and there being no cessation it seemed as though the Almighty had issued forth his mandate of vengeance. The wind was so terrible that many of our tents were blown down. We **[67]** were not able to hold them up; but there being an old meeting house close at hand, many of us fled there to secure ourselves from the storm. Many trees were blown down, and others were twisted and wrung like a withe. The mob came to the river two miles from us, but the river had risen to that height that they were obliged to stop without crossing over. The hail fell so heavily upon them that it beat holes in their hats, and in some instances even broke the stocks off their guns; their horses, being frightened, fled, leaving the riders on the ground. Their powder was wet, and it was evident that the Almighty fought in our defense. This night the river raised forty feet.

"In the morning I went to the river in company with Brother Joseph Smith, Hyrum Smith, Brigham Young and others, as we had it in contemplation to proceed that morning to Liberty, Clay County; but we could not continue our journey as there was no way to cross the river. It was then overflowing its banks; and I have seen the river since and proved that it was fully forty feet from the top of its banks to the bottom. Previous to this rain falling, it was no more than ankle deep. Such a time never was known by us before; still we felt calm all night, and the Lord was with us. The water was ankle deep to us all night, even on that eminence, so we could not sleep.

"At this place W. W. Phelps, S. W. Denton, John Corrill and many others from Liberty joined us; from whom we received much information from the brethren who had been driven from Jackson County, and learned of the fixed determination of our enemies to drive or exterminate them from that county.

"The next day, when we moved into the country we saw that the hail had destroyed the crops, and we saw **[68]** that it had come in some directions within a mile and in other directions within a half mile of our camp. After passing a short distance the ground was literally covered with branches of the trees which had been cut off by the hail. We went a distance of five miles on the prairie to get food for our horses and also to get some provisions for ourselves, and to get into some secure place where we could defend ourselves from the rage of the enemy. We stayed there three or four days, until the rage of the people was somewhat allayed.

"On the 21st Colonel Sconce and two other leading men from Ray County came to see us, desiring to know what our intentions were, 'for,' said he, 'I see that there is an almighty power that protects this people, for I started from Richmond, Ray County, with a company of armed men, having a fixed determination to destroy you, but was kept back by the storm and was not able to reach you.' When he came into camp he was seized with such a trembling that he was obliged to sit down in order to compose himself. When he desired to know what our intentions were, Brother Joseph arose and began to speak; and the power of God rested upon him. He gave a relation of the sufferings of our people in Jackson County, and also many of our persecutions and what we had suffered from our enemies for our religion; and that we had come one thousand miles to assist our brethren, to bring them clothing, and to reinstate them upon their own lands; that we had no intentions to molest or injure any people, but only to administer to the wants of our afflicted brethren; and that the evil reports which were circulated about us were false, and were circulated by our enemies to get us destroyed.

"After he had finished speaking, the power of which melted them into compassion, they arose and offered him **[69]** their hands, and said they would use their influence to allay the excitement which everywhere prevailed against us. They accordingly went forth and rode day and night to pacify the people. They wept because they saw we were an afflicted people, and that our intentions were pure.

"The next day the sheriff of that county, named Neil Gilliam, came to deliver a short address to us. We formed into companies and marched into a grove a little distance from the camp, and there formed ourselves into a circle, and sat down upon the ground. Previous to Mr. Gilliam's address he (Gilliam) said, I have heard much concerning Joseph Smith, and I have been informed that he is in your camp; if he is here I would like to see him.' Brother Joseph arose and said 'I am the man.' This was the first time he was made known during the journey of one thousand miles. Mr. Gilliam then arose and gave us some instructions concerning the manners and customs of the people, their disposition, etc., and what course we should take in order to gain their favor and protection.

"On the Sabbath day while we were in this place, being in want of salt, I took it upon me to go to some of the inhabitants and get some. Brother Cyrus Smalling took his rifle and went along with me. After passing through a path enclosed by hazel bushes, about two miles from the camp, I discovered a deer a little distance ahead of us standing across the path. I made motions to Brother Smalling, and he, drawing up his rifle over my shoulder, which served for a rest, fired and hit the deer just behind the shoulder. It ran a few rods and fell. We cut a pole and fastening the deer on it, got it on our shoulders and carried it along to camp, when we dressed it and divided it among the different companies, and had an excellent feast. **[70]**

"Here Brothers Ezra Thayer and Thomas Hayes were taken sick with the cholera. We left them there, and also brother Joseph Hancock, who had been taken with the cholera during the storm, and who was the first person attacked with it. Brother Joseph called the camp together, and told us that in consequence of the disobedience of some who had not been willing to listen to his words, but had been rebellious, God had decreed that sickness should come upon us, and we should die like sheep with the rot; and said he, 'I am sorry, but I cannot help it.' When he spake these things it pierced me like a dart, having a testimony that so it would be."

## CHAPTER 9

THE FISHING RIVER REVELATION—WHY ZION WAS NOT REDEEMED—THE CHOLERA IN CAMP—THE TEST OF FAITH COMPLETE—THE SHADOW OF A COMING EVENT

HERE, while the Camp rested on Fishing River, the Lord made further known His will concerning the redemption of Zion. The revelation was given on the 22nd of June, the same day that the Prophet repeated his warning in relation to the coming scourge. The points most pertinent to our narrative are here given:

"Behold I say unto you, were it not for the transgressions of my people, speaking concerning the church and not individuals, they might have been redeemed even now; [71]

"But behold, they have not learned to be obedient to the things which I required at their hands, but are full of all manner of evil, and do not impart of their substance, as becometh saints, to the poor and afflicted among them,

"And are not united according to the union required by the law of the celestial kingdom;

"And Zion cannot be built up unless it is by the principles of the law of the celestial kingdom, otherwise I cannot receive her unto myself.

"And my people must needs be chastened until they learn obedience, if it must needs be, by the things which they suffer....

"Therefore, in consequence of the transgression of my people, it is expedient in me that mine elders should wait for a little season for the redemption of Zion....

"But inasmuch as there are those who have hearkened unto my words, I have prepared a blessing and an endowment for them, if they continue faithful....

"I have heard their prayers, and will accept their offering; and it is expedient in me, that they should be brought thus far for a trial of their faith."

Those who had families in the east were then told that they might return, while the rest were required to remain in Missouri. The Saints were instructed to observe wisdom and humility, and "lift up an ensign of peace" to their enemies and to all the world, while awaiting the day of God's power and of Zion's redemption.

The real purpose of the Almighty in relation to this important event was foreshadowed in a revelation given February 24th, 1834, the one calling for the organization of Zion's Camp. Therein the Lord says:

"Behold I say unto you, the redemption of Zion must needs come by power;

"Therefore, I will raise up unto my people a man, who shall lead them like as Moses led the children of Israel, [72]

"For ye are the children of Israel, and of the seed of Abraham, and ye must needs be led out of bondage by power, and with a stretched out arm:

"And as your fathers were led at the first, even so shall the redemption of Zion be."

While there is no doubt that, had the Lord's people been prepared, they might have been redeemed according to His word, it is also evident that the times were not then ripe for that event. This will be shown more plainly as we proceed.

Continuing his narrative, Heber says;

"On Monday, June 23rd, a council of high priests met, according to revelation, to choose some of the first Elders to receive their endowments; being appointed by the voice of the spirit, through Joseph Smith the Prophet. Edward Partridge was called and chosen to go to Kirtland and receive his endowments, with power from on high, and to also stand in his office as a bishop to purchase land in Missouri. Also W. W. Phelps, Isaac Morley, John Whitmer, David Whitmer, Algernon S.

Gilbert, Peter Whitmer, Simeon Carter, Newel Knight, Thomas B. Marsh, Lyman Wight, Parley P. Pratt, Christian Whitmer, and Solomon Hancock were severally called and chosen to receive their endowments in Kirtland with power from on high.

"On the morning of the 24th we started for Liberty, Clay County, where our brethren were residing who had been driven from Jackson County, taking our course round the head of Fishing River, in consequence of high water. When we got within five or six miles of Liberty, General Atchison and several other gentlemen met us, desiring that we would not go to Liberty, as the feelings of the people in that place were much enraged against us. Changing our course and bearing to the left, we [73] pursued our way across a prairie; then passing through a wood we came to Brother Sidney Gilbert's where we camped on the bottom of Rush Creek, in a field belonging to Brother Burgett.

"The destroyer came upon us as we had been warned by the servant of God. About 12 o'clock at night we began to hear the cries of those who had been seized. Even those on guard fell with their guns in their hands, and we had to exert ourselves considerably to attend to the sick, for they were stricken down on every hand. Thus it continued until morning when the camp was separated into several little bands, and dispersed among the brethren.

"I was left at the Camp in company with Joseph B. Noble, John D. Parker, Luke Johnson and Warren Ingalls, in care of those who were sick. We stayed with, and prayed for them, hoping they would recover, but all hope was lost, for about six o'clock in the morning John S. Carter expired. When the cholera first broke out he was the first who came forward to rebuke it; when he was immediately seized by it, and was the first to die. In about thirty minutes after Seth Hitchcock died, and it seemed as though we must all sink under the power of the destroyer.

"We were not able to obtain lumber to make them coffins, but were under the necessity of rolling them up in their blankets and burying them in that manner. We placed them on a sled, which was drawn by a horse about half a mile, and buried them in a little bluff by the side of a small branch of Rush Creek. This was accomplished by dark.

"Our hopes were that no more would die, but while we were uniting in prayer with uplifted hands to God, we looked at our beloved brother, Eber Wilcox, who was gasping his last. At this scene my feelings [74] were beyond expression. Those only who witnessed it can realize anything of the extent of our sufferings; and I felt to weep and pray to the Lord, that he would spare my life that I might behold my dear family again. I felt to covenant with my brethren and my God never to commit another sin while I lived. We felt to sit and weep over our brethren, and so great was our grief that we could have washed them with our tears. To realize that they had traveled a thousand miles through so much fatigue to lay down their lives for their brethren, increased our love for them.

"Brothers Brigham and Joseph Young came from Liberty and assisted us to bury Brother Wilcox. Their presence gave us much consolation. About 12 o'clock at night we placed Brother Wilcox on a small sled which we drew to the place of interment with one hand on the rope and the other bearing our firelocks for defense. While two were digging the grave the others stood with their arms to defend them.

"While Brother Luke Johnson was digging, the cholera attacked him with cramping and blindness. Brother Brigham laid hold of him and pulled him out of the grave, and shook him about, talked to and prayed for him, and exhorted him to jump about and exercise himself, when it would leave him for a few moments, then it would attack him again; and thus we had the greatest difficulty to keep the destroyer from laying us low. Soon after we returned another brother was taken from our little band; thus it continued until five out of ten were taken away.

"After burying these five brethren I was seized by the hand of the destroyer, as I went in the woods to pray. I was instantly struck blind, and saw no way whereby I could free myself from the disease, only by **[75]** jumping and thrashing myself about, until my sight returned to me and my blood began to circulate in my veins. I started and ran some distance, and by this means, through the help of God, I was enabled to extricate myself from the grasp of death. This circumstance took place in a piece of woods behind Brother Gilbert's house.

"On the 26th Algernon Sidney Gilbert, keeper of the Lord's storehouse, signed a letter to the governor, in connection with others, which was his last public act, for he had been called to preach and he said he would rather die than go forth and preach the Gospel to the wicked Gentile nations. The Lord took him at his word; he was attacked with the cholera and died about the 29th.

"Brothers Erastus Budd and Jesse Johnson Smith, a cousin of the Prophet, died at Brother Gilbert's about the same time.

"While we were here, the brethren being in want of some refreshment, Brother Luke Johnson went to Brother Burgett to get a fowl, asking him for one to make a broth for Elder Wilcox and others; but Brother Burgett denied him it, saying, 'In a few days we expect to return back into Jackson County, and I shall want them when I get there.' When Brother Johnson returned he was so angry at Burgett for refusing him, he said, 'I have a great mind to take my rifle and go back and shoot his horse.' I told Luke to never mind; that such actions never fail to bring their reward.

"Judge how we felt, after having left the society of our beloved families, taking our lives in our hands and traveling about one thousand miles through scenes of suffering and sorrow, for the benefit of our brethren, and after all to be denied of a small fowl to make a little **[76]** soup for brethren in the agonies of death. Such things never fail to bring their reward, and it would be well for the Saints never to turn away a brother who is penniless and in want, or a stranger, lest they may one day or other want a friend themselves.

"I went to Liberty, to the house of Brother Peter Whitmer, which place I reached with difficulty, being much afflicted with the disease that was among us. I stayed there until my return home, receiving great kindness at the hands of the brethren.

"The destroyer having afflicted us four days, ceased. Sixty-eight were attacked by the disease, of which number fourteen members of Zion's Camp died.

"June 30th I started for home in company with Lyman Sherman, Sylvester Smith, Alexander Badlam, Harrison Burgess, Luke Johnson and Zera Cole. They elected me their captain.

"We proceeded on our journey daily, the Lord blessing us with strength and health. The weather was very hot, but we traveled from thirty-five to forty miles a day, until about the 26th of July, when we arrived in Kirtland; having been gone from home about three months, during which time, with the exception of four nights, I slept on the ground.

"On my arrival home I found my family well, and I felt to rejoice in the Lord that He had preserved my life through so many dangers. Concluding that I had finished my mission to which the Lord had called me, after resting a few days, I established my pottery and began business."

Thus ended that remarkable expedition; remarkable for its object, for the issues involved, for its tragic episodes, examples of heroism and miraculous manifestations of divine power. What had it achieved? some may [77] ask. Nay, might not many be tempted to query, Was not the mission of Zion's Camp a failure?

"What have you accomplished?" was the sneering taunt of the apostate and of those weak in faith, met by the remnant of the little band on their return to Kirtland. "Just what we went for;" the meek, though firm reply of such men as Heber C. Kimball and Brigham Young.

And they were right. To them it was no failure. The trial of their faith was complete. Their offering, like Abraham's, had been accepted. They had been weighed in the eternal balance, and were not found wanting.

But what of Zion and her redemption?

Let the word of the Lord, the God of Enoch, the God of Joseph give answer:

"THE REDEMPTION OF ZION MUST NEEDS COME BY POWER."

Power dwells in unity, not in discord; in humility, not pride; in sacrifice, not selfishness; obedience, not rebellion.

Zion's Camp, if it failed at all in fulfilling its mission, failed for precisely similar reasons to those which had caused the expulsion of the Saints from Jackson County; reasons which, in ancient times, kept Israel wandering for forty years in the wilderness, within sight of their coveted Caanan, which they were not permitted in that generation to possess. Like Moses, these modern pilgrims beheld, as from Pisgah's top, their promised land: like Moses, on account of transgression, they were not permitted to "cross over." No doubt there were Calebs and Joshuas in the Camp, who were worthy. But the great event, in the wisdom of the Highest, was not then destined to be.

It was left for a future generation and its Joshua to go up in the might of the Lord and redeem Zion. [78]

Yet not alone upon Zion's Camp must rest the responsibility of their failure to redeem Zion. It bears with at least equal weight upon those whom they came to succor.

What said the Lord concerning them?

"Behold, they have not learned to be obedient, ... but are full of all manner of evil, and do not impart of their substance, as becometh Saints, to the poor and afflicted among them."

Is not the episode of the fowl, related by Heber, a tell-tale straw before the wind in this connection? Can a people honey-combed with selfishness build up Zion?

"And are not united according to the union required by the law of the celestial kingdom;"—

Again that injunction of unity, the secret of Zion's redemption. "Except ye are one ye are not mine."

"And Zion cannot be built up unless it is by the principles of the law of the celestial kingdom, otherwise I cannot receive her unto myself."

Wonderful revealing, this. What is it but to say that the United Order, the Order of Enoch, the Order of Zion, is the order of the celestial worlds, where the Gods, a divine brotherhood, have "all things common?"

"Therefore it is expedient in me that mine elders should wait for a little season, for the redemption of Zion."

Is it marvelous that this should be; that a work of such magnitude should require preparation; that Zion, city of holiness, should be built up only by the pure in heart? Ah, reader, the redemption of Zion is more than the purchase or recovery of lands, the building of cities, or even the founding of nations. It is the conquest of the heart, the subjugation of the soul, the sanctifying of [79] the flesh, the purifying and ennobling of the passions. Greater is he who subdues himself, who captures and maintains the citadel of his own soul, than he who, misnamed conqueror, fills the world with the roar of drums, the thunder of cannon, the lightning of swords and bayonets, overturns and sets up kingdoms, lives and reigns a king, yet wears to the grave the fetters of unbridled lust, and dies the slave of sin.

In her children's hearts must Zion first be built up and redeemed; "every man seeking the interest of his neighbor, and doing all things with an eye single to the glory of God." When the fig-tree of Israel's faith puts forth such leaves, then know that the summer is nigh.

"And this cannot be brought to pass, until mine elders are endowed with power from on high."

And yet were these same elders, unendowed, sent forth to redeem Zion? Surely the Lord did not design it then to be. Else, would he not have endowed them before-hand? This admitted, and what becomes of their "failure?"

Ah, there are many such failures in a sublime success. They are but steps in the stairway of triumph and victory.

What did Zion's Camp achieve? It cast the shadow of a coming event; struck the spark that shall kindle to a flame; fixed on the horizon of history a shining star, the herald of a glory yet to come. [80]

## CHAPTER 10

BUILDING THE TEMPLE—JOSEPH AND HEBER WORKING IN THE QUARRY—THE THEOLOGICAL SCHOOL—A LESSON ON FAITH—CALL OF THE TWELVE—HEBER C. KIMBALL ORDAINED AN APOSTLE

THE work now engaging, almost exclusively, the attention of the Church in Kirtland, was the building of the Temple. This edifice was begun in June, 1833. The walls were partly reared when, in the year following, the expedition for the relief of the Missouri Saints took from Kirtland nearly all the able-bodied men whose means and energies, otherwise, would have been employed upon the Lord's House.

But the sacred enterprise was not suffered to languish. The elders left in charge were untiring in their efforts to promote the work. The brethren labored day and night, and the sisters—among the foremost, as ever, in a good cause—were not one whit behind. Says Heber:

"Our women were engaged in knitting and spinning, in order to clothe those who were laboring at the building; and the Lord only knows the scenes of poverty, tribulation and distress which we passed through to accomplish it. My wife had toiled all summer in lending her aid towards its accomplishment. She took a hundred pounds of wool to spin on shares, which, with the assistance of a girl, she spun, in order to furnish clothing for those engaged in building the temple; and although she had the privilege of keeping half the quantity of [81] wool for herself, as a recompense for her labor, she did not reserve even so much as would make a pair of stockings, but gave it for those who were laboring at the house of the Lord. She spun and wove, and got the cloth dressed and cut and made up into garments, and gave them to the laborers on the temple. Almost all the sisters in Kirtland labored in knitting, sewing, spinning, etc., for the same purpose; while we went up to Missouri to endeavor to reinstate our brethren on the lands from which they had been driven.

"Elder Rigdon, when addressing the brethren upon the importance of building this house, spake to this effect: That we should use every effort to accomplish this building by the time appointed; if we did the Lord would accept it at our hands; and on it depends the salvation of the Church, and also of the world. Looking at the sufferings and poverty of the Church, he frequently went upon the walls of the building, both by night and day, and wept, crying aloud to the Almighty to send means whereby we might accomplish the building.

"After we returned from our journey to the West, the whole Church united in this great undertaking, and every man lent a helping hand. Those who had not teams went to work in the stone quarry and prepared the stones for drawing to the house.

"The Prophet, being our foreman, would put on his tow frock and tow pantaloons and go into the quarry. The Presidency, High Priests and Elders all alike assisting. Those who had teams assisted in drawing the stone to the house. These all laboring one day in the week, brought as many stones to the house as supplied the masons through the whole week. We continued in this manner until the walls of the house were reared. The committee who were appointed by revelation to superin[82]tend the building were Hyrum Smith, Reynolds Cahoon and Jared Carter. They used every exertion in their power to forward the work."

During the winter of 1834-5, Heber attended the theological school established in Kirtland. Here originated the lectures on faith, contained in the book of Doctrine and Covenants. It was the custom, at these meetings, to call upon a certain number to speak for the edification of the others. Heber, on one occasion, was invited to address them on the subject of faith. Every passage of scripture bearing on the theme having been quoted by previous speakers, and not wishing to repeat what they had said, he was left to depend entirely upon the Spirit. He began by relating the following anecdote, the incident of which had occurred in his own family:

"My wife, one day, when going out on a visit, gave my daughter Helen Mar charge not to touch the dishes, for if she broke any during her absence she would give her a whipping when she returned. While my wife was absent my daughter broke a number of the dishes by letting the table leaf fall, and then she went out under an apple tree and prayed that her mother's heart might be softened, that when she returned she might not whip her. Her mother was very punctual when she made a promise to her children, to fulfill it, and when she returned she undertook, as a duty, to carry this promise into effect. She retired with her into her room, but found herself powerless to chastise her; her heart was so softened that it was impossible for her to raise her hand against the child. Afterwards, Helen told her mother she had prayed to the Lord that she might not whip her."

Heber paused in his simple narrative. Tears glistened in the eyes of his hearers; the Prophet Joseph was weeping like a child. He told the brethren that that was [83] the kind of faith they needed; the faith of a little child, going in humility to its Parent, and asking for the desire of its heart. He said the anecdote was well-timed.

A grammar school was opened in Kirtland the same winter, taught by Sidney Rigdon and William E. McLellin. Most of the Elders, including the Prophet, attended this school. Some of them were very apt pupils and made rapid headway. Heber's progress, however, was only moderate. Grammar, as a study, afforded him little delight. The mysteries of syntax seemed to elude his mental grasp, as the will-o'-the-wisp the eye and hand of its pursuer. A lover of choice language, and, when loftily inspired, a user of much that was beautiful and sublime; a never-failing fountain of poetic thought and imagery; the technicalities of his mother tongue nevertheless seemed to baffle him. His forte lay elsewhere. He was a philosopher, rather than an orator. Many excelled him in speaking, but few, as thinkers, were his equals. If, in the gift of speech, the power of expression, he fell below many of his confreres, he had thoughts, ideas, inspirations, toward which, as eagles toward the sun, their loftiest oratory soared in vain. His words, though humble, were as sparks of prophecy from the Spirit's flaming forge; his inspired utterances, casual as they sometimes seemed, were like oracles and decrees of fate.

"I used to tell Brother Heber I never wanted him to say anything but good of me," an Apostle once remarked, significantly, in the hearing of the writer.

Some six weeks after the establishment of the grammar school, a meeting of the Camp of Zion was called to assemble, to receive what was termed "a Zion's blessing." At this meeting it was announced by the Prophet that "those who went to Zion with a determination to lay down their lives, if necessary, it was the will of God that **[84]** they should be ordained to the ministry and go forth to prune the vineyard for the last time, or the coming of the Lord, which was nigh—even fifty-six years should wind up the scene."

Foremost of these evangelists, were to be chosen twelve men, to be known as the Twelve Apostles.

The calling of the Twelve had been revealed to Joseph as early as June, 1829. In the same revelation it was given to Oliver Cowdery and David Whitmer—whose calling, the Lord said, was the same as that of the Apostle Paul—to "search out the Twelve," and make known to them their mission.

Little thought Heber that he was to be one of them, and would live to make his name illustrious as a bearer of glad tidings to the nations. It is doubtful that he even knew, at that time, of the intention to choose the Apostles. The revelations were not published then, as now, and few had access to the manuscripts in those early days.

The day set for the choosing of the Twelve was Saturday, February 14th, 1835. The meeting having been duly organized, an expression was taken whereby the Elders present signified their willingness and "anxious desire" to have the Spirit of the Lord dictate in the choice of the Apostles. The three witnesses—Oliver Cowdery, David Whitmer and Martin Harris, each in turn then offered prayer. They were blessed under the hands of the First Presidency, and then proceeded to call forth the Twelve.

The first three chosen were Lyman E. Johnson, Brigham Young and Heber C. Kimball. They were called into the stand, and, after expressing themselves in relation to the holy calling about to be conferred upon them, were ordained under the hands of the First Presi**[85]**dency and the Three Witnesses. "These brethren," says Heber, "ordained us to the Apostleship." Here is a copy of his ordination blessing:

"Heber C. Kimball shall be made like unto those who have been blessed before him, and he shall be favored with the same blessing; that he may receive visions, the ministration of angels, and hear their voices, and even come into the presence of God. That many millions may be converted by his instrumentality, that angels may waft him from place to place, and that he may stand unto the coming of our Lord; that he shall be made acquainted with the day when Christ shall come; that he shall be made perfect in faith; that the deaf shall hear, the lame shall walk, the blind shall see, and greater things than these shall he do; and that he shall have boldness of speech before the nations, and great power." Etc.

The next day Orson Hyde, David W. Patten, Luke S. Johnson, William E. McLellin, John F. Boynton and William Smith were chosen in like manner. The remaining three of the Twelve were Parley P. Pratt, Orson Pratt and Thomas B. Marsh, who were absent at the time of choosing. Parley was ordained an Apostle on February 21st, Thomas B. Marsh on the 25th or 26th of April, and Orson Pratt on the 26th of that month.

No history of this important event would be complete without the famous "Charge to the Twelve," delivered by President Oliver Cowdery. It was as follows:

"DEAR BRETHREN:—Previously to delivering the charge I shall read a part of a revelation. It is known to you that previous to the organization of this Church in 1830, the Lord gave revelations or the Church could not have been organized.

"The people of this Church were weak in faith compared with the ancients. Those who embarked in this cause were desirous to know how the work was to be conducted. They had read many things in the Book of **[86]** Mormon concerning their duty and the way the great work ought to be done; but the minds of men are so constructed that they will not believe without a testimony of seeing or hearing. The Lord gave us a revelation that in process of time there should be twelve chosen to preach His Gospel to Jew and Gentile. Our minds have been on a constant stretch to find who these twelve were.

"When the time should come, we could not tell, but we sought the Lord by fasting and prayer, to have our lives prolonged to see this day, to see you, and to take a retrospect of the difficulties through which we have passed. But having seen the day, it becomes my duty to deliver to you a charge. And first, a few remarks respecting your ministry. You have many revelations put into your hands, revelations to make you acquainted with the nature of your mission. You will have difficulties by reason of your visiting all the nations of the world. You will need wisdom in a two-fold proportion to what you have ever had. You will have to combat all the prejudices of all nations." He then read the revelation and proceeded to say, "Have you desired this ministry with all your hearts? If you have desired it, you are called of God, not of man, to go into all the world." He read again from the revelation, what the Lord said to the twelve brethren. "You have your duty presented in revelation. You have been ordained to the Holy Priesthood. You have received it from those who had their power and authority from an angel. You are to preach the Gospel to every nation. Should you in the least degree come short of your duty, great will be your condemnation, for the greater the calling, the greater the transgression. I, therefore, warn you to cultivate great humility, for I know the pride of the human heart. Beware lest the flatterers of the world lift you up. Beware lest your affections are captivated by worldly objects.

"Let your ministry be first. Remember the souls of men are committed to your charge, and if you mind your calling you shall always prosper. You have been indebted to other men in the first instance for evidence, [87] on that you have acted. But it is necessary that you receive a testimony from Heaven for yourselves, so that you can bear testimony to the truth of the Book of Mormon, and that you have seen the face of God; that is more than the testimony of an angel. When the proper time arrives, you shall be able to bear this testimony to the world. When you bear testimony that you have seen God, this testimony God will never suffer to fall, but will bear you out, although many will not give heed, yet others will. You will therefore see the necessity of getting this testimony from Heaven. Never cease striving until you have seen God face to face. Strengthen your faith, cast off your doubts, your sins and all your unbelief, and nothing can prevent you from coming to God. Your ordination is not full and complete till God has laid His hand upon you. We require as much to qualify us as did those who have gone before us. God is the same. If the Savior in former days laid His hands on His disciples, why not in the latter days?

"With regard to superiority I must make a few remarks. The ancient Apostles sought to be great; but, brethren, lest the seeds of discord be sown in this matter, understand the voice of the Spirit on this occasion, God does not love you better or more than others. You are to contend for the faith once delivered to the Saints. Jacob, you know, wrestled till he obtained. It was by fervent prayer and diligent search that you have obtained the testimony that you are now able to bear. You are as one. You are equal in bearing the keys of the kingdom to all nations.

"You are called to preach the Gospel of the Son of God to the nations of the earth. It is the will of your Heavenly Father that you proclaim His Gospel to the ends of the earth and the islands of the sea. Be zealous to save souls. The soul of one man is as precious as the soul of another. You are to bear this message to those who consider themselves wise, and such may persecute you; they may seek your life. The adversary has always sought the lives of the servants of God. You are, there[88]fore, to be prepared at all times to make a sacrifice of your lives, should the Lord require them in the advancement and building up of His cause. Murmur not at God. Be always prayerful, be always watchful. You will bear with me while I relieve the feelings of my heart. We shall not see another day like this. The time has fully come. The voice of the Spirit has come to set these men apart. You will see the time when you will desire to see such a day as this, and you will not see it. Every heart wishes you peace and prosperity, but the scene with you will inevitably change. Let no man take your Bishopric, and beware that you lose not your crowns. It will require your whole souls. It will require courage like Enoch's. The time is near when you will be in the midst of congregations who will gnash their teeth upon you. This Gospel must roll and will roll till it fills the whole earth.

"Did I say congregations would gnash upon you? Yea, I say nations will gnash upon you. You will be considered the worst of men. Be not discouraged at this. When God pours out His Spirit the enemy will rage, but God, remember, is on your right hand and on your left. A man, though he may be considered the worst, has joy who is conscious that he pleases God. The lives of those who proclaim the true Gospel will be in danger. This has been the case ever since the days of righteous Abel.

"The same opposition has been manifest whenever men came forward to publish the Gospel. The time is coming when you will be considered the worst by many, and by some the best of men. The time is coming when you will be perfectly familiar with the things of God. This testimony will make those who do not believe your testimony, seek your lives. But there are whole nations who will receive your testimony. They will call you good men. Be not lifted up when you are called good men. Remember you are young men, and you shall be spared. I include the other three. Bear them in mind in your prayers, carry their cares to a throne of grace. **[89]** Although they are not present yet you and they are equal.

"This appointment is calculated to create an affection in you, for each other, stronger than death. You will travel to other nations. Bear each other in mind. If one or more is cast into prison, let the others pray for him and deliver him by their prayers.

"Your lives shall be in great jeopardy, but the promise of God is that you shall be delivered. Remember you are not to go to other nations till you receive your endowment. Tarry at Kirtland until you are endowed with power from on high. You need a fountain of wisdom, knowledge and intelligence such as you never had. Relative to the endowment, I make a remark or two, that there be no mistake. The world cannot receive the things of God. He can endow you without worldly pomp or great parade. He can give you that wisdom, that intelligence and that power which characterized the ancient Saints and now characterizes the inhabitants of the upper world. The greatness of your commission consists in this; you are to hold the keys of this ministry. You are to go to the nations afar off; nations that sit in darkness. The day is coming when the work of God must be done. Israel shall be gathered. The seed of Jacob shall be gathered from their long dispersion. There will be a feast to Israel the elect of God. It is a sorrowful tale, but the Gospel must be preached and His (God's) ministers be rejected, but where can Israel be found, and receive your testimony and not rejoice? Nowhere. The prophecies are full of great things that are to take place in the last days. After the elect is gathered out, destruction shall come on the inhabitants of the earth. All nations shall feel the wrath of God after they have been warned by the Saints of the Most High. If you will not warn them others will and you will lose your crowns. You must prepare your minds to bid a long farewell to Kirtland, even till the great day come. You will see what you never expected to see. You will need the mind of Enoch or Elijah and the faith of the brother **[90]** of Jared. You must be prepared to walk by faith, however appalling the prospect to human view. You, and each of you should feel the force of the imperious mandate. Son, go labor in my vineyard, and cheerfully receive what comes, but in the end you will stand while others will fall. You have read in the revelation concerning ordination. Beware how you ordain, for all nations are not like this nation. They will willingly receive the ordinances at your hand to put you out of the way. There will be times, when nothing but the angels of God can deliver you out of their hand. We appeal to your intelligence, we appeal to your understanding, that we have so far discharged our duty to you. We consider it one of the greatest condescensions of our Heavenly Father in pointing you out to us. You will be stewards over this ministry.

"We have work to do that no other men can do. You must proclaim the Gospel in its simplicity and purity, and we commend you to God and the word of His grace. You have our best wishes, you have our most fervent prayers that you may be able to bear this testimony, that you have seen the face of God. Therefore call upon Him in faith and mighty prayer till you prevail, for it is your duty and your privilege to bear such testimony for yourselves. We now expect you to be faithful, to fulfill your calling, there must be no lack here. You must fulfill in all things, and permit us to repeat, all nations have a claim on you. You are bound together as the three witnesses were, you, notwithstanding can part and meet and meet and part again till your heads are silvered o'er with age."

He then took them separately by the hand and said: "Do you with full purpose of heart take part in this ministry, to proclaim the Gospel with all diligence with those your brethren, according to the tenor and intent of the charge you have received." Each of them answered in the affirmative.

Thus were chosen the first Twelve Apostles of the last dispensation. The first quorum of Seventies, their **[91]** co-laborers in the ministry, was called into existence about the same time, its members being selected, as the Twelve had been, from the survivors of Zion's Camp, whose faith and integrity had been tried and proven.

The Apostles assembled from time to time to receive instructions from the Prophet, and strengthen each other in the Lord. One evening when they had met together for this purpose, the grand revelation on Priesthood (now forming the first half of Section 107 of the book of Doctrine and Covenants) was given.

Sunday, April 5th, 1835. Says Heber: "The Twelve had not all, as yet, been together, and as the time drew near that we should travel to the east, we appointed this day to bear our testimony unto our brethren and friends. We were all assembled together with the exception of Brother Orson Pratt, who had not yet been with us. We proceeded to speak according to our ages, the oldest speaking first. This day Brothers Thomas B. Marsh, David W. Patten, Brigham Young and Heber C. Kimball spoke. Sunday, 12th, Brothers Orson Hyde, William E. McLellin, Parley P. Pratt, and Luke S. Johnson spoke. Sunday, 19th, Brothers William Smith, John F. Boynton and Lyman E. Johnson spoke, closing the testimony of the Twelve Apostles to the people in Kirtland at that time. Sunday, 26th, Brother Orson Pratt entered the house while we were opening the meeting and praying and wishing for his arrival. He was ordained an apostle, and we received our charge from Joseph

Smith, the Prophet."

The eldest of the Apostles, Thos. B. Marsh, thus became president of the quorum; though the Twelve were all equal in authority. This order was agreeable to the will of Heaven. [92]

## CHAPTER 11

FIRST MISSION OF THE TWELVE—HEBER REVISITS THE SCENES OF HIS CHILDHOOD—MOBBING AN ABOLITIONIST—"THE ACCUSER OF THE BRETHREN"—DAYS OF REPENTANCE AND REFORMATION

THE Apostles started on their first mission, May 4th, 1835. They traveled through the eastern states and Upper Canada, preaching, baptizing, setting in order the branches of the Church, counseling the Saints to gather westward, and collecting means for the purchase of lands in Missouri and the completion of the Lord's House in Kirtland. Like the Apostles anciently, they went forth two by two, traveling "without purse or scrip," and preaching by the way. Heber's first companion was William Smith, brother to the Prophet.

Separating at Dunkirk, New York, on the 5th of May, the Apostles met in conference on the 9th, at Westfield, Chautauqua County. Here they sat in council upon the first case brought before them for adjudication. A local traveling Elder named Joseph Rose had been teaching erroneous doctrine and perverting the word of God, in that he spiritualized the literal promise of the Savior; that before His second coming the sun should be darkened and the moon turned to blood. Rose asserted that the Jewish church was the sun, darkened, and the Gentile church, the moon, which should be turned to blood. He was shown his error and reproved sharply, whereupon he humbly acknowledged his fault.

At Mendon, his former home, Heber and his companion, Elder Orson Hyde, were confronted by a Bap[93]tist priest named Fulton, who withstood them harshly. Says Heber: "He called us false prophets, and, rejecting our testimony, advised us to go home. We declared unto him that we should go forth preaching the Gospel, and no power should stay us. I told him if he did not repent of his sins and be baptized for the remission of them, he would be damned; which made him angry. We then passed on until we came to a pure stream of water, and there cleansed our feet, bearing testimony against him, as the Lord commanded."

At the Lyonstown conference, on the 6th of June, it was Heber's turn to preside; the Twelve having been instructed by the Prophet to preside in turn at their meetings according to their ages. From here Elder Kimball traveled in company with Elder Luke Johnson towards Pillowpoint, the place of the next conference. In the town of Rose they were cordially received, but in Hewton were turned away from twelve houses, where they had solicited entertainment. At midnight they put up at an inn, retiring supperless to bed, as they had but one shilling with which to pay for their lodging. A walk of six miles before breakfast next morning brought them to Esquire David Ellsworth's where they were warmly welcomed and hospitably entertained. The Apostles blessed the kind souls who thus administered to their wants, and who, on bidding them farewell, gave them money, wished them God-speed and wept at their departure. About one year later the whole family embraced the Gospel.

At Pillowpoint, Jefferson County, a conference was held on the 19th of June. Here the council tried John Elmer, a member of the Church, for holding views and doctrines opposed to the principles of truth. "When called upon, he stated that he had had many visions and **[94]** revelations, and that the Lord had revealed to him of a certainty that He would make His second appearance within fifteen years; also that the Spirit of God often came upon him and threw him down, and caused him to disfigure himself, or die the death of the righteous, or of the wicked, and then come to life again in the presence of others, to convince them that he was a man of God and had great power. He also stated that in one of his visions the Lord Jesus appeared personally and laid His hands upon him and sanctified him, both soul and body, and that he was now immortal or changed, so that he would never die. He stated that he could hold red-hot iron or live coals of fire in his hands without receiving any injury; together with other curious notions and vagaries, ascribing them all to the power of God; and that he never would deny them, although the Council and whole Church should decide against him. The Council endeavored to show him that he was deceived by the adversary, but to no effect. He said he would rather be expelled from the Church than give up any of his views or say they were not of God. Consequently the Church lifted their hands against him."

While at Sackett's Harbor, Heber received a letter from his wife, apprising him of the birth of his son, Heber P., at Kirtland, on the 1st of June. His joy found vent in a characteristic burst of humor. He propounded the following riddle to the brethren: "I have three children now, and have not seen one of them." This was quite a puzzle to them, until he explained that the *one* he referred to was the infant born since he left home.

He next visited his native state, Vermont, and remained several days among the scenes of his childhood, visiting and preaching to his relatives and acquaintances, and wherever opportunity arose. Some believed, **[95]** but did not obey the Gospel. A false prophet named Davison had gone through the country some time before, deceiving the people with pretended miracles. They were therefore prejudiced against the true faith, with its new and strange promises of spiritual gifts and blessings.

Crossing over the Green Mountains, taking a bypath through a lonely and densely timbered wilderness, his only companions the wild animals and screech-owls inhabiting those solitudes, he arrived at St. Johnsbury, and met in council with his brethren on the 17th of July. They held their meetings in a large barn belonging to a Mr. Snow. It was in this neighborhood that the Snow, Farr, Badger and Bingham families embraced the Gospel. Apostle Erastus Snow was born at St. Johnsbury, November 9th, 1818.

With sore and blistered feet, Heber now traveled alone down the Connecticut river into New Hampshire, visiting the town of Plainfield, where his mother was born. He met with considerable opposition, even among his own kindred. At Bradford the Twelve sat in council and tried Elder Gladden Bishop for teaching false doctrine. He was suspended from fellowship. Heber next visited Boston, in company with Apostles Thomas B. Marsh and Brigham Young, and after spending several days with the Saints in that city, where each was presented with a new suit of clothes by Sisters Fanny Brewer, Polly Voce and others, they went northward to the state of Maine. On the way they stopped at Dover, and were shown through a large cotton factory, the work-hands all suspending operations and gazing with much curiosity at the "Mormon Apostles."

The last conference of the year 1835 was held at Farmington, Maine, on the 28th of August. Having fulfilled their mission, the Apostles agreed to return to **[96]** Kirtland, and separated with that understanding, after appointing a day and hour to meet upon the steamboat wharf in Buffalo.

At Concord, New Hampshire, under date of September 3rd, Heber writes thus in his journal: "Here I understood an Abolitionist named Davis was going to deliver a lecture at the Court House. I went with the other stage passengers to hear his principles. After waiting some time for the gentleman, instead of seeing his person as we anticipated, we beheld an uproar among the people, and our ears were saluted with the howls of three or four hundred demons in human shape who were in search of the Abolitionist; and not finding him in the State House, or streets, they commenced demolishing a building and searching others. After a little while the peace officers prevailed on them to desist. They then prepared an effigy, which they carried through the streets on a rail for some time; then forming an assembly before the State House, had an oration delivered on the subject and burned the effigy, while the men of the city dared not open their mouths or say ought to them. They then went to a place where they had three pieces of cannon, which they continued firing until daylight. This was a night of peculiar feeling; reflecting upon the night when my brethren were driven from their homes in Jackson County, Missouri, by a similar mob, and also considering that the time might come when I might fall into the hands of a like band of ruffians, my cry to the Lord was, Save the man from the hands of these foul monsters. There was such an uproar in the city next morning, that it took five men to hold the horses while the passengers got into the stage. This man was one of the first lecturers on Abolitionism in that country, and it was then very unpopular." **[97]**

At Plainfield, Heber tarried two days with his cousin, Charles Spaulding, in the house where his mother was born and reared. From him he received a legacy of seven dollars, left him by his aunt, Speedy Spaulding, who had died a short time before. This money enabled him to pursue his journey. By way of Albany, New York, Palmyra and the hill Cumorah, he proceeded to Canandaigua, where lived his sister Melvina (Mrs. James M. Wheeler) and to Byron, the home of his sister

Abigail (Mrs. Jesse Mum). Thence he rode on to Buffalo, the stage arriving just one hour ahead of the appointed time. His brethren, the Apostles, were all there awaiting him.

Taking passage on board the steamer "United States," they had gone as far as Dunkirk when the vessel struck a rock and sprung a leak. She made for Erie, but reached there with difficulty, being obliged to run upon a sand-bar to keep from sinking. Hailing a passing boat, the Apostles left the disabled steamer, and on board the other arrived at Fairport, from which point they had sailed nearly five months before. Here they hired wagons and drove on to Kirtland, reaching home on the 25th of September.

While the Apostles were absent upon this mission, the "accuser of the brethren" had been busy sowing discord, with a view to causing coldness and estrangement between the First Presidency and the Twelve. Two of the Apostles, Orson Hyde and William E. McLellin, had been suspended during their absence and called home for trial, and, so great was the influence brought to bear by misrepresentation upon the minds of the Presidency, they had been led to mistrust the fidelity of others.

The charge against Elders Hyde and McLellin was for speaking and writing disrespectfully of President Rig[98]don, in his manner of conducting the Kirtland school. The charge was substantiated, and the brethren confessed their fault and were restored to fellowship.

The accusations against the Twelve were more serious. It was said that they had sought to be independent of the presiding quorum of the Church, and had failed to fulfill their mission, in not preaching, at the Freedom conference, the gathering to Zion, or the collection of means for the Kirtland Temple and the purchase of lands in Missouri. Both charges were proved to be groundless.

At the council, where the Apostles laid their grievances before the Presidency, and "all things were reconciled," the Prophet Joseph, it is said, made a covenant with the Twelve that never again would he entertain a charge against them on one-sided testimony, or pass judgment upon them even in thought, without first giving them an opportunity of being heard in their own defense.

If this noble, just, and charitable resolve had always been adhered to by the Saints of God, in whom, if in any people, such a principle should find its exponents and exemplars, how many bitter heart-burnings might have been spared; how many reputations remained unblasted, enmities unaroused, wounds uninfected! Had the idle gossip, the malicious slanderer, the toadying, truckling tale-bearer, who oscillates, pendulum-like, between man and man, seeking occasion against his brother, making him "an offender for a word," coloring all he hears, and pouring into oft too willing ears his insidious tale of derogations and detractions;—had such characters invariably been required to face those whom they accused and to prove their assertions, who can say that the cause of Zion, the unity and purification of God's people, would not have been subserved rather than [99] injured thereby? Are we not too prone to heed the tale-bearer, the secret enemy, who, striking unawares with "the shaft that flies in darkness," perchance seeks to build up his own, upon the ruins of his brother's reputation; and too slow to remember justice and the law of God—that in the mouths of two or three witnesses, and these not enemies of the accused, shall every word be established?

Well might Solomon say, and well may it be believed, that among the things which "the Lord doth hate," are "a false witness that speaketh lies, and he that soweth discord among brethren."

The men who had caused the trouble between the Presidency and the Apostles, or those whom Heber held responsible, were Warren Cowdery, Jared Carter and others, who, using Oliver Cowdery and other influential Elders near the person of the Prophet, as conduits of their ill-will, wrought injury to their brethren who were far away, unable, because absent, to defend themselves.

"I will here remark," says Heber, "that every individual who used an influence against the Twelve on their mission, apostatized and went out of the Church; and this should remain an everlasting warning to all others. In those days there was a continual itching in certain individuals to destroy the union existing between the Twelve and the First Presidency, and the union in the First Presidency, which thing they did at last effect, which broke up the Church for a time; for Oliver Cowdery, Warren Cowdery, Jared Carter, Frederick G. Williams, and six of the Twelve became disaffected, and turned against Joseph and those of the Twelve who sustained him."

As, in the end, good comes of evil, and from the compost-heap springs forth the flower of fragrance and [100] beauty, so from the unhappy event related, issued good and glad results. From the time the reconciliation took place between the Presidency and the Twelve, a reformation commenced in the Church. "Those meetings," says Heber, "of humiliation, repentance, and confessing of sins, were truly the beginning of good days to us, and they continued through the endowment."

## CHAPTER 12

HEBER'S DESCRIPTION OF THE TEMPLE—ITS DEDICATION—ANGELS ADMINISTER—THE "BELOVED DISCIPLE" JOHN SEEN—THE SOLEMN ASSEMBLY—THE ELDERS ENDOWED WITH POWER FROM ON HIGH—HEBER'S LONE MISSION

The Kirtland Temple was dedicated on the 27th of March, 1836. It was yet in an unfinished state, but for some time had been used for meetings and councils of the Priesthood. From Heber's pen we have the following description of the edifice and the ceremonies of its dedication:

"This building the Saints commenced in 1833, in poverty, and without means to do it. In 1834 they completed the walls, and in 1835-6 they nearly finished it. The cost was between sixty and seventy thousand dollars. A committee was appointed to gather donations; they traveled among the churches and collected a considerable amount, but not sufficient, so that in the end they found themselves between thirteen and fourteen thousand **[101]** dollars in debt. This house was 80 x 60 feet, and 57 feet high to the eaves. It was divided into two stories, each 22 feet high and arched overhead. Ten feet were cut off from the front by a partition, and used as an entry or outer court, which also contained the stairs. This left the main room 55 x 65 feet in the clear, both below and above. In each of these rooms were built two pulpits, one in each end. Each pulpit consisted of four different apartments; the fourth standing on a platform raised a suitable height above the floor; the third stood directly behind and elevated a little above the fourth; the second in rear of and elevated above the third; and in like manner the first above the second. Each of these apartments was just large enough and rightly calculated to seat three persons, and the breastwork in front of each of these three last mentioned was constituted of three semicircles joining each other, and finished in good style. The fourth or lower one, was straight in front, and had an elegant table leaf attached to it, that could be raised at pleasure for the convenience of administering the sacrament, etc. These pulpits were alike in each end of the house. One was for the use of the Melchisedek or High Priesthood, and the other for the Aaronic or lesser Priesthood. The first or highest apartment was occupied by the First Presidency over the whole Church; the second apartment by the Melchisedek High Priesthood; the third by the President of the High Priest's Quorum; and the fourth by the President of the Elders and his two counselors. The highest apartment of the other pulpit was occupied by the Bishop of the Church and his two counselors; the next by the President of the Priests and his two counselors; the third by the President of the Teachers and his two counselors; and the fourth by the President of the Deacons and his two counselors. **[102]**

"Each of these apartments had curtains hanging from the ceiling over head down to the top of the pulpit, which could be rolled up or dropped down at pleasure; and when dropped down would completely exclude those within the apartment from the sight of all others. The room itself was finished with slips and seats so calculated that by slipping the seats a little the congregation could change their faces toward either pulpit they chose; for in some cases the high Priesthood would administer, and in other cases the lesser Priesthood would administer. The room was also divided into four compartments by means of curtains or veils hanging from the ceiling over head down to the floor, which could be rolled up at pleasure, so that the house could be used all in one or divided into four rooms and used for different purposes. Thus the house was constructed to suit and accommodate the different quorums of the Priesthood and worship peculiar to the Church. The first story or lower room was dedicated for divine worship alone. The second story was finished similar in form to the first, but was designed wholly for instructing the Priesthood, and was supplied with tables and seats instead of slips. In the attic, five rooms were finished for the convenience of schools and for different quorums of the Church to meet in. There was no baptismal font in this temple, the ordinance of baptism for the dead not having been revealed.

"At the time of dedication the first story was finished, also the attic, but the second story was in an unfinished condition.

"At the dedication an address was delivered by Elder Rigdon, from Matthew 8th chap., 18th, 19th and 20th verses—more particularly the 20th. He spoke two hours and a half. The tenor of his discourse went to [103] show the toils, sufferings, privations, and hardships the brethren and sisters had to endure while building this house, and compared it with the sufferings of the Saints in the days of the Savior. After the address the voice of the assembly was taken in reference to receiving and upholding the several presidents of the different quorums in their standing. The vote was unanimously in the affirmative in every instance. A hymn was sung, and then we had an interesting address from President Joseph Smith, and closed with a dedication prayer written by the Prophet.

"During the ceremonies of the dedication, an angel appeared and sat near President Joseph Smith, sen., and Frederick G. Williams, so that they had a fair view of his person. He was a very tall personage, black eyes, white hair, and stoop shouldered; his garment was whole, extending to near his ankles; on his feet he had sandals. He was sent as a messenger to accept of the dedication. The Priesthood was organized according to the proper order. During the whole of the dedication each quorum was placed in its respective station. Everything was conducted in the best of order, and profound silence maintained."

The Temple having been dedicated, the Apostles and Elders received their endowments, according to the promise of the Lord in Missouri. Says Heber:

"We had been commanded to prepare ourselves for a solemn assembly. At length the time arrived for this assembly to meet; previous to which the Prophet Joseph exhorted the Elders to solemnize their minds, by casting away every evil from them, in thought, word and deed, and to let their hearts become sanctified, because they need not expect a blessing from God without being duly prepared for it, for the Holy Ghost would not dwell in [104] unholy temples. This meeting took place soon after the house of the Lord had been dedicated....

"When the Prophet Joseph had finished the endowments of the First Presidency, the Twelve and the Presiding Bishops, the First Presidency proceeded to lay hands upon each one of them to seal and confirm the anointing; and at the close of each blessing the whole of the quorums responded to it with a loud shout of Hosanna! Hosanna! etc.

"While these things were being attended to the beloved disciple John was seen in our midst by the Prophet Joseph, Oliver Cowdery and others. After this all the quorums arose in order, together with the three Presidencies; and the Twelve then presented themselves separately and individually before the First Presidency, with hands uplifted towards heaven, and asked of God whatever they felt to desire; and after each individual petition the whole of the quorums answered aloud Amen! Hosanna! Hosanna! Hosanna! To God and the Lamb, forever and ever, amen and amen!

"The 6th day of April being the day appointed for fasting and prayer, all the Elders, Priests, Teachers and Deacons, numbering about four hundred, met together in the House of the Lord to attend to further ordinances; none being permitted to enter but official members who had previously received their washings and anointings. Water being provided, the First Presidency, after girding themselves with towels, proceeded to wash the feet of the Twelve. After they got through the Twelve girded themselves and washed the feet of the Seventies. They then took their seats, each quorum seating themselves in their respective places and continued in fasting and prayer, prophesying and exhortation until evening. A sufficient quantity of bread having been provided to feed [105] this whole assembly, it was broken by the First Presidency of the Church and Twelve, after which the congregation knelt while a benediction was pronounced upon it by the First Presidency; and afterwards the Twelve took it and administered to the congregation. Then wine, also being provided, was blessed by the First Presidency and in like manner served to the congregation by the Twelve. This order of things is similar to that which was attended to by the Savior, amongst His disciples, previous to His ascension. The meeting continued on through the night; the spirit of prophecy was poured out upon the assembly, and cloven tongues of fire sat upon them; for they were seen by many of the congregation. Also angels administered to many, for they were also seen by many.

"This continued several days and was attended by a marvelous spirit of prophecy. Every man's mouth was full of prophesying, and for a number of days or weeks our time was spent in visiting from house to house, administering bread and wine, and pronouncing blessings upon each other to that degree, that from the external appearances one would have supposed that the last days had truly come, in which the Spirit of the Lord was poured out upon all flesh, as far as the Church was concerned, for the sons and daughters of Zion were full of prophesying. In this prophesying great blessings were pronounced upon the faithful, and also great cursings upon the ungodly, or upon those who had smitten us. During this time many great and marvelous visions were seen, one of which I will mention which Joseph the Prophet had concerning the Twelve. His anxiety was and had been very great for their welfare, when the following vision was manifested to him, as near as I can recollect: [106]

"He saw the Twelve going forth, and they appeared to be in a far distant land. After some time they unexpectedly met together, apparently in great tribulation, their clothes all ragged, and their knees and feet sore. They formed into a circle, and all stood with their eyes fixed upon the ground. The Savior appeared and stood in their midst and wept over them, and wanted to show Himself to them, but they did not discover Him. He (Joseph) saw until they had accomplished their work, and arrived at the gate of the celestial city; there Father Adam stood and opened the gate to them, and as they entered he embraced them one by one and kissed them. He then led them to the throne of God, and then the Savior embraced each one of them and kissed them, and crowned each one of them in the presence of God. He saw that they all had beautiful heads of hair and all looked alike. The impression this vision left on Brother Joseph's mind was of so acute a nature, that he never could refrain from weeping while rehearsing it."

"I continued through the winter," says Heber, "some of the time going to school, and the residue laboring with my hands, until May, 1836, when I enquired of the Prophet Joseph if I should go on a mission to preach, or go to school; he replied I might do either, for the Lord would bless me in the course I should pursue. Accordingly, on the 10th of May I left Kirtland and proceeded to Fairport, where I took steamboat and arrived in Buffalo the next day. From that place I passed on to the northeast, preaching where doors were open, and baptizing for the remission of sins such as believed.

"June 13th, I arrived at Sackett's Harbor. I had the pleasure of meeting Brothers Luke Johnson and Orson Pratt, who were laboring with all their might for the cause of God in that region. [107]

"From that place I went on the steamer *United States* to Ogdensburg, St. Lawrence Co., N. Y., and from thence passed on about three miles from the village, when I was stopped by a shower of rain, which drove me into the house of Mr. Chapin for shelter, and making known my calling, the people immediately desired a meeting, and called in their neighbors, when I preached to them for about an hour. Many staid until midnight, and before I was up the next morning they called upon me requesting I should preach again that day in the school house, which I did, and at night it was again thronged with those who were eager to hear. The second morning they likewise called on me, and would not let me go until they knew the truth of my testimony, for by this time the country round was in an uproar of excitement. On the fourth morning I was called out of bed, and baptized three. I remained seven days preaching the Gospel of the Kingdom of Heaven, and baptized and confirmed seven. The promise was fulfilled, for those who believed spoke in tongues, and the sick were healed. A woman named Davis had been confined to her bed for five years, not able to do anything during that time, and scarcely able to sit up, who was given up to die by the doctors. I baptized and confirmed her a member of the Church, and at the same time prayed for her, and rebuked the disease, and commanded it to depart from her in the name of the Lord Jesus Christ. She began to amend from that very hour, and in less than one week she was performing her usual household duties, walked into the streets and attended meetings, to the astonishment of the people. Sister Chapin and others were also healed of their infirmities. Sister Davis' husband was considered a staunch Universalist. He was convinced and baptized. [108]

"Thence I journeyed to Plattsburg, where I staid all night with a Mr. Mansfield, who was very friendly to me. I then went in a steamer to St. Albans, Vt., and visited my friends in Sheldon and Bakersfield, traveled through various parts of Vermont, visited Wright's settlement on the top of the Green Mountains, where some were believing. I met Elder Solon Foster at Potsdam, preaching there once, and eight or nine bore testimony to the truth of the Gospel.

"After an absence of about five weeks I returned to Ogdensburg, met the brethren whom I had baptized, and they rejoiced at my return. When I got to the house of Brother Heman Chapin, he was grinding his scythe and fixing his cradle to commence cutting his wheat. I proposed to him if he would furnish me a tow frock and pantaloons to put on, and a rake, I would go into the field and rake and bind all he could cut. He declared there was no man living could do it. Said I, 'never mind, Brother Chapin, its nearly as easy for me to do it as to say it.' The next morning after the dew had passed off we went into the field, commencing at a piece of wheat which he said had three acres in it. Said I, 'go ahead, Brother Heman, we'll cut down this piece before dinner.' About the time he took the last clipp of the three acres I had it bound in a bundle before he had hardly a chance to look round, and about that time the horn blew to call us to dinner. We started back to his house; he never spoke or said one word to me, appearing rather confounded. The next Sabbath such a congregation of hearers I had never seen in the United States; for priests and people had come for twenty-five miles distance, to see and hear that "Mormon" who had performed a thing that had never before been done in that country, for Brother Chapin had proclaimed this **[109]** occurrence unknown to me. I tarried several days in those regions, preaching and baptizing.

"August 25th, while we were assembled for a meeting our hearts were filled with joy by the arrival of Joseph Smith, Sen., the patriarch, and his brother John Smith, who were on a mission to bless the churches in the eastern states.

"On the 27th, the church, numbering twenty, that I had baptized, came together and received patriarchal blessings under the hands of President Joseph Smith, Sen.

"Sunday, 28th, Father John Smith preached at 10 a. m., and four of us bore testimony to the Book of Mormon and the truth of the work. In the afternoon we administered the sacrament, confirmed three and blessed the little children of the branch.

"Monday, 20th, we ordained Levi Chapin a Teacher and Alvin Simons an Elder to watch over the church. I then went to Black Lake, preached and baptized one; then preached at Potsdam and baptized another. Returned to the township of Oswegatchie, called the church together at Ogdensburg, which numbered twenty-eight, and bade them farewell. I left the church rejoicing in the Lord, and many around believing the testimony.

"Thence I pursued my journey to Victor, Ontario County, where I met Vilate, my wife, who was visiting her friends, and I tarried a few days with them. Thence we pursued our journey to Buffalo. Here a magistrate came forward and paid five dollars for our passage to Frankfort, a distance of one hundred and eighty miles. The passengers were chiefly Swiss emigrants. After sitting and hearing them for some time, the Spirit of the Lord came upon me, and I was enabled to preach to **[110]** them in their own language. They seemed much pleased and treated us kindly. We had a very heavy gale while going up the lake, so that every passenger almost and some of the hands were very sick. Many were frightened, and one woman died, she being very feeble when she came on board. But we reached our destination without accident, and arrived in Kirtland, October 2nd. I was gone nearly five months, visited many of my friends, preached much, and baptized thirty. This was the first mission I took alone. The Lord was with me and blessed me, and confirmed the word with signs following."

## CHAPTER 13

THE WORSHIP OF MAMMON—THE TEMPORAL ABOVE THE SPIRITUAL—THE KIRTLAND BANK—FINANCIAL DISASTERS—APOSTASY—HEBER SORROWS OVER THE DEGENERACY OF THE TIMES

"ILL fares the land; to hastening ills a prey,
Where wealth accumulates and men decay."

DURING the absence of Apostle Kimball in the east, a grievous change had come over the Church in Kirtland. The greed of gain, the spirit of speculation was abroad in the land. Mammon had reared his altars on consecrated ground; the money-changer was within the temple. The love of the things of earth had usurped, in many hearts, the love of the things of heaven, and comparatively few were free from the soul-destroying influence of idolatry. Idolatry? Yes: the bowing down to [111] the modern Baal, the worship of wealth—the god of gold—the lust after the ways and pleasures of the world.

The order of Christ's kingdom is the order of creation: firstly spiritual, secondly temporal. When this order is subverted, "chaos is come again." Sorrow is the inevitable consequence of apostasy from the spiritual to the temporal. "To be carnally-minded is death; but to be spiritually-minded is life and peace." Does not the fall of man illustrate this principle? Can he descend from heaven to earth without causing and enduring pain?

The spiritual must sway the temporal, the earthly be ruled by the heavenly. How else shall it be sanctified? It is the spirit in man that moves the body, not the body the spirit. In the Church, Christ's body, the spiritual must reign supreme. The temporal on the heart's throne is ever the usurper; the spiritual crowned and sceptred, ruler by right divine.

Jacob is spiritual; Japheth is temporal. The mission of Israel and the mission of the Gentiles are as the poles antipodal; God's ways and man's ways, as heaven and earth apart.

"We were very much grieved," says Heber, "on our arrival in Kirtland, to see the spirit of speculation that was prevailing in the Church. Trade and traffic seemed to engross the time and attention of the Saints. When we left Kirtland a city lot was worth about $150; but on our return, to our astonishment, the same lot was said to be worth from $500. to $1000., according to location; and some men, who, when I left, could hardly get food to eat, I found on my return to be men of supposed great wealth; in fact everything in the place seemed to be moving in great prosperity, and all seemed determined to become rich; in my feelings they were artificial or imaginary riches. This appearance of prosperity led **[112]** many of the Saints to believe that the time had arrived for the Lord to enrich them with the treasures of the earth, and believing so, it stimulated them to great exertions, so much so that two of the Twelve, Lyman E. Johnson and John F. Boynton, went to New York and purchased to the amount of $20,000 worth of goods, and entered into the mercantile business, borrowing considerable money from Polly Voce and other Saints in Boston and the regions round about, and which they have never repaid."

The Prophet Joseph says of those times: "The spirit of speculation in lands and property of all kinds, which was so prevalent throughout the whole nation, was taking deep root in the Church. As the fruits of this spirit, evil surmising, fault-finding, disunion, dissension and apostasy followed in quick succession, and it seemed as though all the powers of earth and hell were combining their influence in an especial manner to overthrow the Church at once and make a final end. The enemy abroad and apostates in our midst united in their schemes, flour and provisions were turned towards other markets, and many became disaffected towards me, as though I were the sole cause of those very evils I was strenuously striving against, and which were actually brought upon us by the brethren not giving heed to my counsel."

During this period, the Kirtland Safety Society was organized, with a view to controlling the prevailing sentiment and directing it in legitimate channels. The ablest and staunchest men in Israel, including the Prophet and most of the Apostles, were made officers and members of the association.

Then came the financial crash of 1837, by which so many of the banking and business houses of the country **[113]** were prostrated. Nearly all the banks, one after another, suspended specie payment, "and gold and silver rose in value in direct ratio with the depreciation of paper currency." The Kirtland Bank shared a similar fate to many others, and went down in the whirlpool of financial ruin. One of the causes alleged for its failure was the misfeasance of some of those who were entrusted with the funds of the Bank. Heber says that Warren Parrish, one of the clerks, "afterwards acknowledged that he took $20,000, and there was strong evidence that he took more. Those of integrity in the Church replaced the stolen money at the expense of all they had." A counterfeit, falsely reputed to have been issued by the Bank, was also used by its enemies as a means to effect its overthrow.

As usual the onus of responsibility was placed upon the shoulders of the Prophet, although he had withdrawn from the institution some time before. He was falsely accused of dishonesty and fraud, and condemned beyond measure, by men in and out of the Church, as though he were the sole and intentional cause of the catastrophe.

"This order of things," continues Heber, "increased during the winter to such an extent that a man's life was in danger the moment he spoke in defence of the Prophet of God. During this time I had many days of sorrow and mourning, for my heart sickened to see the awful extent that things were getting to. The only source of consolation I had, was in bending my knees continually before my Father in Heaven, and asking Him to sustain me and preserve me from falling into snares, and from betraying my brethren as others had done; for those who apostatized sought every means and opportunity to draw others after them. They also entered into combi[114]nations to obtain wealth by fraud and every means that was evil.

"At this time, I had many dreams from the Lord; one of them I will relate. I dreamed that I entered the house of John F. Boynton, in which there was a panther; he was jet black and very beautiful to look upon, but he inspired me with fear; when I rose to leave the house he stood at the door with the intention to seize on me, and seeing my fear, he displayed his beauty to me, telling me how sleek his coat was, and what beautiful ears he had, and also his claws, which appeared to be of silver, and then he showed me his teeth, which also appeared to be silver. John F. Boynton told me that if I made myself familiar with him he would not hurt me, but if I did not he would. I did not feel disposed to do so, and while the panther was displaying to me his beauty, I slipped through the door and escaped, although he tried to keep me back by laying hold of my coat; but I rent myself from him. The interpretation of this dream was literally fulfilled. The panther represented an apostate whom I had been very familiar with. I felt to thank the Lord for this dream, and other intimations that I had, which, by His assistance, kept me from falling into snares."

The hour was approaching when Heber C. Kimball was destined to make his great mark as an Apostle of the Lord Jesus Christ, to perform a work that would perpetuate his memory, and make his name "a household word" upon the lips of tens of thousands in both hemispheres. [115]

## CHAPTER 14

ZION'S SHIP AMONG THE BREAKERS—"SOMETHING NEW MUST BE DONE TO SAVE THE CHURCH"—HEBER C. KIMBALL APPOINTED TO OPEN THE BRITISH MISSION—SPIRITUAL THINGS TO THE FRONT—RIGHTING THE SHIP—HEBER'S PROPHECY TO WILLARD RICHARDS—"YEA, IN THE NAME OF THE LORD, THOU SHALT GO WITH ME"—THE DEPARTURE FOR ENGLAND

AT this crisis in the affairs of the Church, the Lord revealed to Joseph that "something new" must be done for its salvation. The good ship Zion, storm-tossed and tempest-driven, her sails rent, her timbers sprung, a portion of her officers and crew in open mutiny, was drifting with fearful rapidity toward the rocks and breakers of destruction.

Joseph was denounced as a "fallen prophet" by men who had been his immediate friends and confidential advisers, and the divinity of his mission was being doubted by many who had received through him a testimony of the truth, the gift of the Holy Ghost, a knowledge of God and Christ, whom to know is life eternal.

"No quorum in the Church," says he, "was entirely exempt from the influence of those false spirits who were striving against me for the mastery. Even some of the Twelve were so far lost to their high and responsible calling, as to begin to take sides, secretly, with the enemy."

What "new thing," under these circumstances, was destined to "save the Church?" In what way was Jos[116]eph's mission, as a prophet of the living God, to be revindicated in the eyes of the Saints and of the world?

"On Sunday, the 4th day of June, 1837," says Heber C. Kimball, "the Prophet Joseph came to me, while I was seated in front of the stand, above the sacrament table, on the Melchisedek side of the Temple, in Kirtland, and whispering to me, said, 'Brother Heber, the Spirit of the Lord has whispered to me: 'Let my servant Heber go to England and proclaim my Gospel, and open the door of salvation to that nation.'"

The thought was overpowering. He had been surprised at his call to the apostleship: now he was overwhelmed. Like Jeremiah he staggered under the weight of his own weakness, exclaiming in self-humiliation: "O, Lord, I am a man of stammering tongue, and altogether unfit for such a work; how can I go to preach in that land, which is so famed throughout Christendom for learning, knowledge and piety; the nursery of religion; and to a people whose intelligence is proverbial!"

"Feeling my weakness to go upon such an errand, I asked the Prophet if Brother Brigham might go with me. He replied that he wanted Brother Brigham to stay with him, for he had something else for him to do. The idea of such a mission was almost more than I could bear up under. I was almost ready to sink under the burden which was placed upon me.

"However, all these considerations did not deter me from the path of duty; the moment I understood the will of my heavenly Father, I felt a determination to go at all hazards, believing that He would support me by His almighty power, and endow me with every qualification that I needed; and although my family was dear to me, and I should have to leave them almost destitute, I [117] felt that the cause of truth, the Gospel of Christ, outweighed every other consideration.

"At this time many faltered in their faith; even some of the Twelve were in rebellion against the Prophet of God. John F. Boynton said to me, 'If you are such a fool as to go at the call of the fallen prophet, Joseph Smith, I will not help you a dime, and if you are cast on Van Dieman's land, I will not make an effort to help you.' Lyman E. Johnson said he did not want me to go on my mission, but if I was determined to go, he would help me all he could; he took his cloak from off his back and put it on mine; which was the first cloak I ever had.

"Brothers Sidney Rigdon, Joseph Smith, Sen., Brigham Young, Newel K. Whitney and others said, 'Go and do as the Prophet has told you, and you shall prosper and be blessed with power to do a glorious work.' Hyrum, seeing the condition of the Church, when he talked about my mission, wept like a little child; he was continually blessing and encouraging me, and pouring out his soul in prophecies upon my head; he said: 'Go, and you shall prosper as not many have prospered.'"

Elder Orson Hyde, who had had some disagreement with the authorities and was thought to be disaffected, gave a noble proof of his integrity by asking forgiveness of the brethren, and requesting the privilege of accompanying Apostle Kimball on his mission to England. He was accordingly set apart, with Elder Kimball and Priest Joseph Fielding, for that purpose.

Says Heber: "The Presidency laid their hands on me and set me apart to preside over the mission, and conferred great blessings upon my head; said that God would make me mighty in that nation in winning souls [118] unto Him; angels should accompany me and bear me up, that my feet should never slip; that I should be mightily blessed and prove a source of salvation to thousands, not only in England but America.

"After being called on this mission, I daily went into the east room in the attic story of the temple and poured out my soul unto the Lord, asking His protection and power to fulfill honorably the mission appointed me by His servants. A short time previous to starting, I was laid prostrate on my bed with a stitch in my back, which suddenly seized me while chopping and drawing wood for my family. I could not stir a limb without crying out from the severeness of the pain. Joseph, hearing of it, came to see me, bringing Oliver Cowdery and Bishop Partridge with him; they prayed for and blessed me, Joseph being mouth, beseeching God to raise me up; he then took me by the right hand and said, 'Brother Heber, I take you by your right hand in the name of Jesus Christ of Nazareth, and by virtue of the Holy Priesthood vested in me I command you in the name of Jesus Christ to arise, and be thou made whole.' I arose from my bed, put on my clothes, and started with them and went up to the temple, and felt no more of the pain afterwards."

Though amazed and overwhelmed at his call to this duty, the voice of the Spirit in his own heart had long since told him that he would some day be required to perform just such a work. As with all men of destiny, the mountain of his mission loomed before him dimly in the distance, casting its shadow athwart his soul, and there were times when, worn and wearied with life's common cares, he sought within that shade shelter and repose from the noontide's heat and toil. Thus doth the ideal subserve the real, of which, what is it but the prophecy? [119]

Some months prior to his appointment, in a conversation with Willard Richards in the streets of Kirtland, soon after the latter was baptized, Heber, filled with the spirit of prophecy, had predicted for himself a mission to the shores of Europe.

"Shall I go with thee?" enquired Willard.

"Yea, in the name of the Lord, thou shalt go with me when I go," Heber replied.

But Willard was now in the eastern states, on a special business mission, and the day of Heber's departure was drawing near. Just one day before he left for England, Elder Richards returned, and was reminded by the Apostle of the prediction he had uttered five months before. Willard, being involved in business, and not having received a formal call, did not see how he could go. But, on consulting with the First Presidency, and obtaining their consent, and his partner in business, Brigham Young, agreeing to take charge of their affairs in his absence, he was enabled to fulfill his covenant with Heber, and was set apart the same evening to accompany the mission to England.

Heber received the following letter of recommendation from the First Presidency;

"At a conference of the Elders of the Church of Latter-day Saints, held in Kirtland, Geauga County, Ohio, on the fourth day of June, in the year of our Lord one thousand eight hundred and thirty-seven, Elder Heber C. Kimball, the bearer of this, was unanimously appointed, set apart and ordained to go at the head of this mission to England, to proclaim the Gospel of Jesus Christ to the people of that nation, as it is believed and practiced by us. From the long acquaintance which we have had with this our worthy brother, his integrity and zeal in the cause of truth, we do most cheerfully and confidently recommend him to all candid and upright people as a [120] servant of God and faithful minister of Jesus Christ. We do furthermore beseech all people who have an opportunity of hearing this our brother declare the doctrine believed by us, to listen with attention to the words of his mouth.

"JOSEPH SMITH,
"SIDNEY RIGDON,
"HYRUM SMITH.
"*Presiding Elders of the Church of Jesus Christ of Latter-day Saints.*"

The day of departure came; Tuesday, June 13th, 1837. The solemn scene of Heber's parting with his family cannot be more tenderly or graphically told than in the words of Elder Robert B. Thompson, who thus describes it:

"The day appointed for the departure of the Elders to England having arrived, I stepped into the house of Brother Kimball to ascertain when he would start, as I expected to accompany him two or three hundred miles, intending to spend my labors in Canada that season.

"The door being partly open, I entered and felt struck with the sight which presented itself to my view. I would have retired, thinking that I was intruding, but I felt riveted to the spot. The father was pouring out his soul to that

'God who rules on high,
Who all the earth surveys:
That rides upon the stormy sky,
And calms the roaring seas,'

that he would grant him a prosperous voyage across the mighty ocean, and make him useful wherever his lot should be cast, and that He who 'careth for sparrows, and feedeth the young ravens when they cry' would sup[121]ply the wants of his wife and little ones in his absence. He then, like the patriarchs, and by virtue of his office, laid his hands upon their heads individually, leaving a father's blessing upon them, and commending them to the care and protection of God, while he should be engaged preaching the Gospel in a foreign land. While thus engaged his voice was almost lost in the sobs of those around, who tried in vain to suppress them. The idea of being separated from their protector and father for so long a time was indeed painful. He proceeded, but his heart was too much affected to do so regularly. His emotions were great, and he was obliged to stop at intervals, while the big tears rolled down his cheeks, an index to the feelings which reigned in his bosom. My heart was not stout enough to refrain; in spite of myself I wept, and mingled my tears with theirs. At the same time I felt thankful that I had the privilege of contemplating such a scene. I realized that nothing could induce that man to tear himself from so affectionate a family group, from his partner and children who were so dear to him,—nothing but a sense of duty and love to God and attachment to His cause."

In order to realize the situation so touchingly described, it must be remembered that in those early days, ere the age of steamships and railways had fairly arrived, a mission to Europe, comparatively easy now, seemed almost like a voyage to another world.

Heber continues:

"At 9 a. m., I bade adieu to my family and friends, and in company with Elders Orson Hyde, Willard Richards, and Priest Joseph Fielding, started without purse or scrip on my mission, this being the first foreign mission of the Church of Christ in the last days. We arrived at Fairport on Lake Erie that afternoon, and **[122]** about an hour after took passage on a steamboat for Buffalo.

"We were accompanied by Brothers Brigham Young, John P. Greene, Levi Richards, and Sisters Vilate Kimball, Rhoda Green, Mary Fielding, and others, to Fairport. Sister Mary Fielding gave me five dollars, with which I paid my passage and Brother Hyde's to Buffalo; we were also accompanied to Buffalo by R. B. Thompson and wife, who were on their way to Canada, where he intended to labor in the ministry. After a pleasant voyage we reached Buffalo the next day, where we expected to receive some funds from Canada to assist us on our journey, but were disappointed, as Brothers Goodson, Russell and Snyder did not meet us there according to promise.

"From Buffalo we went down by the canal towards Lyonstown. While walking on its bank I found an iron ring about one and one-fourth inches in diameter, which I presented to Elder Richards, saying, 'I will make you a present of this; keep it in remembrance of me; for our friendship shall be as endless as this ring.' We had but very little means, but determined to prosecute our journey, believing that the Lord would open our way. We accordingly took passage in a line boat on the Erie Canal to Utica, a distance of 250 miles; from thence on the railroad to Albany, where our party divided.

"From Albany I went with Brother Richards about 30 miles, to his father's, in Richmond, Berkshire County, Massachusetts, where we arrived on the 20th, and obtained forty dollars from his brother William which he was owing to him. This enabled us to prosecute our journey. We bade them a last farewell, as Willard's father and mother and sister died a short time afterwards. The next day we returned to Albany and took **[123]** passage in a steamboat to New York, where we arrived on the evening of June 22nd, and again met Orson Hyde and Joseph Fielding. We also met with Brothers John Goodson, Isaac Russell and John Snyder, who had come by the way of Canada to join the mission.

"We found a vessel ready to sail, but not having sufficient means, we were obliged to wait until we could obtain funds to pay our passage, and procure an outfit for the voyage. We found Elder Elijah Fordham, the only member of the Church in that city, who having no house of his own, we lodged at Mrs. Fordham's, Elijah's sister-in-law. Being short of funds, we hired a small room in an unfinished store-house of Brother Fordham's father, who was very wealthy, as he owned many storehouses and buildings, but never invited us into his house to sleep or eat, though he did invite us to assist him two days in raising a building, as a compensation for lying on his store-house floor.

"Brother Fordham seemed to be mute in relation to Mormonism. I told him if he was faithful and remained in New York, there would be a branch of the Church raised up before we returned.

"Sunday, 25th, we fasted, prayed, administered the sacrament, held council for the success of the mission, and had a joyful time. In the afternoon two sectarian priests came in, to find fault, but they were soon confounded, and left.

"On the 28th we deposited 180 of Orson Hyde's "Timely Warnings," in the New York post office, addressed to the priests and ministers of different denominations in the city. We also distributed many to the citizens, and at the same time conversed with them on the subject of the Gospel. Our sojourn in the city opened the door for Brothers Parley and Orson Pratt to **[124]** introduce the Gospel there. Many persons who subsequently came into the Church have referred to the "Timely Warnings" which they had read. We spent considerable time in prayer to our Heavenly Father for His guidance and protection; to make our way plain before us; to bless us with a prosperous voyage across the mighty ocean; make us a blessing to each other, and the captain and crew with whom we should sail.

"In New York we were subject to many inconveniences; had to lay amid straw and blankets upon the ground; to buy our victuals; yet we did not feel discouraged; believing that the Lord would open up our way and guide us to our destination.

"Brother Fordham made me a present of ten dollars, and concluded to accompany us on our mission, but upon mature consideration, we thought it best for him to stay there; believing that the Lord had a people in that city, and that there would be a church built up there before our return.

"Having obtained sufficient money to pay our passage across the Atlantic, eighteen dollars each, we laid in a stock of provisions, and went on board the new packet ship *Garrick*, of 900 tons, bound for Liverpool." **[125]**

# CHAPTER 15

FAREWELL TO NATIVE LAND—"UPON THE WIDE, WIDE SEA"—HEBER'S DREAM OF JOSEPH—A SHIP OUT OF HER RECKONING—A DYING CHILD HEALED—APOSTLE HYDE PREACHES ON BOARD—ARRIVAL AT LIVERPOOL—THE ELDERS LEAP ASHORE

> "ADIEU, adieu, my native shore
>    Fades o'er the waters blue;
> The night-winds sigh, the breakers roar,
>    And shrieks the wild sea-mew.
> Yon sun that sets upon the sea
>    We follow in his flight;
> Farewell, awhile, to him and thee,
>    My native land—Good night!"

AT ten o'clock on the morning of July 1st, 1837, the *Garrick* weighed anchor, and, being towed down the river by a steamer as far as Sandy Hook, set sail oceanward. A few hours later Heber lost sight of his native land. Say he:

"I had feelings which I cannot describe, when I could no longer behold its shores, and when I bade adieu to the land of my birth, I felt to exclaim:

> 'Yes, my native land, I love thee:
> All thy scenes I love them well:
> Friends, connections, happy country,
> Can I bid you all farewell?
>    Can I leave you,
> Far in distant lands to dwell?'

"However, when I reflected on the causes which had induced me to leave it for awhile, and the work which depended upon me, I could likewise say: [126]

> "I go, but not to plough the main,
> To ease a restless mind."

"I was actuated by a different motive than either to please myself, or gain the riches and applause of the world; it was a higher consideration than these that induced me to leave my home. It was because a dispensation of the Gospel had been committed to me; and I felt an ardent desire that my fellow creatures in other lands might hear the sound of the everlasting Gospel, obey its requisitions, rejoice in the fullness and blessings thereof, and escape the judgments which will come upon the ungodly."

Only souls where sentiment and feeling dwell, who have been upon the mighty waters, floating like an insect on a leaf amid the immensity of the liquid waste, can realize that awful loneliness, that sense of helplessness and utter dependency upon a power superior to man's. Atheism, thy home is not the boundless deep! Ocean, thou art religious, thou art worshipful, and throwest heavenward the thoughts of man as though they were thy spray!

Especially was it so with Heber and his companions, God-fearing men, upon whom rested the burden of a mission fraught with salvation to thousands. The solemnities of eternity encompassed them. They felt as little children in the presence of the Infinite. And children they were in their humility. Not in their own strength went they forth, but in the strength of Him who made the seas, and who holdeth their waters in the hollow of His hand.

"Angels shall accompany thee and bear thee up!"

Were they not even now upon the vessel, in mid-ocean, guiding it unerringly toward its destiny? Aye, [127] lest at any time that fated bark should "dash its foot against a stone."

"While crossing the sea," says Heber, "I dreamed that the Prophet Joseph came to me while I was standing upon the forecastle of the ship, and said, 'Brother Heber, here is a rod (putting it into my hands), with which you are to guide the ship. While you hold this rod you shall prosper, and there shall be no obstacles thrown before you but what you shall have power to overcome, and the hand of God shall be with you.' After this I discovered every kind of obstruction was placed before the ship to stop its progress; but the bow being sharp, the obstacles were compelled to move out on either side; and when the ship would come to a mountain, it would plow its course straight through, as though it was in water. This rod which Joseph gave me was about three and a half feet in length. His appearance was just as natural as I ever beheld him in the flesh. He blessed me and disappeared."

It is a singular fact that during fifty years, the period covered by the history of Mormon emigration from the nations abroad, not a ship-load of Latter-day Saints, not a vessel bearing the Elders of Israel to or from foreign shores, has ever been lost at sea. Even rough captains and sailors have learned to regard this with feelings akin to reverential awe, and to accept as a good omen, an assurance of a safe and prosperous voyage, the presence of Mormon Elders or emigrants among their ship's passengers.

In such a light, Heber's dream of Joseph and the rod wherewith he was to "guide the ship," takes on added interest and significance.

Remarkable, too, that this same ship, the *Garrick*, now on its first voyage, after twice ploughing the Atlan[128]tic with Apostles Kimball and Hyde on board—for on this vessel they returned to America—was doomed, on almost its very next voyage, to go down at sea, in the year 1841.

Heber continues his narrative:

"During the voyage we were hailed by a large vessel throwing up a signal of distress. Our captain hauled to, and with his speaking trumpet enquired what was wanted. The answer was, 'we are bound for Quebec, but are lost, having lost our reckoning.' Our captain took an observation, and through his speaking trumpet gave them the latitude and longitude, and the course for them to steer, showing them that they were about a thousand miles from the American shore. They replied that they thought they were close to the shore and were afraid of running on the reefs for several days past. This reminded me that when a person has lost his course, or is out of the way, it is necessary to apply to the Lord, through a Prophet, Seer and Revelator, to put him right.

"Our passage was very agreeable, the winds for the most part being favorable. On the banks of Newfoundland we saw several large fish, called by some, whales, and by others, finners; also many porpoises and different species of fish. We were kindly treated by the officers and crew; their conduct was indeed praiseworthy. Had we been their own relatives, they could not have behaved more kindly, or treated us better. Thus the Lord answered our prayers, for which I desire to praise His holy name.

"The Lord also gave us favor in the eyes of the passengers, who treated us with the greatest respect. During the voyage, a child belonging to one of the passengers was very sick, and given up by the doctor to die; consequently its parents had given up all hopes of [129] its recovery, and expected to have to commit their little one to the ocean. Feeling a great anxiety for the child, I went to its parents and reasoned with them, and laid before them the principle of faith, and told them that the Lord was able to restore their child, notwithstanding there was no earthly prospect of its recovery. To which they listened with great interest. Shortly after, having an opportunity to secretly lay hands upon the child, I did so, and in the name of Jesus Christ rebuked the disease which preyed upon its system. The spirit of the Lord attended the administration, and from that time the child began to recover, and in two or three days after it was running about, perfectly well. Afterwards I informed the parents that I had laid hands on their child, and they acknowledged that it was healed by the power of the Almighty.

"Our health, while on the water, was good, with the exception of Brothers Richards and Fielding, who were sick a day or two.

"Sunday, July 16th, I went to the captain and asked the privilege for one of us to preach on board. He very obligingly agreed, and appointed 1 o'clock, p. m., when it would be most suitable for himself and the crew to attend. I requested Elder Hyde to speak, and notified the captain, crew and passengers of the intended meeting for preaching on the aft quarter deck. At the time appointed there was a congregation of between two and three hundred persons assembled, who listened, with great attention and deep interest, to the discourse. I think I never heard Brother Hyde speak with such power and eloquence. He spoke on the subject of the resurrection, which was necessarily condensed, the time being limited on account of the duties of the crew. The congregation was composed of persons of different faiths, [130] and from different nations, English, Irish, Scotch, French, Germans, etc.,—both Jews and Christians. A great feeling was produced upon the minds of the assembly, who had never heard the subject treated in like manner before; and from the conversation we had afterwards with several of them, I believe that good was done. The congregation appointed a committee who came to us and returned thanks for the favor conferred on them.

"On the 18th, the captain sent a man up to the masthead to look for land. He had not been up long before he cried out, "land," which was the Irish shore. It caused joy and gratitude to arise in my bosom to my heavenly Father for the favorable passage so far, and the prospect of soon reaching our destination. We sailed up the Irish Channel, having Ireland on our left and Wales on our right. The scenery was very beautiful and imposing.

"At daybreak, on July 20th, we arrived in the river Mersey, opposite Liverpool, being eighteen days and eighteen hours from our departure from the anchorage at New York. The packet ship *South America*, which left New York at the same time we did, came in a few lengths behind, thus losing a wager of ten thousand dollars which had been made the day of starting. She had been seen daily during the voyage, but never passed us. The sight was very interesting to see these two vessels enter port with every inch of canvas spread.

"When we first sighted Liverpool I went to the side of the vessel and poured out my soul in praise and thanksgiving to God for the prosperous voyage, and for all the mercies which He had vouchsafed to me, and while thus engaged, and contemplating the scene presented to my view, the spirit of the Lord rested down upon me in a powerful manner, and my soul was filled with love and [131] gratitude. I felt humble, while I covenanted to dedicate myself to God, and to love and serve Him with all my heart.

"Immediately after we anchored, a small boat came along-side, when several of the passengers, with Brothers Hyde, Richards, Goodson and myself got in and went to shore. When we were within six or seven feet of the pier, I leaped on shore, followed by Elders Hyde and Richards, and for the first time in my life I stood on British ground, among strangers, whose manners and customs were different from my own. My feelings at that time were peculiar, particularly when I realized the importance and extent of my mission; the work to which I had been appointed and in which I was shortly to be engaged. However, I put my trust in God, believing that He would assist me in publishing the truth, give me utterance, and be a present help in time of need.

"Elders Hyde, Richards, and myself, being without purse or scrip, wandered in the streets of Liverpool, where wealth and luxury abound, side by side with penury and want. I there met the rich attired in the most costly dresses, and the next minute was saluted with the cries of the poor with scarce covering sufficient to screen them from the weather. Such a wide distinction I never saw before. Looking for a place to lodge in, we found a room belonging to a widow in Union Street, which we engaged for a few days." [132]

# CHAPTER 16

STRANGERS IN A STRANGE LAND—THE ELDERS LED BY THE SPIRIT TO PRESTON—"TRUTH WILL PREVAIL"—THE REVEREND JAMES FIELDING—WONDERFUL FULFILLMENT OF HEBER'S PROPHECIES—A PEOPLE PREPARED FOR THE GOSPEL—THE ELDERS PREACH IN PRESTON

AFTER landing on this foreign shore, Heber's mind for a season was overshadowed with gloom. Among strangers and without money—for he had not a penny in his pocket—and reflecting on the wretched state of affairs in far away Kirtland, where the Prophet of God, whom he loved as his own soul, was surrounded by enemies, and his own family in lowly circumstances in the midst of persecution, his spirits were much depressed. It was then that he had the following night vision. Says he:

"I was in a great water, swimming, and had swam away, trying to make land, although I saw no land, until I had become weary and tired, when I began to sink; then an angel came to me and placed his hand under my chin, for some time keeping me from sinking, until I had rested and gained strength; he blessed me and said, 'Brother Heber, you shall now have strength to swim ashore.' I again began to swim, and it appeared as though every time I stretched forth my arms and feet, I would move rods at each stroke, and continued doing so until I reached land."

This dream, coming as such dreams generally do, in a season of deep depression, was as a spring of pure water in the desert to the parched lips of the weary [133] traveler. As a promise of success, it was amply verified in the subsequent experience of the father and founder of the British mission. "Rods at a stroke" is indeed a strikingly appropriate figure, illustrating the labors in the vineyard of this faithful and mighty servant of the Lord.

"The time we were in Liverpool," he continues, "was spent in council, and in calling on the Lord for direction. While thus engaged, the Spirit of the Lord was with us and we felt greatly strengthened. Our trust was in God, who could make us as useful in bringing down the kingdom of Satan, as He did the ram's horns in bringing down the walls of Jericho; and in gathering out a number of precious souls, who were buried amid the rubbish of tradition, and who had no one to show them the way of truth."

"Go to Preston," said the Spirit of the Lord, and to Preston they went accordingly. The place indicated was a large manufacturing town in Lancashire, thirty-one miles from Liverpool. They arrived there about four o'clock in the afternoon of July 22nd.

It was election day in Preston. Her Majesty, Queen Victoria, who had ascended the throne just three days before the landing of the Elders on her dominions, had ordered a general election for members of Parliament. In the very midst of this busy and interesting scene, Heber and his companions alighted from the coach. He thus describes the spectacle:

"I never witnessed anything like it in my life. Bands of music playing. Flags flying in all directions. Thousands of men, women and children parading the streets, decked with ribbons characteristic of the politics of the several candidates. Anyone accustomed to the peaceable and quiet manner in which the elections in America are conducted, can scarcely have any idea of an election [134] as carried on in England. One of the flags was unrolled before us, nearly over our heads, the moment the coach reached its destination, having on it the following motto: 'TRUTH WILL PREVAIL,' in large gilt letters. It being so very seasonable, and the sentiment being so very appropriate to us in our situation, we cried aloud, 'Amen! Thanks be to God, TRUTH WILL PREVAIL!'"

The Elders took a room in Wilfred Street, in a house belonging to a widow. Joseph Fielding, in the meantime, went in quest of his brother, the Reverend James Fielding, who was pastor of a church in Preston. Returning shortly, he was the bearer of a polite message from the reverend gentleman, inviting the Elders to visit him that evening. Accordingly, Apostles Kimball and Hyde and Elder Goodson went, and were kindly received by Mr. Fielding and his brother-in-law, Mr. Watson, a minister from Bedford. They conversed upon the subject of the Gospel until a late hour. Next morning the Elders received from Mrs. Watson a slight testimonial of her appreciation of their visit, in the shape of a half crown piece.

The Reverend James Fielding, who was destined to be an instrument of Providence for the establishment of Mormonism in Preston—its first foreign foothold—was a brother to Miss Mary Fielding, the same who, with others, accompanied Heber from Kirtland to Fairport, when he started on his mission to England. She subsequently became the wife of Hyrum Smith, the martyr, and mother of Joseph F. Smith, the Apostle.

At this juncture, it will be well to refer to an extraordinary prophecy of Heber C. Kimball's, uttered in the spring of 1836, which connects itself in an interesting manner with the mission he was now about to fulfill. Apostle Parley P. Pratt, over whom the prediction was made, narrates the incident as follows: [135]

"It was now April; I had retired to rest one evening at an early hour, and was pondering my future course, when there came a knock at the door. I arose and opened it, when Elder Heber C. Kimball and others entered my house, and being filled with the spirit of prophecy, they blessed me and my wife, and he prophesied as follows:

"'Brother Parley, thy wife shall be healed from this hour, and shall bear a son, and his name shall be Parley; and he shall be a chosen instrument in the hands of the Lord to inherit the Priesthood and to walk in the steps of his father. He shall do a great work in the earth in ministering the word and teaching the children of men. Arise, therefore, and go forth in the ministry, nothing doubting. Take no thought for your debts, nor the necessaries of life, for the Lord will supply you with abundant means for all things.

"'Thou shalt go to Upper Canada, even to the city of Toronto, the capital, and there thou shalt find a people prepared for the fullness of the gospel, and they shall receive thee, and thou shalt organize the Church among them, and it shall spread thence into the regions round about, and many shall be brought to the knowledge of the truth and shall be filled with joy; and from the things growing out of this mission shall the fullness of the Gospel spread into England, and cause a great work to be done in that land.'

"This prophecy was the more marvelous because, being married near ten years, we had never had any children; and for near six years my wife had been consumptive, and had been considered incurable. However, we called to mind the faith of Abraham of old, and judging him faithful who had promised, we took courage."

Both these prophecies, the one relating to the birth [136] of his son, and the other to his Canadian mission, were literally and marvelously fulfilled. Parley P. Pratt, jun., was born March 25th, 1837, eleven months after the event was thus foretold. Among the "people prepared for the fullness of the Gospel" whom Parley the Apostle found "in the city of Toronto," in strict accordance with Heber's inspired words, was John Taylor, afterwards an Apostle and the President of the Church, and a powerful champion of Mormonism in the British Isles; also Joseph Fielding, Heber's fellow missionary, and his sisters, Mary and Mercy, who had lately emigrated from England. The Fieldings of Canada wrote to their reverend brother in Preston an account of the rise and progress of the latter-day work, and thus prepared him for the advent of the Elders upon British shores. He, in turn, told his congregation and exhorted them to pray to the Lord to send His servants unto them. Obedient to his counsel, the worthiest and most pious members of his flock commenced praying for the coming of the Elders from America. Their faith shook the heavens, and in dreams and visions many were shown the very men whom the Lord was about to send into their midst. Heber C. Kimball, especially, on his arrival in Preston was recognized by persons who had never until then beheld him in the flesh.

Thus, "from things growing out of this mission" to Canada, had the fullness of the Gospel "spread into England," according to Heber's prediction. Thus, like Parley in the city of Toronto, had Heber found in Preston, souls who were prepared to receive his message. The angels of God had been before him, and left their foot-prints upon the people's hearts.

The day after their arrival in Preston, being the Sabbath, the brethren, on the invitation of Mr. Fielding, [137] repaired to Vauxhall Chapel, where he held forth from his own pulpit. "We sat before him," says Heber," praying to the Lord to open up the way for us to preach." At the close of the service, the reverend gentleman, of his own accord—for no one had requested it—gave notice that an Elder of the Latter-day Saints would preach in his chapel at 3 o'clock in the afternoon. The news spread rapidly, and a large congregation assembled at the appointed hour, to hear the Elders from America.

The first speaker was Heber C. Kimball. Says he: "I declared that an angel had visited the earth, and committed the everlasting Gospel to man; called their attention to the first principles of the Gospel; and gave them a brief history of the

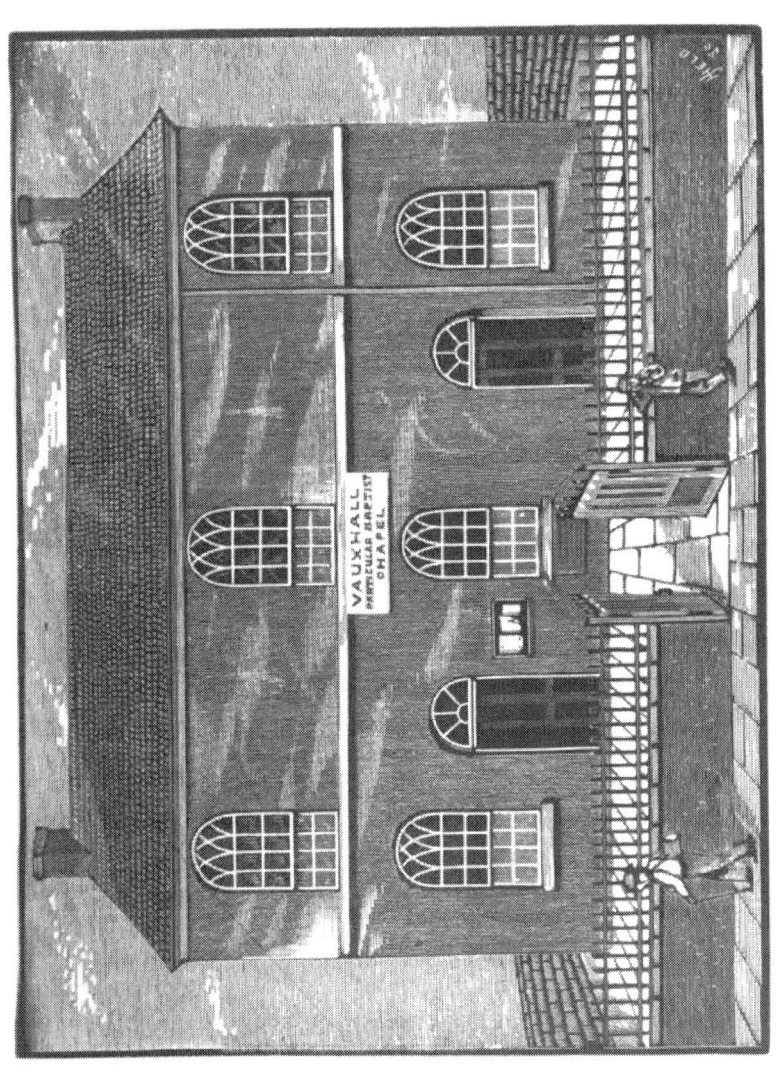

Vauxhall Chapel, 1875

nature of the work which the Lord had commenced on the earth; after which Elder Hyde bore testimony to the same, which was received by many with whom I afterwards conversed; they cried 'glory to God,' and rejoiced that the Lord had sent His servants unto them. Thus was the key turned and the Gospel dispensation opened on the first Sabbath after landing in England."

Another appointment was given out for the brethren in the evening, when Elder Goodson preached, and Joseph Fielding bore testimony, and still another for the Wednesday night following, when Apostle Hyde held forth and Elder Richards added his testimony. The chapel was filled to overflowing, and many were "pricked in their hearts," being convinced of the truth, "and began to praise God and rejoice exceedingly."

Thus was the first opening made for the preaching of the Gospel in the British Isles and on the continent of Europe. Thus it was—to use the Reverend Fielding's famous phrase—that "Kimball bored the holes, Goodson drove the nails, and Hyde clinched them." **[138]**

———•••———

## CHAPTER 17

SATAN ALARMED—THE POWERS OF EVIL CONSPIRE AGAINST THE ELDERS—CHAPELS AND CHURCHES CLOSED AGAINST THEM—THE REVEREND MR. FIELDING IN HIS REAL COLORS—THE WORK CONTINUES TO SPREAD—AN ARMY OF DEMONS ATTACK THE ELDERS—THE DAWN AND VICTORY

MEANWHILE, the powers of darkness had taken counsel against these servants of the Lord. Not without a struggle would Satan loose his hold, and permit the gates of salvation to open for the eastern, as they had already opened for the western hemisphere. The evil one had seen that the Church in America was trembling on the verge of dissolution. To give it fresh impetus, and infuse new life into the seemingly sinking system, was the object of the Apostles' mission to the shores of Albion. The opening of that mission it was Satan's fell purpose to thwart, and for which he was now gathering, far and near, the embattled hosts of hell.

The Elders might be said to have "stolen a march" on the Adversary, in securing, already, three hearings at Vauxhall Chapel, with the favorable results before noted. This much could not be retrieved, but the enemy of righteousness hoped to prevent a repetition of such scenes, and to hinder those who believed, from obeying the Gospel by going down into the waters of baptism. For know, O reader—if thou art a stranger to this truth—that Satan is well satisfied with their condition who "only believe" in Jesus, if they are not "born of the water" according to His righteous example and holy will. **[139-141]**

Acting on the principle, it may be presumed, that a thing to be recovered should first be sought for where it was lost, the evil one determined to use for his purpose the Reverend James Fielding, the very man who had befriended the Elders, and given them their first public opportunity of declaring the message they had been sent to deliver. Strange enough after what had passed—though sufficiently frequent, in similar phases, since those days, to be no longer a cause of wonderment—he found that reverend gentleman in precisely the mood best suited to his dark design. Like all who fear man more than they love the Lord, preferring the praise and honors of the world to the approval of a good conscience and the favor of their Maker, the Reverend James Fielding, when he had noticed the marvelous effect of the Elders' preaching, and contemplated the present and prospective results, in the leading away of his flock to drink at other fountains and browse in other pastures, shrank back appalled from the picture presented to his view. Willing to sate his appetite for the new and marvelous, and even obey a doctrine which promised worldly honors and emoluments, he was not willing to humble himself "even as a little child" and seek the kingdom of God at the sacrifice of every earthly consideration.

Had he forgotten the text which, perchance, he had a hundred times preached glibly from: "He that taketh not his cross and followeth after Me, is not worthy of Me"? Or, like many other Christian divines, "having a form of godliness, but denying the power thereof," was he satisfied to believe that those words had lost their meaning for this generation? Be it as it may, here is the record that will meet him at the day of judgment:

"The Rev. James Fielding, who had so kindly invited us to preach in his chapel, learning that a number of his [142] members believed our testimony, and that some had requested to be baptized, shut his doors against us and would not suffer us to preach in his chapel any more; alleging for an excuse that we had preached the doctrine of baptism for the remission of sins, contrary to our arrangement with him.

"I need scarcely assure my friends that nothing was said to him from which any inference could be drawn that we should suppress the doctrine of baptism. We deem it too important a doctrine to lay aside for any privilege we could receive from mortals. Mr. Fielding had been apprised of our doctrines before we saw him, having received several communications from his brother Joseph, and his two sisters, Mary and Mercy, who wrote to him from Canada, in which letters our doctrines were clearly laid down. We likewise conversed with him on the subject at our interview. He, having been traditioned to believe in infant baptism, and having preached and practised the same a number of years, saw the situation he would be placed in if he obeyed the Gospel; that notwithstanding his talents and standing in society, he would have to come into the sheepfold by the door, and after all his preaching to others, have to be baptized himself for the remission of sins by those who were ordained to that power. These considerations no doubt had their weight upon his mind, which caused him to act as he did; and notwithstanding his former kindness he soon became one of our most violent opposers.

"However, his congregation did not follow his example, they having some time been praying for our coming, and having been assured by Mr. Fielding that he could not place more confidence in an angel than he did in the statements of his brother Joseph, respecting this people; consequently they were in a great measure **[143]** prepared for the reception of the Gospel, probably as much so as Cornelius was anciently.

"Having now no public place to preach in, we began to preach at night in private houses, which were opened in every direction, when numbers came to hear and believed the Gospel."

Thus was Satan unsuccessful in stopping the spread of the work. The smoking flax was bursting into flame, and all his efforts could not quench it. Chapels and churches he might close, for of them he held the keys, but the hearts of the humble and pure were in God's keeping, and to these sacred temples His servants had ready access.

Then came the stroke climacteric; the *dernier ressort* of satanic hostility.

"Saturday evening," says Heber C. Kimball, "it was agreed that I should go forward and baptize, the next morning, in the river Ribble, which runs through Preston.

"By this time the adversary of souls began to rage, and he felt determined to destroy us before we had fully established the kingdom of God in that land, and the next morning I witnessed a scene of satanic power and influence which I shall never forget.

"Sunday, July 30th, about daybreak, Elder Isaac Russell (who had been appointed to preach on the obelisk in Preston Square, that day,) who slept with Elder Richards in Wilfred Street, came up to the third story, where Elder Hyde and myself were sleeping, and called out, 'Brother Kimball, I want you should get up and pray for me that I may be delivered from the evil spirits that are tormenting me to such a degree that I feel I cannot live long, unless I obtain relief.'

"I had been sleeping on the back of the bed. I immediately arose, slipped off at the foot of the bed, and **[144]** passed round to where he was. Elder Hyde threw his feet out, and sat up in the bed, and we laid hands on him, I being mouth, and prayed that the Lord would have mercy on him, and rebuked the devil.

"While thus engaged, I was struck with great force by some invisible power, and fell senseless on the floor. The first thing I recollected was being supported by Elders Hyde and Richards, who were praying for me; Elder Richards having followed Russell up to my room. Elders Hyde and Richards then assisted me to get on the bed, but my agony was so great I could not endure it, and I arose, bowed my knees and prayed. I then arose and sat up on the bed, when a vision was opened to our minds, and we could distinctly see the evil spirits, who foamed and gnashed their teeth at us. We gazed upon them about an hour and a half (by Willard's watch). We were not looking towards the window, but towards the wall. Space appeared before us, and we saw the devils coming in legions, with their leaders, who came within a few feet of us. They came towards us like armies rushing to battle. They appeared to be men of full stature, possessing every form and feature of men in the flesh, who were angry and desperate; and I shall never forget the vindictive malignity depicted on their countenances as they looked me in the eye; and any attempt to paint the scene which then presented itself, or portray their malice and enmity, would be vain. I perspired exceedingly, my clothes becoming as wet as if I had been taken out of the river. I felt excessive pain, and was in the greatest distress for some time. I cannot even look back on the scene without feelings of horror; yet by it I learned the power of the adversary, his enmity against the servants of God, and got some understanding of the invisible world. We distinctly **[145]** heard those spirits talk and express their wrath and hellish designs against us. However, the Lord delivered us from them, and blessed us exceedingly that day."

Elder Hyde's supplemental description of that fearful scene is as follows, taken from a letter addressed to President Kimball:

"Every circumstance that occurred at that scene of devils is just as fresh in my recollection at this moment as it was at the moment of its occurrence, and will ever remain so. After you were overcome by them and had fallen, their awful rush upon me with knives, threats, imprecations and hellish grins, amply convinced me that they were no friends of mine. While you were apparently senseless and lifeless on the floor and upon the bed (after we had laid you there), I stood between you and the devils and fought them and contended with them face to face, until they began to diminish in number and to retreat from the room. The last imp that left turned round to me as he was going out and said, as if to apologize, and appease my determined opposition to them, 'I never said anything against you!' I replied to him thus: 'It matters not to me whether you have or have not; you are a liar from the beginning! In the name of Jesus Christ, depart! He immediately left, and the room was clear. That closed the scene of devils for that time."

Years later, narrating the experience of that awful morning to the Prophet Joseph, Heber asked him what it all meant, and whether there was anything wrong with him that he should have such a manifestation.

"No, Brother Heber," he replied, "at that time you were nigh unto the Lord; there was only a veil between you and Him, but you could not see Him. When I heard of it, it gave me great joy, for I then knew that the work of God had taken root in that land. It was **[146]** this that caused the devil to make a struggle to kill you."

Joseph then related some of his own experience, in many contests he had had with the evil one, and said: "The nearer a person approaches the Lord, a greater power will be manifested by the adversary to prevent the accomplishment of His purposes."

An answer this, for the unbelieving and sophistical, who argue, with the shallow reasoning of Job's comforters, that they have sinned most who suffer most, and are ever ready to ascribe spiritual manifestations, good or evil, to madness, drunkenness or imbecility. It is needful, we are told, to experience opposites, to be enabled to choose intelligently between them; and to those who have this experience, and who "take the Holy Spirit for their guide," the way to judge is as plain "as the daylight from the dark night."

> 'Tis Contrast sways unceasing sceptre
> O'er vast Appreciation's realm;
> E'en Gods, through sacrifice descending,
> Triumphant rise to overwhelm.

So was it with the Apostles and Elders in Preston, after their terrible encounter with the powers of evil, at Sunday day-break, July 30th, 1837. The Spirit of the Lord, with peace and joy that "passeth understanding," dawned with the Sabbath sun upon their souls. They had tasted of the bitter, and would thenceforth more fully know the sweet; encompassed about by "the horror of darkness," they hailed with ecstacy till then unknown, the glory of the golden morn. [147]

## CHAPTER 18

THE REVEREND MR. FIELDING FORBIDS THE ELDERS TO BAPTIZE THEIR CONVERTS—APOSTLE KIMBALL'S ANSWER: "THEY ARE OF AGE AND CAN ACT FOR THEMSELVES"—PREMIER GLADSTONE AND SECRETARY EVARTS—FREE AGENCEY AND UNRIGHTEOUS DOMINION—HEBER C. KIMBALL BAPTIZES IN THE RIVER RIBBLE—A MIRACLE

THE Reverend James Fielding, finding, notwithstanding his opposition, that the Elders prospered in their labors, and were preparing to lead into the waters of baptism a number of his flock who had applied to them for that privilege, wrought himself into "a fine frenzy." He had even been to the Elders' lodgings, and, confronting Apostle Kimball, forbidden him to baptize them.

"They are of age," answered Heber, "and can act for themselves; I shall baptize all who come unto me, asking no favors of any man."

"On hearing this," he adds, "Mr. Fielding trembled and shook as though he had a chill."

"They are of age and can act for themselves." A similar answer to that given, nearly half a century later, by the greatest of England's living statesmen, when asked by the representative of "the freest government on earth," to aid in the suppression of Mormon emigration from Europe. An answer worthy of "the grand old man," as it was worthy of the grand Apostle, Heber C. Kimball, and in consonance with the spirit of liberty, the genius of the Gospel, and that sublime Mormon doctrine, the free agency of man.

The destruction of human agency is Satan's peculiar [148] mission; a doctrine of devils from the beginning, it will be so unto the end. Force can never win in a controversy involving the conscience, or soul of man. "It may compel the body, but it cannot convince the mind." Thought is forever unfettered; as free to the Siberian serf, as to Columbia's proudest son, or the monarch on his throne. Freedom to believe, man cannot give; the right to act, where action injures no one, he cannot in justice take away. They who do so follow after Lucifer, who rebelled against God, and was hurled with his doctrine of tyranny from heaven's battlements, drawing down to perdition a third of its spirit hosts, "because of their agency;" the very eternal principle he had vainly sought to destroy.

The Prophet Joseph, speaking of the power of the Priesthood, the power which governs and controls all things, says:

"No power or influence can or ought to be maintained by virtue of the Priesthood, only by persuasion, by long suffering, by gentleness, and meekness, and by love unfeigned.

"When we undertake to cover our sins, or to gratify our pride, our vain ambition, or to exercise control, or dominion, or compulsion, upon the souls of the children of men, in any degree of unrighteousness, behold the heavens withdraw themselves; the Spirit of the Lord is grieved; and when it is withdrawn, Amen to the Priesthood, or the authority of that man."

A sublime enunciation, worthy the inspired mind of an American Prophet, cradled in the lap of liberty, and born to bring truth to light. Thine was a noble thought, Bartholdi, noble though only half expressed. Not liberty alone, not truth alone, but truth and liberty, Liberty with Truth, shall yet "enlighten the world."

**[149]**

Referring to the morning of his contest with the demons, Apostle Kimball says:

"Notwithstanding the weakness of my body from the shock I had experienced, I had the pleasure, about 9 a.m, of baptizing nine individuals and hailing them brethren and sisters in the kingdom of God. These were the first persons baptized into the Church in a foreign land, and only the eighth day after our arrival in Preston."

"A circumstance took place which I cannot refrain from mentioning, for it will show the eagerness and anxiety of some in that land to obey the Gospel. Two of the male candidates, when they had changed their clothes at a distance of several rods from the place where I was standing in the water, were so anxious to obey the Gospel that they ran with all their might to the water, each wishing to be baptized first. The younger, George D. Watt, being quicker of foot than the elder, outran him, and came first into the water."

"The circumstance of baptizing in the open air being somewhat novel, a concourse of between seven and nine thousand persons assembled on the banks of the river to witness the ceremony. It was the first time baptism by immersion was administered openly, as the Baptists in that country generally have a font in their chapels, and perform the ordinance privately."

"In the afternoon Elder Russell preached in the market place to a congregation of about five thousand persons, numbers of whom were pricked to the heart.

"I had visited Thomas Walmesley's house, whose wife was sick of the consumption and had been for several years; she was reduced to skin and bones, a mere skeleton; and was given up to die by the doctors. I preached the Gospel to her, and promised her in the name **[150]** of the Lord Jesus Christ if she would believe, repent and be baptized, she should be healed of her sickness. She was carried to the water, and after her baptism began to amend, and at her confirmation she was blest, and her disease rebuked, when she immediately recovered, and in less than one week after she was attending to her household duties."

Sister Walmesley, the subject of this episode, is still living. She resides in Bear Lake County, Idaho, and though far advanced in years, at last accounts was hale and hearty.

Thus was a miracle wrought that day, and nine souls initiated into the kingdom of God; the first fruits of the Gospel in a foreign land. The names of those baptized were George D. Watt, Miller, Thomas Walmesley. Ann Elizabeth Walmesley Miles Hodgen, George Wate, Henry Billsbury, Mary Ann Brown and Ann Dawson. [151]

## CHAPTER 19

THE ELDERS SEPARATE FOR THE BETTER PROSECUTION OF THEIR WORK—JENNETTA RICHARDS—THE PRESTON BRANCH ORGANIZED—HEBER GOES TO WALKERFOLD—ANOTHER MINISTER'S "CRAFT IN DANGER"—MORE OF HEBER'S PROPHECIES—"WILLARD, I BAPTIZED YOUR WIFE TO-DAY"

HAVING gained a foothold in Preston, and lifted the ensign of the latter-day work, around which the ransomed of the Lord were beginning to rally, the Elders decided to separate and carry the Gospel into other counties. They met in council the day after the first baptisms in the River Ribble, and "continued in fasting and prayer, praise and thanksgiving until two o'clock in the morning." Elders Richards and Goodson were appointed to go on a mission to the city of Bedford, and Brothers Russell and Snyder to Alston, in Cumberland. Apostles Kimball and Hyde, with Priest Fielding, were to remain and labor in and around Preston. A day or two later the brethren departed for their fields of labor.

The second important step in the founding of the British mission was now taken.

"On Wednesday, August 2nd," says Elder Kimball, "Miss Jennetta Richards, a young lady, the daughter of a minister of the Independent Order, who resided at Walkerfold, about fifteen miles from Preston, came to the house of Thomas Walmesley, with whom she was acquainted. Calling in to see them at the time she was there, I was introduced to her, and we immediately entered into conversation on the subject of the Gospel. [152] I found her very intelligent. She seemed very desirous to hear the things I had to teach and to understand the doctrines of the gospel. I informed her of my appointment to preach that evening, and invited her to attend. She did so; and likewise the evening following. After attending these two services she was fully convinced of the truth.

"Friday morning, 4th, she sent for me, desiring to be baptized, which request I cheerfully complied with, in the river Ribble, and confirmed her at the water side. Elder Hyde assisting. This was the first confirmation in England. The following day she started for home, and wept as she was about to leave us. I said to her, 'Sister, be of good cheer, for the Lord will soften the heart of thy father, that I will yet have the privilege of preaching in his chapel, and it shall result in a great opening to preach the Gospel in that region.' I exhorted her to pray and be humble. She requested me to pray for her, and gave me some encouragement to expect that her father would open his chapel for me to preach in. I then hastened to my brethren, told them of the circumstances and the result of my visit with the young lady, and called upon them to unite with me in prayer that the Lord would soften the heart of her father, that he might be induced to open his chapel for us to preach in.

While awaiting the issue of this event, the brethren continued their ministerial labors. The record resumes:

"Sunday, 6th, Elder Hyde preached in the marketplace to a numerous assemblage, both rich and poor, who flocked from all parts 'to hear what these dippers had to say.' After he was through with his discourse I gave an exhortation, and when I had concluded a learned minister stepped forth to oppose the doctrines we advanced, but more particularly the doctrine of baptism, he being a great stickler for infant baptism. The people thinking that he intended to offend us, would not let him proceed, but seemed determined to put him down, and undoubtedly would have done so had not Brother Hyde interposed and begged permission for the gentleman to speak; telling the congregation that he was prepared to meet any arguments he might advance. This appeased the people, who listened to the remarks of the reverend gentleman, after which Brother Hyde spoke in answer to the objections which had been offered, to the satisfaction of nearly all present, and the minister appeared somewhat ashamed. Some of the people hissed at him and told him not to do the like again. One individual came up and asked him what he now thought of his baby baptism; when another took him by the hand and led him out of the throng."

It was now deemed advisable to confirm all who had been baptized and organize them into a branch, twenty-eight persons having been baptized in Preston, but only one confirmed. The converts were accordingly requested to meet at the house of Sister Ann Dawson, where the Elders had their lodgings. It was the evening of the third Sabbath they had spent in England. The meeting having convened, after some preliminary remarks by the Elders, they confirmed twenty-seven members and organized the Preston branch, the first branch of the Church of Jesus Christ of Latter-day Saints in a foreign land. While attending to these sacred duties, the Spirit of the Lord was poured out upon them in a powerful manner, causing them to rejoice exceedingly.

And now came the fulfillment of Heber's prophecy to Jennetta Richards, daughter of the minister of Walkerfold. The early part of the week brought two letters to Elder Kimball, one from Miss Richards, and the other from her father. The latter read as follows:

*Mr. H. C. Kimball,*

Sir:—You are expected to be here next Sunday. You are given out to preach in the forenoon, afternoon and evening. Although we be strangers to one another, yet,

I hope we are not strangers to our blessed Redeemer, else I would not have given out for you to preach. Our chapel is but small and the congregation few,—yet if one soul be converted it is of more value than the whole world.

"I remain, in haste,
"JOHN RICHARDS."

Taking coach from Preston on the following Saturday afternoon, a little before dark Heber arrived at the door of the Revered John Richards, in Walkerfold. On entering the house he was warmly greeted by Mr. Richards, who said: "I understand you are the minister lately from America?" Heber replied in the affirmative. The reverend gentleman then bade him welcome and exclaimed: "God bless you!" Refreshments were served and conversation ensued until a late hour, to the satisfaction of the whole family.

"Next morning," says Heber, "I accompanied the reverend gentleman to his chapel at the hour appointed. He gave out the hymns and prayed, and I preached to an overflowing congregation on the principles of salvation. I likewise preached in the afternoon and evening, and they seemed to manifest great interest in the things which I laid before them. Nearly the whole congregation were in tears. After I had concluded the services of the day Mr. Richards gave out another appointment for me to preach on Monday evening, which I attended [155] to. By request of the congregation I likewise preached on Wednesday evening. A number believed the doctrines I advanced, and on Thursday, 17th, six individuals, all members of Mr. Richards' church, came forward for baptism. James Smithies and his wife Nancy were two of the number.

This result was more than the good pastor had anticipated. He had listened with deep interest to, and had been willing for his congregation to hear, the simple yet powerful testimony of the Mormon Apostle, who, fired with the Holy Ghost, and all unmindful of the studied arts and graces of pulpit oratory, spake, like his Master of yore, "as one having authority." But conversions of this kind he had not counted upon. Fearful of losing his entire flock, and also his salary, if any more such preaching were to be heard in his chapel, he informed Elder Kimball that he would be obliged to close his pulpit against him. Unlike Mr. Fielding, however, he manifested no bitterness of spirit, but after denying him this privilege, continued to treat his Mormon guest with great kindness and hospitality.

Heber's mind had been prepared for the change. "One night," says he, "while at Mr. Richards' house, I dreamed that an elderly gentleman came to me and rented me a lot of ground, which I was anxious to cultivate. I immediately went to work to break it up; and observing young timber on the lot, I cut it down. There was also an old building at one corner of the lot which appeared ready to fall. I took a lever and endeavored to place the building in a proper position, but all my attempts were futile, and it became worse. I then resolved to pull it down, and with the new timber build a good house on a good foundation. While thus engaged, the gentleman of whom I had rented the place [156] came and found great fault with me for destroying his young timber, etc.

"This dream was fulfilled in the following manner: After Mr. Richards let me preach in his chapel, I baptized all of his young members, as I had before baptized his daughter. He then reflected upon himself for letting me have the privilege of his chapel; told me that I had ruined his church, and had taken away all his young members. I could not but feel pity for the old gentleman, but I had a duty to perform which outweighed all other considerations."

Heber now began to preach in private houses, which were opened in the neighborhood, and "ceased not to declare the glorious tidings of salvation." Among his interested auditors, still, was the Reverend John Richards. His daughter Jennetta was very sorrowful over the turn affairs had taken, and wept much at his refusal to allow Elder Kimball to preach in his chapel. Heber told her to be of good cheer, for he believed that the Lord would soften her father's heart, and cause him to reopen his chapel.

The fulfillment is noted as follows:

"Sunday, 27th, I went along with him to his meeting, feeling a desire to hear him preach. After he had finished his discourse, I was agreeably surprised to hear him give out another appointment for me to preach in his chapel. I accordingly preached in the afternoon and evening. The words were with power. The effect was great upon the people, for they were in tears, and the next day I baptized two more, both of them members of Mr. Richards' church. Although he had preached in that parish upwards of thirty years, and his members, as well as the inhabitants of the place and vicinity, were very much attached to him, yet when the fulness of the **[157]** Gospel was preached, the people, notwithstanding their attachment to and regard for their venerable pastor, when convinced of their duty came forward and followed the footsteps of the Savior, by being buried in the likeness of His death."

While laboring in this neighborhood, Heber had a dream in which Willard Richards appeared to him and said: "You are wanted at Preston, and we cannot do without you any longer."

"The next morning," says he, "I started for Preston where I found that I was anxiously expected by the brethren, who had received a letter from Brother Richards, and one from Brother Russell, giving an account of their proceedings since they left Preston. There was also a letter from my wife, which contained many precious items of news from Kirtland. Elder Hyde praised the Lord on seeing me. Brother Goodson had likewise returned from Bedford, where he and Brother Richards had labored; he gave us an account of their mission and success in raising up a little branch of nineteen."

Another of Heber's prophecies—one of those seemingly casual though fateful utterances for which he was famous—must here be mentioned.

"Willard, I baptized your wife to-day," were his words addressed to Elder Richards just after Jennetta Richards joined the Church. Willard and Jennetta had not yet seen each other. The sequel is in Willard's own words, taken from his diary. Time: March, 1838:

"I took a tour through the branches, and preached. While walking in Thornly

I plucked a snowdrop, far through the hedge, and carried it to James Mercer's and hung it up in his kitchen. Soon after, Jennetta Richards came into the room, and I walked with her and Alice [158] Parker to Ribchester, and attended meeting with Brothers Kimball and Hyde at Brother Clark's.

"While walking with these sisters, I remarked, 'Richards is a good name; I never want to change it: do you, Jennetta.' "No: I do not,' was her reply, 'and I think I never will.'"

"Sept. 24th, 1839, I married Jennetta Richards, daughter of the Rev. John Richards, independent minister at Walkerfold, Chaigley, Lancashire. Most truly do I praise my Heavenly Father for His great kindness in providing me a partner according to His promise. I receive her from the Lord, and hold her at His disposal. I pray that He may bless us forever. Amen!"

## CHAPTER 20

THE MISSION OF ELIAS—THE SYMBOLISM OF THE UNIVERSE—THE PAST PREPARATORY TO THE PRESENT AND FUTURE—THE WAY PREPARED FOR THE FULNESS OF THE GOSPEL—THE "LESSER LIGHTS" OF ENGLAND—FIELDING, MATTHEWS AND AITKEN—THE STARS PALING BEFORE THE SUN

THE mission of Elias is the mission of preparation, the lesser going before the greater, opening up the way. The day-star heralding the dawn. The wedge of truth piercing the wall of prejudice, cleaving the ranks of error, creating the gap through which shall ride on victory's flaming wheels, the chariot of Righteousness. [159]

"Behold I will send my messenger, and he shall prepare the way before me."

What Christ is to the Father, Elias is to the Son; messenger and symbol of His Majesty. And hath not Elias also his fore-runner? The mantle of Elias falls on many shoulders; the shadow of that mantle on many more.

Life, the universe, is one vast symbolism. Earth fore-shadows heaven. The stars, the worlds on high, are of higher worlds typical; a climax of constellations, a ladder of light, a burning stairway of immortal glories.

> "System on system, countless worlds and suns,
> Linked in division, one yet separate,
> The silver islands of a sapphire sea,
> Shoreless, unfathomed, undiminished, stirred
> With waves which roll in restless tides of change."

Planet above planet, step by step, lustre upon lustre "until thou come nigh to Kolob;" Kolob, lord of light, king of kokaubeam, nearest unto the throne of God.

And shall it not be seen when all history is written, on earth as in heaven, where it exists as a prophecy; when all secrets are revealed and hidden things made known; that Time with all its ages is a chain, a climax, an ascending scale of dispensations, merging in each other, and all into one, like rills and rivers mingling with the ocean;

that men and nations from the beginning have carved out the way for other men and nations; that human lives and human events, like sections of machinery turned by the enginery of Omnipotence, have fitted into and impelled each other, under the controlling, guiding master mind and hand that "doeth all things well?"

Was not the past all preparatory to the present? Does not the present foreshadow the future? Are not **[160]** influences at work, even now; doctrines being taught, truths put forth by pulpit, play and press; discoveries made in art and science; antiquities unveiled and mysteries brought to light, that are surely paving the way for the revelations of Jesus Christ, past, present and to come? Is not the knowledge now possessed by the Saints, glorious though it be, but a foretaste, the ante-past of a greater feast of knowledge yet to follow?

The mission of Elias is the mission of preparation, the lesser going before the greater, opening up the way.

The mantle of Elias falls on many shoulders; the shadow of that mantle on many more.

In America, it was Sidney Rigdon, Alexander Campbell and other orators and divines, who prepared the way before Joseph Smith and the fullness of the everlasting gospel. In England, the Fieldings, the Matthews, the Aitkens and other lights, shed the lustre of advanced thought over the path-way soon to be brightened by the beams of eternal truth. Receiving not the light themselves, they nevertheless bore witness of its approach, and unknowingly made ready the minds of many for its acceptance. The more lustrously they shone, the greater their measure of power, the higher, wider, deeper, more advanced and more liberal their doctrines, the nearer they approximated, although they knew it not, to what the world terms "Mormonism," what men in other ages called "Christianism," but what the Gods in eternity have glorified as the Gospel of life and salvation.

This preparatory work, like the work which was to follow, was both spiritual and temporal. In America, the sword of a Washington, the pen of a Jefferson had carved out the legend of liberty, "All men are equal," ere the Gospel trump was heard again proclaiming, to high **[161]** and low, rich and poor, "Peace on earth, good will to men." In England, Victoria had ascended the throne, and the spirit of reform, in church and state, was rolling, a billow of victory, over the land. Society was moved to its center. Old institutions were crumbling. The iconoclast was abroad. Steam and electricity had begun their miracles; science was exploding superstition; tyrant's thrones were tottering; Liberty's upheaval in the west had shaken the very pillars of the east; the "former things" were passing away; He that "sat upon the throne" was making "all things new."

Thus had God prepared the way for the advent of the everlasting Gospel.

As we have seen, the man chosen to pioneer the work on Europe's shores, to lead the assault on Satan's strongholds in the old world, and wave back over the Atlantic to his chief the signal of truth triumphant among the nations, was Heber C. Kimball.

Speaking of those "lesser lights" who went before him and his brethren and unwittingly helped them to establish Mormonism in the British Isles, Heber says, referring now to the mission of Elders Richards and Goodson to the city of Bedford:

"A minister by the name of Timothy R. Matthews, a brother-in-law to Joseph Fielding, received them very kindly, and invited them to preach in his church, which was accepted, and in it they preached several times, when a number, amongst whom were Mr. Matthews and his lady, believed their testimony, and the truths which they proclaimed. Mr. Matthews had likewise borne testimony to his congregation of the truth of these things, and that they were the same principles that were taught by the Apostles anciently; and besought his congregation to receive the same. Forty of his members went **[162]** forward and were baptized, and the time was appointed when he was to be baptized. In the interval, however, Brother Goodson, contrary to my counsel and positive instructions, and without advising with any one, read to Mr. Matthews the vision seen by President Joseph Smith and Sidney Rigdon, which caused him to stumble, and darkness pervaded his mind; so much so, that at the time specified he did not make his appearance, but went and baptized himself in the river Ouse; and from that time he began to preach baptism for the remission of sins. He wrote to Rev. James Fielding saying that his best members had left him."

"Mr. Matthews was a gentleman of considerable learning and talent. He had been a minister in the established church of England, but seeing many things in that church contrary to truth and righteousness, and feeling that an overturn was nigh at hand, and that the church was destitute of the gifts of the Spirit, and was not expecting the Savior to come to reign upon the earth, as had been spoken by the prophets; he felt led to withdraw from that body, and gave up his prospects in that establishment. He then began to preach the things which he verily believed, and was instrumental in raising up quite a church in that place."

This of the Reverend Mr. Fielding, in Preston: "Mr. James Fielding had been a minister in the Methodist Church, but for some of the above causes had withdrawn from that society, and had collected a considerable church in Preston. Those gentlemen, with their congregations at the time we arrived were diligently contending for that faith which was once delivered to the saints; but they afterwards rejected the truth. Notwithstanding they did not obey the Gospel, the greater portion of their members received our testimony, obeyed **[163]** the ordinances we taught, and are now rejoicing in the blessings of the new and everlasting covenant."

Of the Rev. Robert Aitken, the most famous of these reform ministers, Tullidge, our local historian, says:

"He seems to have been almost a Whitefield in his eloquence and magical influence over the people. He was emphatically the most popular 'new light' of the period in England. For years he had been preaching very successfully against 'the corruptions of the established church.' His mission had been quite a crusade against the English Episcopacy, and he had established many flourishing chapels in Liverpool, Preston, Manchester, Burslem, London and elsewhere. In the metropolis he founded 'Zion's chapel' and what is interesting in the case was that his themes on the ancient prophecies and their fulfillment in 'these latter days' were very like what might have been heard from Alexander Campbell or the eloquent Sidney Rigdon, before as well as after he became a Mormon Elder. The Rev. Robert Aitken was also powerful in his 'warnings to the Gentiles,' and his sermons were often glorious outbursts of inspiration, when he dwelt upon the prospect of a latter-day church rising in fulfillment of the prophets."

But the power and influence of this brilliant star were about to wane. A greater luminary had arisen—the very Latter-day Church of which he had spoken—before whose rays the light of "Zion's Chapel" must pale as pales the starlight before the morn.

Concerning this celebrated expounder of the Bible, and *pounder* of the Book of Mormon—for such it seems he literally was—Apostle Kimball writes:

"Soon after our arrival in England, many of the Aitkenites embraced the Gospel, which caused considerable feeling and opposition in the ministers belonging [164] to that sect. Having lost quite a number of members, and seeing that more were on the eve of being baptized, the Rev. Robert Aitken came to Preston, and gave out that he was going to put down Mormonism, expose the doctrines, and overthrow the Book of Mormon. He made a very long oration on the subject, was very vehement in his manner, and pounded the Book of Mormon on the pulpit many times. He then exhorted the people to pray that the Lord would drive us from their coast; and if the Lord would not hear them in that petition, that He would smite the leaders.

"The next Sunday Elder Hyde and myself went to our meeting room, read the thirteenth chapter of first Corinthians, and strongly urged upon the people the grace of charity which is so highly spoken of in that chapter, and made some remarks on the proceedings of the Reverend Robert Aitken, who had abused us and the Book of Mormon so very much. In return for his railing we exhorted the Saints to pray that the Lord would soften his heart and open his eyes that he might see that it was hard to 'kick against the pricks.' This discourse had a very good effect, and that week we had the pleasure of baptizing fifty into the kingdom of Jesus, a large number of whom were members of Mr. Aitken's church."

Thus did the sheep of Israel, straying in Idumean pastures, continue flocking back into the Master's fold. They knew the voice of their Shepherd when He called, and a stranger they would no longer follow. [165]

# CHAPTER 21

THE TEMPERANCE REFORM IN PRESTON—A WORK PREPARATORY TO THE GOSPEL—PREACHING IN THE "COCK PIT"—HEBER WRITES HOME AN ACCOUNT OF HIS MISSION—THE WORK IN CUMBERLAND—EPISODE OF MARY SMITHIES—"SHE SHALL LIVE TO BECOME A MOTHER IN ISRAEL"

ONE of the great movements in England, commenced just prior to the landing of the Elders, was the temperance reform. Undoubtedly this was a work preparatory to the advent of the Gospel, and one recognized as such, not only by the Elders, but by their converts connected with the temperance cause.

"In almost every place we went," says Elder Kimball, "where there was a temperance hall, we could get it to preach in, many believing that we made men temperate faster than they did; for as soon as any obeyed the Gospel they abandoned their excesses in drinking; none of us drank any kind of spirits, porter, small beer, or even wine; neither did we drink tea, coffee or chocolate."

It is an interesting fact that this temperance movement began in Preston, where later was first proclaimed in Britain the glad tidings of the Gospel. Very fitting and appropriate, and quite in keeping with our theme, that the lesser movement should thus precede the greater, and from the same starting-point go forth preparing the way.

Herein, too, is sound Gospel philosophy. The spirit of the Lord and the demon of alcohol are essentially antagonistic. That which corrupts the body or darkens the mind, has nothing in common with Mormonism. [166] The Holy Ghost dwelleth not in unclean tabernacles. To be ready for the reception of that spirit which maketh manifest the things of God, and retain its light within the lamp of the soul, the heart must be pure, the mind unclouded, the body clean and undefiled.

On the first Sunday in September, 1837, the Saints in Preston commenced holding meetings in what was known as the "Cock Pit." It was a large and commodious place, capable of seating eight hundred persons, and situated in the center of the town. It had formerly been used by the sporting fraternity for the purpose indicated by its name, but recently had been converted into a temperance hall. Says Heber, describing this unique, historic edifice:

"The space for cock-fighting was an area of about twelve or fifteen feet in the center, around which the seats formed a circle, each seat rising about a foot above another, till they reached the walls of the building. When we leased it the area in the center was occupied by the singers, and our pulpit was the place where the judges formerly sat, who awarded the prizes at cockfights. We had to pay seven shillings per week for the use of it, and two shillings per week for lighting; it being beautifully lit up with gas. The building was about twenty-five feet from 'the Old Church,' probably the oldest in Lancashire."

On the 6th of September Elder Kimball paid a visit to the little branch in Walkerfold, where the Saints were suffering much persecution. Some had been driven from their homes, and otherwise ill treated for the cause of Christ, by their own fathers and mothers. The sight of Heber's face revived their sinking spirits, and they again rejoiced in the Lord. Later in the month he again visited the branch at Longridge and Walkerfold, and found it **[167]** prospering. Several more were added to the Church during his stay. He next visited and preached at Barshe Lees and Ribchester, baptizing two persons at the former place, and then returned to Preston.

About this time Heber wrote a letter to his wife, in Kirtland, giving some account of his mission. In it the following passages occur:

"You stated in your letter that some of the Twelve were coming to England next spring, calculating to bring their wives with them. This I have no objections to, but if they do they had better bring money to support them. They had better take Brother Joseph's advice and leave their wives at home, for if they bring them here they will repent the day they did so. I do not wish to bring my wife to this country to suffer. If they could see the misery that I do they would not think of such a thing. The Savior says, 'he that is not willing to leave father and mother, wife and children, brothers and sisters, houses and lands, for my sake and the Gospel, is not worthy of me.' We have hired our lodgings since we have been here and bought our own provisions. We eat but one meal a day at home, for the brethren invite us to dinner and supper with them, and they frequently divide their last loaf with us. They do all in their power, and I feel to bless them in the name of the Lord. There are 55 baptized in Preston, and it is as much as they can do to live, and there are but two or three that could lodge us over night if they should try; in fact there are some that have not a bed to sleep on themselves. The Lord says 'take no thought for the morrow,' and this is the way I feel for the present. I commit myself into His hands, that I may always be ready to go at His command. I desire to be content with whatsoever situation I am placed in. **[168]**

"I feel contented about you. I know the Lord will take care of you, and preserve you until I come home, and feed you and clothe you, and the children. Give me your prayers and you shall have mine. Be faithful, my dear companion; our labors will soon be over, when we shall meet to part no more forever."

Thus, it appears, the work in England was beginning to attract the attention of the Church at home, and stirring a desire in the breasts of the Apostles to "thrust in their sickles and reap" where the field was so "white unto the harvest." Heber's practical advice about leaving their wives at home while they went forth in the ministry, had its effect upon the minds of the brethren, and the custom has prevailed from that day to this, almost universally throughout the foreign missions of the Church.

In the meantime how fared it with the brethren in the north, Elder Russell and Priest Snyder, who had been sent with the Gospel into Cumberland?

"Brother Snyder returned from the north where he had traveled in company with Brother Russell. He stated that they met with considerable opposition while preaching the gospel, that they had baptized about thirty, and that others were investigating. After spending a few days with us," says Elder Kimball, "he and brother Goodson took their leave for America. Brother Goodson pretended to have business of importance which called him home. He had over 200 books of Mormon and Doctrine and Covenants which he refused to let me have, although I proffered to pay him the money for them on my return to America. He carried them back, and on arriving in Iowa Territory he burned them, at which time he apostatized and left the Church.

"Although we were deprived of the labors of Brothers Goodson and Snyder, the work of the Lord continued [169] to roll forth with great power, for those of us who remained received greater strength. Calls from all quarters to come and preach were constantly sounding in our ears, and we labored night and day to satisfy the people, who manifested such a desire for the truth as I never saw before. We had to speak in small and very crowded houses, and to large assemblies in the open air. Consequently our lungs were often very sore, and our bodies worn down with fatigue. Sometimes I was guilty of breaking the priestly rules. I pulled off my coat and rolled up my sleeves and went at my duty with my whole soul, like a man reaping and binding wheat, which caused the hireling priests to be very much surprised. They found much fault with us, and threatened us continually, because we got all of their best members. We told them all we wanted was the wheat; they could keep the rest."

Next comes an interesting incident in Heber's ministry, relating closely to one branch of his numerous family. Says he:

"I will mention a circumstance in relation to the first child born in the Church of Jesus Christ of Latterday Saints in Great Britain, which was on the 7th of October, 1837, at Barshe Lees. She was the daughter of James and Nancy Smithies, formerly Nancy Knowles. After she was born her parents wanted to take her to the church to be sprinkled, or christened, as they call it. I used every kind of persuasion to convince them of their folly; it being contrary to the scriptures and the will of God; the parents wept bitterly, and it seemed as though I could not prevail on them to omit it. I wanted to know of them why they were so tenacious. The answer was, 'if she dies she cannot have a burial in the churchyard.' I said to them, 'Brother and Sister Smithies, [170] I say unto you in the name of Israel's God, she shall not die on this land, for she shall live until she becomes a mother in Israel, and I say it in the name of Jesus Christ and by virtue of the Holy Priesthood vested in me.' That silenced them, and when she was two weeks old they presented the child to me; I took it in my arms and blessed it, that it should live to become a mother in Israel. She was the first child blessed in that country, and the first born unto them."

The child's name was Mary Smithies. She grew to womanhood, emigrating with her parents to America, and became Heber's wife, and the mother of five of his children.

Apostle Kimball next took a tour through some villages south of Preston, in company with Brother Francis Moon. The people "flocked in crowds" to hear him. At Longridge five preachers were among the large congregation of interested listeners. At Eccleston he had the privilege—a rare one—of preaching in a Methodist chapel. During this journey he baptized ten persons, two of whom were

Methodist preachers.

By this time the Church in Preston had become numerous, and it was found necessary to organize them into five branches, which was accordingly done on the 8th of October. Priests and Teachers were ordained to take charge of the branches. Thursday evenings were set apart for prayer meetings in various places, and on the Sabbath the whole body assembled at the main hall to partake of the sacrament, and receive general instructions. The greatest harmony and love prevailed, and "as little children" the Saints rejoiced in doing the will of God. Heber spent the principal part of his time in the country, "leaving Preston Monday mornings, and returning on Saturday evenings." [171]

# CHAPTER 22

HEBER WRITES TO WILLARD IN BEDFORD—THE ELDERS BECOME LICENSED PREACHERS—THE "MILK" AND "MEAT OF THE WORD"—RAPID SPREAD OF THE WORK—MIRACLES—HEBER'S DREAM OF THE BULL AND FIELD OF GRAIN—A DISAPPOINTED MOB

FEELING some anxiety about the work in Bedford, where Elder Richards was still laboring, Heber wrote to him as follows:

"PRESTON, Oct. 12th, 1837.

*"Dear Brother Richards:*

"With pleasure I take my pen in hand to let you know that I have not forgotten you. Brother Hyde and myself have labored all the time, night and day, so that we have not had much time to sleep. There are calls on the right and left. In Preston there are about one hundred and sixty members. At Walkerfold I have built up one branch; one in Barshe Lees, in Yorkshire; one in Ribchester; one in Penwortham, and one in Thornley. We have built up those branches besides laboring in Preston nearly all the time; so you can judge whether or no we have been idle. There are ten calls where we can only fill one. Have had a very bad cold on my lungs, so that I have had to hold up for a few days, to recruit my health. Our congregations have been so large that our lungs have failed to make all the people hear. Brother Fielding has been with me part of the time; he has not preached much, but has baptized, and visited from house to house.

"The harvest is ripe and many are thirsting for the word of life. May God give you energy to go forth in His name, and cry aloud and spare not; and I say unto you, Brother Richards, if you stay in that place much [172] longer there will contentions arise, until the little branch will be broken up and scattered to the four winds. And I say this in the name of the Lord: go forth into the country without purse or scrip, as God has commanded, and if you should leave the branch two or three weeks the Saints will take no harm, and the Lord will bless you in so doing. Go fifteen or twenty miles; cry repentance, and let the big things alone; for this is the way that the hearts of the people are closed up in Bedford, by Elder Goodson preaching those things he was commanded to let alone. I have scarcely meddled with the prophecies; I have only preached the first principles of the Gospel to the people, doing the same that I teach you to do. The churches in the country I stay with a few days, and then leave them two or three weeks; they are praising the Lord and are glad to see me when I visit them.

"Brother Richards, I am not forgetful of your kindness to me and the brethren while with us; but I have a godly jealousy over you for your welfare and prosperity in the cause of Christ.

"Heber C. Kimball."

Willard, it appears, had been praying to receive the mind and will of the Lord through his brethren, the Apostles, to direct him in his labors. His prayer being answered, he went forth with renewed energy, preaching and baptizing, laboring diligently and with success, until March, 1838, when he returned to Preston.

Heber continues: "The effect of the Gospel of Jesus Christ now began to be apparent, not only in the hearts of believers, but likewise in the hearts of those who rejected it. Our meeting in Preston being disturbed by the Methodist ministers, we got our hall licensed, and two gentlemen named Joseph Brown and Arthur Burrows, who were policemen, proffered their services to preserve the peace, and protect us from any further dis[173]turbance; which they continued to do as long as we stayed in that land. Many began to persecute us for preaching without a license from the authority of the nation. This idea of obtaining a license from the secular authority was somewhat novel to us; but after consulting our friends, amongst whom was Mr. John Richards' son, an attorney practising in Preston, we found it was according to the laws of England. Brothers Hyde and I therefore made application to the Quarter Sessions and obtained licenses, by the assistance of Mr. Richards; and for which service he refused compensation.

"The following is a copy of my license:

"'Lancashire to wit

This is to certify that at the General Quarter Sessions of the Peace, held, by adjournment at Preston in and for said county, the eighteenth day of October, in the first year of the reign of Her Majesty, Queen Victoria, Heber Chase Kimball came before the Justices present, and did then and there in open court, take the oaths appointed to be taken, instead of the oaths of allegiance and supremacy; and also the abjuration oath; and subscribed his name thereto, pursuant to the several laws in that behalf made and provided.

"'E. Gorst,
"'Deputy Clerk of the Peace in and
for said county.'

"Having now obeyed the requisitions of the law, we felt ourselves tolerably secure, knowing that our enemies could not lawfully harm us. I wrote to Brother

Richards that I had taken the oath to be true to Her Majesty and see that the laws were executed, also the abjuration oath provided for foreigners who were not naturalized, and obtained a license as a preacher of the Gospel; and recommended him to do the same at Bed[174]ford: but they made him take the oath of allegiance before they granted him his license to preach. After we had obtained our licenses, to our surprise we found there were only a few licensed preachers in Preston; and when they abused me I told them if they did not cease their abuse I would see the laws put in force according to the oaths I had taken; and this generally silenced them.

"Although we had many persecutors who would have rejoiced at our destruction, and who felt determined to overthrow the work of the Lord, yet there were many who were friendly, who would have stood by us under all circumstances, and would not have been afraid to hazard their lives in our behalf. The church in Preston now numbered two or three hundred souls, with more being added continually.

"November 14th, I wrote to Willard Richards, exhorting him to teach the first principles of the Gospel only; telling him that if the people would not receive them they would not receive anything else; the more simple he could be, the better it would be for his hearers, Brother Goodson having left about 20 Books of Mormon in his possession, I told him to sell all that he could, either to saint or sinner; to get him some clothes, and to make himself warm and comfortable."

The wisdom of the Apostle's counsel to give first the "milk of the word" to those who were infants in faith, reserving the "meat" for such as became strong, is self-evident. No vessel can contain beyond its capacity. Food, in kind and quantity, must ever keep pace with the growth, and be suited to the condition of the one to whom it is administered.

It is human nature to oppose that which is new. The pride of man revolts at the idea of admitting himself [175] in error, and his preconceived notions to be false, or even defective. The flesh, naturally inert, dislikes change that brings toil and study, even for the soul's salvation. Self-interest pleads in various ways, in favor of the old, and against the new. Thus hoary tradition, antique error, sits warmed and comforted, a welcome guest, alike in palace and in hovel, while Truth, a pilgrim, hungry and cold, without stands shivering in the frosty air.

All truth may be new to the ignorant, though old as eternity to the Gods, and whom the Gods make wise. Much that is true, is not expedient. The Prophet Joseph could not tell all he knew, even to the Elders; nor the Elders all they knew to the people, Paul, caught up unto "the third heaven;" Joseph, unto "the seventh heaven," saw and heard things unspeakable, things "unlawful to be uttered." The mysteries of God's kingdom are not for the world, nor for novices in the faith until it is wisdom in the Lord, "lest they perish."

The effect of Elder Goodson's folly in reading to the Reverend Mr. Matthews the vision of the triple glories, when his mind was just beginning to grasp the Gospel's first principles—sufficiently novel and far enough advanced to test his neophyte faith to the utmost—is only one of many like instances in Mormon missionary experience. Prudence demands that truth be inculcated by gradual degrees. "Cry nothing but repentance to this generation," is a word of supreme wisdom to the Lord's servants, laboring in His vineyard among the tender vines and fragile flowers of humanity. Eagles build their nests in strong and high places. Truth is loftier and mightier than many eagles.

The Apostle's record continues:

"Having an appointment to preach in the village of Wrightington, while on the way I stopped at the houses **[176]** of Brothers Francis Moon and Amos Fielding, when I was informed that the family of Matthias Moon had sent a request for me to visit them, that they might have the privilege of conversing with me on the subject of the Gospel. Accordingly Brother Amos Fielding and I paid them a visit that evening. We were very kindly received by the family, and had considerable conversation on the subject of my mission to England, and the great work of the Lord in the last days. They listened with attention to my statements, but at the same time they appeared to be prejudiced against them. We remained in conversation until a late hour, and then returned home. On our way Brother Fielding observed that he thought our visit had been in vain, as the family seemed to have considerable prejudice. I answered, 'be not faithless but believing; we shall yet see great effects from this visit, for I know that some of the family have received the testimony, and will shortly manifest the same;' at which remark he seemed surprised.

"The next morning I continued my journey to Wrightington and Hunter's Hill. After spending two or three days in that vicinity preaching, I baptized seven of the family of Benson, and others, and organized a branch.

"I returned by the way of Brother Fielding's, with whom I again tarried for the night. The next morning I started for Preston, but when I got opposite the lane leading to Mr. Moon's, I was forcibly led by the Spirit of the Lord to call and see them again. I therefore directed my steps to the house. On my arrival I knocked at the door. Mrs. Moon exclaimed, 'come in! come in! You are welcome here! I and the lassies (meaning her daughters) have just been calling on the Lord, and praying that He would send you this way.' She then **[177]** informed me of her state of mind since I was there, and said she at first rejected my testimony, and endeavored to think lightly on the things I had advanced, but on trying to pray, the heavens seemed to be like brass over her head, and it was like iron under her feet. She did not know what was the matter, saying, 'certainly the man has not bewitched me has he?' and upon inquiring she found it was the same with the lassies. They then began to reflect on the things I told them, and thinking it possible that I had told them the truth, they resolved to lay the case before the Lord, and beseech Him to give them a testimony concerning the things I had testified of. She then observed that as soon as they did so light broke in upon their minds; they were convinced that I was a messenger of salvation; that it was the work of the Lord, and they had resolved to obey the Gospel. That evening I baptized Mr. Moon and his wife, and four of their daughters.

"The same night I went to Leyland, and stayed with Francis Moon, and the next morning I went to Preston where I stayed about three weeks with Brother Hyde.

"During this time our enemies were not idle; they heaped abuse upon us with an unsparing hand and issued torrents of lies concerning us, which I am thankful to say did not injure us. Among those most active in publishing falsehoods against us and the truth were many of the clergy, who were afraid to meet us face to face in honorable debate, although particularly requested so to do. We only asked three days' notice of the time of discussion, so as to notify the people. But they sought every opportunity to try to destroy our characters, and propagate their lies concerning us, thus showing that they loved darkness rather than light. We frequently called upon the ministers of various denominations, who [178] had taken a stand against us, to come forward and investigate our religion before the world, in an honorable manner, and bring forth their strong reasons to disprove the things we taught, and convince the people by sound argument and the word of God, if they could, that we did not preach the Gospel of Jesus Christ. This they declined. They kept at a respectful distance, and only came out when they knew we were absent, with misrepresentations and abuse. It is true we suffered some from the statements which they thought proper to make, when we could not get an opportunity to contradict them; but generally their reports were of such a character as carried their own refutation with them.

"I visited Mr. Moon again, and baptized the remainder of his family, consisting of thirteen souls, the youngest of whom was over twenty years of age. They received the Gospel as little children, and rejoiced exceedingly in its blessings. The sons were very good musicians, and the daughters excellent singers. When they united their instruments and voices in the songs of Zion, the effect was truly transporting.

"Before I left England there were about thirty of that family and connections baptized, five of whom, Hugh, John, Francis, William and Thomas Moon, were ordained to be fellow laborers with us in the vineyard, and I left them rejoicing in the truths they had embraced.

"In all my labors I was greatly assisted by the Spirit of the Lord, and my soul was comforted exceedingly; for the sick were healed, the lame walked, and in several cases where persons had lain upon their beds in a consumptive state for many years and were not able to sit up, they would be taken in a carriage, perhaps a mile, to the water, where I baptized, laid my hands upon them and confirmed them, that they might receive the Holy [179] Ghost, and rebuked their disease in the name of Jesus Christ, and said unto them 'be thou made whole,' and they would leap and shout glory to God, and begin to mend from that hour. This was a common occurrence on our first mission to England. Many scores of persons were healed by our sending a handkerchief to them.

"I was instrumental in building up churches in the following places, viz.; Eccleston, Wrightington, Askin, Dauber's Lane, Exton, Chorley, Whittle, Hunter's Hill, and Leyland Moss, after laboring about four weeks, and baptizing in the neighborhood of two hundred persons, which caused me to rejoice that I had not labored in vain. More loving and affectionate Saints I never saw before; they were patterns of humility. All the above villages are within a short distance of each other, and near to Preston.

"After my return from those places I took a tour to the northeast of Preston, in company with Brother Joseph Fielding, where we labored a short time with considerable success, and raised up churches in Ribchester, Thornley, Stoney Gate Lane, and at Clithero, a market town containing several thousand inhabitants. At Clithero I baptized a preacher named Thomas Smith and six members of the Methodist Church, immediately after I had preached the first time.

"One night while at the village of Ribchester I dreamed that in company with another person I was walking, and we saw a very extensive field of wheat; more so than the eye could reach; such a sight I had never witnessed. The wheat appeared perfectly ripe and ready for harvest. I was very much rejoiced at the glorious sight which presented itself; but judge of my surprise, when on taking some of the ears and rubbing them in my hands, I found nothing but smut; not any sound grain could I find. I marveled exceedingly and **[180]** felt very sorrowful, and exclaimed 'what will the people do for grain! Here is a great appearance of plenty, but there is no sound wheat.'

"While contemplating the scenery, I looked in another direction, and saw a small field in the form of the letter L, which had the appearance of something growing in it. I immediately directed my steps to it, and found that it had been sown with wheat, some of which had grown up six inches high, other parts of the field not quite so high, and some had just sprouted. This gave me some encouragement to expect that at the harvest there would be some good grain. While thus engaged, a large bull, looking very fierce and angry, leaped over the fence, ran through the field, and stamped down a large quantity of that which had just sprouted, and after doing considerable injury he leaped over the fence and ran away. I felt very much grieved that so much wheat should be destroyed when there was such a prospect of scarcity.

"When I awoke next morning the interpretation was given me. The large field with the great appearance of grain, so beautiful to look upon, represented the nation in which I then resided; which had a very pleasing appearance and a good show of religion; which made great pretensions to piety and goodness, and consequently of the gifts of the Spirit. The small field I saw, clearly represented the region of country where I was laboring, and where the word of truth had taken root, which was in the shape of the letter L, and it was growing in the hearts of those who had the gospel, some places having grown a little more than others. The village I was in was that part of the field where the bull did so much injury; for during my short visit there, most of the inhabitants were believing, but as soon as I **[181]** departed, a clergyman belonging to the Church of England came out and violently attacked the truth, made a considerable noise, crying, "False Prophet! Delusion!" and after trampling on truth and doing all the mischief he could before I returned, he took shelter in his pulpit.

"However he did not destroy all the seed, for after my return I was instrumental in building up a branch in Ribchester. A mob of Catholics had combined, that when I went to baptize any persons they would pelt me with stones. I made arrangements with each of the candidates to go singly to the place of baptism, and about the time the last one got there I started quickly, got to the place and baptized them all. As I was baptizing the last one the mob came up and were disappointed in their vengeance, for I came out of the water, and they did not know how many I had baptized."

## CHAPTER 23

THE VOICE OF THE GOOD SHEPHERD—HEBER CONVERTS WHOLE VILLAGES—THE SPIRIT OF THE MASTER UPON HIS SERVANT—THE CHRISTMAS CONFERENCE IN PRESTON

"MY sheep know my voice, and a stranger they will not follow." So said the Shepherd of Israel.

The test is true in all time. How many in these latter days bear witness, that, until Mormonism came, they had no religion, and desired none, but were instantly converted on first hearing it proclaimed. Again, **[182]** how many wandered in quest of it, from church to church, from creed to creed, scarce knowing what they sought, yet conscious of "an aching void" which nothing else could fill, and only happy when at last it was supplied.

"My sheep know my voice, and a stranger they will not follow."

A remarkable instance of this truth now occurred in Heber's ministry. Says he:

"Having mentioned my intention of going to Downham and Chatburn, to several of the brethren, they endeavoured to dissuade me from going, informing me there could be no prospect of success whatever, as several ministers of different denominations had endeavored in vain to raise churches in these places, and had frequently preached to them, but to no effect, as they had resisted all the efforts and withstood the attempts of all sects and parties for the last thirty years, who, seeing all their attempts fail, had given them up to hardness of heart. I was also informed they were very wicked places. However this did not discourage me, believing that the Gospel of Jesus Christ could reach the heart, when the gospels of men proved abortive; I consequently told those brethren that these were the places I wanted to go to, for that it was my business not to call the righteous but sinners to repentance.

"The next day we received a very pressing invitation to preach in Chatburn, but having given out an appointment to preach in Clithero that evening, I informed them that I would not be able to comply with their request that night; this did not satisfy them, they continued to solicit me with the greatest importunity, until I was obliged to consent to remain with them, and requested Elder Fielding to attend to the appointment at **[183]** Clithero; there was a feeling of reluctance on his part to go, as he feared the rabble might break up his meeting; but seeing the importunity of the people that I should stay with them in Chatburn, he consented to go to Clithero alone. As he feared it might be, so it was; his meeting was broken up.

"In Chatburn I was cordially received by the inhabitants, who turned out in great numbers to hear me preach. They procured a large tithing barn, placing a barrel in the center, upon which I stood. I preached to them the first principles of the Gospel, spoke in simplicity upon the principles revealed by our Lord and Savior Jesus Christ, the conditions of pardon for a fallen world and the blessings and privileges of those who embraced the truth; I likewise said a little on the subject of the resurrection. My testimony was accompanied by the Spirit of the Lord, and was received with joy, and these people who had been represented as being hard and obdurate, were melted into tenderness and love. I told them that, being a servant of the Lord Jesus Christ, I stood ready at all times to administer the ordinances of the Gospel, and explained what was necessary to prepare them for baptism; that when they felt to repent of and forsake their sins, they were ready to be baptized for the remission of sins, like the jailor and his household, and Cornelius and his house. When I concluded I felt someone pulling at my coat, exclaiming, 'Maister, Maister,' I turned round and asked what was wanted. Mrs. Elizabeth Partington said, 'Please sir, will you baptize me?' 'And me?' And me?' exclaimed more than a dozen voices. Accordingly I went down into the water and baptized twenty-five. I was engaged in this duty, and confirming them and conversing with the people until after midnight. [184]

"The next morning I returned to Downham, and baptized between twenty-five and thirty in the course of the day.

"The next evening I returned to Chatburn. The congregation was so numerous that I had to preach in the open air, and took my stand on a stone wall, and afterwards baptized several. These villages seemed to be affected from one end to the other; parents called their children together, spoke to them on the subjects which I had preached about, and warned them against swearing and all other evil practices, and instructed them in their duty.

"We were absent from Preston five days, during which time Brother Fielding and I baptized and confirmed about 110 persons; organized branches in Downham, Chatburn, Waddington and Clithero; and ordained several to the lesser Priesthood, to preside. This was the first time the people in those villages ever heard our voices, or saw an American.

"I cannot refrain from relating an occurrence which took place while Brother Fielding and myself were passing through the village of Chatburn on our way to Downham: having been observed approaching the village, the news ran from house to house, and immediately the noise of their looms was hushed, and the people flocked to their doors to welcome us and see us pass. More than forty young people of the place ran to meet us; some took hold of our mantles and then of each others' hands; several having hold of hands went before us singing the songs of Zion, while their parents gazed upon the scene with delight, and poured their blessings upon our heads, and praised the God of heaven for sending us to unfold the principles of truth and the plan of salvation to them. The children continued with us to Downham, a mile dis[185]tant. Such a scene, and such gratitude, I never witnessed before. 'Surely,' my heart exclaimed, 'out of the mouths of babes and sucklings thou hast perfected praise.' What could have been more pleasing and delightful than such a manifestation of gratitude to Almighty God; and from those whose hearts were deemed too hard to be penetrated by the Gospel, and who had been considered the most wicked and hardened people in that region of country."

A rare scene, indeed, and a suggestive one, for the parallel of which the mind must leap backward nigh two thousand years:

"On the next day, much people that were come to the feast, when they heard that Jesus was coming to Jerusalem.

"Took branches of palm trees, and went forth to meet him, and cried, Hosanna; Blessed is the King of Israel that cometh in the name of the Lord.

"The Pharisees therefore said among themselves, Perceive ye how ye prevail nothing? behold, the world is gone after him."

So was it with this servant of Christ, this brother of Jesus in the British Isles. The hireling priests, the pharisees of Christendom, prevailed nothing. The "world went after him," whole villages at a sweep, singing praises, and shouting in tones of rapture: "Blessed is he that cometh in the name of the Lord."

There was divine harmony in all this. In Heber, his character, manner and methods—we say it reverently—there was much of the Christ; the might of the lion, with the meekness of the lamb. His, also, was the Savior's lineage; in his heart a kindred spirit, in his veins the self-same blood. Where causes are similar, should there not spring similar results? [186]

And is it not truly a Christ-like sentiment, with which he concludes his description of that wonderful scene:

"In comparison to the joy I then experienced, the grandeur, pomp and glory of the kingdoms of this world shrank into insignificance, and appeared as dross, and all the honor of man aside from the Gospel as vanity. The prayer of my heart was, 'O Lord do thou bless this people, save them from sin, and prepare them for Thy celestial kingdom, and that Thy servant may meet them round Thy throne; and grant, O Lord, that I may continue to preach the Gospel of Christ, which shall cause the hearts of the poor to rejoice, and the meek to increase their joy in the Lord; which shall comfort the hearts of the widows and cheer the soul of the orphan; and that I may be an instrument in Thy hands of bringing them to Zion, that they may behold Thy glory and be prepared to meet the Savior when He shall descend in the clouds of heaven."

On Christmas a special conference was held in Preston by the Apostles. About three hundred of the Saints assembled, delegates being present from the various branches in and around Preston, extending some thirty miles. Joseph Fielding was ordained an Elder, and ten Priests and seven Teachers were ordained and set apart to take charge of the several branches where they resided.

At this conference, the Word of Wisdom, the temperance revelation of the Church, was first publicly taught in Great Britain. The Elders had taught it more by example than precept heretofore. It became almost universally observed among the brethren. In the "Cock Pit," where this conference was held, had first been lifted the standard of temperance reform. It was the motto [187] on one of the banners of this movement, "Truth will Prevail," which greeted the Elders so opportunely, as an omen of success now verified, on their arrival in Preston from Liverpool, five months before. Says Apostle Kimball:

"The Spirit of the Lord was with us; and truly the hearts of the Elders were rejoiced beyond measure when we contemplated the glorious work which had been done, and we had to exclaim, 'Blessed be the name of the Lord, who has crowned our labors with such success!' During the conference we confirmed fourteen members and, blessed about one hundred children."

One hundred little children blessed in Preston, Christmas, 1837!

A beautiful and fitting celebration of that blessed day of days, when "unto us a Child was born" to take away the sins of the world; when God descended from His throne and took upon Him flesh, exchanging crown for cross, and sceptred rule for martyrdom, in the cause of man's redemption. Shine out, ye blazing stars, and sun and moon give forth your warmth and lustre! Ye cannot dim the glory, nor vie the matchless love, of Him who set you there to light and cheer, on, onward to celestial heights the world He died to save! [188]

## CHAPTER 24

THE WORK OF GOD NOT DEPENDENT UPON MAN—HUMILITY A SOURCE OF POWER—EVERY MAN CHOSEN AND FITTED FOR HIS SPHERE—EXAMPLE OF PAUL THE APOSTLE—HEBER "HITS THE ROCK" IN LONGTON—THE APOSTLES VISIT THE BRANCHES PRIOR TO RETURNING TO AMERICA.

PREACHING the Gospel and converting sinners unto Christ never yet depended for success upon man's learning or the music of oratory. The unlettered fishermen of Galilee, proclaiming in simple words "Christ crucified," were far more powerful in winning souls from error's ways and melting the hearts of the multitude, than would all the orators have been; the Herods, Ciceros, or Demosthenes, of Judea, Greece and Rome.

The reason is not, as some suppose, that learning and oratory are valueless in the cause of Christ, or necessarily a hindrance, as was Saul's armor upon youthful David. The example of the eloquent and erudite Paul suffices to disprove such a fallacy. The secret is simply this: that God had chosen those humble fishermen, and not the learned orators of the age, for that especial work, and endowed them with power from on high. No man, learned or unlearned, can build up God's Kingdom, except He be with him, and the Holy Ghost work through him. God is the doer of

His work, not man, and no flesh can glory in His presence. It was the Holy Ghost in Paul, as it was the Holy Ghost in Peter, not the learning or illiteracy of either, that wrought the wonders of which they were capable. [189]

The Holy Ghost dwells only in hearts that are pure and humble. Humility, next to virtue, is the one grand requisite of a servant of God. Pride and vanity are synonyms of weakness; humility, another name for strength. Men of learning and language, whom nature and education have made "spokesmen," need not be any less humble—though men of little learning and much language are very apt to be. Pride, in rags or in purple, is the offspring of ignorance; while learning is the parent of humility.

The eloquent and learned man, humble and filled with the Holy Ghost, is manifestly more capable, in his sphere, and more successful, than one without his advantages would be. But turn the tables, reverse the conditions, and, in his sphere, the unlearned man, intelligent, God-fearing and inspired, looms a giant, where his more polished brother might seem a pigmy by comparison. The faculty of adapting self to circumstances is invaluable for the missionary to possess. In saying that he was "all things to all men," the brave and faithful Paul did not brand himself a hypocrite. Rather, did he not mean he could accommodate himself to his surroundings; enter into the feelings and sympathies of "all men:" the high, the low, the rich, the poor, the learned and the illiterate; at home in palace or in hovel; feasting in gratitude at luxury's board, or sharing thankfully the crust of poverty; holding spell-bound by his oratory the charmed sages of Athens, or melting his jailor's heart with the simple pathos of his tale.

Such was Paul, the eloquent and learned Apostle; a vessel formed and fashioned, like all others, for his work. It was his mission to be "brought before Caesar"; the mission of most of his brethren to preach, like their Master, "the Gospel to the poor." It will yet fall to the [190] lot of God's servants to stand before kings and rulers, as did Elijah, Nathan and Daniel of old. But in the days of Heber, of Joseph, and of Brigham, the Gospel was chiefly to the poor and humble, who received it gladly and rejoiced in the God of their salvation.

Returning now to the Apostles in Preston:

"Immediately after the conference," wrote Heber, "Elder Hyde and I went to a village near the sea shore called Longton, where we published to the listening crowds the glad tidings of salvation. Brothers Hyde and Goodson had preached several discourses there, and numbers were believing, but none had been baptized. The people asked Brother Hyde why he did not 'bring Kimball down, to hit the rock a crack with his big sledge and let the water flow out.' I preached from Hebrews 6th chapter, 1st verse: 'Therefore not leaving the principles of the doctrine of Christ, let us go on unto perfection; not laying again the foundation of repentance from dead works, and of faith toward God.' I preached a plain and simple discourse, and according to my calling I taught them to repent and be baptized, that they might be saved, and if they did not they would be damned. Elder Hyde bore testimony. After meeting I baptized ten, and in the morning after, several more. It being very cold weather—the streams all frozen over—we had to repair to the sea to administer the ordinance.

"January 24th, I left Preston and went to Longton with Brother Hyde. We preached once each, and baptized ten; from thence returned to Preston and stayed two or three days. Then I started on a mission to Eccleston and other places, visiting six branches and strengthening them. I was absent about eighteen days and baptized fifteen; the weather being so cold that many dared not go into the water. Returned to [191] Preston and stayed three days. On the Sabbath Elder Hyde and myself administered the sacrament and confirmed twelve. From thence went to Longton and baptized three, ordained one priest, one teacher, and one deacon, and blessed about thirty children. Again returned to Preston. From thence went to Whittle; preached once, and baptized five; and returned to Preston February 23rd.

"From this time to our departure from England we were continually engaged in the work of the ministry, proclaiming the everlasting Gospel in all the regions round, and baptizing all who believed and repented of their sins. The Holy Ghost, the comforter, was given to us and abode with us in a remarkable manner."

"The time when we expected to return to our native land being near at hand, it was considered best for us to spend the short time we had to remain in visiting and organizing the branches; placing such officers over them, and giving such instructions as would be beneficial to them during our absence. Accordingly Brothers Hyde, Fielding and myself visited a branch nearly every day, and imparted such instructions as the Spirit directed. We first visited the branches south of Preston, and after spending some time in that direction we journeyed to the north, accompanied by Brother Willard Richards, who had returned from Bedford March 7th, where he had been proclaiming the Gospel. In consequence of sickness his labors had not been so extensive as they otherwise would have been, and were confined within a short distance of the city of Bedford, where he raised up two small branches of about forty members, which he set in order, and ordained James Lavender an Elder, and other officers to preside. He had labored under considerable difficulty in consequence [192] of the conduct of Elder Goodson, who taught many things which were not in wisdom, and which proved a barrier to the spread of the truth in that region. His health being poor, he was not able to preach much.

"While we were attending to our duties in that section we received a very pressing invitation from a Baptist church, through the medium of their deacon, to pay them a visit, stating that the society were exceedingly anxious to hear from our lips the wonderful things we had proclaimed in the regions round about. We endeavored to excuse ourselves from going, as our engagements were such that it would require the short time we had to stay to attend them. They seemed determined not to take a denial and pleaded with such earnestness that we could not resist their entreaties, and we finally consented to go and preach once. Having arrived at the village, which was between Downham and Burnley, we found a large congregation already assembled in the Baptist chapel, anxiously waiting our arrival. The minister gave out the hymns and Elder Hyde spoke on the resurrection with great effect, after which the minister gave out another hymn, which was sung by the assembly, and then he requested me to address them. I spoke briefly on the first principles of the Gospel. During the services the congregation was overjoyed, tears ran down their cheeks, and the minister could not refrain from frequently clapping his hands for joy, while in the meeting. After the service was over he took us to his house where we were very kindly entertained. After partaking of his hospitality, he with some more friends accompanied us to our lodgings, where we remained in conversation until a very late hour. The next morning while we were preparing to depart we were waited upon by several of the citizens who requested us to preach again that day, [193] stating that great interest was felt by the inhabitants, many of whom were in tears, fearing they should hear us no more, and that a number of influential men had suspended operations in their factories to allow their workmen the privilege of hearing us preach; but we were obliged to deny them, as it was necessary to attend to the appointments we had previously made. We could scarcely go away from them, and when we did so they wept like little children. Such a desire to hear the Gospel I never saw equalled before.

"After commending them to the grace and mercy of God, we went to Downham, where we preached in the afternoon, after which we baptized several and confirmed forty. In the evening we called the churches of Chatburn, Downham, Clithero and Waddington together, and after confirming some, we ordained Priests, Teachers and Deacons to preside over the branches.

"From thence we went to Preston, and after a short stay visited Penwortham and Longton, and organized the churches in those places, which numbered about fifty members each." [194]

## CHAPTER 25

CONDITION OF THE CHURCH AT HOME—PRUNING OFF THE DEAD BRANCHES—A DAY OF CHOOSING—APOSTATES CONSPIRE TO OVERTHROW THE CHURCH—FLIGHT OF THE PROPHET FROM KIRTLAND—FALL OF OLIVER COWDERY AND OTHER APOSTLES—"SHOW UNTO US THY WILL, O LORD, CONCERNING THE TWELVE!"

WHILE the Apostles are setting in order the Church in England, preparatory to their departure for America, let us fly before them over the sea and note some of the changes which have taken place since they left Kirtland.

The Church had suffered terribly from the ravages of apostasy. At no time in its history has it seemed so near destruction, as in the early part of 1837, the period of the opening of the British Mission. The causes are noted elsewhere in these pages, and deserve a niche in the temple of memory for all time. The Ohio mobbings, the Missouri persecutions, the martyrdom, the exodus, nor all that Zion's cause has suffered since, have imperilled it half so much as when mammon and the love of God strove for supremacy in the hearts of His people, and the

Saints, for a time forgetful of their high calling, laid aside their spiritual mission and went groveling after "the beggarly elements of the world."

Only once in the history of the work, has its almighty Author found it necessary to reveal that "something new must be done for the salvation of the Church." **[195]**

That "something new," as we have seen, was a great spiritual movement, to counteract the tendency to carnal or temporal things, which was resting like the sleep of death upon the drooping eyelids of the Zion of God.

To root out the deadly Upas-tree, rouse Zion from her slumber beneath its pestilential shade, and prune off the withered branches from the Tree of Life, was the first care of the Prophet after despatching the Elders for England.

A conference assembled "in committee of the whole Church" at Kirtland, on Sunday, September 3rd, 1837. At this conference the various quorums of the Priesthood were presented to the people for their action.

President Sidney Rigdon presented the name of Joseph Smith, junior, to the Church, to know if they still looked upon him as the President of the whole Church, and would receive and sustain him in that position. The vote was unanimous in the affirmative.

President Smith then presented Sidney Rigdon and Frederick G. Williams as his counselors, and to constitute with himself the three first Presidents of the Church. Elder Rigdon was sustained unanimously, but the motion failed as to F. G. Williams. President Smith then put in nomination Oliver Cowdery, Joseph Smith, senior, Hyrum Smith, and John Smith, as assistant counselors; these four, together with the first three, to be considered the heads of the Church. Carried unanimously.

It was voted that Newel K. Whitney continue to hold his office as Bishop in Kirtland, and that Reynolds Cahoon and Jared Carter continue to act as the Bishop's counselors.

The Twelve Apostles were then presented, one by **[196]** one, when Thomas B. Marsh, David W. Patten, Brigham Young, Heber C. Kimball, Orson Hyde, Parley P. Pratt, William Smith and William E. McLellin, were received and unanimously sustained in their Apostleship. Luke Johnson, Lyman Johnson and John F. Boynton were rejected and cut off, though given the privilege of confessing and making satisfaction. The cause of the difficulty with Elders Boynton and Johnson was their "leaving their calling to attend to other occupations."

Five members of the High Council were also objected to by the people, and new ones chosen in their stead. John Gaylord, James Forster, Salmon Gee, Daniel S. Miles, Joseph Young, Josiah Butterfield and Levi Hancock were retained in office as Presidents of the Seventies, while John Gold was rejected.

A similar conference was held at Far West, Caldwell County, Missouri, then the head-quarters of the Church in that region, on the 7th of November 1837, and another on the 5th of February, 1838. The Priesthood was reorganized and the Church set in order, in the same manner as had been done in Kirtland. Hyrum Smith was sustained, in lieu of Frederick G. Williams, as one of the three First

Presidents, in which office he had before been acting. Elder Boynton and the two Elders Johnson were reinstated in the Quorum of the Twelve, though later they again fell away. Bishops Edward Partridge, Isaac Morley and Titus Billings were retained in office; while Presidents William W. Phelps and John Whitmer were severed from the Church; the former afterwards returned.

Against these brethren "Elder Lyman Wight stated that he considered all other accusations of minor importance, compared to their selling their lands in Jackson County; that they had set an example which all **[197]** the Saints were liable to follow. He said that it was a hellish principle, and that they had flatly denied the faith in so doing."

Thus was the line of demarcation being drawn. Thus were "the inhabitants of Zion" commencing to "judge all things pertaining to Zion." There had been a day of calling; a day of choosing now had come, and they who were "not Apostles and Prophets" were beginning to be known.

During the absence of the Prophet and Elder Rigdon in Missouri, whither they had gone to superintend the work of purification, Warren Parrish, John F. Boynton, Luke Johnson, Joseph Coe, and others, in Kirtland, dissented from the Church and combined together for its overthrow. They were encouraged and assisted by apostates and prominent Elders of the Church in Missouri. These dissenters called themselves "the Church of Christ," the "old standard," openly renouncing the Church of Jesus Christ of Latter-day Saints, and denouncing the Prophet Joseph and all who adhered to him, as heretics.

So bitter became the apostate and mobocratic spirit in Kirtland, that they who raised their voices in defense of the Prophet of God, at once endangered their lives. Apostle Brigham Young, who stood firm and immovable at Joseph's side, was forced to flee to save himself from the fury of the enemy, who were enraged at his bold, outspoken stand in favor of the Prophet, and against his foes and traducers. Three weeks later, on January 12th, 1838, the Prophet and President Rigdon also fled from Kirtland, for Missouri, followed by human blood-hounds, armed and thirsting for their lives, a distance of two hundred miles.

Kirtland was now no longer a fit abiding place for **[198]** the Saints. The faithful of the body of the Church commenced migrating to Missouri, where the work of purification went on.

At Far West, in April, 1838, Presidents Oliver Cowdery and David Whitmer were excommunicated from the Church. The charges sustained against the former were for urging vexatious law-suits against the brethren, slandering President Joseph Smith, contempt of the Church in not attending meetings, leaving his calling in which God had appointed him by revelation, for the sake of filthy lucre, and turning to the practice of law; disgracing the Church by being connected in the bogus business, dishonesty, and, finally, for "leaving or forsaking the cause of God, and returning to the beggarly elements of the world, and neglecting his high and holy calling, according to his profession."

President Whitmer was charged with not observing the Word of Wisdom;

# CHAPTER 25

neglecting meetings and possessing the same spirit as the dissenters, writing letters to the dissenters in Kirtland, unfavorable to the cause of God and the character of His Prophet, neglecting the duties of his calling and separating himself from the Church, and signing himself President of the Church of Christ, after being cut off from the Presidency, in an insulting letter to the High Council.

On the same day Apostle Lyman E. Johnson was excommunicated, and soon after Apostle William E. McLellin fell away.

On the 8th of July, 1838, at Far West, the Prophet Joseph and the remainder of the Twelve met in solemn council and unitedly besought the Throne of Grace for guidance, light and help.

"Show unto us Thy will, O Lord, concerning the Twelve!" **[199]**

Such was the burden of their prayer, to which the Lord made answer as follows:

"Verily, thus saith the Lord, let a conference be held immediately, let the Twelve be organized, and let men be appointed to supply the place of those who are fallen. Let my servant Thomas remain for a season in the Land of Zion, to publish my word. Let the residue continue to preach from that hour, and if they will do this in all lowliness of heart, in meekness and humility, and long suffering, I, the Lord, give unto them a promise that I will provide for their families, and an effectual door shall be opened for them, from henceforth; and next spring let them depart to go over the great waters, and there promulgate my Gospel, the fullness thereof, and bear record of my name. Let them take leave of my Saints in the city Far West, on the 26th day of April next, on the building spot of my house, saith the Lord. Let my servant, John Taylor, and also my servant John E. Page, and also my servant Wilford Woodruff, and also my servant Willard Richards, be appointed to fill the places of those who have fallen, and be officially notified of their appointment."

John Taylor and John E. Page were ordained Apostles December 19th, 1838, and Wilford Woodruff on the 26th of the following April. Willard Richards received his ordination in Preston, England, after the arrival there of the Apostles in April, 1840. George A. Smith was added to the quorum the same day that Wilford Woodruff was ordained, to fill a vacancy caused by the fall of another of the Twelve. All, save John E. Page, who fell from grace a few years later, have won immortal fame in Israel, and left to posterity the legacy of a spotless name.

Let us now return to the Apostles and their work in England. **[200]**

# CHAPTER 26

HEBER'S FAREWELL TO CHATBURN—AN AFFECTING SCENE—HIS SYMPATHY FOR THE POOR OF ENGLAND—THE APRIL CONFERENCE IN PRESTON—TWO THOUSAND SAINTS ASSEMBLE—JOSEPH FIELDING APPOINTED TO PRESIDE OVER THE BRITISH MISSION

WE left Apostles Kimball and Hyde, with their associates in the ministry, visiting the various branches of the mission they had founded, preparatory to taking farewell leave of the Saints and sailing for America. They agreed to hold a general conference in Preston on the 8th of April, the day before their departure.

"In the interval," writes Heber, "I went and visited the branches in the regions of Clithero and Chatburn, and on the morning when I left Chatburn many were in tears, thinking they should see my face no more. When I left them, my feelings were such as I cannot describe. As I walked down the street I was followed by numbers; the doors were crowded by the inmates of the houses to bid me farewell, who could only give vent to their grief in sobs and broken accents. While contemplating this scene I was constrained to take off my hat, for I felt as if the place was holy ground. The Spirit of the Lord rested down upon me and I was constrained to bless that whole region of country. I was followed by a great number to Clithero, a considerable distance from the villages, who could then hardly separate from me. My heart was like unto theirs, and I thought my head was a fountain of tears, for I wept for several miles after I bid [201] them adieu. I had to leave the road three times to go to streams of water to bathe my eyes."

"Who can read this," says Tullidge, beautifully, "without a feeling of profound veneration for the great and good man whose memory is enshrined in the hearts of the British Saints as their spiritual father? That touching scene is enough to immortalize the character of Heber C. Kimball as a true apostle of Christ; and the pathos is actually heightened when he is seen alone by the wayside weeping, or by the streams washing away those sacred tears."

Heber C. Kimball was indeed a true apostle of Christ, one of the called and chosen; a prophet and a servant of God, in nature as well as name.

The Prophet Joseph told him in after years that the reason he felt as he did in the streets of Chatburn was because the place was indeed "holy ground," that some of the ancient prophets had traveled in that region and dedicated the land, and that he, Heber, had reaped the benefit of their blessing.

It being known that the Elders were about to leave England, great numbers flocked to hear them, and many were baptized. Their labors were consequently very arduous. Says Elder Kimball:

"Some days we went from house to house, conversing with the people on the things of the kingdom, and would sometimes be instrumental in convincing many of the truth: and I have known as many as twenty persons baptized in one day, who have been convinced on such occasions. I have had to go into the water to administer the ordinance of baptism six or seven times a day, and frequently after having come out of the water and changed my clothes, I have had to turn back to the water before I reached my lodgings; this, too, when the [202] weather was extremely cold, the ice being from twelve to fourteen inches thick. The weather continued so about twelve weeks, during which time I think there were but ten days in which we were not in the water baptizing. The harvest was indeed plenteous, but the laborers were few."

The following passage of reflections on the poor of England is worthy of the great philanthropic heart of Heber C. Kimball:

"This was very extraordinary weather for that country, as I was informed that some winters they had scarcely any frost or snow, and the oldest inhabitants told me that they never experienced such a winter before. In consequence of the inclemency of the weather, several manufacturing establishments were shut up, and several thousands of men, women and children were thrown out of employment, whose sufferings during that time were severe; and I was credibly informed, and verily believe, that many perished from starvation. Such sufferings I never witnessed before. The scenes which I daily beheld were enough to chill the blood in my veins. The streets were crowded with men, women and children who begged from the passengers as they walked along. Numbers of those poor, wretched beings were without shoes or stockings, and scarcely any covering to screen them from the inclemency of the weather; and daily I could discover delicate females walking the streets gathering up the animal refuse, and carrying it to places where they could sell it for a penny or half-penny. And thus they lived through the winter. At the same time there were hundreds and thousands living in wealth and splendor. I felt to exclaim, O Lord, how long shall these things exist! How long shall the rich oppress the poor, and have no more care or interest for them than the [203] brutes of the field, nor half so much! When will distress and poverty cease, and peace and plenty abound! When the Lord Jesus shall descend in the clouds of heaven, then the rod of the oppressor shall be broken. Hasten the time, O Lord, was frequently the language of my heart when I contemplated the scenes of wretchedness and woe which I daily witnessed.

"Great numbers were initiated into the Kingdom of Heaven; those who were sick were healed; those who were diseased flocked to us daily; and truly their faith was great, such as I hardly ever witnessed before, consequently many were healed of their infirmities. We were continually employed day and night, some nights hardly closing our eye-lids. The task was almost more than we could endure; but realizing the circumstances of this people, their love of the truth, their humility and unfeigned charity, caused us to use all diligence and make good use of every moment, for truly our bowels yearned over them."

Touching the prospects of the missionary work in England, he adds:

"The work kept spreading; the prospect of usefulness grew brighter and brighter, and the field opened larger and larger; while the cries of 'Come, and administer the words of life unto us,' were more and more frequently sounding in our ears. I do not remember during the last six months I was in England of retiring to my bed earlier than midnight, which was also the case with Brothers Hyde and Fielding.

"Sunday, April 8th, the day of the conference, came. The Saints began to assemble at an early hour. By nine o'clock there were from six to seven hundred present from various parts of the country. After the meeting was opened by singing and prayer, we had a repre[204]sentation of the following branches, viz.: Preston, Penwortham, Walkerfold, Thornley, Ribchester, Chatburn, Clithero, Barshe Lees, Waddington, Leyland Moss, Leyland Lane, Eccleston, Hunter's Hill, Euxton, Whittle, Dauber's Lane, Bamber Bridge, Longton, Southport, Downham, Burnley, Bedford, Alston, Brampton, Bolton, Chorley. The total number of Saints represented were about two thousand, which, with the exception of the branches in Preston, Bedford and Cumberland, were principally raised up by my own labors, as I spent my time in the branches, except on Sundays, when I preached in Preston. The branch in Preston numbered about four hundred, that in Bedford forty, and the branch in Cumberland sixty."

All this was the work of only eight months. Two thousand had been baptized and enough branches organized to form the base work of three or four conferences, incorporating in the missionary work about that number of the counties of England. Thus the work had already widely spread, yet only three or four Elders had been out in the ministry. Heber C. Kimball himself had converted in eight months about one thousand five hundred souls. He continues:

"We gave instructions to the official members, reminding them of their several duties and callings, and the responsibilities which rested upon them; pressing upon them the necessity of being humble and faithful in the discharge of their duties, so that by patience, meekness and love unfeigned, they might commend themselves to God, and the Church of Jesus Christ, over whom the Holy Ghost had made them guardians.

"Feeling it necessary for the good of the kingdom to leave someone in authority over the whole church, I nominated Joseph Fielding to preside, with Willard [205] Richards as his first counselor, and William Clayton his second counselor. The nominations met with the approbation of the whole assembly, who agreed to hearken to their instructions and uphold them in their offices. These brethren were then ordained to the High Priesthood, and set apart to preside over the Church in England. Eight Elders, several Priests, Teachers and Deacons, were set apart and ordained to the several offices to which they were called. One of the brethren ordained was going to Manchester, and another to the city of London."

"We then confirmed forty individuals, after which about one hundred children were blessed. The same day twenty persons were baptized for the remission of sins. We then proceeded to administer the sacrament to the numerous assembly, and gave some general instructions to the whole church respecting their duty to God and to each other, which were listened to with great attention.

"At this conference we were favored with the company of Elder Willard Richards, also Elder Russell, who had returned from Cumberland. He met with considerable opposition from his own kindred, as well as from ministers of the different denominations, who sought every opportunity to destroy his influence. Notwithstanding the great opposition he was instrumental in bringing upwards of sixty souls into the kingdom of God, and left them rejoicing in the truth, under the watchcare of Elder Jacob Peart. Thus the great work was commenced in three places, Preston, Bedford and Alston, which forcibly reminds me of the parable of the leaven which the woman hid in the three measures of meal."

The conference closes with another of those almost dramatic pictures with which this eventful history abounds. [206]

"At 5 p. m.," says the Apostle, "we brought the conference to a close, having continued without interruption from 9 a. m., and appointed 7 o'clock the same evening to deliver our farewell addresses. At the appointed time we repaired to the 'Cock Pit' which was crowded to excess. Brother Hyde and myself spoke to them concerning our labors in that land, the success of the ministry, and the kindness we had experienced at their hands, and told them we expected before long to see them again, after we had visited the Church and our families in America. When we spoke of our departure their souls were melted; they gave vent to their feelings and wept like little children, and broke out in lamentations like the following: 'How can we part with our beloved brethren!' 'We may never see them again!' 'O, why must you leave us!' I could not restrain my feelings, and they found vent in a flood of tears. It would have been almost an impossibility for us to have left this affectionate people, if we had not had the most implicit confidence in the brethren who had been appointed to preside over them in our absence; but knowing they had the confidence of the Church, we felt that affairs would be conducted in righteousness.

"Immediately after dismissing the congregation we met the official brethren, about eighty, and instructed them in their duties, and dismissed at 1 o'clock the next morning." [207]

## CHAPTER 27

DEPARTURE FOR LIVERPOOL—HEBER'S LETTER TO THE SAINTS IN CHATBURN AND DOWNHAM—HIS PREDICTION CONCERNING THOMAS WEBSTER—ITS STRICT FULFILLMENT

AT nine o'clock on the morning of April 9th, Elders Kimball, Hyde and Russell left Preston for Liverpool. Through the kindness of the Saints, many of whom assembled to bid them farewell, they were provided with means to take them back to Kirtland. With tearful eyes they were gazed at by the multitude until the coach was lost to view.

"Notwithstanding the variegated scenery of the country," says Heber, "which in England is very beautiful, my mind reverted back to the time when I first arrived in that country, and the peculiar feelings that possessed me when I traveled from Liverpool to Preston eight months before. Then I was a stranger in a strange land,

and had only to rely upon the kindness and mercy of that God who had sent me there. While I mused on these things, my soul was humbled within me, for I had now hundreds of brethren to whom I was united in bonds the most endearing and sacred, and who loved me as their own souls, and whose prayers would be continually offered up for my welfare and prosperity.

"After a ride of about four hours we arrived at Liverpool, and ascertaining that the ship in which we intended to sail would not leave port as early as **[208]** expected, in consequence of a great storm, in which several vessels had been wrecked and many lives lost, we took lodgings for a few days until the vessel should depart.

"We were accompanied by Elders Fielding and Richards, who felt desirous to obtain all the information they could respecting the government of the Church, as our opportunities of instruction had been limited while in Preston, it being almost impossible to have much private intercourse, as there were so many who wished to converse with us on the subject of the Gospel, etc. But in this they were disappointed, for as soon as it was known in Preston and other places that our departure was delayed, Elder Clayton and numbers of the brethren came to visit us in Liverpool.

"I wrote the following farewell to the Church of Latter-day Saints in Chatburn and Downham:

"'LIVERPOOL, April 15, 1838.

"'*Beloved Brethren:*

"'Having given all diligence to make known unto you the common salvation of our Lord Jesus Christ, which ye have so joyfully received from my lips, I feel now to write to you a few words for your consolation, and the confirming of that hope which is possessed by you, that ye may be steadfast and immovable, always abounding in the work of the Lord, that it may be made manifest unto all men that our labors have not been in vain.

"'Be kind and affectionate one towards another, manifesting your faith by your works—doing as well as saying. If there is any one among you destitute of daily food, feed him; if any one be naked, clothe him; if any one be cast down, raise him up; if any among you are sick, send for the Elders, or Priests, that they may come and pray for you, and lay their hands upon you, and the prayer of faith shall heal the sick; therefore, brethren, **[209]** let your faith be centered in God, for He is able to do all things, to forgive sins and heal the sick, for you know this, that God has said *these signs shall follow them that believe.*

"'Now, brethren, I exhort you in the name of my Master, to contend for that faith which was once delivered to the Saints; for the same faith will produce the same effects; for God has not changed, neither has His word changed; heaven and earth shall pass away, but there shall not one jot or tittle of His word fail; all shall be fulfilled, whether it be by His own voice or the voice of His servants, it is all the same; therefore, brethren, do not live by bread alone, but by every word that proceedeth forth from the mouth of God.

"'Dear brethren and sisters, be patient, be humble, be prayerful, visit your secret places. Pray in your families morning and evening, ye who are heads of families, and neglect not the assembling of yourselves together; but speak often one to another concerning the things of the kingdom, and diligently follow after every good thing, remembering that the diligent hand maketh rich. Let these things be and abound with you, and ye shall be neither barren nor unfruitful in the knowledge of God. Let your eyes be single, and your bodies shall be filled with light.

"'Now, to you, brethren, who have been ordained to watch over the flock, I would say, stand in your places and magnify the offices which ye have received of the Lord Jesus, to feed His sheep. Feed the lambs; watch over the flock in all things; be not partial to any one; remember these things, and the blessing of God shall attend you in all things.

"'Dear brethren and sisters, I give you the gratitude of my heart for the kindness which you have bestowed upon me and my brethren; for when I was hungry, ye fed me; when I was naked, ye clothed me; when I was destitute, ye gave me money; when I was a stranger, ye took me in and lodged me; and, as ye have done these things to me and my brethren in our necessities, my heavenly Father shall minister unto you in your [210] necessities; for I am not forgetful of those things and I do ever remember you in my prayers, praying my heavenly Father to sustain you, and enable you to walk worthy of the holy vocation unto which ye have been called, unto the end. Amen.

"' Finally, brethren and sisters, farewell. Pray for me and my brethren; and may the God of all grace sanctify you wholly, and bring you into my Father's kingdom.

"'Adieu. This from your beloved brother in Christ,

"'HEBER C. KIMBALL.'"

One more incident remains to be told, ere with the Elders we take leave of England. At Liverpool, April 13th, "Good Friday," Apostle Kimball penned the following:

*"Dear Brothers and Sisters in Preston:*

"It seemeth good unto us and also unto the Holy Spirit to write you a few words which cause pain in our hearts, and will also pain you when they are fulfilled before you; yet you shall have joy in the end. Brother Webster will not abide in the Spirit of the Lord, but will reject the truth, and become the enemy of the people of God, and expose the mysteries which have been committed to him, that a righteous judgment may be executed upon him, unless he speedily repent.

"When this sorrowful prediction shall be fulfilled, this letter shall be read to the Church, and it shall prove a solemn warning to all to beware.

"Farewell in the Lord."

This letter, signed by the two Apostles, Heber C. Kimball and Orson Hyde, was sealed in the presence, and committed to the care, of Elders Joseph Fielding and Willard Richards. These brethren, on returning to Preston, had Elder William Clayton and Deacon Arthur Burrows examine the sealed missive critically, and placed [211] marks and dates upon it, in order to be able to testify, if necessary, that it had not been opened.

The fulfillment of the prediction was most accurate. Thomas Webster, the individual referred to in the epistle, was a member of the Preston branch, a man of promise and ability, quite popular with the Saints, and his integrity at the time unquestioned. Desiring that he should prosper. Presidents Fielding and Richards watched over and prayed for him, and "he continued to grow in the knowledge of the kingdom, and spoke with power for some months." A change then came over him; he became dissatisfied, and preferred certain charges against the presiding Elders. These charges were proven to be false, or of no account, and Webster was required to acknowledge his error, or cease acting in his office. He refused to do either. On the following Sunday, in a private house, he administered the sacrament to six of his followers, one of whom had been excommunicated from the Church, while another had not even been baptized. For this offense Webster was deprived of his membership.

The letter of the Apostles was then opened and read to the Church, Brothers Clayton and Burrows first testifying publicly that the seal had never been broken. It was feared that Webster's popularity would draw many after him, but the reading of the prediction concerning him utterly destroyed his influence, and more fully confirmed the Saints in their faith.

Webster, ambitious to create a following, and well aware of his popularity, applied for permission to come before the Church and publicly plead his cause, which request was wisely denied, as he had refused to appear, when required, the Sabbath before. Soon after placards were posted up in different parts of Preston reading as [212] follows; "A lecture will be delivered at Mr. Giles' chapel, to expose the mysteries of Mormonism, by Thomas Webster." This announcement he fulfilled, though with little effect, thus making good in strictest detail the prophecy of Heber C. Kimball, uttered six months before.

Return we now to the Apostles and Elder Russell, in Liverpool, about to take passage on board the *Garrick*, bound for New York.

# CHAPTER 28

THE ELDERS SAIL FOR HOME—A STORM AT SEA—HOW HEBER FOUND FAVOR WITH THE STEWARD—ARRIVAL AT NEW YORK—THE "GARRICK" AGAIN VICTORIOUS—JOURNEY TO KIRTLAND—ON TO FAR WEST—HAPPY MEETING WITH JOSEPH AND THE BRETHREN

HOMEWARD bound!
Sheathed the sword and furled the banner.
The battle won, the fortress stormed and taken.
For a little season, rest and change, ere again the trumpet sounds, and the warrior is resummoned to the fray.

It was indeed a campaign of victory from which the Elders were returning. The laurel wreath was theirs, bravely and fairly earned.

Yet not for worldly honors and applause had they been striving. These, to the true servant of Christ, are ever the last consideration. The praise of man they neither expected nor desired. Their reward was with [213] them, a reward never wrongly bestowed; the approval of a good conscience and the favor of their Maker; meed only of worthy motives, and of duty well performed.

Again on board the *Garrick*, upon the bosom of the heaving main.

It was on the 20th of April, 1838, that the Elders embarked for home.

"Soon after we left Liverpool," says Heber, "a great storm came on, with a head wind, which continued without cessation for several days, and did considerable damage to the vessel; the bowsprit was broken twice, by the force of the wind, with only the jib sail set; the boom likewise came down with great force, near where the captain was standing, but he fortunately escaped; several other parts of the rigging were much torn and injured. During the continuance of the storm, Brothers Hyde and Russell were very sick. After this we had more favorable weather.

"When we had been on the water two weeks, I asked permission of the captain for one of us to preach, which request was cheerfully complied with, and the second cabin was prepared for the occasion. Brother Russell preached, after which Brother Hyde made some observations; they were listened to with great attention, and the congregation appeared very much satisfied.

"The Lord gave us favor in the eyes of the captain and passengers, who treated us with respect and kindness. One reason for obtaining this universal favor of the ship's company was, the steward of the ship had charge of a fine Durham cow, which was larger than the medium size of our oxen; the cow became sick and the steward was very sorry, because she was their only dependence to supply the cabin passengers with milk. I went and looked at the cow and discovered that she [214] could not raise her cud. I told the steward to cut for me a half dozen slices of fat pork, as large as my hand, which he did; and I gave them to the cow, when she soon got well. From that time forth the steward sent us turtle soup, wine, and every luxury the ship afforded, and made us many presents.

"May 12th, we came in sight of New York, and in the evening secured a landing, after a passage of twenty-two and a half days."

It will be remembered that the *Garrick*, on its first voyage, bearing these Elders to England, won a wager of ten thousand dollars, arriving at Liverpool a few lengths ahead of the packet ship *South America*, both vessels having left New York at the same time, and keeping in sight of each other during the whole of the way. Another victory was now scored by the *Garrick* in arriving at the port of New York.

Was it because these Mormon Apostles were again on board, returning themselves from a great spiritual contest, in which God had given them the victory? Judge, reader, for yourself. Here is the Apostle Heber's record of the event:

"There was a wager made at Liverpool whether the *New England* or the *Garrick* would arrive in port first. When we passed Sandy Hook the *New England* was four or five miles ahead of us; some of our officers remarked she would go in before us, but I told them she would not, as I had said at Liverpool we would go in first. At this time neither of the ships were sailing more than three knots an hour, when suddenly the wind left the sails of the *New England*, and a fair wind struck our sails, and we ran in one hour ahead of her."

Continuing, the prophet Heber says:

"We landed and went into the city of New York **[215]** with several of the passengers, who purchased some refreshments, and after we returned, bade us partake with them, and we all rejoiced together; we then bowed before the Lord and offered up the gratitude of our hearts for all His mercies, in prospering us on our mission, and bringing us safely across the mighty deep, to behold once more the land of our nativity, and the prospect of soon embracing our families and friends.

"Sunday, 13th, we went in search of Brother Fordham, whom we found after some trouble. He was glad to see us, and immediately took us to the house of Brother Wandel Mace, where we were glad to see our beloved brother Orson Pratt, who was then laboring in that city, and who, with his brother Parley P. Pratt, had been instrumental in bringing many into the kingdom there. And now I had the pleasure of witnessing the fulfillment of the prophecy I delivered to Brother Fordham when I started for England.

"We accompanied Brother Orson Pratt to the house where the Saints assembled to worship. We found about eighty persons assembled, all of whom had recently joined the Church. After singing and prayer, I was requested to give an account of our mission to England, which I did. In the evening Elders' Russell and Hyde preached; afterwards some came forward and offered themselves as candidates for baptism. The short time we were in New York was spent very agreeably with the Saints.

"On the 14th we bade adieu to the brethren, and continued our journey by steamboat, railroad and canal, and arrived at Kirtland May 22nd, having been absent eleven months and nine days.

"I found my family in good health, and as comfortably situated as I could expect; our joy was mutual. **[216]** The Saints likewise welcomed us home, for which I felt thankful to my heavenly Father.

"But my journey was not yet ended; for soon after my arrival in Kirtland I commenced making preparations to move my family to the State of Missouri, where Brother Joseph and the greater part of the authorities of the Church, and almost all the members who had any faith in Mormonism, had already removed. The cause of their removal to the west was the persecutions to which they were subject in Kirtland. The brethren who yet resided there, although very kind and affectionate, were weak in the faith, in consequence of trials and temptations. This caused us to grieve exceedingly, and we resolved to cheer them up as much as we possibly could. We preached in the house of the Lord a few times, recounted our travels and the great success that had attended our labors; also the marvelous work which the Lord had commenced in England. They began to take courage, their confidence increased, their faith was strengthened, and they again realized the blessings of Jehovah.

"About the 1st of July I commenced my journey with my family, accompanied by Elders Orson Hyde, Erastus Snow and Winslow Farr, two brothers by the name of Badger, and the widow Beeman, with their families, numbering about forty souls. We took wagons to Wellsville, on the Ohio River, about a hundred and thirty miles; then took steamboat to St. Louis, also thence to Richmond on Missouri River. Elder Hyde stayed at Richmond several days. We there procured wagons and went to Far West, where we arrived in safety on the twenty-fifth of July, and had a happy meeting with Joseph, Hyrum and Sidney, some of the Twelve, and numbers of our friends and brethren, some of whom were so [217] glad to see us, that tears started in their eyes when we took them by the hand.

"During our journey from Kirtland to Missouri, the weather was extremely warm, in consequence of which I suffered very much, my body being weakened by sickness, and I continued very feeble for a considerable length of time.

"Sunday July 20th, I met Joseph, Sidney and Hyrum on the public square, as they started for Adam-Ondi-Ahman. Joseph requested me to preach to the Saints and give them a history of my mission, saying, 'It will revive their spirits and do them good,' which I did, although I was scarcely able to stand. I related many things respecting my mission and travels, which were gladly received by them, whose hearts were cheered by the recital, while many of the Elders were stirred up to diligence, and expressed a great desire to accompany me when I should return to England." [218]

## CHAPTER 29

THE LAND WHERE ADAM DWELT—THE SAINTS IMPELLED TOWARD THEIR DESTINY—PERSECUTION REVIVES—ADAM-ONDI-AHMAN—THE ALTAR OF THE ANCIENT OF DAYS

THE land where Adam dwelt. The site of the Garden of Eden. The place where the Ancient of Days shall sit, and the God of heaven shall again visit His people. As saith the prophet Daniel:

"I beheld till the thrones were cast down and the Ancient of Days did sit, whose garment was white as snow, and the hair of his head like the pure wool: his throne was like the fiery flame, and his wheels as burning fire.

"A fiery stream issued and come forth from before him: thousand thousands ministered unto him, and ten thousand times ten thousand stood before him: the judgment was set, and the books were opened....

"I saw in the night visions, and behold one like the Son of man came with the clouds of heaven, and came to the Ancient of Days, and they brought him near before him.

"And there was given him dominion, and glory, and a kingdom, that all people, nations, and languages should serve him: his dominion is an everlasting dominion, which shall not pass away, and his kingdom that which shall not be destroyed....

"I beheld and the same horn made war with the Saints, and prevailed against them;

"Until the Ancient of Days came, and judgment was given to the Saints of the Most High; and the time came that the Saints possessed the kingdom." [219]

Here, in this most ancient region, where, parallel with the stream of Time, the great river of mortal life arose, had pitched their tents the Saints of latter days.

Here dwelt Adam and Eve in the world's infancy; here they tasted of the fruit forbidden, and were driven forth from Eden, their fall predestined that mortal man might be. Here the great sire of mankind built altars unto God, offering sacrifice unto the Father in commemoration of the atonement of the Son. Here fell the first martyr; here righteous Abel's blood was spilt; here burst the awful thunders of heaven's awakened wrath upon the guilty head of earth's first murderer. Here Adam, bowed with age, blessed the righteous residue of his seed, and predicted whatsoever should befall his posterity to the latest generation.

All this ere the days of Peleg, in whose days "was the earth divided;" ere Enoch's city rose to heaven, or the ark of Noah floated over a wave-buried world. Ere Babel's towering folly mocked the skies; ere wrecked was language on confusion's strand; ere the great river of humanity, dividing into rills, went forth to water with the streams of life the soil of every land.

Here, in the times of restitution, when all things in Christ are gathered in one, Adam, Michael, the great Prince, Ancient of Days, is to come in power and glory, revisiting the scenes of his earthly pilgrimage.

America, the old world, not the new! Cradle of man, mother of nations, grave of empires!

Unto Missouri, land of promise; the ancient, the chosen, the favored above all other lands, had the Lord's Prophet, Joseph, led His covenant people.

Spring Hill, Daviess County, Missouri, one of the settlements of the Saints in this region, had been renamed by revelation, Adam-ondi-Ahman, because, said [220] the Lord, "it is the place where Adam shall come to visit his people, or the Ancient of Days shall sit, as spoken of by Daniel the Prophet."

Verily were the Saints of the Most High being driven toward their destiny. The "horn" that made war with them and "prevailed against them," was surely pushing them on to final victory. Was it not destiny, too, that they should thus retrace the steps of their great ancestor, who, driven forth from Eden,[1] dwelt in Adam-ondi-Ahman?

Heber was now with his people at Far West, in "the land where Adam dwelt," ready to perform his part of the labor in preparing the kingdom of the Son of God for the coming of the Ancient of Days.

"Soon after my arrival," says he, "Bishop Partridge gave me a lot and sufficient

---

[1] Jackson County, Missouri, from whence the Saints were driven, is reputed to be the ancient site of the Garden of Eden.

lumber to build a house. Charles Hubbard made me a present of forty acres of land, and another brother gave me a cow. All the brethren were remarkably kind in contributing to my necessities. About the last of August, after I had spent much labor, and nearly finished my house, I was obliged to abandon it to the mob, who again commenced persecuting the Saints, driving off their cattle and destroying their property."

The origin of this persecution was much the same as that of the Jackson County trouble, five years before. The thrift and enterprise of the Saints, with their growing power and influence, had aroused the jealous fears of their Gentile neighbors, and what the scheming villainy of political demagogues left undone, the malice of sectarian priests accomplished, in kindling the wrath of the ignorant and fanatical against them. **[221]**

An election riot in Gallatin, Daviess County, on the 6th of August, 1838, where a combined effort was made to prevent the Mormons from voting, and several of the brethren were under the necessity of using force to defend themselves against their bullying assailants, was made the pretext for further outrages against the community to which they belonged. The Saints in that locality being helplessly in the minority, were at the mercy of the mob which now rose against them.

One of the methods employed by the leaders of the lawless banditti to enlist sympathy for their own cause, and arouse the public mind against their victims, was to destroy property belonging to non-Mormons, their own followers in some instances, and then ride through the country advertising it as the work of Mormons, against whom any tale, however false or atrocious, was readily believed. Some of the mob even fired upon a church while its occupants were worshiping on the Sabbath day, and then spread the alarm that the Mormons had "riz" and were destroying property, demolishing churches and interfering with free religious worship.

These atrocious falsehoods, worthy only of fiends incarnate, bore legitimate fruit in deeds equally devilish and appalling. The people rose *en masse;* the Saints were driven from their homes, their houses plundered and burned, their fields laid waste, and men, women and children fled for their lives in all directions, pursued by their merciless oppressors.

What followed, Heber's record thus relates:

"After hearing of the mobbing, burning and robbing in Gallatin, Daviess Co., and the region round about, the brethren of Caldwell went directly to Adam-ondi-Ahman, which is on the west fork of Grand River. Thomas B. Marsh, David W. Patten, Brigham Young, **[222]** myself, Parley P. Pratt and John Taylor amongst the number. When we arrived there we found the Prophet Joseph, Hyrum Smith and Sidney Rigdon, with hundreds of others of the Saints preparing to defend themselves from the mob who were threatening the destruction of our people. Men, women and children were fleeing to that place for safety from every direction; their houses and property were burnt and they had to flee half naked, crying, and frightened nigh unto death, to save their lives.

"While there we laid out a city on a high elevated piece of land, and set the stakes for the four corners of a temple block, which was dedicated, Brother Brigham Young being mouth; there were from three to five hundred men present on the occasion, under arms. This elevated spot was probably from two hundred and fifty to five hundred feet above the level of Grand River, so that one could look east, west, north or south, as far as the eye could reach; it was one of the most beautiful places I ever beheld.

"The Prophet Joseph called upon Brother Brigham, myself and others, saying, 'Brethren, come, go along with me, and I will show you something.' He led us a short distance to a place where were the ruins of three altars built of stone, one above the other, and one standing a little back of the other, like unto the pulpits in the Kirtland Temple, representing the order of three grades of Priesthood; 'There,' said Joseph, 'is the place where Adam offered up sacrifice after he was cast out of the garden.' The altar stood at the highest point of the bluff. I went and examined the place several times while I remained there."

An episode of peace in time of war. A glimpse of heaven's blue through a rift in the gathering storm. **[223]**

A fiery ordeal was before the Saints. The Church, tried with poverty and tempted by the prospect of wealth, had survived and maintained its integrity. It had also withstood the world's scorn, the wrath and ridicule of the ungodly. Nor had fiery trials been wanting, whereby the faith of some had been proven, the supposed faith of others weighed in the balance and found wanting. A general test was now to be applied. The faith and integgrity of the whole Church were about to pass through the fierce flames of affliction; between the upper and nether millstones of official tyranny and mob violence.

---

# CHAPTER 30

TIMES THAT TRIED MEN'S SOULS—THE MOB GATHERING AGAINST FAR WEST—BATTLE OF CROOKED RIVER—DEATH OF DAVID W. PATTEN—DAYS OF DARKNESS AND DISASTER

THE fall and winter of 1838 was one of the darkest periods in Church history. Mobocracy on one hand, and apostasy on the other, dealt the cause of God cruel blows, such as no human work could hope to withstand. The tempest of persecution, briefly lulled, burst forth with tenfold fury; no longer a city or county—a whole state rose in arms against God's people, bent upon their destruction. "The dogs of war" were loosed upon the helpless Saints, and murder and rapine held high carnival amid the smoking ruins of peaceful homes and ravaged fields. **[224]**

Then fell the mask from the face of hypocrisy. Treason betrayed itself. Apostles, Presidents, and Elders fell from the faith and joined hands with the robbers and murderers of their brethren. Satan laughed! The very mouth of hell seemed opening to engulf the Kingdom which He who cannot lie has sworn shall stand forever.

Truly, those were "times that tried men's souls."

Like a rock in mid-ocean, facing the storm, unmoved by wind or wave, stood Heber C. Kimball; among the truest true, among the bravest brave.

Referring to the time of his visit to Adam-ondi-Ahman, he says:

"In a few days an express came with the news that the mob was gathering in every part of Missouri to come against the Saints in Far West. We therefore returned to Caldwell County.

"Thomas B. Marsh left the day previous to the rest of the Twelve, pretending there was something very urgent at home, and when we arrived at Far West, October 22nd, we learned that he and Orson Hyde had left the city. Brother Hyde was sick when we went to Diahman.

"The Saints, tenacious of their liberties and sacred rights, resisted the unlawful designs of the mob, and with courage worthy of them guarded their families and their houses from their aggressions. But not without the loss of several lives, among whom was my much esteemed and lamented friend David W. Patten, who fell a sacrifice to the spirit of persecution and a martyr to the cause of truth. The circumstances of his death I will briefly relate.

"It being ascertained that a mob had collected on Crooked River, led by the Rev. Samuel Bogard, a Metho[225]dist preacher, a company of sixty or seventy persons immediately volunteered in Far West to watch their movements, and if necessary repel their attacks. They chose Elder Patten for their leader, and commenced their march about midnight, and came up to the mob at the dawn of October 25th. As the brethren were marching quietly along the road near the top of the hill, they were fired upon, when young O'Banyon reeled out of the ranks, and fell mortally wounded. Thus the work of death commenced, when Captain Patten ordered his men to charge the mob, who proved to be on the creek below. It was yet so dark that little could be seen, looking to the west; but the mob could see Captain Patten and his men in the dawning light, when they fired a broadside and three or four of the brethren fell. Captain Patten ordered the fire returned, giving the watchword, 'God and Liberty.' The brethren charged the camp, when the mob were soon put to flight and crossed the river at the ford. One of the mob fired from behind a tree, and shot Captain Patten, who instantly fell mortally wounded, the ball having pierced his abdomen.

"Immediately on receiving the intelligence that Brother Patten was wounded, I hastened to see him and found him in great pain, but still he was glad to see me; he was conveyed about four miles to the house of Brother Stephen Winchester; during his removal his sufferings were so excruciating that he frequently desired us to lay him down that he might die; but being desirous to get him out of the reach of the mob, we prevailed upon him to let us carry him among his friends. We carried him on a kind of bier, fixed up from poles.

"Although he had medical assistance, his wound was such that there was no hope entertained of his recovery, and this he was perfectly aware of. In this situation, **[226]** while the shades of time were lowering, and eternity with all its realities opening to his view, he bore a strong testimony to the truth of the work of the Lord, and the religion he had espoused. He was perfectly sensible and collected until he breathed his last, which occurred at about ten o'clock in the evening. Stephen Winchester, Brother Patten's wife, Bathsheba W. Bigler, with several of her father's family were present at David's death.

"The principles of the Gospel which were so precious to him before, afforded him that support and consolation at the time of his departure, which deprived death of its sting and horror. Speaking of those who had fallen from their steadfastness he exclaimed, 'O that they were in my situation! For I feel that I have kept the faith, I have finished my course, henceforth there is laid up for me a crown, which the Lord, the righteous Judge, will give me.' Speaking to his beloved wife, he said, 'whatever you do else, O do not deny the faith.' He all the time expressed a great desire to depart. I said to him 'Brother David, when you get home, I want you to remember me.' He replied, 'I will.' At this time his sight was gone. A few minutes before he died, he prayed as follows, 'Father, I ask Thee in the name of Jesus Christ, that Thou wouldst release my spirit, and receive it unto Thyself.' And he then said to those who surrounded his dying bed, 'Brethren, you have held me by your faith, but do give me up, and let me go, I beseech you.' We accordingly committed him to God, and he soon breathed his last, and slept in Jesus without a groan.

"This was the death of one who was an honor to the Church and a blessing to the Saints; and whose faith, virtues and diligence in the cause of truth will be had in remembrance by the Church of Jesus Christ from generation to generation. It was a painful way to be deprived **[227]** of the labors of this worthy servant of Christ, and it cast a gloom upon the Saints; yet the glorious and sealing testimony which he bore of his acceptance with heaven and the truth of the Gospel was a matter of joy and satisfaction, not only to his immediate friends, but to the Saints at large.

"I took Dr. Avard with me to Far West, a distance of three miles, to Elder Rigdon's house, where we found Brother Patrick O'Banyon, who was wounded in nearly the same manner as Brother Patten. He also died in a short time, firm and steadfast in the faith. He was perfectly calm and composed, and bore a strong testimony to the truth of Mormonism.

"Gideon Carter, who was also a faithful Saint, was shot in the head, and left dead on the ground, so defaced that the brethren did not at first know him.

"This was a gloomy time!" **[228]**

# CHAPTER 31

THE FALL OF FAR WEST—JOSEPH AND HIS BRETHREN BETRAYED TO THE ENEMY—HEBER FACING THE TRAITORS—HIS FEARLESS DENUNCIATION AND FIRM TESTIMONY—ATROCITIES OF THE MOB—HEBER'S PROPHECY OF RETRIBUTION—HE VISITS THE PROPHET IN RICHMOND JAIL

THE thunder-cloud of war now rolled upon the doomed city of Far West. Heber's narrative continues:

"On the 30th we discovered several thousand of the mob coming to Far West, under pretence of being government troops; they passed through our corn and wheat fields, making a complete desolation of everything they came across.

"Brother Brigham and I were appointed captains of fifty, in a hurry, and commanded to take our position, right in the thoroughfare on which the mob was advancing to the city, momentarily anticipating the awful tragedy of a bloody massacre. Joseph was with us giving counsel.

"The army came up to within good rifle shot, and halted; seeing our temporary fortifications, which we had thrown up the night previous, by pulling down some of our houses, and fixing up our wagons; they dared not approach nearer, but retreated to Goose Creek, about three-fourths of a mile, screaming, hallooing and screeching; the devils in hell could not have made a more hideous howling. The mob declared there were fifteen hundred of us; but to my certain knowledge there were only about one hundred and fifty in that line. [229]

"The word came to us that Joseph Smith and several others were to be given up, otherwise they would massacre every man, woman and child. In order to prevent this horrible threat from being executed, Joseph gave himself up, with Elders Sidney Rigdon, Parley P. Pratt, Lyman Wight, and George W. Robinson, they having been betrayed into the mob camp by Col. George M. Hinkle and other apostates, on the 31st of October.

"November 1st, the mob, professing to be the regular militia of the state of Missouri, numbering about 7,000, surrounded Far West, we were all taken prisoners and then marched a short distance into a hollow, where Col. Lucas had previously pointed his cannon, in full range, so that if we had not laid down our arms, he could easily sweep us into eternity, which was his design. We were then formed into a hollow square, and commanded by Col. Lucas to ground arms and deliver up our weapons of war, although they were our own private property. We were then marched back a short distance, on the public square in Far West, where we were again formed into a hollow square, near the house of Brother Beeman.

"The mob then commenced plundering the citizens of their bedding, clothing, money, wearing apparel, and everything of value they could lay their hands upon; and also attempting to violate the chastity of the women in sight of their husbands, pretending they were hunting for prisoners and fire-arms.

"The most of us had not had any food for twenty-four hours, not having time to go to our houses to get it. When these troops surrounded us, and we were brought into a hollow square, the first persons that I knew were men who had once professed to be beloved **[230]** brethren, and they were the men who piloted these mobs into our city, namely William McLellin and Lyman E. Johnson, two of the twelve; John Whitmer and David Whitmer, two of the witnesses to the Book of Mormon; William W. Phelps and scores of others, hail fellows well met. A portion of the troops were painted like Indians, and looked horrible, led by Neil Gillium, who styled himself 'The Delaware Chief;' who, with many others cocked their guns upon us and swore they would blow our brains out, although we were disarmed and helpless.

"William E. McLellin wanted to know where Heber C. Kimball was. Some one pointed me out to him as I was sitting on the ground. He came up to me and said: 'Brother Heber, what do you think of the fallen prophet now? Has he not led you blindfolded long enough? Look and see yourself, poor, your family stripped and robbed, and your brethren in the same fix; are you satisfied with Joseph?' I replied, 'Yes, I am more satisfied with him a hundred fold than ever I was before, for I see you in the very position that he foretold you would be in; a Judas to betray your brethren, if you did not forsake your adultery, fornication, lying and abominations. Where are *you*? What are you about? You, and Hinkle, and scores of others; have you not betrayed Joseph and his brethren into the hands of the mob, as Judas did Jesus? Yes, verily, you have; I tell you Mormonism is true, and Joseph is a true prophet of the living God; and you with all others that turn therefrom will be damned and go to hell, and Judas will rule over you.'

"Soon after this, when things began to be a little more quiet, I desired to go to my home to get something to eat as I had not eaten anything for many hours. I asked some of the mob standing near, if I could not have **[231]** the privilege to go to my house, a little distance off; they referred me to their captain, who was Bogard, the Methodist preacher. I went to him and told him what I wanted. He first spoke of sending some one with me, as I would be liable to be shot if found alone. In a short time says he, 'I will go with you.' He went down to my house; my wife prepared some dinner, and he ate with me; then we returned, and I took my seat on the ground with my brethren who were under guard.

"The next day, and, I was permitted to return to my house, but was told not to leave the city, as it was surrounded by a strong guard to prohibit anyone leaving the place; they were engaged in taking every man who seemed to have any influence, and putting them in chains to stand a trial. They were pointed out by the apostate allies of the mob.

"We were brought up at the point of the bayonet and compelled to sign a deed of trust, transferring all our property to defray the expenses of this war made on us by the State of Missouri. This was complied with, because we could not help ourselves. When we walked up to sign the deeds of trust to pay these assassins for murdering our brethren and sisters, and their children; ravishing some of our sisters to death; robbing us of our lands and possessions and all we had on earth, and other similar "services," they expected to see us cast down and sorrowful, but I testify as an eye witness that the brethren rejoiced and praised the Lord, for His sake taking joyfully the despoiling of their goods. Judges and magistrates, Methodist, Presbyterian, Campbellite and other sectarian priests stood by and saw all this going on, exulting over us, and it seemed to make them more angry that we bore our misfortunes so cheerfully. Judge Cameron said, with an oath, 'See them laugh **[232]** and kick up their heels. They are whipped, but not conquered.'

"On the 6th, Gen. Clark delivered his noted extermination speech, and read over the names of the brethren who were made prisoners, to await a trial for something, they knew not what, and placed under a strong guard. In order that the tyrant may not be forgotten I insert a portion of his speech:

"Gentlemen, you whose names are not attached to this list of names, will now have the privilege of going to your fields and of providing corn, wood, etc., for your families. Those who are now taken will go from this to prison, be tried and receive the due demerit of their crimes. But you (excepting such as charges may be hereafter preferred against) are at liberty as soon as the troops are removed that now guard the place, which I shall cause to be done immediately. It now devolves upon you to fulfill the treaty that you have entered into, the leading items of which I shall now lay before you.

"The first requires that your leading men be given up to be tried according to law; this you have complied with.

"The second is that you deliver up your arms—this has also been attended to. The third stipulation is that you sign over your properties to defray the expenses that have been incurred on your account; this you have also done. Another article yet remains for you to comply with, and that is, that you leave the State forthwith; and whatever may be your feelings concerning this, or whatever your innocence is, it is nothing to me. General Lucas (whose military rank is equal to mine) has made this treaty with you, and I approve of it. I should have done the same had I been here, and am therefore determined to see it executed.

"The character of this State has suffered almost beyond redemption, from the character, conduct and influence that you have exerted; and we deem it an act **[233]** of justice to restore her character by every proper means.

"The order of the Governor to me was that *you should be exterminated,* and not allowed to remain in the State. And had not your leaders been given up, and the terms of the treaty complied with before this time, *your families would have been destroyed and your houses in ashes.*

"There is a discretionary power vested in my hands, which, considering your circumstances, I shall exercise for a season. You are indebted to me for this clemency. I do not say that you shall go now, but you must not think of staying here another season, or of putting in any crops; for the moment you do this the citizens will be upon you; and if I am called here again, in case of non-compliance with the treaty made, do not think I shall act as I have done now. You need not expect any mercy, but *extermination, for I am determined the Governor's order shall be executed.*

"As for your leaders, do not think, do not imagine for a moment, do not let it enter your minds that they will be delivered and restored to you again, for their *fate is fixed, the die is cast, their doom is sealed.*

"I am sorry, gentlemen, to see so many apparently intelligent men found in the situation that you are; and oh! if I could invoke that great Spirit of the unknown God to rest upon and deliver you from that awful chain of superstition, and liberate you from those fetters of fanaticism with which you are bound—that you no longer do homage to a man.

"I would advise you to scatter abroad and never again organize yourselves with Bishops, Priests, etc., lest you excite the jealousies of the people and subject yourselves to the same calamities that have now come upon you.

"You have always been the aggressors, you have brought upon yourselves these difficulties, by being disaffected, and not being subject to rule, and my advice is, that you become as other citizens, lest by a recurrence of these events you bring upon yourselves irretrievable ruin." [234]

"He also said: 'You must not be seen as many as five together, if you are, the citizens will be upon you and destroy you, but you should flee immediately out of the state. There is no alternative for you but to flee, you need not expect any redress; there is none for you.'"

"I was present," continues Heber, "when that speech was delivered, and I can truly say 'he is a liar and the truth is not in him,' for not one of us had made any such agreement with Lucas, or any other person; what we did was by compulsion in every sense of the word, and as for Gen. Clark and his 'unknown God,' they had nothing to do with our deliverance, but it was our Father in heaven, the God of Abraham, of Isaac, and of Jacob, in whom we trust, who liveth and dwelleth in the heavens, and the day will come when our God will hold him in derision with all his coadjutors."

"Joseph Smith, Sidney Rigdon, Hyrum Smith, Parley P. Pratt, Lyman Wight, Amasa Lyman and George W. Robinson were marched off for Independence, Jackson County. It was rumored that all of the men who were in the Crooked River battle would be taken prisoners, therefore many of them fled to the north, before the guards were placed around the city.

"I have no doubt that I would also have been taken a prisoner, for every means was adopted by Hinkle to have me taken, but he could not remember me. The mob had not become acquainted with Brother Brigham, as he lived three or four miles from the city on Mill Creek; and I had not been there over three weeks when the mobbing commenced, and was only known by the brethren, and many of them I had not seen since my arrival."

Heber's wonderful influence over men, that power of controlling and subduing their passions which won [235] for him from the Prophet Joseph the surname of "peace-maker," here found an opportunity for its exercise.

"One afternoon," says he, "I sent my son William on an errand, a short distance, when one of the guards drew up his rifle and threatened to blow out his brains if he stepped one inch further towards the house. Through the agency of some of my brethren I was notified of it. I went to the man and spoke to him in a friendly manner, and conversed with him about the beautiful country, it being more beautiful than England and the nations I had been traveling in. He became very much interested; in a short time I pointed out my son William; says I, 'that is my son.' He said, 'if that is one of your sons, he may pass, he may go home;' afterwards the man came to my house several times and became very friendly.

"I merely mention this, to show the perils we were in, men, women and children; death and destruction waiting on us; and this spirit aroused by apostates such as Hinkle, who sold Joseph and his brethren, and actually received money for betraying them.

"The murders, house-burnings, robberies, rapes, drivings, whippings, imprisonments, and other sufferings and cruelties inflicted upon the people of God, under the illegal orders of Missouri's Executive, have only in part been laid before the world, and form a page in history unsurpassed and unparalleled in the history of religious persecution—that foulest of all crimes. This historic page alone can credit Lilburn W. Boggs and his minions with feeding the ministers of the proscribed religion on the flesh of their murdered brethren; the odium of which is fully shared by the ministers of different denominations who participated in these vile atrocities. If hell can furnish a parallel where is it? **[236]**

"I have not the ability to write what I saw and felt and realized, but will leave it to eternity to reveal the scenes of those days. I can say before God, angels, heaven and earth, that I am innocent of violating any law of the state of Missouri, and my brethren are equally innocent and virtuous, true to their God and their country.

"The measure they meted to the Latter-day Saints shall be measured to them again, and upon all those who had a hand in our persecution and expulsion, and those who consented to it, four-fold, full, running over, and pressed down; and AS THE LORD GOD ALMIGHTY LIVETH, I SHALL LIVE TO SEE IT COME TO PASS![2]

"After the mob departed, I accompanied Brother Brigham to Richmond Jail, to see our brethren. We found Joseph, Hyrum, Sidney and others chained together in one room, and others confined in other places, amongst the most dissolute asociations. We scarcely had the privilege of speaking to our brethren more than to say, 'how do you do,' every eye being upon us in suspicion. We put up at a public house for the night, and I bear testimony, from our feelings and the spirit manifested in that house, that there were legions of devils present; I do not remember that either of us slept any that night.

"November 29th, the brethren were removed to Liberty Jail, in Clay County, and put in close confinement." **[237]**

---

[2] During the great Civil War (1861-65) this region was literally baptized in fire and blood.

# CHAPTER 32

MEMORIAL TO THE MISSOURI LEGISLATURE—A CHAPTER OF INFAMY—HOW MISSOURI REDRESSED THE WRONGS OF THE SUFFERING SAINTS—BRIGHAM AND HEBER SETTING IN ORDER THE CHURCH—ARRANGING FOR THE EXODUS

THE brethren who retained their liberty addressed a memorial to the Missouri Legislature, setting forth the wrongs that the Saints had suffered in that state, and humbly petitioning for redress of grievances. As a concise statement of the Missouri persecutions, with much of which the history of Heber C. Kimball is identified, and himself being one of the signers of the document, it is here given a place in this volume:

"We, the undersigned petitioners and inhabitants of Caldwell County, Missouri, in consequence of the late calamity that has come upon us, taken in connection with former afflictions, feel it a duty we owe to ourselves and our country to lay our case before your honorable body for consideration.

"It is a well known fact, that a society of our people commenced settling in Jackson County, Missouri, in the summer of 1831, where they, according to their ability, purchased lands and settled upon them, with the intention and expectation of becoming permanent citizens in common with others.

"Soon after the settlement began, persecutions began; and as the society increased persecution also increased, until the society at last was compelled to leave the county; and although an account of these persecutions has been published to the world, yet we feel that it will not be improper to notice a few of the most prominent items in this Memorial. [238]

"On the 20th of July, 1833, a mob convened at Independence, a committee of which called upon a few of the men of our Church there, and stated to them that the store, printing office, and indeed all other mechanic shops must be closed forthwith and the society leave the county immediately.

"These propositions were so unexpected that a certain time was asked for to consider the subject, before an answer should be returned, which was refused, and our men being individually interrogated, each one answered that he could not consent to comply with their propositions. One of the mob replied that he was sorry, for the work of destruction would commence immediately. In a short time the printing office, which was a two-story building, was assailed by the mob and soon thrown down, and with it much valuable property destroyed. Next they went to the store for the same purpose; but Mr. Gilbert, one of the owners, agreeing to close it, they abandoned their design. Their next move was the dragging of Bishop Partridge from his house and family to the public square, where, surrounded by hundreds, they partially stripped him of his clothes, and tarred and feathered him from head to foot. A man by the name of Allen was also tarred at the same time. This was Saturday and the mob agreed to meet the following Tuesday, to accomplish their purpose of driving or massacreing the society.

"Tuesday came, and the mob came also, bearing with them a red flag in token of blood. Some two or three of the principal men of the society, offered their lives if that would appease the wrath of the mob, so that the rest of the society might dwell in peace upon their lands. The answer was that unless the Society would leave *en masse,* every man should die for himself. Being in a defenseless situation, to save a general massacre, it was agreed one half of the society should leave the county by the 1st of January, and the remainder by the first of the following April. A treaty was entered into and ratified and all things went on smoothly for awhile. But some time in October, the wrath of the mob began again [239] to be kindled, insomuch that they shot at some of our people, whipped others, and threw down their houses and committed many other depredations; indeed the society of Saints were harassed for some time both day and night, Their houses were brick-batted and broken open, women and children insulted, etc.

"The store-house of A. S. Gilbert and Co. was broken open, ransacked and some of the goods strewed in the streets.

"These abuses, with many others of a very aggravated nature, so stirred up the indignant feelings of our people, that when a party of them, say about thirty, met a company of the mob of about double their number, a skirmish took place, in which some two or three of the mob, and one of our people were killed. This raised, as it were, the whole country in arms, and nothing would satisfy them but the immediate surrender of the arms of our people, and they forthwith to leave the county. Fifty-one guns were given up, which have never been returned or paid for, to this day.

"The next day parties of the mob, from fifty to seventy, headed by priests, went from house to house, threatening women and children with death if they were not off before they returned. This so alarmed them that they fled in different directions: some took shelter in the woods, while others wandered on the prairies till their feet bled. In the meantime, the weather being very cold, their sufferings in other respects were very great.

"The society made their escape to Clay County as fast as they possibly could, where the people received them kindly and administered to their wants. After the society had left Jackson County, their buildings, amounting to about two hundred, were either burned or otherwise destroyed; and much of their crops, as well as furniture, stock etc., which if properly estimated would make a large sum, for which they have not as yet received any remuneration.

"The Society remained in Clay County nearly three years, when at the suggestion of the people there, they [240] removed to that section of the country known now as Caldwell County. Here the people purchased out most of the former inhabitants, and also entered much of the wild land. Many soon owned a number of eighties, while there was scarcely a man that did not secure to himself at least a forty.

"There we were permitted to enjoy peace for a season; but as our society increased in numbers and settlements were made in Daviess and Carroll Counties, the mob spirit spread itself again.

"For months previous to our giving up our arms to General Lucas' army, we heard little else than rumors of mobs collecting in different places, and threatening our people. It is well known that the people of our Church, who had located themselves at De Witt, had to give up to a mob, and leave the place, notwithstanding the militia were called out for their protection.

"From De Witt the mob went towards Daviess County, and while on their way there took two of our men prisoners and made them ride upon the cannon, and told them they would drive the Mormons from Daviess to Caldwell and from Caldwell to hell, and that they would give them no quarter, only at the cannon's mouth. The threats of the mob induced some of our people to go to Daviess to help to protect their brethren, who had settled at Diahman on Grand river. The mob soon fled from Daviess County; and after they were dispersed and the cannon taken, during which time no blood was shed, the people of Caldwell returned to their homes, in hope of enjoying peace and quiet; but in this they were disappointed, for a large mob was soon found to be collecting on the Grindstone forks of Grand River, from ten to fifteen miles off, under the command of Cornelius Gillium, a scouting party of which came within four miles of Far West and drove off stock belonging to our people in open day light.

"About this time word came to Far West, that a party of the mob had come into Caldwell County to the south of Far West, and were taking horses and cattle, burning houses and ordering inhabitants to leave their **[241]** homes immediately; and that they had then actually in their possession three men prisoners. This report reached Far West in the evening and was confirmed about midnight. A company of about sixty men went forth under the command of David W. Patten to disperse the mob as they supposed. A battle was the result, in which Captain Patten and two of his men were killed and others wounded. Bogart, it appears, had but one killed and others wounded. Notwithstanding the unlawful acts committed by Captain Bogart's men previous to the battle, it is now asserted and claimed that he was regularly ordered out as a militia captain to preserve the peace along the line of Ray and Caldwell Counties. That battle was fought four or five days previous to the arrival of General Lucas and his army. About the time of the battle with Captain Bogart a number of our people who were living near Haun's mills, on Shoal Creek, about twenty miles below Far West, together with a number of emigrants who had been stopped there in consequence of the excitement, made an agreement with the mob which was about there, that neither party should molest the other, but dwell in peace. Shortly after this agreement was made a mob party of from two to three hundred, many of whom are supposed to be from Chariton County, some from Daviess, and also those who had agreed to dwell in peace, came upon our people there, whose number in men was about forty, at a time when they little expected any such thing and without any ceremony, notwithstanding they begged for quarter, shot them down as they would tigers or panthers. Some few made their escape by fleeing, eighteen were killed and a number more were severely wounded.

"This tragedy was conducted in the most brutal and savage manner. An old man, after the massacre was partially over, threw himself into their hands and begged for quarter when he was instantly shot down; that not killing him they took an old corn cutter and literally mangled him to pieces. A lad of ten years of age, after being shot down also begged to be spared, when one of **[242]** them placed the muzzle of his gun to his head and blew out his brains.

"The slaughter of these not satisfying the mob they then proceeded to rob and plunder.

"The scene that presented itself after the massacre to the widows and orphans of the killed is beyond description. It was truly a time of weeping, of mourning and of lamentation.

"As yet we have not heard of any being arrested for these murders, notwithstanding there are men boasting about the county that they did kill on that occasion more than one "Mormon;" whereas all our people who were in the battle with Captain Patten against Bogart, that can be found, have been arrested, and are now confined in jail to await their trial for murder.

"When General Lucas arrived near Far West and presented the Governor's order, we were surprised greatly, yet we felt willing to submit to the authorities of the state. We gave up our arms without reluctance. We were then made prisoners and confined to the limits of the town for about a week, during which time the men from the country were not permitted to go to their families many of whom were in a suffering condition for the want of food and firewood, the weather being very cold and stormy. Much property was destroyed by the troops in town during their stay there, such as burning house logs, rails, corn cribs, boards, etc., the using of corn and hay, the plundering of houses, the killing of cattle, sheep, and hogs and also the taking of horses not their own; and all this without regard to owners or asking leave of anyone. In the meantime men were abused, women insulted and abused by the troops—and all this while we were kept prisoners.

"Whilst the town was guarded we were called together by the order of General Lucas, and a guard placed close around us, and in that situation were compelled to sign a deed of trust for the purpose of making over our individual property, all holden as they said, to pay all the debts of every individual belonging to the Church, and also to pay for all damages the old **[243]** inhabitants of Daviess may have sustained in consequence of the late difficulties in that county.

"General Clark now arrived and the first important move made by him was collecting of our men together, on the square, and selecting out about fifty of them' whom he immediately marched into a house and confined close. This was done without the aid of the sheriff or any legal process. The next day forty six of those taken were driven, like a parcel of menial slaves, off to Richmond, not knowing why they were taken, or what they were taken for. After being confined in Richmond more than two weeks, about one half were liberated. The rest, after another week's confinement, were most of them required to appear at court and have since been let to bail.

"Since General Clark withdrew his troops from Far West, parties of armed men have gone through the county, driving off horses, sheep and cattle and also plundering houses. The barbarity of General Lucas' troops ought not to be passed over in silence. They shot our cattle and hogs merely for the sake of destroying them, leaving them for the ravens to eat.

"They took prisoner an aged man named Tanner, and without any reason for it, he was struck on the head with a gun, which laid his skull bare. Another man by the name of Carey was also taken prisoner by them and without any provocation had his brains dashed out by a gun. He was laid in a wagon and there permitted to remain for the space of twenty-four hours, during which time no one was permitted to administer to him comfort or consolation; and after he was removed from that situation, he lived but a few hours.

"The destruction of property at and about Far West is very great. Many are stripped bare as it were and others partially so. Indeed, take us as a body, at this time we are a poor and afflicted people, and if we are compelled to leave the state in the spring, many, yes a large portion of our society, will have to be removed at the expense of the state, as those who might have helped them are now debarred that privilege in consequence of the deed of trust we are compelled to sign, which deed **[244]** so operated upon our real estate that it will sell for little or nothing at this time.

"We have now made a brief statement of some of the most prominent features of the troubles that have befallen our people since our first settlement in the state, and we believe these persecutions have come in consequence of our religious faith, and not for immorality on our part. That instances have been, of late, when individuals have trespassed upon the rights of others and thereby broken the laws of the land, we will not attempt to deny; but yet we do believe that no crime can be substantiated against any of the people who have a standing in our Church of an earlier date than the difficulties in Daviess County.

"And when it is considered that the rights of this people have been trampled upon from time to time with impunity, and abuses heaped upon them almost innumerable, it ought in some degree to palliate for any infraction of the law which may have been made on the part of our people.

"The late order of Governor Boggs to drive us from this state, or exterminate us, is a thing so novel, unlawful, tyrannical and oppressive, that we have been induced to draw up this memorial, and present this statement of our case to your honorable body, praying that a law may be passed, rescinding the order of the Governor to drive us from the state, and also giving us the sanction of the Legislature to inherit our lands in peace.

"We ask an expression of the Legislature, disapproving of the conduct of those who compelled us to sign a deed of trust, and also disapproving of any man or set of men taking our property in consequence of that deed of trust, and appropriating it to the payment of damage sustained in consequence of trespasses committed by others.

"We have no common stock; our property is individual property and we feel willing to pay our debts as other individuals do. But we are not willing to be bound for other peoples' debts also. The arms which were taken from us here, which we [245] understand to be about six hundred and thirty, besides swords and pistols, we care not so much about, as we do the pay for them, only we are bound to do military duty, which we are willing to do, and which we think was sufficiently manifested by the raising of a volunteer company last fall at Far West, when called upon by General Parkes to raise troops for the frontier.

"The arms given up by us we consider were worth between twelve and fifteen thousand dollars; but we understand they have been greatly damaged since taken, and at this time probably would not bring near their former value. And as they were both here and in Jackson County, taken by the militia, and consequently by the authority of the state, we therefore ask your Honorable Body to cause an appropriation to be made by law, whereby we may be paid for them, or otherwise have them returned to us and the damages made good. The losses sustained by our people in leaving Jackson County, are so situated that it is impossible to obtain any compensation for them by law, because those who have sustained them are unable to prove those trespasses upon individuals. That the facts do exist that the buildings, crops, stock, furniture, rails, timber, etc., of the society, have been destroyed in Jackson County, is not doubted by those who are acquainted in this upper country; and since trespasses cannot be proven upon individuals, we ask your Honorable Body to consider this case and if in your liberality and wisdom you can conceive it to be proper to make an appropriation by law to these sufferers, many of whom are still pressed down with poverty in consequence of their losses, would be able to pay their debts, and also in some degree be relieved from poverty and woe; whilst the widow's heart would be made to rejoice, and the orphan's tears measurably dried up and the prayers of a grateful people ascend on high, with thanksgiving and praise to the author of our existence for that beneficent act.

"In laying our case before your Honorable Body, we say that we are willing, and ever have been, to conform to the Constitution and laws of the United States, and [246] of this state. We ask in common with others the protection of the laws. We ask for the privilege guaranteed to all free citizens of the United States and of this state, to be extended to us, that we may be permitted to settle and live where we please, and worship God according to the dictates of our conscience without molestation. And while we ask for ourselves this privilege we are willing all others should enjoy the same.

"We now lay our case at the feet of your Legislature, and ask your Honorable Body to consider it, and do for us, after mature deliberation, that which your wisdom, patriotism and philanthropy may dictate.

"And we as in duty bound will ever pray.

"A committee appointed by the citizens of Caldwell County, to draft this memorial and sign it in their behalf.

⎧ EDWARD PARTRIDGE,
⎪ HEBER C. KIMBALL,
⎪ JOHN TAYLOR,
⎪ THEODORE TURLEY,
⎨ BRIGHAM YOUNG,
⎪ ISAAC MORLEY,
⎪ GEORGE W. HARRIS,
⎪ JOHN MURDOCK,
⎩ JOHN M. BURK,

"Far West, Caldwell County, Missouri, Dec. 10, 1838."

The only recognition given by the Legislature to this pathetic appeal, this soul-harrowing recital of "bitter, burning wrongs," enough to melt a heart of stone,

"To stir a fever in the blood of age,
And make the infant's sinews strong as steel,"

was the appropriation of the paltry sum of two thousand dollars, to be distributed among the people of Daviess and Caldwell Counties, "*the Mormons not excepted.*"

O lavish generosity! Two thousand dollars for a city sacked and pillaged, fields and farms laid waste, and homes given to the flames; not to mention murders, rapes, expulsions and other outrages nameless [247] for their enormity, committed upon a helpless people by a ruthless mob, in the sovereign name of the state of Missouri!

"THE MORMONS NOT EXCEPTED!"

O world-wide philanthropy! Magnanimity unparalleled! As though the Mormons had not been the main, and well-nigh only sufferers from this horrible and hellish invasion. Indeed, the only other losses sustained—barring those inflicted by the oppressed people in sheer self-defense—were from depredations by the mobocrats themselves upon their own sympathizers, committed in such a way as to seem the work of Mormons, who were falsely accused of the devilish deeds and the public mind thus inflamed against them.

And then, the manner of distributing this princes' ransom! Surely the tactics of the average Indian agent and post-trader there had their origin. The notorious Judge Cameron had charge of the distribution; a wretch whose unpitying gaze had surveyed complacently the wrongs and cruelties heaped upon the helpless Saints, his serene equanimity of temper being disturbed only by the patience and superhuman cheerfulness of the brethren when compelled at the point of the bayonet to sign away their property to pay the expenses of the war waged against them. He was assisted by a man named McHenry.

Says Heber C. Kimball:

"Judge Cameron drove in the hogs belonging to the brethren (many of which were identified) shot them down in the streets, and, without further bleeding they were half-dressed, cut up and distributed by McHenry to the poor, charging four or five cents per pound; which, together with a few pieces of refuse calicoes, at double and treble price, soon consumed the appropriation."

And thus did the great state of Missouri redress the wrongs of ten thousand innocent people, robbed and [248] trampled on without provocation by its mob militia, led on and fired to their deeds of blood and plunder by political demagogues and hireling priests of Christendom. And this in the broad daylight of the nineteenth century, in a land of religious liberty, on soil consecrated by the blood of patriots—ancestors of the people thus trampled on and despoiled—and in the presence of American judges, magistrates and priests, affecting the calling, but disgracing the name, of Christian!

Brigham and Heber, in the absence of their fellow Apostles—the remainder of the Twelve who had not gone over to the enemy, being in prison for the Gospel's sake, or away on missions—proceeded to set in order the Church at Far West, which was more or less scattered and demoralized from the effects of the recent persecution. They were obliged to move secretly and with the utmost caution, their lives and liberties being in jeopardy from apostate spies and prowling mobocrats. They reorganized the High Council, "expressed their fellowship with all who desired to do right," and filled the vacancies occasioned by the absence of brethren who had fled out of the state to save their lives.

On the nineteenth of December, they ordained John Taylor and John E. Page to the apostleship.

The next step of the Apostles was to arrange for the exodus of the Saints en masse, from this land of tyrants, traitors and mobocrats, the blood-stained soil of Missouri. [249]

## CHAPTER 33

THE FIRST PRESIDENCY INSTRUCT THE APOSTLES—BRIGHAM YOUNG CHOSEN PRESIDENT OF THE TWELVE—THE EXODUS BEGUN—HEBER TARRIES IN MISSOURI TO MINISTER TO HIS IMPRISONED BRETHREN—HIS FAITHFUL BUT FRUITLESS EFFORTS FOR THEIR RELEASE—THE LORD SPEAKS TO HEBER

FROM Liberty Jail, January 16th, 1839, the First Presidency addressed the following letter of instructions to the Apostles:

"BROTHERS, H. C. KIMBALL AND B. YOUNG:

"*Joseph Smith Jun., Sidney Rigdon and Hyrum Smith, prisoners for Jesus' sake, send greeting:*

In obedience to your request in your letter, we say to you as follows: It is not wisdom for you to go out of Caldwell with your families yet for a little season, until we are out of prison, after which you may act at your pleasure; but though you take your families out of the State, it will be necessary for you to return, and leave as before designed, on the 26th of April.

"Inasmuch as we are in prison, for a little season, if need be, the management of the affairs of the Church devolves on you, that is the Twelve.

"The gathering of necessity is stopped; but the conversion of the world need not stop, but under wise management can go on more rapidly than ever.

"Where churches are built, let them continue where they are, until a door is open to do otherwise, and let every Elder occupy his own ground, and when he builds a church, let him preside over it, and let not others run in to trouble him; and thus let every man prove himself unto God that he is worthy. If we live, we live; and if we [250] die for the testimony of Jesus, we die; but whether we live or die, let the work of God go on.

"Let the churches in England continue there till further orders—till a door can be opened for them, except they choose to come to America and take their chance with the Saints here. If they will do that let them come; and if they choose to come, they would do well to send their wise men before them, and buy out Kirtland, and the regions round about, or they may settle where they can till things may alter.

"It will be necessary for you to get the Twelve together, ordain such as have not been ordained, or at least such of them as you can get, and proceed to regulate the Elders as the Lord may give you wisdom. We nominate George A. Smith and Lyman Sherman to take the places of Orson Hyde and Thomas B. Marsh.

"Brethren, fear not, but be strong in the Lord and in the power of His might. What is man that the servant of God should fear him, or the son of man, that he should tremble at him. Neither think it strange concerning the fiery trials with which we are tried, as though some strange thing had happened unto us. Remember that all have been partakers of like afflictions. Therefore, rejoice in your afflictions, by which you are perfected and through which the Captain of our Salvation was perfected also. Let your hearts and the hearts of all the Saints be comforted with you, and let them rejoice exceedingly, for great is our reward in heaven, for so the wicked persecuted the prophets which were before us. America will be a Zion to all that choose to come to it, and if the churches in foreign countries wish to come, let them do so. Say to Brother P. P. Pratt that our feelings accord with his; he is as we are, and we as he. May peace rest upon him in life and in death.

"Brethren, pray for us, and cease not till our deliverance comes, which we *hope* may come. We hope, we say, for our families' sake.

"Let the Elders preach nothing but the first principles of the Gospel, and let them publish our afflictions—the injustice and cruelty thereof, upon the house tops. [251] Let them write it and publish it in all the papers where they go. Charge them particularly on this point.

"Brethren we remain yours in hope of eternal life,

"SIDNEY RIGDON.
"JOSEPH SMITH, JR.
"HYRUM SMITH.

"N. B. Appoint the oldest of those of the Twelve, who were first appointed, to be the president of your quorum."

"J. S.
"S. R.
"H. S."

Agreeable to the instruction contained in the postscript of this letter, Brigham Young was sustained by the Apostles as president of their quorum. There were but two, it will be remembered, of the original Twelve, who were his seniors. One of these, Thomas B. Marsh, had apostatized, and the other, the lamented David W. Patten, was now filling a martyr's grave.

"On February 7th," says Apostle Kimball, "I accompanied Brother Brigham to Liberty to visit Joseph and the brethren in prison. We had the privilege of going in to see and converse with them; stayed at Liberty over night. Next morning we were permitted to visit the prisoners again while they were at breakfast, and returned during the day to Far West. When we left there Lyman Sherman was somewhat unwell. In a few days after our return he died. We did not notify him of his appointment.

"I fitted up a small wagon, procured a span of ponies, and sent my wife and three children in company with Brother Brigham Young and his family, with several others, who left Far West, Feb. 14th. Everything my family took with them out of Missouri could have been packed on the backs of two horses: the mob took all the rest. [252]

"Being a stranger there, I was requested by Joseph, Brigham and others, to tarry and assist in getting the brethren and families out of Missouri, and to wait upon those brethren who were in prison.

"I went to Liberty almost every week to visit the brethren; generally the only way I had to communicate with them was through the grates of their prison. Many times, after I had traveled forty or fifty miles to see them, I was denied the privilege by the jailor and the guards.

"I sent one hundred dollars by Brother Stephen Markham to Joseph, and also various sums at different times by other individuals.

"March 15th, the Prophet Joseph and others petitioned Judge Tomkins, or either of the Supreme Judges of the state of Missouri, for a state's writ of *habeas corpus*, that he and his brethren might be brought before either of those judges, that justice might be administered. I was requested by Joseph to go to Jefferson City and present the petition. Theodore Turley was appointed to accompany me. We took copies of the papers by which the prisoners were held, with the petition to the Supreme Judges, and immediately started a distance of 300 miles; visited the judges, and laid the whole matter before them individually, according to our best abilities; neither of them would take any action in the case, although they appeared friendly, and acknowledged that the brethren were illegally imprisoned. We also presented a petition to the Secretary of State, the Governor being absent. He appeared very kind, but like the other officers he had no power to do good!

"We immediately returned to Liberty, where we arrived on the 30th and made Joseph and the rest of the prisoners acquainted with the result of our mission, through the grate of the dungeon, as we were not per[253]mitted to enter the prison. Joseph told us to be of good cheer, for the Lord would deliver him and his brethren in due time; he also told us to tell the brethren to be of good cheer, and get all the Saints away as fast as possible.

"In company with Brother Turley, I visited Judge Austin A. King, who was angry with us for presenting his illegal papers to the Supreme Judges. He treated us very roughly. I returned to Far West, April 5th.

"My family having been gone about two months, during which time I heard nothing from them; our brethren being in prison; death and destruction following us everywhere we went; I felt very sorrowful and lonely. The following words came to my mind, and the Spirit said unto me, 'write,' which I did by taking apiece of paper and writing on my knee as follows:

"FAR WEST, April 6th, 1839.
*A word from the Spirit of the Lord to my servant, Heber C. Kimball:*
"Verily I say unto my servant Heber, thou art my son, in whom I am well pleased; for thou art careful to hearken to my words, and not transgress my law, nor rebel against my servant Joseph Smith, for thou hast a respect to the words of mine anointed, even from the least to the greatest of them; therefore thy name is written in heaven, no more to be blotted out for ever, because of these things; and this Spirit and blessing shall rest down upon thy posterity for ever and ever; for they shall be called after thy name, for thou shalt have many more sons and daughters, for thy seed shall be as numerous as the sands upon the sea shore; therefore, my servant Heber, be faithful, go forth in my name and I will go with you, and be on your right hand and on your left, and my angels shall go before you and raise you up when you are cast down and afflicted; remember that I am always with you, even to the end, therefore be of [254] good cheer, my son, and my spirit shall be in your heart to teach you the peaceable things of the kingdom. Trouble not thyself about thy family, for they are in my hands; I will feed them and clothe them and make unto them friends; they never shall want for food nor raiment, houses nor lands, fathers nor mothers; brothers nor sisters; and peace shall rest upon them forever; if thou wilt be faithful and go forth and preach my gospel to the nations of the earth; for thou shalt be blessed in this thing: thy tongue shall be unloosed to such a degree that has not entered into thy heart as yet, and the children of men shall believe thy words, and flock to the water, even as they did to my servant John; for thou shalt be great in winning souls to me, for this is thy gift and calling; and there shall be no gift withheld from thee, if thou art faithful. Therefore, be faithful, and I will give thee favor in the eyes of the people; be humble and kind and you shall obtain kindness; be merciful and you shall obtain mercy; and I will be with you even unto the end. Amen.[255]

# CHAPTER 34

A WORD FOR THE FALLEN—ONLY GOD KNOWETH THE WHEREFORE AND WHY—ORSON HYDE'S REPENTANCE AND RETURN TO THE CHURCH—HEBER C. KIMBALL AND HYRUM SMITH HIS CHAMPIONS—ISAAC RUSSELL'S APOSTASY—HEBER WRITES TO THE CHURCH IN ENGLAND

"BE merciful and you shall obtain mercy." The word of the Lord unto His servant Heber. The word of the Lord unto His disciples in days of old. The voice of universal charity, breathing forth the spirit of Christ upon a weak, a sinful and a fallen world.

"Blessed are the merciful, for they shall obtain mercy."

Why should we rail at the fallen? Why not rather weep, when a brother or a sister sins? Why hate them for what is their misfortune? The heavens wept over fallen Lucifer, and even Michael, the archangel, contending with him for the body of Moses, "durst not bring against him a railing accusation?"

None but the tempted know what trials are; none but the fallen what the fallen suffer, or how they endured ere they fell. None but God can fully know the why and wherefore of their fall.

> "We see but half the causes of our deeds,
> Seeking them wholly in the outer life."

What we deem chance, may be destiny; what we term accident, design. A greater knowledge than man's, the knowledge of a God, can alone elucidate the mystery **[256]** of mortal actions, as seen by the dim uncertain light of the flickering lantern of human wisdom.

He who is the Judge; who "putteth down one and setteth up another;" who is angry with none save with those who will not in all things acknowledge and obey Him; who bringeth order out of chaos, light out of darkness, strength from weakness, life from death, and victory from seeming failure and defeat; He only can entirely tell why some succeed where others fail, why some are weak and some are strong, why false and true are found together; why "there must needs be an opposiin all things;" why demons as well as angels are essential; why sun and shadow cross each other; why joy and sorrow, sweet and bitter, wine and wormwood, are in life's cup commingled; why the beacon lights the breaker's foam; why the stranded wreck, and the bark safely anchored, each must tell its tale and point its moral for the welfare of future generations.

"Blessed are the merciful, for they shall obtain mercy."

"To err is human; to forgive divine."

"And now abideth faith, hope, charity, these three; but the greatest of these is charity."

"About this time," says Heber, "Orson Hyde came to me feeling very sorrowful for the course he had pursued the past few months; he said it was because of fear (Brother Hyde was sick just before the Far West troubles commenced), and now lamented his folly and asked me what he should do. I told him to give up his school, remove his family and gather with the Church. He wanted to know if I thought the brethren would forgive him. I said, 'Yes.' He then asked, 'Will you defend my case?' And I promised him I would."

Heber was as good as his word, and through his [257] mediation Brother Hyde was forgiven, after a humble confession, and restored to fellowship. He was also reinstated in his Apostleship, which he thenceforth magnified unto the end of his days.

Heber enlisted as his fellow champion of the cause of Brother Hyde, President Hyrum Smith, great-hearted and merciful as himself, and when, at the next conference of the Church, Joseph presented the name of Orson Hyde to the congregation for their action, Hyrum and Heber pleaded for him so earnestly that the Prophet said: "If my brother Hyrum and Heber C. Kimball will defend Orson Hyde, I will withdraw my motion,"

Thus did the voice of mercy, the voice of God, in two of His noblest sons, plead and not in vain for the fallen.

And what of Oliver, and David, and Sidney, and scores of others who fell from grace, but many of whom, penitent at life's eleventh hour, returned to lay the offering of a broken heart and a contrite spirit upon the altar of God's infinite love? Will they not find mercy, and meet a judgment more just, than we in our narrow charity know how to mete out to the erring?

Verily they will; and more joy will there ever be in the mansions of our Father, over the returning prodigal, the soul that was lost and is found, than in the steadfast faith of the righteous multitude, whose reward is that they need no repentance.

Another Elder who fell away during this time of trouble, was Isaac Russell, Heber's fellow missionary to England. About thirty families followed him, accepting him as their leader. Viewing with sorrow the fall of such men, his former faithful companions in the ministry, Heber's mind turned with some solicitude to the church in England, which they, with himself, had been instrumental in found[258]ing. He wrote to Joseph Fielding, President of the Church in that land, as follows:

"I have only received two letters from you since I came here. If you knew the feelings I have for the welfare of that people your pen would not be so idle. May God stir you up to diligence to feed His sheep; for they are children of my begetting through the Gospel. Think it not strange that I speak thus; for you know the feelings that a father has for his children.

"Now, brethren, be faithful and visit the churches, and exhort the Saints to be faithful in all things, and not lay down their watch for a moment; for there is great danger of falling beneath the powers of darkness. Don't think hard of me, brethren, for my plainness, for I am a plain man, and God requires it of me, and the same of you. Don't keep the Saints in ignorance of those things I have made you acquainted with—that is, our sufferings, for they will know them when I come, and they will have to pass through similar scenes. Don't be selfish; for it will not impoverish you to tell them all that I tell you.

"Your sister Mary left here about eight weeks ago, also the rest of the wives of the prisoners, thinking that they would be out in a few days. There are ten in prison; they are all well and in good spirits. I am going to see them to-morrow if the Lord will.

"Mobs are common in this country; it is getting so that there is no safety anywhere in this land. Prepare yourselves for trouble wherever you go, for it awaits you and all others that love the Lord and keep His commandments.

"Brethren, I want you to go to the north where Brother Russell labored, and see what situation the Saints are in, for I have some fears about them. Go and strengthen them in the name of the Lord, for I think that Russell is leading them astray.[3]

"Brethren, I can truly say that I have never seen the Church in a better state since I have been a member **[259]** of it. What there are left are firm and steadfast, full of love and good works.

"They have lost all their earthly goods, and are now ready to *go and preach the Gospel to a dying world!*

"We have ordained about one hundred Elders into the Seventies. There are about one hundred and fifty who have gone into the vineyard this winter to preach the Gospel, and many more will go in the spring, and several will come to England with me in the summer or fall.

"Elder Rigdon was bailed out of prison, and has left Missouri. About ten thousand had gathered to this state. By the first of May, next, there will not be one left who has any faith. Not one-fourth part had any teams to move with, and we had two hundred miles to travel before we could get out of the state. I think their deliverance is a great miracle."

---

## CHAPTER 35

THE BRETHREN IN LIBERTY JAIL—JUDGE KING'S COUP D'ETAT—THE MOB AGAIN THREATEN FAR WEST—FIENDS IN HUMAN FORM—THE PROPHET REGAINS HIS FREEDOM—THE APOSTLES FULFILL REVELATION—FIRST CONFERENCE OF THE CHURCH IN ILLINOIS.

JOSEPH and his brethren were still in the hands of the enemy, but the hour of their deliverance was drawing nigh. They had suffered severely in their confinement from the cruelty of their captors, but most of them had borne up bravely. Elder Rigdon, whose faith was beginning to fail under the terrible tension of trial, rashly exclaimed in a moment of despair: "Jesus Christ was a **[260]** fool to me in suffering." Soon after, he was released on bail and set at liberty. The others were

---

[3] This letter preceded, only by a few weeks, an epistle from Isaac Russell to the Saints in Alston, England, of a nature "calculated to deceive and lead astray."

destined to tarry in chains a little longer.

Judge King now ordered the removal of the prisoners from Liberty to Daviess County, fearing a change of venue might be obtained to some other place where the feeling against them was less intense, and the prospect for a fair trial more favorable.

Heber C. Kimball and another of the brethren were appointed to visit Judge Hughes, a friend of Joseph's, and get him to attend the sitting of the court in Daviess County.

"The Judge," says Heber, "who had formerly been an Indian agent, and was a very rough man in his language, cursed the judges, the governor, and everybody else who would not step forward and help the brethren out of the hands of their persecutors, for he did not believe they were guilty of any of the crimes alleged against them; he said there was no proof that they had committed any crime worthy of imprisonment or death, and that the Mormons had been meanly treated in Missouri.

"There were several men in Liberty who were very friendly to the brethren. I called on them when I went there, and they treated me with great civility. General Doniphan and General Atchison and several of the foremost men of the town were among them.

"Those I have mentioned and several others, revolted at the scenes enacted against the Mormons, and would have liberated the brethren had it not been for 'outside pressure,'—that is, the strong prejudice against us by the people, and their bloodthirstiness to kill the prophets."

Meanwhile, the mob, not content with the ruin they had wrought, continued to threaten the few Saints who [261] remained in Far West, evidently determined to carry out the order of their chief, Governor Boggs, to "exterminate the Mormons, or drive them from the state." The main body of the Church, numbering from ten to twelve thousand souls, had already left the state, and were beyond the reach of Missourian mobs, encamped upon the hospitable shores of Illinois.

"On the 14th of April, 1839," continues Heber, "the committee who had been left to look after the wants of the poor, removed thirty-six of the helpless families into Tenney's grove, about twenty-five miles from Far West. I was obliged to secrete myself in the corn-fields and woods during the day and only venture out in the evening, to counsel the committee and brethren in private houses.

"On the morning of the 18th, as I was going to the committee room to tell the brethren to wind up their affairs and be off, or their lives would be taken, I was met on the public square by several of the mob. One of them asked, with an oath, if I was a Mormon.

"I replied, 'I am a Mormon.'

"With a series of blasphemous expressions, they then threatened to blow my brains out, and also tried to ride over me with their horses, in the presence of Elias Smith, Theodore Turley and others of the committee.

"It was but a few minutes after I had notified the committee to leave, before the mob gathered at the tithing house, and began breaking clocks, chairs, windows, looking-glasses and furniture, and making a complete wreck of everything they could move, while Captain Bogart, the county judge, looked on and laughed. A mobber named Whittaker threw an iron pot at the head of Theodore Turley and hurt him considerably, when Whittaker jumped about and laughed like a madman; [262] and all this at the time when we were using our utmost endeavors to get the Saints away from Far West. The brethren gathered up what they could, and fled from Far West in one hour. The mob staid until the committee left, and then plundered thousands of dollars worth of property which had been left by the brethren and sisters to assist the poor to remove.

"One mobber rode up, and, finding no convenient place to fasten his horse to, shot a cow that was standing near, while a girl was milking her, and while the poor animal was struggling in death, he cut a strip of her hide from the nose to her tail, to which he fastened his halter.

"During the commotion of this day, a great portion of the records of the committee, accounts, history, etc., were destroyed or stolen.

"Hearing that Joseph and the brethren had escaped from their guard while they were on their way from Daviess to Boone County, to which place they had obtained a change of venue, I called upon Shadrach Roundy, with whom I started immediately towards Quincy.

"On reaching Keetsville, I stopped at the house of Col. Price. The Colonel, hearing of my arrival, came directly into the house, and discovering who I was, said, 'Joseph and Hyrum Smith and the other prisoners have escaped.' I enquired what he knew about them. He answered, 'their guard took breakfast here this morning; they have turned back, saying they were going to Richmond, by way of Tenney's Grove. I know that the guard has been bribed, or they would evince more interest by pursuing them.' After we had partaken of refreshment, Brother Roundy and I pursued our course towards Quincy about fourteen or fifteen miles.

"Being thoroughly satisfied that the prisoners had escaped, we turned back towards Far West. When we [263] arrived at Tenney's Grove a man came to me and presented an order drawn on me by Joseph Smith for $500, saying it was for horses furnished him. I immediately raised $400, which I paid him, when he proceeded to Richmond, Ray County, where he paid out some of the money to secure lands that we had been driven from.

"Brother Roundy and myself started a few hours after for Richmond, being on our way to Far West, for the purpose of visiting Parley P. Pratt and others, in jail, On our arrival at Richmond, I went directly to the prison to see Parley, but was prohibited by the guard, who said they would blow my brains out if I attempted to go near him. In a few minutes Sister Morris Phelps came to me in great agitation, and advised me to leave forthwith, as Parley P. Pratt had told her that a large body of men had assembled with tar, feathers and a rail, who swore they would tar and feather me, and ride me on a rail, suspecting I was the one who assisted Joseph and the other prisoners to escape. I immediately informed Brother Roundy, we jumped on our horses and fled towards Far West, which was distant; we rode all night, and reached Far West about the break of day, expecting Brother Brigham Young and the Twelve to arrive there that day."

April 26th, 1839, was the day appointed by revelation for the Apostles to take leave of Far West on the building spot of the Lord's House. As usual, when times and seasons are given—for foreknowledge is power, with evil spirits as well as good—Satan had diligently sought to make the word of God of no effect. The mob, with their apostate allies who had betrayed to them the secrets of the kingdom, had sworn that this revelation should not be fulfilled; and having driven the Saints from their homes, leaving only a few scattered **[264]** families in and around Far West, and imprisoned the Church leaders, they flattered themselves that their wicked oath had been verified.

Little knew they the men they were dealing with, still less that God whose word they had vainly sought to falsify; Him who hath said: "Heaven and earth shall pass away, but my word shall not pass away."

Heber continues: "I kept myself concealed in the woods, and passed round the country, notifying the brethren and sisters to be on hand at the appointed time for the laying of the corner stone.

"April 25th. This night, which was a beautiful, clear moonlight, Elders Brigham Young, Orson Pratt, John E. Page, John Taylor, Wilford Woodruff, George A. Smith, and Alpheus Cutler, arrived from Quincy, Illinois, and rode into the public square early on the morning of the 26th. All seemed still as death.

"April 26th, we held a conference at the house of Brother Samuel Clark, cut off 31 persons from the Church, and then proceeded to the building spot of the Lord's house, where, after singing, we recommenced laying the foundation, agreeably to the revelation given July 8th, 1838, by rolling a stone, upwards of a ton weight, upon or near the south-east corner.

"In company with Brother Brigham Young, we ordained Wilford Woodruff and George A. Smith (who had been previously nominated by the First Presidency, accepted by the Twelve, and acknowledged by the Church at Quincy) members of the quorum of the Twelve Apostles; and Darwin Chase and Norman Shearer, (who were liberated from Richmond prison on the 24th inst, where they had been confined about six months for the cause of Christ) Seventies. They sat on the south-east corner stone while we ordained them. **[265]**

"The Twelve then individually called upon the Lord in prayer, kneeling on the corner stone; after which 'Adam-ondi-Ahman' was sung.

"The brethren wandered among our deserted houses, many of which were in ruins, and saw the streets in many places grown over with weeds and grass.

"We went to Father Clark's, breakfasted, and before sunrise departed. I accompanied my brethren, riding thirty miles that day. We continued our journey to Quincy, where I found my family well and in good spirits, on the 2nd of May.

"On reading the words of inspiration which I had written, my wife bore record to the truth of that part which says, 'trouble not thyself about thy family for they are in my hands; I will feed them and clothe them, and make unto them friends; for they never shall want for food nor raiment.' I learned from her that my family continued with Brother Brigham until they crossed the Mississippi, to the town of Atlas, in Illinois, where, through the instrumentality of George Pitkin, my wife got introduced to a widow Ross, who let her have a very nice comfortably fitted up room, and who was as kind to her as an own mother or sister; here my wife tarried seven weeks. At the end of that time John P. Greene took his horses and wagon and carried my family up to Quincy, forty miles, and rented a good house, where I found her on my leaving Missouri. She had had no lack of friends, and had every comfort bestowed on her that she could have had among her own kindred. And I can say in my heart, God bless them all, and my Brother Brigham for his great kindness in assisting them into Illinois. In relation to that part which said I should have many sons and daughters, she rather doubted that, as the thought had never entered into her head, or mine, that the Lord **[266]** would establish in this Church the doctrine of plurality of wives, in my day; still I believed it would be restored to the earth in some future time.

"May 3rd, I went in company with Elder Brigham Young, Orson Pratt, John Taylor, Wilford Woodruff and George A. Smith, and rode four miles to Mr. Cleveland's to visit Joseph and Hyrum, who were as glad to see us as we were to see them, once more enjoying their liberty. I spent the day with them, and it was one of the greatest days of rejoicing in my life, to once more have the privilege of conversing with the Prophet, in freedom.

"May 4th, I attended a general conference of the Church near Quincy, at which the Saints from all the regions round about assembled It was a time which will long be remembered by the Saints, being the first conference held after their expulsion. The cases of Brothers William Smith and Orson Hyde were brought up. The conference granted them the privilege of appearing personally before the next conference of the Church to give an account of their conduct, but in the meantime they were suspended from exercising the functions of their office. The conference sanctioned the proceedings of the Twelve on the Temple block at Far West, and also sanctioned the intended mission of the Twelve to Europe.

"The meetings continued for three days. Elder Rigdon was appointed delegate to go to Washington and lay the grievances of the Saints before the general government. It was also resolved that a number of Elders should accompany the Twelve on their mission to Europe." **[267]**

# CHAPTER 36

NAUVOO THE BEAUTIFUL—HEBER'S PREDICTION OVER THE FATED CITY—ELDER RIGDON'S ALARM—HEBER'S SECOND ENCOUNTER WITH EVIL SPIRITS—PARLEY P. PRATT ESCAPES FROM PRISON, FULFILLING HEBER'S PROPHECY

THE scene now changes to Commerce, afterwards named Nauvoo, the famous gathering place of the Saints in Illinois. Situated in a graceful bend on the east bank of the Mississippi, on an eminence commanding a noble view of the broad river and beyond, Nauvoo, even as the site of the lovely city it soon became, well merited its appellation of "the Beautiful."

It was forty miles above Quincy, in which hospitable town the exiled Saints had found a resting place and kindly welcome, after their expulsion from Missouri.

In this region the Saints had commenced gathering, and, having purchased lands, were now busily engaged building up the new stake of Zion. The Church had been purified by its baptism of fire, and much of its human dross "burnt and purged away." Most of its members that remained were of the pure gold, refined by suffering, and throughout the community a better feeling prevailed than ever before.

Heber's first visit to Commerce was on Sunday the 12th of May. On the 25th he again went up the river, with several others of the Twelve, and spent the day in council with Joseph and the brethren. While on the water, standing by the railing of the boat, gazing in admiration at the beautiful site of Nauvoo, Heber [268] observed: "It is a very pretty place, but not a long abiding home for the Saints."

This remark was carried to the ears of Elder Rigdon and his family, who were comfortably quartered in a nice stone house built by Dr. Isaac Galland, from whom the Saints had purchased some of their lands. Heber's reputation as a prophet was by this time pretty well established in Israel, and Sidney, who had had about as much persecution as he could stand, and was in nowise hankering after a repetition of the Missouri scenes, was considerably alarmed at his words, dreading their prophetic potency. At the council, which was held at the house of the Prophet Joseph, Sidney remarked that he had some feelings against Elder Kimball, and then, referring to the prediction of the latter in relation to the city of the Saints, said, petulantly:

"I should suppose that Elder Kimball had passed through sufferings and privations and mobbings and drivings enough, to learn to prophesy good concerning Israel."

With a mixture of meekness and humor, Heber replied:

"President Rigdon, I'll prophesy good concerning you all the time—if you can get it."

The retort amused Joseph, who laughed heartily with the brethren, and Elder Rigdon yielded the point.

Joseph now advised the Apostles, such as had not done so already, to move their families up to Commerce. Says Heber:

"I immediately went and moved my family up in a wagon, to a place belonging to Brother Bozier, about one mile from Commerce, where I pulled down an old stable, and laid up the logs at the back end of the Bozier house, putting a few shakes on to cover it; but it had **[269]** no floor nor chinking; and in this condition I moved my family into it; whenever it rained, the water stood near ankle deep on the ground. There were some half dozen families in the Bozier house.

"One night I was awakened out of my sleep by my wife making a noise as if choking; I asked what was the matter; she replied that she had dreamt that a personage came and seized her by the throat and was choking her. I immediately lit a candle, and saw that her eyes were sunken and her nose pinched in, as if she was in the last stage of the cholera. I laid my hands upon her and rebuked that spirit in the name of Jesus and by the power of the holy Priesthood, and commanded it to depart. In a moment afterwards I heard some half a dozen children in different parts of the Bozier House crying as if in great distress; the cattle began to bellow and low; the horses neighed and whinnied; the dogs barked, and hogs squealed; the hens cackled, and the roosters crowed, and everything around was in great commotion. In a few minutes afterwards I was sent for to lay hands on Sister Bentley, formerly the wife of David W. Patten, who was seized in a similar manner to my wife. My wife continued quite feeble for several days from the shock.

"One day while visiting Joseph, he took me a walk by the river side, when he requested me to relate the occurrence at Brother Bozier's. After I had done so, I also told him of our vision of the evil spirits in England, on the opening of the Gospel to that people. He then gave me a relation of many contests that he had had with Satan, and his power that had been manifested from time to time since the commencement of bringing forth the Book of Mormon. I will relate one circumstance that took place at Far West, in a house that Joseph had **[270]** purchased, which had been formerly occupied as a public house by some wicked people. A short time after he got into it, one of his children was taken very sick; he laid his hands upon the child, when it got better; as soon as he went out of doors, the child was taken sick again; he again laid his hands upon it, so that it again recovered. This occurred several times, when Joseph inquired of the Lord what it all meant; then he had an open vision, and saw the devil in person, who contended with Joseph, face to face, for some time. He said it was his house, it belonged to him, and Joseph had no right there. Then Joseph rebuked Satan in the name of the Lord, and he departed and touched the child no more.

"July 2nd, I went with Joseph, Hyrum, Sidney and others, over the river to Montrose; rode four miles and looked out the site of the town of Zarahemla. We dined at Brother Woodruffs. After dinner we all went to Brigham Young's, when Wilford Woodruff and George A. Smith were blessed as two of the Twelve Apostles; and Theodore Turley was blessed as a Seventy. Brother Hyrum gave the Twelve some good advice on the nature of their mission; to practice prudence and humility in their preaching, and to strictly hold on to the authority of the Priesthood. Brother Joseph taught many glorious and important principles to benefit and bless them on their mission; teaching them to observe charity, wisdom, and a fellow feeling for each other, and love one towards another, in all things, and under all circumstances, unfolding keys of knowledge, to detect Satan, and preserve us in the favor of God."

Some time before Heber had written to Elder Parley P. Pratt, who was still in prison in Missouri, giving him the particulars of the conference at Far West, on the 26th of April, with the resolution of the Priest[271]hood that the Twelve should have their shackles stricken off, and go forth preaching the Gospel to the world, leaving their families to be provided for, in their absence, by the Bishops. He added:

"The Presidency feel well towards you. They say you must come out of that place, and so I say; for I do not feel as though I can go to England until I take you by the hand. When this takes place my joy will be full. Be of good cheer, brother; a few days now, and you shall see the salvation of God; and I shall see you in other lands, publishing peace to the captives. My determination is to be a man of God, and to try to save souls from their sins, let others do as they may. I will try to keep my eye on the mark, that is, Christ, the Son of the living God, His grace assisting me. The Twelve have all left Quincy. Your brother Orson is about twenty-five miles from here. Whatever you do, do quickly!

"July 10th," continues the prophet Heber, "Elder Parley P. Pratt arrived from his imprisonment in Missouri. When I heard that he was in Quincy I went there and assisted him and Orson Pratt up to Commerce. His escape caused much rejoicing among the Saints. A few days afterwards he and I purchased five acres each, of woodland, from Hyrum Kimball. They lay adjoining each other, one mile from the river. He and I went to work to cut each a set of logs fourteen by sixteen feet in length, which we cut in one day. We then invited some of the old citizens, viz., Brother Bozier, D. H. Wells, Lewis Robison and others to come and assist us to put them up; as our people were mostly prostrate by sickness. We drew them and put them up the next day. I got a man to assist me to hew puncheon for the floor, and to make some shakes to cover the roof, which were similar to a shingle, or a stave for a barrel. I drew the rock [272] and built a chimney, and just got to the ridge of the house, when I was taken down prostrate by the chills and fever. My wife was also laid prostrate. In the meantime Brother Orson Pratt moved his family into the little shanty with me."

---

## CHAPTER 37

AN EPIDEMIC OF DISEASE—JOSEPH HEALS THE MULTITUDE—BRIGHAM AND HEBER START ON THEIR MISSION TO ENGLAND—SICKNESS BY THE WAY—HEBER POISONED—HIS LIFE SAVED BY BRIGHAM

TWELVE months had elapsed since the word of the Lord came for the Apostles to depart and "go over the great waters" to promulgate the Gospel. They had

Joseph Smith

Hyrum Smith

fulfilled the revelation in so far as to take leave of the Saints in Far West, at the time and place appointed, but the toils and trials incident to settling their new home had unavoidably delayed their departure from America.

One of these trials was an epidemic which swept over Nauvoo and the neighboring towns, prostrating many of the inhabitants with sickness; partly due, no doubt, to the moist, malarial nature of the soil in and around the lower portions of the new settlement, but greatly enhanced by the physical weakness of the Saints, resulting from their recent privations and sufferings in Missouri. So general and widespread was the sickness that scarcely a family in Nauvoo or the vicinity entirely escaped the scourge. [273]

But this unhappy condition of affairs—rendered doubly disheartening from following so closely upon the Missouri troubles—was not without its recompense. It was the occasion of a marvelous and miraculous display of divine power in behalf of the Lord's afflicted people. Heber thus describes the event:

"July 22nd, the Prophet Joseph arose from his bed of sickness, when the power of God rested upon him, and he went forth administering to the sick. He commenced with the sick in his own house, then visited those who were camping in tents in his own dooryard, commanding the sick in the name of the Lord Jesus Christ to arise from their beds and be whole; when they were healed according to his words. He then went from house to house, and from tent to tent, upon the bank of the river, healing the sick by the power of Israel's God, as he went among them. He did not miss a single house, wagon or tent, and continued this work up to 'the upper stone house,' where he crossed the river in a boat, accompanied by Parley P. Pratt, Orson Pratt, John E. Page, John Taylor and myself, and landed at Montrose. He then walked into the cabin of Brother Brigham Young, who was lying very sick, and commanded him in the name of the Lord Jesus Christ to arise and be made whole. He arose, healed of his sickness, and then accompanied Joseph and his brethren of the Twelve, and went into the house of Brother Elijah Fordham, who was insensible, and considered by his family and friends to be in the hands of death. Joseph stepped to his bedside, looked him in the eye for a minute without speaking, then took him by the hand and commanded him in the name of Jesus Christ to arise from his bed and walk. Brother Fordham immediately leaped out of his bed, threw off all his poultices and bandages, dressed himself, called for a [274] bowl of bread and milk, which he ate, and then followed us into the street. We then went into the house of Joseph B. Noble, who was also very sick, and he was healed in the same manner.

"Joseph spoke with the voice and power of God.

"When he had healed all the sick by the power given unto him he went down to the ferry boat, when a stranger rode up almost breathless, and said that he had heard that Joseph Smith was raising the dead, and healing all of the sick, and his wife begged him to ride up and get Mr. Smith to go down and heal her twin children, about three months old. Joseph replied, 'I cannot go, but will send some one.' In a few minutes he said to Elder Woodruff, 'You go and heal those children, and take this pocket handkerchief, and when you administer to them, wipe their faces with it, and they shall recover.' Brother Woodruff did as he was commanded, and the children were healed.

"The mob spirits, when they saw men whom they thought were dying, arise from their beds, and pray for others, stood paralyzed with fear; yet those same men would have killed Joseph and his brethren if they had had an opportunity. Joseph recrossed the river to his own home and I returned to mine, rejoicing in the mercies and goodness of God. This was a day never to be forgotten by the Saints; nor by the wicked; for they saw the power of God manifest in the flesh."

"August 4th, being Sunday, the Saints met to partake of the sacrament, and received an exhortation from the Prophet Joseph, impressing upon them the necessity of being righteous and clean of heart before the Lord. He also commanded the Twelve to go forth without purse or scrip, according to the revelations of Jesus Christ. [275]

"During the night of August 23rd, my son, David Patten, was born in Commerce, in the log cabin I had put up at the end of the Bozier house. We had a heavy thunderstorm that night, but the hand of the Lord was over us. As soon as my wife was able I moved my family into the new log house that I had built."

September came, and the Apostles prepared to take leave of their families and friends and depart on their mission to Europe. Again the evil one laid his plans to circumvent them. As he once afflicted righteous Job, striving to overthrow his trust in God, he now sought by similar means to undermine the faith and integrity of these latter-day servants of the Lord. But his efforts were unavailing; he had the same class of spirits to contend with as in days of old; men who could say with the patient man of Uz, though bowed in sorrow and humiliation: "I know that my Redeemer liveth," and "though He slay me, yet will I trust in Him."

"September 14th," says Heber, "President Brigham Young left his home at Montrose to start on the mission to England. He was so sick that he was unable to go to the Mississippi, a distance of thirty rods, without assistance. After he had crossed the river he rode behind Israel Barlow on his horse to my house, where he continued sick until the 18th. He left his wife sick with a babe only three weeks old, and all his other children were sick and unable to wait upon each other. Not one soul of them was able to go to the well for a pail of water, and they were without a second suit to their backs, for the mob in Missouri had taken nearly all he had. On the 17th Sister Mary Ann Young got a boy to carry her up in his wagon to my house, that she might nurse and comfort Brother Brigham to the hour of starting. [276]

"September 18th, Charles Hubbard sent his boy with a wagon and span of horses to my house; our trunks were put into the wagon by some brethren; I went to my bed and shook hands with my wife who was then shaking with a chill, having two children lying sick by her side; I embraced her and my children, and bade them farewell. My only well child was little Heber P., and it was with difficulty he could carry a couple of quarts of water at a time, to assist in quenching their thirst.

"It was with difficulty we got into the wagon, and started down the hill about ten rods; it appeared to me as though my very inmost parts would melt within me at leaving my family in such a condition, as it were almost in the arms of death. I felt as though I could not endure it. I asked the teamster to stop, and said to Brother Brigham, 'This is pretty tough, isn't it; let's rise up and give them a cheer.' We arose, and swinging our hats three times over our heads, shouted: 'Hurrah, hurrah for Israel.' Vilate, hearing the noise, arose from her bed and came to the door. She had a smile on her face. Vilate and Mary Ann Young cried out to us: 'Good bye, God bless you.' We returned the compliment, and then told the driver to go ahead. After this I felt a spirit of joy and gratitude, having had the satisfaction of seeing my wife standing upon her feet, instead of leaving her in bed, knowing well that I should not see them again for two or three years.

"We were without purse or scrip, and were carried across the prairie, about fourteen miles, to a shanty near the railway, where Brother O. M. Duel lived. We were unable to carry our small trunks into the house; Sister Duel seeing our feeble condition, assisted the boy to carry them in. [277]

"Sep. 19th, Brother Duel took us in his wagon to Lima, about twelve miles. When he left us he gave each of us a dollar. Brother Bidwell then carried us in his wagon to John A. Mickesell's, near Quincy, about twenty miles, The fatigue of this day's journey was too much for our feeble health; we were prostrated, and obliged to tarry a few days in Quincy.

"Sep. 25th, we left Quincy about 11 a. m., as we felt considerably better. My sorrow was great, to see so many of our brethren sick and dying, in consequence of being driven, and exposed to hunger and cold. Brother Lyman Wight took us in a one horse wagon and carried us to Brother C. C. Rich's at Burton, where we slept through the night. Brother Wight predicted many things, and left his blessings with us when he bade us farewell.

"Sep. 26th, Brother Rich carried us to Brother Wilber's; while on the road the chills came on me again, and I suffered much pain and fatigue.

"Sep. 27th, Brother Wilber took us in a buggy about twenty-five miles to the house of James Allred, in Pittsfield.

"Sep. 28th, Father Allred carried us to the place where Brother Harlow Redfield lived. There we preached to a small branch of the Church, on Sunday, 29th.

"Sep. 30th, Brother Rodgers carried Brother Brigham to Brother Decker's, and myself to Mr. Roswell Murray's; they were living within a few rods of each other, near Winchester in Scott County.

"Here we also found a few brethren in the Church, who had been smitten and robbed of their property in Missouri; who were once more in comfortable circumstances, rejoicing in the Lord. [278]

"Oct. 1st, we were carried to Lorenzo D. Young's, a brother of Brigham Young, where we stayed and recruited our strength until the 4th, when he carried us to Jacksonville, where we stayed the night.

"Oct. 5th, a sister in the Church hired a horse and buggy to carry us to

Springfield, and Brother Babcock drove us there, a distance of thirty-five miles, where we were gladly received by the brethren and nursed. Brother Brigham was confined to his bed by sickness. Brother Libius T. Coon, who was practicing medicine, attended upon him. Here we found Brothers G. A. Smith, Turley, and R. Hedlock.

"I went from house to house, strengthening the brethren and teaching them the things of the kingdom. I was so far recovered that I preached on the Sabbath. They got a two horse wagon and harness, for which they paid fifty-five dollars, and collected thirty-five dollars in money, for the company.

"Judge Adams, one of the judges of the Supreme Court, took me to his house; I stayed with him three nights and the most part of three days. He gave me five dollars when I left. My father-in-law, Roswell Murray, went with us on a visit to his friends in the East.

"Oct. 11th, resumed my journey in company with Brothers Young, Turley, Smith, Hedlock and Murray. The brethren exchanged horses in Springfield, and with the assistance we received from the brethren living there, we succeeded in obtaining one horse and a two-horse wagon, in which the sisters fitted up a bed for Brother Brigham to ride on, as he was unable to sit up. We traveled eight miles with the three-horse team, and put up at the house of Father Baker. When we went into the house, Brother George A. Smith, while stooping down to warm him at the fire, dropped a small flask [279] bottle, containing tonic bitters, out of his pocket, on the hearth, and broke it; at this occurrence Father Baker was very much astonished, and said, 'You're a pretty set of Apostles, to be carrying a bottle of whisky with you.' We explained to him that the bottle contained some bitters which the brethren at Springfield had prepared for George A. because of his sickness; this appeased his righteous soul, so that he consented to allow us to stay through the night.

"Oct. 12th, we pursued our journey towards Terre Haute; traveled all day; most of the brethren being very sick I walked most of the way; at night I slept in the wagon with my father-in-law and Brother Hedlock, and caught cold; the next morning I had to go until twelve o'clock before I had anything to eat, and then it was transparent pork and corn dodger. My health again began to fail; the wagon broke down twice, and the chills came on me about two in the afternoon, and held me till night; then the fever held me all night. I had the chills and fever three days, and lost my appetite. The third chill was so severe that it seemed as though I could not live till night. We arrived at Terre Haute about dusk on the 17th; Brother Young and I put up at Dr. Modisett's. In the evening I became very ill. The doctor said he could give me something that would do me good, that would relieve me of my distress, and I would probably get a nap; but the old man was so drunk that he did not know what he did, and he gave me a tablespoonful of morphine; his wife saw him pour it out, but dared not say a word, although she believed it would kill me. In a few minutes after I took it, I straightened up in my chair, complaining of feeling very strange, and felt as though I wanted to lie down. On my attempting to go to the bed, I reeled and fell to the floor. There was hardly a [280] breath of life in my body. Brother Brigham rolled me over on my back, put a pillow under my head, and inquired of the doctor what he had given me, and then learned that he had given me morphine. I lay there for a long time; when I came to, Brother Brigham was attending to me with a fatherly care, and manifesting much anxiety in my behalf. I told him, 'Don't be scared, for I sha'n't die.' In a short time after he had got me on the bed, I commenced vomiting, and continued doing so most of the night. It was through the closest attention of Brother Young and the family that my life was preserved through the night. In the morning Brothers Smith, Turley, Hedlock and Murray came to see us. They laid their hands on me and prayed for me. When they left they wept. Father Murray felt very sorrowful; said he, 'we shall never see Heber again; he will die.' I looked up at them and said, 'Never mind, brethren, go ahead, for Brother Brigham and I will reach Kirtland before you will.' Brother Brigham gave them all the money we had except five dollars, and told them to take good care of the team, and make all possible speed to Kirtland. They started the same day. In about an hour after they departed I arose from my bed." [281]

## CHAPTER 38

ON TO KIRTLAND—MIRACULOUSLY SUPPLIED WITH MONEY—CONDITION OF AFFAIRS AT THE OLD CHURCH HEADQUARTERS

HAVING partly recovered from the effects of this narrow escape from death, Heber and his fellow Apostle resumed their journey to Kirtland. The record continues:

"October 23rd, Brother James Modisett took us in his father's carriage twenty miles, to the house of Brother Addison Pratt. From thence we were carried by Dr. Knight to Pleasant Garden, and put up with Brother Jonathan Crosby. We found a few brethren who were well and in good spirits. We remained there three days, preaching to the few brethren, and those who wished to hear. Dr. Knight and some others gave us some money to assist us on our mission.

"Oct. 25th, I received a letter from my wife, giving an account of her sickness since I left; also of our children William and Helen.

"Oct. 26th, Brother Babbitt took us in his buggy twelve miles, to the house of Brother Scott; they were very glad to see us, and we tarried with them through the night.

"Oct. 27th, Brother Scott sent his little son John, who carried us to Belleville, fifteen miles—several miles of the journey in a rain storm, which obliged us to put up at an inn for the remainder of the day and night. Brother Brigham was very sick and obliged to go to bed. I sat up and waited upon him, and spent the evening with the [282] landlord and his lady, preaching to them; they received our testimony and were very kind to us.

"The next morning we took stage, and started on our way towards Kirtland.

While in Pleasant Garden we obtained some money, so that with the five dollars we had left when the brethren left us on the 18th it amounted to $13.50. When we got into the stage we did not expect to ride many miles. We rode as far as Indianapolis, paid our passage, and found we had sufficient means to carry us to Richmond, Indiana.

"When we arrived at Richmond we found we had means to take us to Dayton, to which place we proceeded and tarried over night, waiting for another line of stages. We expected to stop here and preach until we got means to pursue our journey. Brother Brigham went to his trunk to get money to pay the bill, and found we had sufficient to pay our passages to Columbus, to which place we took passage in the stage and tarried over night. When he paid the bill he found he had sufficient means to pay our passage to Worcester. We tarried till the after part of the day and then took passage to Worcester. When we arrived there, Brother Brigham went to his trunk again to get money to pay our bill, and found sufficient to pay our passages to Cleveland. When we reached a little town called Strongsville, about twenty miles from Cleveland, towards evening, Brother Brigham had a strong impression to stop at a tavern when we first came into the town; but the stage did not stop there, so we went on. We arrived at Cleveland about 11 o'clock at night, took lodgings, and remained till next morning.

"Nov. 3rd, being Sunday, in the morning we went to the Episcopalian church. While returning to the hotel we met my father-in-law, and learned that Elders Turley, [283] Smith and Hedlock had just arrived in Cleveland. Father Murray was as much astonished to see me alive as though he had seen one risen from the dead. I don't think I ever saw a man feel better than he did when I met him in the street. We walked with him a short distance, and met the brethren who were in good health, compared with what they had been, and in fine spirits. We learned that they stopped at the tavern in Strongsville, where Brother Brigham had such strong impressions to stop the night previous. They had picked up Elder John Taylor, at Dayton, where he was left at a tavern very sick with the ague and fever a few days before, by Father Coltrin, who proceeded to Kirtland.

"Brothers Taylor and Hedlock got into the stage with us, which left early in the afternoon; they rode as far as Willoughby. We proceeded to Kirtland and arrived the same evening, thus fulfilling the prediction made on my sick bed.

"Brother Brigham had one York shilling left, and on looking over our expenses we found we had paid out over $87.00 out of the $13.50 we had at Pleasant Garden, which is all the money we had to pay our passages with. We had traveled over 400 miles by stage, for which we paid from 8 to 10 cents a mile, and had eaten three meals a day, for each of which we were charged fifty cents, also fifty cents for our lodgings. Brother Brigham often suspected that I put the money in his trunk, or clothes; thinking that I had a purse of money which I had not acquainted him with; but this was not so; the money could only have been put in his trunk by some heavenly messenger, who thus administered to our necessities daily as he knew we needed.

"I made my home at Dean Gould's at the house of Ira Bond. The family were all very kind to me, and **[284]** made me as comfortable as they could. I remained with them most of the time I was in Kirtland, two days of which I was sick with chills and fever.

"There was a division of sentiment among the brethren in Kirtland, many of whom had lacked the energy to move to Missouri, while some lacked the inclination. On Sunday, Elder Taylor preached in the Temple in the forenoon and I preached in the afternoon. I compared the people there to a parcel of old earthen pots that were cracked in burning, for they were mostly apostates who were living there. Martin Harris, Cyrus Smalling and others were much offended at what I said, and asked me whom I referred to in my comparisons. 'No one in particular,' said I, 'but to anyone whom the coat fits.' John Moreton and others declared I should never preach in the house again. On the Sunday following, Brother Brigham and Brother Taylor were the speakers.

"While we tarried, a council was held with Brothers Kellogg, Moreton and others who took the lead in Kirtland. We proposed that some of the Elders should remain there and preach for a few weeks. John Moreton replied that they had had many talented preachers, and he considered that men of such ordinary talents as were on this mission could do no good in Kirtland. He thought probably Brother John Taylor might do, but he was not sure." **[285]**

## CHAPTER 39

THE APOSTLES SAIL FOR ENGLAND—GROWTH OF THE BRITISH MISSION DURING HEBER'S ABSENCE—LABORS OF ELDERS WOODRUFF AND TAYLOR—FIRST COUNCIL OF THE TWELVE AMONG THE NATIONS—WILLARD RICHARDS ORDAINED AN APOSTLE

JOURNEYING eastward, the Apostles arrived in New York, where they tarried for some time, preaching the Gospel and adding new members to the Church in that city. On the 19th of December, 1840, Apostles John Taylor and Wilford Woodruff, with Elder Theodore Turley and others, sailed for Liverpool on board the *Oxford*. Three months later to a day, Apostles Young and Kimball, Parley P. Pratt, Orson Pratt, George A. Smith and Elder Reuben Hedlock followed in their wake on board the *Patrick Henry*.

After a very stormy passage, they reached Liverpool on the sixth of April, the anniversary of the organization of the Church, ten years before. They there found Elder John Taylor with about thirty Saints who had just received the Gospel in that place. A day or two later they went on to Preston by railroad, where Heber and his companions were warmly welcomed by a multitude of Saints who had assembled there to meet them. They arrived in Preston on the anniversary of Heber's departure in 1838.

It will now be proper to take a brief retrospective view of the progress of the

British Mission during the two years interim between the departure of Elders Kim[286]ball and Hyde for America, and the return of Heber to the scene of his former successful labors. The most important event that had taken place in this interval was the planting of the Gospel standard in the great manufacturing town of Manchester. This opening was made by Elder William Clayton, in October, 1838. The branch in that place grew so rapidly as to soon rival Preston, and in a short time it became the headquarters of the whole British Mission.

Scotland had also been opened by Elders Mulliner and Wright, though the work had as yet taken little root in that land.

In and around Preston and the other towns and villages opened during the first mission of the Elders to England, the work had gradually spread under the presidency of Elders Fielding, Richards and Clayton.

During the stormy period which had just spent its fierceness upon the Saints in America, the Church in England had not escaped persecution, though, compared with the sufferings of the former, the trials of the British Saints were a mere bagatelle. A novel incident connected with the death of one of the Saints—the first death that occurred in the mission—is thus related:

"Sister Alice Hodgin died at Preston, September 2nd, 1838, and it was such a wonderful thing for a Latter-day Saint to die in England that Elder Richards was arraigned before the Mayor's Court at Preston, October 3rd, charged with 'killing and slaying the said Alice with a black stick,' etc., but was discharged without being permitted to make his defense, as soon as it was discovered that the iniquity of his accusers was about to be made manifest.

The arrival of Apostles Taylor and Woodruff at Liverpool on the 11th of January, 1840, opened the [287] second period of the British Mission. They were welcomed by Mr. George Cannon, brother-in-law of Elder Taylor and father of George Q. Cannon, the present Apostle, then a mere youth, and not yet connected with the cause in which he was destined to play so important a part. Sunday they spent in Liverpool, and the next day proceeded on to Preston.

At a council held at the house of Willard Richards, after the arrival of these Apostles, it was arranged that Elders John Taylor and Joseph Fielding should go to Liverpool, and lift the standard of Mormonism in that important city; Hyrum Clark to Manchester, where Elder Clayton was given charge of Church affairs; and Wilford Woodruff and Theodore Turley to the Potteries in Staffordshire, and to Birmingham if the Spirit so led. Elder Richards was to have the privilege of "moving wherever the Spirit directed." The Elders were instructed to report to their respective presidents.

On the following day, January 18th, after meeting and blessing each other, the brethren separated and departed for their various fields of labor.

The marvelous success of Apostle Woodruff in Staffordshire and Herefordshire, in the latter of which counties, in a little over one month, he converted several hundred souls, including upwards of forty preachers of the United Brethren; with the important labors of Elder Taylor in Liverpool and vicinity, and of Elder Turley in Birmingham, (which town became a Mormon stronghold second only in importance to London) would fill a volume in themselves. We can barely glance at such achievements in following the individual history of Heber C. Kimball.

Immediately upon the arrival of President Young and the Apostles who accompanied him, a council of the **[288]** Twelve and a conference of the Saints was called to convene at Preston on the 14th of April.

At this gathering there were present of the Apostles, Brigham Young, Heber C. Kimball, Parley P. Pratt, Orson Pratt, John Taylor, Wilford Woodruff and George A. Smith. Brigham Young was called to the chair, and was unanimously sustained as the standing President of the Twelve. Willard Richards was ordained an Apostle and added to the quorum by unanimous voice, and according to previous appointment by revelation.

It was moved by Heber C. Kimball and seconded by Willard Richards that twenty of the Seventies, or more at the discretion of the President, be sent for to assist in the work of the ministry.

On the second day of the council Heber C. Kimball was the presiding Apostle. The various branches of the Church in England and Scotland were represented, showing an aggregate membership of 1671 souls, including the Priesthood. The official numbers were as follows: Elders, 34; Priests, 52; Teachers, 38; Deacons, 8. Total of Priesthood, 132. President Kimball laid before the meeting the importance and propriety of ordaining a Patriarch to give patriarchal blessings to the Saints, and Bleazard Corbridge was accordingly chosen for that office.

It was decided that the Saints who wished to emigrate should receive recommends from the Church in Britain to the Church in America, and that no persons should receive such recommends who had money, unless they assisted the poor according to the counsel of the Twelve.

It was further determined that a monthly periodical be published, to be known as *The Latter-day Saints' Millennial Star*, with Parley P. Pratt as its editor; and that **[289]** a committee of three, namely, Brigham Young, Parley P. Pratt and John Taylor be appointed to make a selection of hymns for the use of the Saints.

The conference closed on the 16th of April, having been in session three days.

The time had now come for the Apostles to separate, to go into different parts of the Lord's vineyard. It was thought wisdom for Elder Heber C. Kimball to visit the churches which he had built up while in England on his former mission; for Orson Pratt to go north on a mission to Scotland, John Taylor to continue his labors in Liverpool, Parley P. Pratt to proceed to Manchester to begin the publication of the *Star*, George A. Smith to go into the Potteries, and Brigham Young and Willard Richards to accompany Elder Woodruff into his field of labor. These arrangements were at once carried out by the brethren, and the work spread on every hand, with redoubled energy and multiplied success. **[290]**

# CHAPTER 40

HEBER VISITS THE BRANCHES RAISED UP DURING HIS FORMER MISSION—HIS REPORT OF THEIR CONDITION AND STANDING—FIRST GENERAL CONFERENCE AT MANCHESTER

PURSUANT to the appointment of his quorum at the conference, Heber visited the Saints whom he had brought into the Church during his former mission. Elder Willard Richards accompanied him, pending preparations for his mission to Herefordshire.

They first visited the branch in Walkerfold, the home of the Rev. John Richards, whose daughter Jennetta Willard had married, in fulfillment of Heber's prediction. They found Sister Richards in a very low state of health, but after they had anointed and laid hands upon her, according to the ordinance of the Church, she immediately began to amend.

The Reverend Mr. Richards, who was feeling very sorely the effects of the preaching of Mormonism in his pastorate, on seeing Elder Kimball in his house, ordered him to leave. Heber meekly complied, much to the grief of Sister Richards and her aged mother, who wept aloud at his departure. The Walkerfold branch, though small, had suffered more persecution in proportion to its numbers than any other, but its members, with scarcely an exception, had remained steadfast in the faith.

Heber's report continues:

"From thence we returned to Preston, where I left Brother Richards to prepare for his mission to Herefordshire, and proceeded from thence to Dauber's Lane and Eggleston. We found there two branches rejoicing in [291] the Lord. After a short visit with them, I returned to Preston; and after two days I started on a visit to the north. I went alone, by way of Walkerfold, on my way to Clithero, where I held meetings on the Sabbath, and administered the sacrament to nearly two hundred Saints. It was a time of refreshing to them and to myself, as I had not seen them for more than two years. It had been said there, as in other places, that I would never return to them again; but they now saw me again, and knew that myself and many of my fellow laborers had come; and that our message and our zeal were the same as formerly, and therefore I was received with greater joy than ever. I stayed at Elder T. Smith's, where on Monday I was joined by Elder Fielding from Preston.

"On Wednesday we went to Chatburn and held meeting in the evening. There was great joy in the place. The next day we went to Downham and held meeting that evening and many came to hear. We bore testimony to the Gospel, and of the work of the Lord in these last days. The people were very attentive. When we had closed, a certain man wished to ask a few questions; he appeared much agitated; in fact we were reminded of the prediction in the Book of Mormon, that 'men would anger and tremble because of the truth.' He demanded some evidence of the truth of the Gospel, or message, of which we testified; but would not tell us what evidence would satisfy him, so we could only repeat our testimony to him, and let him go, with no other evidence than what ourselves and tens of thousands of others had believed and were satisfied with. The Saints had a time of rejoicing. On Saturday we returned to Chatburn and held meeting, after which three persons were baptized and added to the Church. On the Sabbath the meeting was held in a large barn, no house [292] being sufficiently large to convene the people. There were many to hear, who were very attentive. We ordained two Priests. In the evening four others were baptized. Some who had left the society, wished they had been faithful, and some of them returned by humble repentance and being re-baptized. There appears to be something peculiar in the people of this place; others had tried in vain to enlist them into their folds; but on hearing the first preaching of the fullness of the Gospel they were overwhelmed in tears of repentance, and more than twenty were immediately baptized. It is a small village, but the number of members soon increased to about ninety. They have mostly stood fast. We have never received anything like an insult all the time we visited the place, and we feel bound to bless them.

"On Monday we returned to Clithero; after meeting five more were baptized. On Tuesday evening two were baptized in Waddington. Since then we have heard that eight more have been baptized, and others ready.

"The next day we started for Ribchester, calling at Walkerfold on our way, where we found Sister Richards in good health. We reached Ribchester on Friday, and held meeting in the evening; the Saints were comforted. The next day we returned to Preston. I consider that I have never seen the Saints in better spirits. They say it seems like old times; they can receive their patriarchal blessings under the hand of Brother Mellin, as he is ordained to the office of an Evangelist. Some speak in tongues and prophesy, and others have visions, etc., as was foretold by the Prophet Joel, concerning the last days. We can truly say the Lord has begun to restore all things, as spoken by the prophets.

"After this we went to Longton, and held meeting, and the next day started for Southport, many of the [293] brethren accompanying us as far as the river Astlam. There was no bridge, and to save us the trouble of going round, a brother carried us over on his shoulders. We held one meeting in Southport, and one in Churchtown. At Southport there was a sister sick and not expected to live. She was healed by administering the ordinance, and next day she went with us two miles on foot. We ordained one Elder and one Teacher, and on our way back preached to the Saints in Longton, exhorting them to have their lamps trimmed and burning, ready to go forth to meet the Bridegroom. We then returned to Preston. On Saturday we met the officers in council, and on the Sabbath met with the Church as usual.

"On Monday evening a number of the Saints met at Brother T. Moon's, in Penwortham, to receive their patriarchal blessings. We were with them, and gave them such instruction as was necessary.

"Wednesday, I accompanied Elder Clayton to Manchester; found Elders Young, P. P. Pratt and J. Taylor there; tarried there with them till Saturday the

30th, when Elders Young, Taylor and myself took the train for Liverpool; met with the Church there on the Sabbath, and had a good time, the Saints rejoiced, and others believed.

"A number of the Saints had taken their passage for America on board the ship *Britannia*. We spent some time with them for several days. June 5th we took leave of them. They were in good spirits, expecting to move from the dock at 2 p. m. We blessed them, and commended them to the Lord. I then took leave of Elders Young and Taylor, and returned by train to Preston. I found Brother Fielding and the Saints rejoicing in the Lord. At this time I can truly say that I never felt more to rejoice than I have done in my late visits to **[294]** the churches. The Saints, in general, as they have been baptized into one body, are partakers of one spirit, whether they be Jew or Gentile, bond or free. I also take this opportunity to say, that I have lately received a letter from my wife, giving us good tidings from America. The work is moving steadily, but not slowly through that land, bearing on its way through the states and cities of that vast continent. The Saints are getting over their pains and sufferings, at least in a great measure, and are enjoying health. I would say to my brethren in the ministry that their families are well, and I feel to congratulate them on the hope and glorious prospect of one day not far remote when we shall rest from our labors in the kingdom of God. It is evident our labor is not in vain in the Lord. In almost every branch I have visited the numbers are increasing. The stone is actually growing into a mountain, and we know that it must soon fill the whole earth. May the Lord hasten the time. Amen."

Heber rejoined his quorum at Manchester, where a general conference convened on the sixth of July. The meetings were held in "Carpenter's Hall," a building almost as famous in the history of the British Mission as the celebrated "Cock Pit" in Preston.

The Apostles in the mission were all present excepting Orson Pratt, who was in Edinburgh, unable to attend on account of the great distance, and his arduous labors in opening the Scottish Mission. Parley P. Pratt was chosen to preside.

The new hymn-book was introduced and received the unanimous approbation of the meeting. A number of brethren were ordained to the ministry and then President Young called upon those officers whose circumstances would permit them to devote themselves entirely **[295]** to the work of the ministry, and who would volunteer to do so, to stand up, when the following names were taken: B. Young, H. C. Kimball, John Taylor, Wilford Woodruff, Willard Richards, G. A. Smith, Wm. Clayton, Reuben Hedlock, H. Clark, Theodore Turley, Joseph Fielding, Thomas Richardson, Amos Fielding, John Parkinson, John Wytch, John Needham, H. Royle, John Blezard, D. Wilding, Charles Price, Joseph Knowles, William Kay, Samuel Heath, Wm. Parr, R. McBride and James Morgan.

President Fielding and his counselors were relieved of the charge of presiding over the mission, and several Elders were appointed to various fields of labor in England, Scotland and Ireland.

President Young gave administrative directions to the Elders previous to their separation. He then blessed the congregation and the conference adjourned. [296]

## CHAPTER 41

FOUNDING THE LONDON CONFERENCE—APOSTLES KIMBALL, WOODRUFF AND SMITH CHOSEN FOR THE WORK—SEEKING FOR A MAN WITH THE SPIRIT OF GOD—THE FIRST CONVERT—THE ELDERS HOLD OPEN-AIR MEETINGS IN TABERNACLE SQUARE

THE next notable movement determined on by the Apostles was the founding of the London Conference. The men chosen for this work were Heber C. Kimball, Wilford Woodruff and George A. Smith. Leaving Manchester on the 4th of August, Heber joined his companions in Herefordshire, whence the three proceeded on to London, preaching and baptizing by the way.

They reached their destination about four o'clock in the afternoon of the 18th, and were kindly received by a Mrs. Allgood, of No. 19, King Street, Borough, who gave them needed refreshments and directed them to lodgings in the neighborhood. Two days later they reported to the *Millennial Star* as follows:

"We are well and in good spirits, and are going to see the people in different parts, and see what we can do in this small world; for London looks like a small world. Give us your prayers and direct your letters as above."

It was well ordered that three such characters as these, with their indomitable will power and perseverance, added to child-like faith and humility, were sent to break Gospel ground in the British Metropolis. The task was no easy one. London, with all its churches [297] and cathedrals, its high-priced ministers and princely churchmen, its Bibles, missions, schools, and evangelical agencies of every description, was the devil's stronghold, nevertheless; and the prospect might have dismayed, with its hardships, spirits less valiant, souls less faithful, than those selected for the ordeal.

For days the Apostles wandered through the streets of the great city, viewing its wonderful sights, visiting its places of interest and historic note, and all the while looking for an opportunity to deliver their message, and for souls to receive their testimony. Among other places they went to "Zion's Chapel" and heard the Reverend Robert Aitken, the same great preacher from whom Heber, on his former mission, had won so many disciples in Preston. They were profoundly impressed with his eloquence and the sublime truths he uttered, but to them his efforts were those of one who was "building without the foundation." They had previously heard an Aitkenite preacher at Union Chapel, Waterloo Road, and had also called on the Reverend J. E. Smith, of Lincoln's-Inn-Fields, their object being to find an opening for their ministry.

Still following very much the example of Heber's first mission to England, the three Elders next attended a meeting of the Temperance Society in Temperance Hall, St. George's Row, near the Elephant Castle. Here Elder George A. Smith was given the privilege of making a short speech. It was the first public effort of a Mormon Elder in London, though it was more in the nature of a temperance testimony than the introduction of Mormonism to the metropolis. Subsequently the brethren addressed another meeting at the same place on the subject of temperance, and succeeded in engaging the hall for preaching purposes, though they **[298]** were not permitted to occupy it immediately. They gave out an appointment to preach the Gospel there on the 7th of September.

One day, as they were strolling through the streets, "to see if they could find a man with the Spirit of God," Heber accosted an amiable looking stranger and asked him if he was a preacher. He replied that he was, and informed the brethren that he had been in America, and had come to London for the purpose of going to South Australia; but had suffered much from sickness in his family, having just buried one child, while another was then lying at the point of death.

"Your child shall live," said Heber C. Kimball.

The stranger then gave them some information in regard to places for preaching, and they parted from him. On the same day they called at his house; he was not at home, but his child was better.

The next day the servants of the Lord went again over the city. This time they found the object of their search; "a man in whom was the Spirit." His name was Corner. He lived at No. 52 Ironmonger Row, St. Luke's Parish, near the Church. He and his household received the testimony of the Elders and opened their doors for the preaching of the Gospel.

This, however, was not enough; though the brethren praised God for this manifestation of His favor. They longed to reach the ears of the multitude, and declare to them the message that "burned like fire in their bones." At the expiration of twelve days, finding no immediate prospect for an indoor opening of the kind they were in quest of, they determined to go into the streets and lift up their voices.

It was Sunday morning, August 30th, 1840. Wending their way through the crowded streets and winding **[299]** thoroughfares, in search of some public place where they knew the common people were wont to assemble on the Sabbath, to hear all sorts of harangues from all sorts of speakers, the three Apostles, after walking three miles, stopped in Tabernacle Square, "Old Street." A promiscuous assembly had gathered there—men of all creeds and opinions—and an "open-air" meeting was in progress. It was an Aitkenite preacher who was addressing them. Mixing with the multitude, the Elders listened respectfully to what he was saying, and gradually edged their way towards the spot where he was standing.

When the Aitkenite minister had concluded his discourse a Presbyterian preacher took his place and was about to begin.

"Sir!" exclaimed a voice in the crowd, addressing the preacher. All eyes were turned in the direction of the sound. A man stepped forward. It was Heber C. Kimball. "Sir," he said, "There is a preacher from America present, who would like to speak to the assembly when you have got through your service."

The Presbyterian, not to be outdone in courtesy, and perhaps proud of the honor of introducing an American preacher to a British public, addressing the people, said:

"I am informed that there is a minister from America present. I propose that he shall speak first."

The proposition was readily accepted, and the people drew near, alive with curiosity at the novelty of hearing a preacher from America.

Apostle George A Smith was the one selected for the occasion. He mounted the chair resigned by the Presbyterian, and addressed the audience for about twenty minutes. [300]

Next came the Presbyterian, and at the close of his remarks Heber C. Kimball again advanced.

"Will there be any objection to our preaching here at 3 o'clock"? he inquired.

"No; not at all," answered the Presbyterian. "What denomination do you belong to"?

"To the Church of Jesus Christ of Latter-day Saints," Heber replied.

"Oh, I have heard of them," exclaimed the Presbyterian quickly, his countenance and whole manner changing. "They are a bad people; they have done much hurt; they divide churches; we don't want to hear you."

He then mounted the chair again and said to the people:

"I have just heard that the last man who spoke belongs to the Latter-day Saints." And then he began to rail against the Apostles and their faith.

After he had thus vented himself, Elder Kimball mildly inquired:

"Will you let me step into the chair to give out an appointment for a 3 o'clock meeting?"

But the minister angrily refused, whereupon Heber raised his voice and informed the people that some American preachers would preach there at 3 o'clock.

A vast congregation assembled at the appointed hour to hear them, the conduct of the Presbyterian and the excitement of the morning having helped to increase it materially.

Elder Wilford Woodruff was the first preacher. After singing and prayer, he read from the first chapter of Paul's Epistle to the Galatians, the 8th and 9th. verses;

"But though we, or an angel from heaven, preach any other Gospel unto you than that which we have preached unto you, let him be accursed. [301]

"As we said before, so say I now again, if any man preach any other Gospel unto you than that ye have received, let him be accursed."

A direct thrust at apostate Christendom, with its multitudinous variety of "other gospels," all differing from each other and from the great original.

Brother Woodruff did not fail that day to hold them up a glass wherein they might see the "inmost parts" of Paul's dread meaning, made applicable in words of telling force to the Christian denominations of that great city.

Then came Heber C. Kimball with his sledge-hammer blows of testimony, driving home the truth of the Apostle's words, as with a mallet of mighty power. He told them of the great apostasy that had taken place since the days of Paul, and of the restoration of the Gospel in the latter days, closing with an earnest testimony to the divine mission of Joseph Smith, the great Prophet whom God had raised up in the land of America.

The people gave good attention and seemed much interested in what they had heard.

After the meeting Mr. Corner, the person already noticed, invited the three Apostles home to his house; so, withdrawing from the crowd, they went to 52 Ironmonger Row, St Luke's Parish.

But Heber was not yet satisfied. The inward monitor which he knew never erred told him that his day's labor was not accomplished. Scarce knowing why, but surrendering himself to the dictates of the Spirit, he retraced his steps and wended his way alone back to Tabernacle Square, leaving Elders Woodruff and Smith at "Father Corner's," conversing on the things of the Kingdom.

The crowd had not yet dispersed from the Square, but stood in groups here and there, discussing eagerly [302] the events of the day, and the strange things told them by the American preachers. As Heber approached he was immediately recognized—and, indeed, his was a presence, once seen, not easily to be forgotten—and the surprised and pleased multitude, thronging round him, besought him to speak to them again.

He willingly complied and addressed them long and earnestly. More powerful than ever was his testimony. He was alone, but the Spirit was with him, and with the Spirit Heber C. Kimball was a host. Breathlessly they listened, and at the close several men whom he had never seen until that afternoon, came forward and invited him home to their houses.

The ice was broken. His testimony had prevailed. The good seed sown by the wayside had taken root, as it were, in the very crevices of the stony pavements of the world's metropolis. [303]

## CHAPTER 12

FATHER CORNER BAPTIZED—THE APOSTLES VISIT THE REVEREND ROBERT AITKEN—HEBER ATTACKED WITH CHOLERA—THE WORK IN OTHER PARTS—SECOND CONFERENCE AT MANCHESTER—BRIGHAM ACCOMPANIES HEBER TO LONDON—CONVERSION OF THE REV. JAMES ALBION

THE first baptism in London took place on Monday the 31st of August, the day following the events related in the last chapter. It was "Father Corner" who offered himself as a convert to the Elders, and it was Heber C. Kimball who baptized him. The ceremony was performed at the Public Baths, after which the new member was confirmed under the hands of the three Apostles at his own house.

Thus was laid the foundation of the London Conference.

Leaving Elder Woodruff for several days, Heber and George A. went to

Deptford, for the purpose of establishing a branch there. While they were gone, Brother Woodruff made the second convert—a woman. He also obtained from the directors of a Methodist chapel permission to preach in a school-house at Bowl Court, Shoreditch.

Sunday morning, September 6th, the Apostles filled the appointment made by Elder Woodruff, who preached first, followed by Elders Kimball and Smith. These were the first gospel sermons delivered by the Elders in a meeting house in London, though they had each [304] addressed an audience briefly, at Temperance Hall, on the subject of temperance.

In the afternoon they preached again out of doors in Tabernacle square; and in the evening returned to preach in the Methodist school house. When they arrived, however, they discovered that a plan had been formed by several preachers of that denomination for one of their own number to occupy the evening, fearing lest some should receive the testimony of these "dangerous men" from America. Already had the Methodists of London taken the alarm.

Discovering this ministerial intrigue against them the three Apostles went their way, but that evening they found four persons who received their testimony and offered themselves for baptism.

On the Monday following, Heber and George A. visited the celebrated Robert Aitken. He received them courteously, and acknowledged that their doctrines were scriptural, but said he was fearful of deception. At this period he was in a very disturbed state of mind concerning Mormonism, for the mission which the Apostles brought from America seemed so much like a surprise-fulfillment to him of the glowing sermons of his own ministry. Probably Mormonism troubled Robert Aitken more than it did any other man in England, and it is not a little singular that soon afterwards he returned to the Orthodox Established Church from which he had dissented, and became again one of its ministers.

On the evening of the day they visited the Rev. Mr. Aitken the Elders opened their course of sermons in Temperance Hall, St. George's Road, but they had no audience worthy the occasion. About thirty only were said to be present; but Apostle Woodruff preached to them for over an hour, and then Heber followed. At the close [305] they paid "seven and sixpence" for the hall for the evening—a large sum from the pockets of these Evangelists at that time, yet they trusted in the Lord for future results.

Thus having made an opening in London, Wilford Woodruff returned a while to superintend his former field of labor; but Heber C. Kimball and George A. Smith remained to hold the situation.

On the 19th of September Heber was stricken down with cholera. The attack was so severe that it seemed as if he could not live till morning. He rallied, however, and by the blessing of God was raised up to continue his labors. The next morning, being the Sabbath, he went into the water and baptized four persons.

Meanwhile the work in other parts had been making rapid headway. After much labor it had at length been firmly established in Scotland, under the presidency of Orson Pratt; and had been carried into Ireland and the Isle of Man by Apostle John Taylor. Several of the native Elders had also penetrated Wales. President Brigham Young, in the absence of Parley P. Pratt, who had gone to America to bring his family to England, had been busy publishing the *Millennial Star*, the hymn book and Book of Mormon, in which labors he was assisted by Willard Richards. The emigration of the Saints to America had also commenced. Thus was the good work rolling on.

On the 6th of October, 1840, was held the second general conference at Manchester. There were present of the Twelve, Brigham Young, Heber C. Kimball, Willard Richards, Orson Pratt, George A. Smith, and Wilford Woodruff. Orson Pratt presided.

It was found that twenty-seven conferences had been **[306]** organized at this period, besides many branches not then incorporated. The representation showed an increase since the last general conference of one thousand one hundred and thirteen members; twenty-five Elders; ninety-six Priests; fifteen Teachers, and thirteen Deacons. Several places of special interest may be noted as represented: London, by Heber C. Kimball; members, eleven, Priests, two; Birmingham, four members; Glasgow, by Elder Mulliner, one hundred and ninety-three members, eight Elders, seven Priests, five teachers and three Deacons; Edinburgh,. by Orson Pratt, forty-three members and two Priests; Manchester, by Brigham Young, members, three hundred and sixty-four; Elders, four; Priests, twenty-seven; Teachers, six; and one Deacon; Wilford Woodruffs Conferences, members, one thousand and seven; Elders, nineteen; Priests, seventy-eight; Teachers, fifteen, and one Deacon. Altogether three thousand, six hundred and twenty-six members of the Church were represented, more than double the number reported at the Conference six months before.

After this Conference Elders Woodruff and Smith returned to London, while Heber remained for a time with President Young in Manchester, waiting to accompany him to the metropolis; the latter having resolved to visit London and assist his co-laborers in the arduous work of building up that important conference.

The two Apostles set out upon their journey on the 25th of November, 1840. On their way they stopped at the Potteries in Staffordshire, where they met Elder George A. Smith, who was paying a visit to his former field of labor, having left Brother Woodruff in London. They also went to Birmingham, where Elder Lorenzo Snow was then laboring. On the 30th they took train for London, and arrived there the same evening. **[307]**

They found Brother Woodruff "well and in good spirits," but with a tale to tell of his experience since he saw them last, "whose lightest word" was well calculated to "harrow up the soul."

It will be remembered that Heber C. Kimball and his confreres, who opened the British Mission in 1837, had a terrible encounter with evil spirits on the day of the first baptisms in Preston. A similar ordeal had been experienced by Apostle Woodruff on the night of the first Sabbath after his return from Manchester.

Himself and Elder Smith had held a sacrament meeting that day at Father Corner's, with a few Saints who had gathered there, during which "the Spirit bore testimony that there would be a great work done in London."

Satan, it seems, was also aware of this fact, and it displeased him mightily.

That night, while lying in his bed, meditating upon the mission in that city and determining to warn its inhabitants, and "overcome the powers of darkness," a personage appeared to the Apostle Wilford whom he took to be the "Prince of darkness." "He made war with me," says the Apostle, "and attempted to take my life. As he was about to overcome me I prayed to the Father in the name of Jesus Christ for help. I then had power over him, and he left me, though much wounded. Afterwards three persons, dressed in white, came to me and administered to me, when I was immediately healed and delivered of all my troubles."

Such, in brief, was the thrilling tale told by Apostle Woodruff to his fellow servants in Christ, on their arrival in the British capital.

The next evening, December 1st, President Young preached his first sermon in London at Barnett's Acad[308]emy, 57 King's Square, Goswell Road. Heber C. Kimball followed him. The President remained about ten days in London, and then returned to Manchester.

In a letter to his wife, written about this time, Heber gives somewhat of a detailed account of the President's visit to the metropolis, and other events that were happening in different parts of the mission:

LONDON, December 3rd, 1840.

MY DEAR VILATE:—

"I feel to rejoice to hear from you once more. Elders Young and Woodruff and myself have been traveling all day to see some of the sights of this great city. We visited the Tower of London. We entered into one room 150 feet by 33; there, arranged in regular and chronological order, were no less in number than twenty-two equestrian figures, representing many of the most celebrated kings of England, accompanied by their favorite lords and men of rank, all of them, together with their horses, in the armor of the respective periods when they flourished,—many, indeed, in the identical suits in which they appeared while living, There were 500,000 stands of arms, and cannon, taken from all parts of the world, in their conflicts with other nations; and all the jewelry and crowns of the kings and queens. I wish you could see them, for we can see better than we can write about them. We went to see the Thames tunnel; from thence returned home to our lodgings. Mrs. Morgan presented me with a letter from you, dated Oct. the 11th.... I felt to rejoice at hearing from you, that you are still alive and in good spirits, and to hear of the good times that you have in Nauvoo, and the good tidings that President Smith is laying before the Saints; I should like to be there if it was right in the sight of God. But I feel no liberty as yet to come home, but I think I shall soon. I want to see you and my little children, and I want to see Brother Joseph, Brother Rigdon and Brother Hyrum, and all of my old friends [309] that have gained my affections, that have stood through thick and thin, through evil reports as well as good; they are the ones that I wish to live with on earth, and I believe I shall; for I have no desire for anything else but to press forward for the celestial world. I don't expect to find much rest this side of that, but I feel to prepare for the worst and hope for the better. I have strong sensations of what is coming on the earth. I shall not be disappointed if I get home about the time to have a little sport with my brethren. As you say, a hint to the wise is sufficient. I am sorry to hear that some of our brethren have denied the faith, that is, some of them that went from this country, but it is just what I expected, and told them so; they thought they were going to be fostered by the Church in that place; they might have known better, for they knew the Saints had been driven, and robbed of all their goods, and they could not expect help from them, but rather the reverse. I don't know but they think it will hinder the work of the Lord if they turn away; they are mistaken there, for it will advance the work just as much for them to turn away as it will for them to remain; so it is all the same with the Lord. The Savior says we cannot do anything against the truth, but for it. I have got so I feel perfectly easy about these things, for they are the work of God and not the work of man. I know no other way than to be subject to the powers that be. I pray my Father will give me this disposition, for I wish to be in the hand of God as the clay in the hands of the potter. The Lord has His own way of doing His own work, and we have got to submit to Him instead of His submitting to us. I feel well in mind—never felt better in my day—but I am afflicted in body with bad colds. The weather is cold and wet, and the smoke is so bad some of the time that they have to light up their lamps in the middle of the day, it is so dark. It is very unhealthy for me, and it is so for my brethren. Times grow worse and worse in this country; the people are driven almost to desperation; the times appear sad and gloomy. I had some conversation with a Frenchman the other evening; he says it is hard times in France; all **[310]** lands seem to share in the same fate; distress on all sides.

"I will begin where I left off at Liverpool on the 31st. I stated to you that Elder Young and myself were going to Wales. This was on Saturday,—the distance of twenty miles, seven miles by steamboat, and the rest by coach. Got there in the evening—at the town of Harder. On the Sabbath we preached twice; had as many as could hear us; it appeared that everyone believed our testimony. We were called to pray for the sick. One young man lay sick with the fever, and a Methodist preacher received a blessing, and one woman. They were healed, and began to proclaim it aloud to be the power of God. Sunday was the 1st day of November; on the 2nd we started back to Manchester by the way of Lynn; there were some baptized the day we left. I heard there were about thirty others ready to go forward the first opportunity. The six Methodist preachers that sent for us are going to be baptized if they have not been already. There has another work broke out in Wales, fourteen miles from the place where we went. The last news we had from them, there were fifty-two baptized. We received a line from Elder Pratt yesterday, stating that there were about ninety baptized in those two places. After we got to Manchester on the 5th, I took coach for Clithero in Yorkshire, thirty miles distant.

I preached four times in Clithero, once in Waddington, once in Chatburn, once in Downham. I remained with them six days, and baptized several while there. In a few weeks' time there have been about forty baptized; these are some of them from the old churches; the excitement seems to be as great as it was when I first went into that place. There were scores that believed my testimony that had formerly been much opposed to this work. The opposition is great in that part. They collected in mobs to break up my meetings, but did not carry their designs into execution. The devil is mad, and the work spreads in all parts. They are publishing pamphlets in all directions, and the papers are full of all kinds of lies. If things continue as they [311] have for a short time past, we shall be driven from this country. In the places that I have mentioned the spirit has been poured out upon them; they speak in tongues, interpret, prophesy, dream dreams, see visions, and there seems to be great humility. There seems to be a revival through this land....

"On the 25th of November Elder Young and myself started for London. I felt quite feeble when we started. I will continue my epistle from the 5th of December. The day we started we went twenty miles to Macklesfield, and stayed all night. There is a church of nearly one hundred members there. It is a silk manufacturing town of about 60,000 inhabitants. The next morning we went to the potteries; stayed two nights; preached to the Saints; the world's people came in throngs; they acted more like devils than like men. There are many coming into the Church in this place. The gifts are among the Saints; this makes the devil mad. Many are turned out of their work because of their religion. Many go hungry and look pale for the want of a little food to eat. When I have a penny in my pocket it goes freely. I have taken pains to ask them; some tell me they have not half enough to eat—and have a little child to the breast at the same time. These things are hard. I will stop, for I cannot paint the scenes that are before me daily; these things grow worse and worse. From there we went to Birmingham; found Elder Snow; on Sunday evening heard him preach for the first time. After he got through Elder Young and myself bore testimony. The Saints felt to rejoice, and some believed. There are 300,000 inhabitants in that city and only eighteen Saints....

"Sunday, the 6th. I have been to St. Paul's Church this forenoon with the brethren. It was so dark they had to light up the church with gas. A considerable part of this letter I have written in the day time, and have had to write by a candle. It is very disagreeable to me, and makes me feel bad and sick. Not one of us feels well. Brother Smith's lungs are very bad; he will not be able [312] to stay in this country. He is at the potteries, where he will remain until he goes home....

"December 12th. You will think I have been lazy since I commenced this. Elder Young left here yesterday for Herefordshire; it was thought best for me to remain here for a short time with Elder Woodruff. The prospect seems to be better than it has been. There was one man baptized this week, and several more are believing. I shall stay here about three weeks if all things go well. Now, my dear Vilate, be of good cheer, for all things will go well; and pray much, and hearken to counsel from those that are over you.... My love to all of the Saints in Christ. Remember me to my little children, and kiss them for me. Oh, how I want to see you all!

I am your husband forever,<br>H. C. KIMBALL.

About this time the Reverend James Albion, an independent minister, with his wife and daughter became favorably impressed with Mormonism. He offered his chapel to Elders Kimball and Woodruff for them to preach in, and told his congregation that he was a Latter-day Saint, and should be baptized, and that they were no longer to consider him their minister unless they followed his example and joined the Saints. This made a great stir among his committee and congregation.

On the evening of the closing Sunday of the year, the Elders preached by appointment of Mr. Albion in his chapel, to the largest congregation they had addressed in London. There were present priests and people of many denominations. While Elder Woodruff was speaking a Wesleyan minister arose and opposed him, "which had a good effect, for the congregation seeing the Spirit he was of, turned against him, and the committee refused him permission to speak there any more." Thus ended the Apostolic labors of the year. [313]

## CHAPTER 13

OPENING OF THE YEAR 1841 IN LONDON—ENCOURAGING SUCCESS OF THE ELDERS—HEBER C. KIMBALL BLESSES THE QUEEN OF ENGLAND—THE WOOLWICH BRANCH ORGANIZED—ORGANIZATION OF THE LONDON CONFERENCE—THE PROSPECT OF WAR BETWEEN GREAT BRITAIN AND THE UNITED STATES HASTENS THE RETURN OF THE APOSTLES TO AMERICA

THE new year opened auspiciously for the work of God in the great city of London. On the first of January, the Church there numbered twenty-one souls, and ere another day had dawned two more were added unto the fold of Christ.

As usual the converts were mostly of the poor and lowly classes, willing indeed to share their last crust with the Lord's servants, who had sacrificed so much to bring the Gospel to their doors, but unable, in their extreme poverty, to render much assistance in a pecuniary way. Everything was dear in London. While exercising the most rigid economy the Elders found it impossible to subsist upon much less than a pound per week, individually. They had hired lodgings at No. 40, Ironmonger Row, near Father Corner's, and were keeping up a regular meeting house,—the Academy in Goswell Road. Never before were they so straitened financially.

But conversions and baptisms were becoming more frequent, and the clouds of discouragement which had so long hung over them, were beginning to clear away.

Apostle Woodruff baptized the daughter of the Reverend James Albion, who had been so friendly to [314] the Elders, and soon afterwards Heber C. Kimball baptized the minister himself.

Heber visited Woolwich, where he preached once and converted four persons, who immediately offered themselves for baptism. They wandered up and down the Thames until 9 o'clock at night, seeking for a suitable place to administer the ordinance, but were unsuccessful owing to the mud and ice on the banks of the river. Next day Heber brought his converts to London and baptized them at the public baths in Tabernacle Square. Dr. William Copeland was also baptized that day.

Concerning this time, Heber writes:

"The waters have begun to be troubled, and I pray that they may continue until the Lord gathers out His people from this city, I can say I never felt a greater desire for a place than I have for London; it is the metropolis of the world and the depot of wickedness. All manner of debauchery that can be thought of is practiced here.

"But the ice is broken in London, and the Gospel has got such a hold that the devil can not root it out."

Satan, however, continued to do all that he could in opposition to the Elders, by stirring up the wrath of sectarian priests and bigoted people against them.

It seems that prior to starting on this mission, Heber had been promised by the Prophet that he should see the Queen of England. The fulfillment occurred as follows: On the 26th of January Victoria opened the British Parliament. Apostles Kimball and Woodruff, with Dr. Copeland and several other friends, started out for the purpose of witnessing the royal pageant. Arriving at St. James' Park at 10 a. m., they beheld an immense concourse of people, extending in two [315] unbroken lines from Buckingham Palace to the House of Lords. It was estimated that from three to four hundred thousand people were assembled. Through the courtesy of one of the Queen's life-guards—and no small favor was it on that day—Heber and his party succeeded in getting a place in the front line, past which the grand procession was to move. The royal cortege passed within ten feet of where they stood, so that they obtained a fair view of Her Majesty, both going to and returning from the Houses of Parliament. The Queen sat in a gorgeous state carriage, drawn by eight cream colored horses, richly caparisoned. At her left hand sat Albert, the Prince Consort. Following were six carriages, each drawn by six horses, containing members of the royal family, lords and nobles.

Says Heber: "We saw her, as the Prophet Joseph had told us. She made a low bow to us, and we returned the compliment. She looked pleasant; small of stature; with blue eyes; an innocent looking woman. Prince Albert is a fine looking man. All things went on pleasantly. No accidents."

It was on this occasion that Heber C. Kimball blessed Queen Victoria, with the tradition of which so many of the Saints are familiar. Passing so close to them, and seemingly bowing directly and personally to the Apostles, Heber returned the royal salute with a hearty "God bless you," addressed to the Queen as she passed. Her Majesty of course is not aware of the fact that on that day she received an Apostle's benediction, but no one who has noted in faith the prophetic potency of Heber C.

Kimball's words uttered on less occasions, will doubt the efficacy of such a blessing, even on the head of a queen of England.

Baptisms continued in London, and the Elders now **[316]** had good congregations. Heber organized a branch in Woolwich of those whom he had baptized there.

On the 8th of February a package of the Book of Mormon was received, when Elders Kimball and Woodruff went to Stationers' Hall and secured the copyright of the book in the name of Joseph Smith, Jun.

At this time there was a strong probability of war between Great Britain and the United States, and the Elders began to think of returning to their native land. President Young wrote to Heber and Wilford to prepare for an early departure.

The cause of the threatened war was the imprisonment of Mr. McLeod, a British officer, in Lockport jail, New York, which state was trying him for arson; and the Americans seemed resolved on executing him. The case at issue was the burning of the *Caroline* on Lake Erie, in 1837, during the troubles in Canada. Great Britain maintained that he was acting under British orders and demanded his release.

On the 11th of February, Elder Lorenzo Snow arrived in London to take charge of the Church there after the departure of Elders Kimball and Woodruff. Heber and Lorenzo together visited Woolwich, which was fast developing into an important branch, and on their return the first London conference was held in Barnett's Academy.

It was Sunday, February 14th, 1841. On this day the London Conference was organized. There were present at the organization Elders Heber C. Kimball, Wilford Woodruff, Lorenzo Snow, William Pitt and four Priests. The meeting was called to order by Elder Kimball, and after singing and prayer the President called upon the official members to represent their respective branches. They were as follows: **[317]**

The Church at Ipswich, represented by Elder Pitt, consisting of twelve members, one Elder, one Priest and one Teacher.

The Church at Bedford, represented by Robert Williams, Priest, consisting of forty-two members and one Priest; seven had moved and two died.

The Church at Woolwich, represented by John Griffith, Priest, consisting of six members, one Priest.

The Church in London, represented by Elder Kimball, consisting of forty-six members, one Elder, two Priests; generally in good standing; excellent prospect of a continued increase.

James Albion was ordained an Elder; Thomas Barnes a Teacher; R. Williams an Elder to oversee the Church at Bedford; Richard Bates a Priest in the Church at Woolwich; John Sheffield a Teacher in the branch at Bedford and A. Painter a Teacher at Woolwich.

The above named persons were ordained under the hands of Elders Kimball, Woodruff and Snow.

It was then moved by Elder Kimball and seconded by Elder Woodruff, that Elder Lorenzo Snow be appointed President of the London Conference, and also to take the superintendency of the Church in London.

Much valuable instruction was given by Apostles Kimball and Woodruff in relation to the duties of the official members, and the conference then adjourned to Sunday, the 16th of May.

Immediately after the conference Heber started for Manchester to join President Young. He had just received a letter from his wife, Vilate, saying that the Prophet Joseph was very anxious for the return of the Twelve, as both countries were then in the greatest excitement over the prospect of war. As for the Apostles themselves, they could not but realize that their situation [318] as American missionaries was very precarious, and that their immigration of that year was in imminent danger of being interrupted by the British government.

## CHAPTER 44

HEBER ORGANIZES THE BIRMINGHAM CONFERENCE—MEETING OF THE APOSTLES IN MANCHESTER PRIOR TO RETURNING TO AMERICA—ORSON HYDE PRESENT ON HIS WAY TO PALESTINE—THE EXTENSIVE WORK OF ONE YEAR

On his way to Manchester Heber tarried a few days at Bedford, strengthening the Saints in that place, and adding new members to the Church. He also visited Birmingham and there organized a conference. One hundred and seven members were represented, and nine persons ordained to the ministry. Elder Alfred Cordon was appointed president. The Birmingham Conference became one of the largest and most important conferences in the mission.

On the 6th day of April, 1841, the Apostles met as a quorum in Manchester, for the transaction of business prior to their departure for America. The meetings, which were open to the Saints, were held in Carpenter's Hall. The members of the quorum present were Brigham Young, Heber C. Kimball, Orson Hyde, Parley P. Pratt, Orson Pratt, Wilford Woodruff, John Taylor, Willard Richards and George A. Smith. Orson Hyde had lately arrived from America on his way to Jerusalem, [319] whither he had been sent on a mission to the house of Judah.

The representation of the churches and conferences throughout the mission being called for, it was found that thirty-three conferences and branches were represented, aggregating a membership of five thousand eight hundred and fourteen, with one hundred and thirty-six Elders, three hundred and three Priests, one hundred and sixty-nine teachers, and sixty-eight Deacons. This enumeration did not include some fifty members not connected with any branch, and nearly eight hundred Saints who had emigrated to America during the year.

Several ordinations were performed, and the following business was transacted:

"Resolved, That Manchester, Stockport, Dukinfield, Oldham, Bolton and all the neighboring branches be organized into one conference to be called the Manchester Conference.

"That the church in Brampton, Alston, and Carlisle be included in one conference;

"That the churches of Liverpool, Isle of Man, Wales, viz., Overton, Harding and Elsmere, be organized into one conference, to be called the Liverpool Conference;

"That the Macclesfield Conference include Macclesfield, Northwich, Middlewich, and Lostock;

"That the Edinburgh Conference include Edinburgh and vicinity, and that the conference of Glasgow include Glasgow, Paisley, Bridge of Weir, Johnston, and Thorny Bank.

"Resolved, that G. D. Watt preside over the Edinburgh Conference; that Thomas Ward preside over the Clithero Conference; that Lorenzo Snow preside over the London Conference; that J. Gaily preside over **[320]** the Macclesfield Conference; that A. Cordon preside over the Staffordshire Conference; that J. Riley be ordained a High Priest and preside over the Birmingham Conference; that J. McAuley preside over the Glasgow Conference; that Thomas Richardson preside over the Gadfield Elm Conference; that Wm. Kay preside over the Froomes Hill Conference; that Levi Richards have the superintendence of the Garway Conference; that P. Melling, Patriarch, continue to preside over the Preston Conference, and that J. Sanders preside over the Brampton Conference."

The above resolutions were adopted unanimously. Elder J. Albertson was then given a patriarchal blessing, under the hands of Father Melling, after which he was himself ordained a Patriarch by the Apostles.

During the meeting a very richly ornamented cake, a present from New York, from a Sister Adams to the Twelve, was exhibited and then divided among the congregation. While the distribution was going on, several appropriate hymns were sung, and a powerful and general feeling of delight pervaded the meeting. Under the inspiration of the moment, Elder Parley P. Pratt composed the following lines and handed them to the clerk who read them to the congregation:

> "When in far distant regions
>    As strangers we roam,
> Far away from our country,
>    Our friends and our home;
> When sinking in sorrow,
>    Fresh courage we'll take,
> As we think on our friends,
>    And remember the cake."

Several discourses were then delivered, and this memorable and happy meeting—the first and last at **[321]** which so many members of the early Twelve met together in a foreign land, came to a close.

The Apostles next issued their first general epistle to the Saints in England, Scotland, Ireland, Wales and the Isle of Man. It was a well-worded, even eloquent document, full of wise counsel and timely instruction. Having now set in order the affairs of the Church throughout the mission, the Apostles, all save Orson Hyde, who was bound for Palestine, and Parley P. Pratt, who was left to preside over the British mission, prepared to return to America.

A great work had been accomplished by these faithful and devoted men of God, during the past year. The mission founded by Heber C. Kimball and his brethren in 1837, was now established upon a broad and permanent basis, and the mighty stream of Israel's emigration from foreign shores set in motion. **[322]**

## CHAPTER 15

THE APOSTLES SAIL FOR HOME—ARRIVAL AT NEW YORK—HEBER'S LETTER TO THE "MILLENNIAL STAR"—HAPPY MEETING WITH THE PROPHET AND THE SAINTS AT NAUVOO—LABORS SPIRITUAL AND TEMPORAL—HEBER'S PHRENOLOGICAL CHART

ON the 20th day of April, 1841, Brigham Young, Heber C. Kimball, Orson Pratt, John Taylor, Wilford Woodruff, George A. Smith and Willard Richards, with a company of Saints, sailed from Liverpool on board the ship *Rochester*, bound for New York. They landed there on the 20th of May, having been just one month upon the water, and remained in that city until the 4th of June.

In a letter to the editor of the *Millennial Star*, Heber thus relates what followed:

"On the 4th of June I started for home, in company with Elders Young and Taylor. Elder O. Pratt remained in New York to republish the book he had printed in Edinburgh, Scotland, giving a history of the coming forth of the Book of Mormon, and of which he intended to publish 5,000 copies. Elders G. A. Smith and Hadlock stayed in Pennsylvania, not having the means of getting home. I had to borrow four pounds myself, and the Saints in New York gave us some help. May the Lord bless them fourfold.

"We went by way of Philadephia to Pittsburg, the distance being four hundred miles by railway and canal. We went on the swift line, for which we paid fourteen dollars, the slow line carrying for nine dollars. After **[323]** staying four days at Pittsburg, we set sail on board the steamboat *Cicero* on the 12th of June, and when we had proceeded about fifteen miles she ran on a sand bank, where we were detained three days; in fact the boat ran aground several times, the water was so low. We were three weeks on board before we arrived at Nauvoo. I never experienced warmer weather at this season before, and many persons are dying of cholera on board the steamboats on the river. I would advise persons coming by way of the rivers to start earlier in the spring. It will be much cheaper for the Saints to come by way of New Orleans, the cost of which is about five pounds ten shillings, and they will come much quicker and with greater ease. If they prefer coming by way of New York, they will do well to go from thence by way of Chicago, as it will be both cheaper and quicker than by way of Philadelphia. I would advise the Saints to come in the cool part of the season, on account of their health.

"We landed in Nauvoo on the 1st of July, and when we struck the dock I think there were about three hundred Saints there to meet us, and a greater manifestation of love and gladness I never saw before. President Smith was the first one that caught us by the hand. I never saw him feel better in my life than he does at this time; this is the case with the Saints in general. When we got in sight of Nauvoo we were surprised to see what improvements had been made since we left home. You know there were not more than thirty buildings in the city when we left about two years ago, but at this time there are twelve hundred, and hundreds of others in progress which will be finished soon. On Friday last seventy Saints came to Nauvoo, led by Lorenzo Barnes, from Chester County, Pennsylvania, in wagons, living in tents by the way. On the next day a company came in wagons **[324]** from Canada, all in good spirits; and in two or three days after they all obtained places to live in. They are coming in from all parts of this vast continent daily and hourly, and the work is spreading in all of this land, and calls for preaching in all parts. You will recollect that when we built our houses in the woods there was not a house within half a mile of us. Now the place, wild as it was at that time, is converted into a thickly populated village. Our old friends who were driven from Missouri are my neighbors; for instance, the Allreds, Charles Hubbard, Charles Rich, and hundreds of others that I could mention that you know. I wish you were here, if it were right. I can say with propriety, as to the knowledge I have of things, I never knew the Church in so good a state as at the present time; they feel well and in good spirits, and filled with love and kindness. Most of our English brethren have got themselves places and houses built for them, and others building, and many of them say they never felt better in their lives and have no desire to return to their native land, for they have houses and land of their own, what they never before were in possession of. They are generally enjoying good health and spirits. There has been some sickness among them during their long journey, and a few deaths. I will mention some names. Thomas Smith and his wife, and his daughter Diana; she died the day I got home. Brother Smith and his wife died before they got to St. Louis. They were from Clithero, Lancashire. Brother Henry Nightingale. He got shot through his thigh; it was an accident. He survived the misfortune only two weeks. His wife was at my house this week. He died about the time I got home. He was from Preston. John Stevenson, from Longton; also Sister Wyche, from the Potteries; William Blacast's wife, from Longton, is dead; also **[325]** Brother Rigby's wife, from Clayton, and James Carlbridge, from Thornby. The sickness is generally among the new comers.

"On the 3rd of July the Nauvoo Legion was called out to celebrate our independence. There was judged to be about 8,000 people present. There was an oration delivered by President Rigdon to the satisfaction of all present. We had a heavenly time; all was peace and harmony; there was no drunkenness on that day as I discovered; there is no public house that keeps spirits, nor grocery, and in fact none except in case of sickness is used in the city of Nauvoo. You will not find a more temperate people than the Latter-day Saints in this or any other country.

"I never saw crops look better than they do in this place at present. The wheat is in general cut, and secured. Provisions are cheaper; flour is $2.25 a hundred and will be less soon. Corn is brought into the city for twenty-five cents a bushel; bacon from seven to eight cents per pound; butter ten cents; other things in proportion. The whole country for many miles is cultivated with corn, wheat, potatoes, and all kinds of produce; it looks as though the blessing of God rested upon the crops in this region, and it is noticed by the inhabitants that come from other parts, for the crops are better here than in other parts of the country, or counties around this place. Most of the Saints have plenty growing to last them for a year, and to spare; and the blessing of God rests on this people, and I know for one that God is here, and that to bless his people, and the devil cannot hinder, for it is the work of the great God, and it must and will roll forth.

"On the 4th of July, being the Sabbath day, the Saints came together to the amount of 5,000 to hear us [326] give a detail of our mission to England. Then was a time of rejoicing I assure you. Our place of meeting was in a grove close by the temple, as we have no other place at present. There is every effort made to complete the house of the Lord; they devote every tenth day for that purpose. The basement story is nearly finished, which is considered to be half of the stone work. It is going to be very magnificent. They intend to have the walls finished this fall if possible. Elders G. A. Smith and Hadlock got here on the 14th, both well. We found our families well, except Sister Taylor, who was quite low. She has now recovered.

"Elders Young and Taylor send much love to you all, and I am sure all would if they knew that I was writing to you. Give my love to Elders Snow, Richards and Adams, and to all of the officers and members in that land. Please to give my respects to Sister Pratt and to Sister Olive and to all your families. My wife joins with me in love to you both and to Sister Olive and Mary Ann, and may the Lord bless you with long life and good days, and keep you safe till you return to your own country with your own family, is the wish and prayer of your brother in Christ. Elder Orson Pratt arrived here this week; he went to Sackett's Harbor; his wife's sister came with him, He and his family are well. Your brother William is well.

"As to crops that are growing in the Iowa, there is thought to be enough to supply all the Saints in Nauvoo and Iowa for one year. Such sights you never saw before. There is a greater improvement by one half than there was in Far West in the same time. Our enemies begin to threaten us, for you know they cannot bear to see us prosper.

"I must now come to a close. There are five of the [327] Twelve got home. We are all well and in good spirits. We think much about you and yours, and our brethren and sisters in that land. I hope we shall see them all soon, and hope also that they may be faithful, and hearken unto counsel, for they that hearken to counsel will be wise, and their lives will be prolonged on the earth. I exhort them to observe these things, and to be subject to the powers that be. They have my best wishes for their welfare both temporal and spiritual. Now, fare you well a little season, my dear brother in Christ."

Heber's time was now more or less taken up with temporal affairs. The work of God was growing so rapidly that the Prophet, in order to devote more of his time to spiritual concerns, was obliged to roll some of the burden of the public business from his own shoulders upon those of the Twelve. At a conference held on the 16th of August, 1841, Joseph remarked "that the time had come when the Twelve should be called upon to stand in their place next the First Presidency, and attend to the settling of immigrants, and the business of the Church at the Stakes, and assist to bear off the kingdom victorious to the nations." They were also directed to build the cities which Joseph had designed, namely, Nauvoo, Zarahemla, Warren, Nashville and Ramus, and while attending to these duties in person, to send missionaries into different parts to preach the gospel.

Brigham and Heber also served in a semi-military capacity, being made chaplains in the Nauvoo Legion soon after their return from England.

At intervals, while engaged in the new labors assigned them, the Twelve continued to send their general epistles to the churches abroad.

At the close of the April conference of 1842, Presi[328]dents Young, Kimball and others of the Twelve ordained two hundred and seventy-five Elders, the largest number ordained in one day since the formation of the Church. Thus, in labors spiritual and temporal, under the direction of the Prophet of God, Heber and his brethren continued to fulfill their sacred mission.

About this time there came to Nauvoo a celebrated phrenologist of the period, who applied to the Prophet for the privilege of examining the heads of himself and several of his chief Apostles, designing to publish their charts. Joseph, Brigham, Heber and Willard were chosen for types, and their charts were incorporated in the Prophet's history. Here is Heber's:

*Phrenological Chart of Elder Heber C. Kimball; by A. Crane, M. D., Professor of Phrenology.*

## PROPENSITIES.

Amativeness.—10, large. Extreme susceptibility; passionately fond of the company of the other sex.

Philoprogenitiveness.—7, full. Interested in the happiness of children; fond of their company.

Inhabitiveness.—4, medium or small. Somewhat indifferent to places as such; easily changes location.

Adhesiveness.—8, f. Solicitous for the happiness of friends, and ardent attachments to the other sex.

Combativeness.—7, f. Great powers of exertion and sustaining under opposition and difficulties.

Destructiveness.—6, m. Ability to control the passions, and is not disposed to extreme measures.

Secretiveness.—9, l. Great propensity and ability to conceal feelings, plans, etc.

Acquisitiveness.—6, m. Freeness to spend money; love of it chiefly for its uses and what it will buy. [329]

Alimentativeness.—7, f. A good appetite, but not excessive; partiality for a variety of rich, hearty dishes.

Vitativeness.—6, m. or s. Indifferent to life; views the approach of death without fear.

## FEELINGS

Cautiousness.—8, f. Provision against prospective dangers and ills, without hesitation or irresolution.

Approbativeness.—10, l. Ambition for distinction; sense of character; sensibility to reproach, fear of scandal.

Self-esteem.—9, l. High-mindedness, independence, self-confidence, dignity, aspiration for greatness.

Concentrativeness.—7, f. Can dwell on a subject without fatigue, and control the imagination.

Benevolence.—9, l. Kindness, goodness, tenderness, sympathy.

Veneration.—8, f. Religion, without great awe or enthusiasm; reasonable deference to superiority.

Firmness.—10, l. Stability and decision of character and purpose.

Conscientiousness.—9, l. High regard for duty, integrity, moral principle, justice, obligation, truth, etc.

Hope.—7, f. Reasonable hopes, a fine flow of spirits; anticipation of what is to be realized.

Marvelousness.—7, f. Openness to conviction without blind credulity; tolerable good degree of faith.

Imitation.—10, f. A disposition and respectable ability to imitate, but not to mimic, or to act out.

Prepossession.—7, l. or f. Attached to certain notions; not disposed to change them, etc.

Ideality.—10, l. Lively imagination; fancy, taste love of poetry, elegance, eloquence, excellence, etc. [330]

## PERCEPTIVES.

Admonition.—7, f. or m. Desirous to know what others are doing; ready to counsel, and give hints of a fault or duty, etc.

Constructiveness.—9, l. Great mechanical ingenuity, talent and skill.

Tune.—9, v. l. or l. Great musical taste and talent; conception of melody.

Time.—4, s. or v. s. Forgetfulness of dates, ages, appointments, day of the month, etc.

Locality.—11, v. l. or l. Great memory of places and position.

Eventuality.—10, l. Retentive memory of events and particulars.

Individuality.—8, f. With very large causality, and comparison, great observation, with deep thought, etc.

Form.—8, f. Cognizance, and distinct recollection of shapes.

Size.—5, m. s. or v. s. Inaccurate measurement of magnitude, distance, etc.

Weight.—11, v. l., l. or f. Knowledge of gravitation, momentum, etc.

Color.—9, f. or m. Moderate skill in judging of colors, comparing and arranging them.

Language.—7, f. Freedom of expression, without fluency or verbosity; no great loquacity.

Order.—9, l. Love of arrangement, everything in its particular place.

Number.—8, f. Respectable aptness in arithmetical calculations, without extraordinary talent.

### REFLECTIVES.

Mirthfulness.—10, l. Wit, fun, mirth, perception and love of the ludicrous.
[331]
Causality.—9, l. Ability to think and reason clearly, and perceive the relations of cause and effect.

Comparison.—10, l. A discrimination; power of illustration; ability to perceive and apply analogies.

This chart is not only worth preserving as a curiosity, but it is, in many respects, an excellent index of Heber's character and idiosyncrasies.

## CHAPTER 46

REVELATION OF CELESTIAL MARRIAGE—SECRECY THE PRICE OF SAFETY—JOSEPH TESTS HEBER AND MAKES HIM HIS CONFIDANT—HOW VILATE KIMBALL WAS CONVERTED—HEBER AND VILATE GIVE THEIR DAUGHTER HELEN TO THE PROPHET IN CELESTIAL MARRIAGE

A STARTLING innovation, a test designed to try, as never before, the faith and integrity of God's people now came upon them. Not in the shape of fire and sword, nor toilsome pilgrimage, nor pestilence, nor wealth, nor poverty. Ah! no; something far different from these, and far more difficult to bear.

A grand and glorious principle had been revealed, and for years had slumbered in the breast of God's Prophet, awaiting the time when, with safety to himself and the Church, it might be confided to the sacred keeping of a chosen few. That time had now come. An angel with a flaming sword descended from the courts of glory and, confronting the Prophet, commanded him in the name of the Lord to establish the principle so [332] long concealed from the knowledge of the Saints and of the world.

That principle was the law of celestial or plural marriage!

Well knew the youthful Prophet the danger of his task. Well knew he the peril and penalty of disobedience. Fearing God, not man, he bowed to the inevitable, and laid his life—aye, was it not so?—upon the altar of duty and devotion.

Among those to whom Joseph confided this great secret, even before it was committed to writing, was his bosom friend, Heber C. Kimball. Well knowing the integrity of his heart, so many times tested and found true, he felt that he ran no risk in opening to Heber's eyes the treasured mysteries of his mighty soul.

But why careful, among so many friends, to select only a few as the recipients of such a favor? Would not the Saints have died to a man in defense of their Prophet—God's seer and revelator? Alas, none knew so well as Joseph the frailty of man, the inherent weakness and wickedness of the human heart.

"Many men," said he, "will say, 'I will never forsake you, but will stand by you at all times.' But the moment you teach them some of the mysteries of the kingdom of God that are retained in the heavens, and are to be revealed to the children of men when they are prepared for them, they will be the first to stone you and put you to death.

"It was this same principle that crucified the Lord Jesus Christ, and will cause the people to kill the Prophets in this generation."

What! would even the Saints have so done? Did not some of those who *were* Saints then, so do?

Had not Joseph said many times—are not men now **[333]** living who heard him say: "Would to God, brethren, I could tell you who I am! Would to God I could tell you what I know! But you would call it blasphemy, and there are men upon this stand who would want to take my life."

"If the Church," said he, "knew all the commandments, one half they would reject through prejudice and ignorance."

No wonder, then, that he should choose his confidants; for their sakes no less than his own. For these also are Joseph's words:

"When God offers a blessing, or knowledge to a man, and he refuses to receive it, he will be damned."

Revelation is ever the iconoclast of tradition; and such is the bigotry of man, his natural hatred of the new and strange, as opposed to his personal interests or private views, that the very lives of those whose mission is to introduce and establish new doctrines, though designed as a blessing to humanity, are ever in danger from those whose traditions would thus be uprooted and destroyed.

Joseph was not a coward; it was he who said that a coward could not be saved in the kingdom of God; but neither was he lacking in caution, especially when warned of the Lord of the necessity for its exercise. Therefore, was he now revealing, to a chosen few, whom God had prepared to receive what he should tell them, one of the grand principles of the everlasting Gospel, "unlawful to be uttered" to the multitude, yet one day to be thundered from the house-tops in the ears of all living, with many other mighty truths locked in the treasure house of future time, of which eternity still holds the key.

Before he would trust even Heber with the full secret, however, he put him to a test which few men would have been able to bear. [334]

It was no less than a requirement for him to surrender his wife, his beloved Vilate, and give her to Joseph in marriage!

The astounding revelation well-nigh paralyzed him. He could hardly believe he had heard aright. Yet Joseph was solemnly in earnest. His next impulse was to spurn the proposition, and perhaps at that terrible moment a vague suspicion of the Prophet's motive and the divinity of the revelation, shot like a poisoned arrow through his soul.

But only for a moment, if at all, was such a thought, such a suspicion entertained. He knew Joseph too well, as a man, a friend, a brother, a servant of God, to doubt his truth or the divine origin of the behest he had made. No; Joseph was God's Prophet, His mouth-piece and oracle, and so long as he was so, his words were as the words of the Eternal One to Heber C. Kimball. His heart-strings might be torn, his feelings crucified and sawn asunder, but so long as his faith in God and the Priesthood remained, heaven helping him, he would try and do as he was told. Such, now, was his superhuman resolve.

Three days he fasted and wept and prayed. Then, with a broken and a bleeding heart, but with soul self-mastered for the sacrifice, he led his darling wife to the Prophet's house and presented her to Joseph.

It was enough—the heavens accepted the sacrifice. The will for the deed was taken, and "accounted unto him for righteousness." Joseph wept at this proof of devotion, and embracing Heber told him that was all that the Lord required. He had proved him, as a child of Abraham, that he would "do the works of Abraham," holding back nothing, but laying all upon the altar for God's glory.

The Prophet joined the hands of the heroic and [335] devoted pair, and then and there, by virtue of the sealing power and authority of the Holy Priesthood, Heber and Vilate Kimball were made husband and wife for all eternity.

Heber's crucial test was in part over. Vilate's trial was yet to come. The principle of celestial marriage was now known to them, so far as their own eternal covenant was concerned, but the doctrine of plurality of wives which it involves, was yet to be revealed. How Heber and Vilate received and embraced this feature of the principle is thus tenderly told by their daughter Helen:

"My mother often told me that she could not doubt the plural order of marriage was of God, for the Lord had revealed it to her in answer to prayer.

"In Nauvoo, shortly after his return from England, my father, among others of his brethren, was taught the plural wife doctrine, and was told by Joseph, the Prophet, three times, to go and take a certain woman as his wife; but not till he commanded him in the name of the Lord did he obey. At the same time Joseph told him not to divulge this secret, not even to my mother, for fear that she would not receive it; for his life was in constant jeopardy, not only from outside influences and enemies, who were seeking some plea to take him back to Missouri, but from false brethren who had crept like snakes into his bosom and then betrayed him.

"My father realized the situation fully, and the love and reverence he bore for the Prophet were so great that he would sooner have laid down his life than have betrayed him. This was one of the greatest tests of his faith he had ever experienced. The thought of deceiving the kind and faithful wife of his youth, whom he loved with all his heart, and who with him had borne so patiently their separations, and all the trials and sacrifices **[336]** they had been called to endure, was more than he felt able to bear.

"He realized not only the addition of trouble and perplexity that such a step must bring upon him, but his sorrow and misery were increased by the thought of my mother hearing of it from some other source, which would no doubt separate them, and he shrank from the thought of such a thing, or of causing her any unhappiness. Finally he was so tried that he went to Joseph and told him how he felt—that he was fearful if he took such a step he could not stand, but would be overcome. The Prophet, full of sympathy for him, went and inquired of the Lord; His answer was, 'Tell him to go and do as he has been commanded, and if I see that there is any danger of his apostatizing. I will take him to myself.'

"The fact that he had to be commanded three times to do this thing shows that the trial must have been extraordinary, for he was a man who, from the first, had yielded implicit obedience to every requirement of the Prophets

"When first hearing the principle taught, believing that he would be called upon to enter into it, he had thought of two elderly ladies named Pitkin, great friends of my mother's, who, he believed, would cause her little, if any, unhappiness. But the woman he was commanded to take was an English lady named Sarah Noon, nearer my mother's age, who came over with the company of Saints in the same ship in which father and Brother Brigham returned from Europe. She had been married and was the mother of two little girls, but left her husband on account of his drunken and dissolute habits. Father was told to take her as his wife and provide for her and her children, and he did so.[4] **[337]**

"My mother had noticed a change in his manner and appearance, and when she inquired the cause, he tried to evade her questions. At last he promised he would tell her after a while, if she would only wait. This trouble so worked upon his mind that his anxious and haggard looks betrayed him daily and hourly, and finally his misery became so unbearable that it was impossible to control his feelings. He became sick in body, but his mental wretchedness was too great to allow of his retiring, and he would walk the floor till nearly morning, and some times the agony of his mind was so terrible that he would wring his hands and weep like a child, and beseech the Lord to be merciful and reveal to her this principle, for he himself could not break his vow of secrecy.

"The anguish of their hearts was indescribable, and when she found it was useless to beseech him longer, she retired to her room and bowed before the Lord and poured out her soul in prayer to Him who hath said: 'If any lack wisdom let

---

[4] Heber was told by Joseph that if he did not do this he would lose his Apostleship and be damned.

him ask of God, who giveth to all men liberally and upbraideth not.' My father's heart was raised at the same time in supplication. While pleading as one would plead for life, the vision of her mind was opened, and, as darkness flees before the morning sun, so did her sorrow and the groveling things of earth vanish away.

"Before her was illustrated the order of celestial marriage, in all its beauty and glory, together with the great exaltation and honor it would confer upon her in that immortal and celestial sphere, if she would accept it and stand in her place by her husband's side. She also saw the woman he had taken to wife, and contemplated with joy the vast and boundless love and union which this order would bring about, as well as the increase of **[338]** her husband's kingdoms, and the power and glory extending throughout the eternities, worlds without end.

"With a countenance beaming with joy, for she was filled with the Spirit of God, she returned to my father, saying: 'Heber, what you kept from me the Lord has shown me.' She told me she never saw so happy a man as father was when she described the vision and told him she was satisfied and knew it was from God.

"She covenanted to stand by him and honor the principle, which covenant she faithfully kept, and though her trials were often heavy and grievous to bear, she knew that father was also being tried, and her integrity was unflinching to the end. She gave my father many wives, and they always found in my mother a faithful friend."

Helen also refers in her narrative to the sensation caused in Nauvoo, one Sabbath morning, prior to the return of the Twelve from England, by a sermon of the Prophet's on "the restoration of all things," in which it was hinted that the patriarchal or plural order of marriage, as practiced by the ancients, would some day again be established, The excitement created by the bare suggestion was such that Joseph deemed it wisdom, in the afternoon, to modify his statement by saying that possibly the Spirit had made the time seem nearer than it really was, when such things would be restored.

These facts serve to show something of the nature and extent of the sacrifice made by the Saints in accepting this principle, and likewise the pure, lofty, religious motives actuating both men and women who could thus heroically embrace a doctrine against which—as is generally the case with the gospel's higher principles—their traditions and preconceived notions instinctively rebelled. **[339]**

Soon after the revelation was given, a golden link was forged whereby the houses of Heber and Joseph were indissolubly and forever joined.[5] Helen Mar, the eldest daughter of Heber Chase and Vilate Murray Kimball, was given to the Prophet in the holy bonds of celestial marriage.

---

[5] The Prophet Joseph, I am informed, in blessing Heber C. Kimball, told him that his inheritance in Zion should adjoin his on the north.

# CHAPTER 17

JOHN C. BENNETT'S APOSTASY—HEBER AND THE TWELVE SENT OUT TO REFUTE HIS SLANDERS—HEBER'S FAMOUS SERMON: "THE CLAY IN THE HANDS OF THE POTTER"—INCEPTION OF THE RELIEF SOCIETY—VILATE'S VOW AND HEBER'S PRAYER

WITHOUT doubt, the revelation of the great principle of plural marriage was a prime cause of the troubles which now arose, culminating in the Prophet's martyrdom and the exodus of the Church into the wilderness. True, the old causes remained, sectarian hatred and political jealousies, and these were the immediate reasons for such results. But back of all was the eternal warfare of truth and error, battling each for the world's supremacy, and the mailed hand of Omnipotence pushing the chosen people along the thorn-strewn, blood-sprinkled path of a glorious destiny.

John C. Bennett, an individual who had wormed [340] himself into the good graces of the Saints, like the serpent of old among the flowers of Eden, at this juncture apostatized, not finding the Church of God, with its pure and wholesome laws, a safe refuge for vice, or a suitable arena for the antics of rascality. Excommunicated for his vile practices, he at once entered the lecture field—that favorite resort of vengeful apostates—and sought to abuse the public mind in relation to the Latter-day Saints and their religion. His charges were so atrocious as to half defeat their own purpose, the more intelligent at once rejecting them for what they were—outrageous fabrications. Many of the ignorant and fanatical, however, believed them. The Prophet therefore called a council of leading Elders, including Heber C. Kimball and others of the Twelve, to consider the advisability of sending missionaries through the states to preach the gospel—the principles which the Saints really believed and were authorized to teach—and expose and refute the slanderous charges of the man Bennett and other apostates.

This council was held in the latter part of August, 1842. It was decided to hold a special conference at once and nominate the Elders who were to go upon this mission. Accordingly, on the 29th of August a conference convened at Nauvoo, at which three hundred and eighty Elders volunteered for the purpose.

One of these was Heber C. Kimball. He, in company with Brigham Young, George A. Smith and Amasa Lyman (who had lately been ordained an Apostle under the hands of the other three), having been instructed by the Prophet, set out upon this mission early in September. They held their first meeting at Lima, where they addressed a large assembly in a grove, in relation to the slanderous reports of John C. Bennett. Their labors [341] and subsequent movements were outlined as follows in a letter to the editor of the *Times and Seasons:*

"DEAR BROTHER:

"Having commenced our mission yesterday, we held our first conference at Elder Isaac Morley's. We had a good time. The brethren here are in good spirits.

We ordained nineteen Elders and baptized twelve. We expect next Saturday and Sunday to hold a two days' meeting in Quincy, being the 17th and 18th instant; on the 24th and 25th at Payson; the 1st and 2nd of October at Pleasant Vale; the 8th and 11th of October at Pittsfield; the 15th and 16th of October at Apple Creek, in Green County. From thence we shall proceed to Jacksonville and Springfield.

"If you please, notice the above in your paper, for the benefit of those friends scattered abroad. "Yours in the everlasting covenant,

BRIGHAM YOUNG,<br>H. C. KIMBALL,

"MORLEY SETTLEMENT,
September 12, 1842."

Having fulfilled their mission, Brigham and Heber returned together to Nauvoo on the 4th of November.

The opening of the year 1843 was a period of rejoicing to the Saints at Nauvoo, the Prophet having been honorably discharged from his arrest under the Missouri writ, by the U. S. District Court of Illinois, Judge Pope presiding. Grateful for this, the Twelve issued a proclamation to the Saints to observe the 17th of January as a day of fasting, prayer and thanksgiving for the Prophet's deliverance. On the next day Joseph invited his friends to a feast to commemorate the event, Heber being one of the number.

On the evening of March 7th a meeting was held at the house of Elder Kimball, which was crowded. Heber addressed the assembly, taking for his text, Jeremiah [342] xviii, 2-5, on the figure of the clay in the hands of the potter. Joseph was so pleased with his sermon that he deemed it worthy of special notice in his history. This was the origin of Heber's famous sermon—"the clay in the hands of the potter," so familiar to the Saints, and well worthy of remembrance, not only for the masterly way in which it was presented, but for the depth of the doctrine therein contained.

Probably it was Heber's early profession—it will be remembered that he was by trade a potter—that first impressed him with this important theme, with its train of associate thoughts and images. And herein was shown the thoughtful, observant nature of his mind, which drew from simplest as well as sublimest objects that wealth of simile, the rich fund of metaphor and comparison in which his sayings were so prolific. Thus also was evinced the poet nature of the man, though he probably never wrote a line of verse.

Heber's powers as a speaker—though he never sought the distinction or claimed the title of orator—were well recognized, even at that early day. As a persuader, not with tinkling phrases and flowery rhetoric, to please the ear, but by simple words and the power of the Holy Ghost, to move the heart, he had few equals.

Some days after the meeting referred to, a petition reached Nauvoo from Boston, signed by twelve hundred names, asking for Elders Heber C. Kimball and Orson Hyde to come and labor in that city. A similar petition was also sent from

Salem, Massachusetts, by Elder Erastus Snow. Before going on another mission, however, Heber, in connection with the Prophet, took an active part in creating an organization which has since become famous in the midst of Israel. It was no other than the Relief Society, the preliminary meeting of which [343] was held at the house of Heber C. Kimball in Nauvoo. In view of the scarcely less famous organizations which have sprung up since, known as the Young Men's and Young Ladies' Mutual Improvement Associations of the Latter-day Saints, it is interesting to note that the former movement originated among the young people, for whose welfare Heber was at that time specially and zealously laboring. We quote from the Prophet's history:

A SHORT SKETCH OF THE RISE OF THE YOUNG GENTLEMEN AND LADIES' RELIEF SOCIETY.

"In the latter part of January, 1843, a number of young people assembled at the house of Elder H. C. Kimball, who warned them against the various temptations to which youth is exposed, and gave an appointment expressly for the young at the house of Elder Billings; and another meeting was held in the ensuing week at Brother Farr's school-room, which was filled to overflowing. Elder Kimball delivered addresses, exhorting the young people to study the scriptures, and enable themselves to give a reason for the hope within them, and to be ready to go on to the stage of action, when their present instructors and leaders had gone behind the scenes; also to keep good company and to keep pure and unspotted from the world.

"The next meeting was appointed to be held at my house; and notwithstanding the inclemency of the weather, it was completely filled at an early hour. Elder Kimball, as usual, delivered an address, warning his hearers against giving heed to their youthful passions, and exhorting them to be obedient and pay strict attention to the advice and command of their parents, who were better calculated to guide the pathway of youth than they themselves.

"My house being too small, the next meeting was appointed to be held over my store. I addressed the young people for some time, expressing my gratitude to [344] Elder Kimball for having commenced this glorious work, which would be the means of doing a great deal of good, and said the gratitude of all good men and of the youth would follow him through life, and he would always look back upon the winter of 1843 with pleasure. I experienced more embarrassment in standing before them than I should before kings and nobles of the earth; for I knew the crimes of which they were guilty, and knew precisely how to address them; but that my young friends were guilty of none of them, and therefore I hardly knew what to say.

"I advised them to organize themselves into a society for the relief of the poor, and recommended to them a poor lame English brother [Maudesley], who wanted a house built, that he might have a home amongst the Saints; that he had gathered a few materials for the purpose, but was unable to use them, and had petitioned for aid. I advised them to choose a committee to collect funds for this purpose, and perform this charitable act as soon as the weather permitted. I gave them such advice as I deemed was calculated to guide their conduct through life and prepare them for a glorious eternity.

"A meeting was appointed to carry out these suggestions, at which William Cutler was chosen president, and Marcellus L. Bates, clerk. Andrew Cahoon, C. V. Spencer and Stephen Perry were appointed to draft a constitution for the society, and the meeting adjourned to the 28th of March, when the said committee submitted a draft of a constitution, consisting of twelve sections. The report was unanimously adopted, and the meeting proceeded to choose their officers. William Walker was chosen president; William Cutler, vice-president; Lorin Walker, treasurer; James M. Monroe, secretary; Stephen Perry, Marcellus L. Bates, R. A. Allred, Wm. H. Kimball and Garret Ivans, were appointed a committee of vigilance. The meeting then adjourned until the next Tuesday evening.

"The next meeting was addressed by Elders Brigham Young, Heber C. Kimball and Jedediah M. Grant, whose instructions were listened to with breathless attention." [345]

The Relief Society afterwards became distinctively a woman's organization.

Heber's next mission was through the eastern states, in company with President Young and others, collecting means for the temple and the Nauvoo House, which were then in course of erection. They left Nauvoo early in June, 1843. The day before starting, Vilate Kimball penned these tender lines and presented them as a token of love to her husband:

"Nauvoo, June 8th, 1843.
"My Ever Kind and Affectionate Companion:

"I write these few lines for you to look upon when you are far distant from me, and when you read them remember they were penned by one whose warm, affectionate heart is ever the same towards you; *yea, it is fixed, firm as a decree which is unalterable.* Therefore, let your heart be comforted, and if you never more behold my face in time, let this be my last covenant and testimony unto you: that I am yours in time and throughout all eternity. This blessing has been sealed upon us by the Holy Spirit of promise, and cannot be broken only through transgression, or committing a grosser crime than your heart or mine is capable of, that is, murder.

> "So be of cheer, my dearest dear,
> For we shall meet again
> Where all our sorrows will be o'er,
> And we are free from pain.
> "V. Kimball."

Heber's full heart responded as follows:

"O God, the Eternal Father, in the name of Jesus Christ wilt Thou bless her with peace and with a long life; and when Thou shalt see fit to take her, let Thy servant go with her; and dwell with each other throughout all eternity; that no power shall ever separate us from each other; for Thou, O God, knowest we love each **[346]** other with pure hearts. Still, we are willing to leave each other from time to time, to preach Thy word to the children of men. Now, O God, hear Thy servant, and let us have the desires of our hearts; for we want to live together, and die, and be buried, and rise and reign together in Thy kingdom with our dear children; in the name of Jesus Christ of Nazareth. Amen."

This tender interchange of affection, be it remembered, was after Heber and Vilate had embraced the principle of plural marriage; a point which fails to sustain the position assumed by most Christian philosophers, as to the "brutalizing and debasing effects of Mormon polygamy."

Here is another little gem of Vilate's, written several years later:

LINES WRITTEN BY VILATE KIMBALL TO HER COMPANION HEBER C. KIMBALL

"No being round the spacious earth
    Beneath the vaulted arch of heaven,
Divides my love, or draws it thence,
    From him to whom my heart is given.

"Like the frail ivy to the oak,
    Drawn closer, by the tempest riven,
Through sorrow's flood he'll bear me up
    And light with smiles my way to heaven.

"The gift was on the altar laid;
    The plighted vow on earth was given;
The seal eternal has been made,
    And by his side I'll reign in heaven.

WINTER QUARTERS,
    January 17, 1847."

The last verse of this beautiful little poem delicately tells the whole story of the sacrifice made by this noble and devoted pair, and the reward of their fidelity in **[347]** accepting the great principle whose "seal eternal" had bound them together for time and all eternity.

The Apostles returned from their mission to the east on the 22nd of October, 1843. Heber's purely missionary labors were drawing to a close. The hour of the Prophet's martyrdom was approaching, and upon the shoulders of the Twelve, as the First Presidents of the Church, was about to roll the burden of the kingdom of the latter days.

# CHAPTER 48

HEBER'S LAST MISSION TO THE GENTILES—JOSEPH SMITH A CANDIDATE FOR THE PRESIDENCY OF THE UNITED STATES—THE APOSTLES HIS ELECTIONEERERS—THE MARTYRDOM—RETURN OF THE TWELVE TO NAUVOO

ON the 21st of May of the fateful year 1844, Heber C. Kimball left Nauvoo on his last mission to the Gentiles. He accompanied President Brigham Young and other Apostles and Elders, about one hundred in all. The object of their mission was unique. It was to present to the nation the name of Joseph Smith as a candidate for the presidency of the United States.

The steamer *Osprey*, on which the Elders took passage for St. Louis, left the wharf at Nauvoo amid the cheers and acclamations of those on shore, who shouted: "Joseph Smith, the next President of the United States!"

Alas! little knew those faithful souls, who went forth full of hope and patriotism that bright May morning, [348] that they had looked their last upon the living features of their beloved Prophet, whom they were thus offering as a political savior to the nation; that within six weeks, while they were yet absent on their errand, a deed would be done which, for cruelty and atrocity, and for fearful consequences upon the guilty—shedders of innocent blood!—must stand without a parallel in the annals of modern crime.

Doubtless there was a destiny in the absence from the Prophet's side, at such a time, of men like Heber C. Kimball and Brigham Young. Of all those about him, upon these men, as upon two pillars of power, Joseph at that time most leaned. Of the original Twelve Apostles, according to the Prophet's own testimony, this twain alone had never "lifted up their heels against him." Satan knew best when to strike, and chose the fell moment to lay his fatal snare when Brigham, Heber and others of Joseph's wisest counselors were away. God had so ordered and permitted.

St. Louis was reached by the Apostles on the 22nd of May. Calling the Church together in that city, Elders Young and Kimball instructed them spiritually and politically. The Saints there numbered nearly seven hundred souls. Thence, a journey of thirteen days brought them to the capital of the nation.

Heber C. Kimball and Lyman Wight were now traveling together. Following is a digest of their letters to the Prophet, Elder Wight acting as scribe:

"We have got a petition signed, with our names attached, in behalf of the Church, asking for a remuneration for our losses, and not for our rights, or redress, for they would not receive such a petition from us. It was thought by Judge Semple, Judge Douglas, General Atchison, and Major Hughes, that our petition would [349] carry if it was not too late in the season. Judge Semple handed it to the committee on public lands. He said he would do the best he could for us. General Atchison is of the opinion if we could sue the state of Missouri for redress of grievances, that there was virtue enough in the state to answer our demands, 'for,' said he, *'they are ashamed of their conduct.'* Douglas and Semple are of the same opinion. Brother Kimball and myself spared no pains during our stay at Washington. We left on the 11th inst. for Wilmington, Delaware. Thence journeying to Philadelphia on the 13th.

"On the 21st we shall attend conference at Wilmington, and go thence to New York and Boston, and so continue from place to place until we shall have accomplished the mission appointed unto us.... Just returned from Wilmington Conference, accompanied by several of the brethren and sisters who went from this place. We can truly say that this was one of the most pleasant trips in our life. We went down on the steamer *Balloon*, and returned by railway.

"Our Conference commenced on Saturday, the 22nd. The brethren came in from the adjacent country, and after much instruction from Brothers Kimball and Wight, we took a vote to know whether they would go whithersoever the Presidency, Patriarch and Twelve went, should it be to Oregon, Texas or California, or any other place directed by the wisdom of Almighty God. The Saints, numbering about one hundred, rose to their feet and exclaimed, 'whithersoever they go, we go,' without a dissenting voice. This was truly an interesting meeting. We have not the least idea that any one will back out; they are nearly all men of wealth and have commenced this morning to offer all surplus property for sale, that whenever you say go, they are ready. We ordained ten as promising young Elders as we ever laid hands upon. They pledged themselves to start this week and go through the state of Delaware from house to house, and proclaim that the Kingdom of Heaven is at hand.

"On Sabbath, the 23rd, we preached alternately to **[350]** a large and respectable congregation, and left the warmest of friends in that place, both in and out of the Church.

"Yours as ever,
"H. C. KIMBALL,
"LYMAN WIGHT."

A letter from Vilate Kimball to her husband, from which we make the following extracts, describes the scenes that were then taking place in Nauvoo;

"June 7th, 1844.
"MY DEAR HUSBAND:

"Nauvoo was never so lonesome since we lived here as it is now. I went to meeting last Sunday for the first time since conference. Neither Joseph, nor Hyrum, nor any of the Twelve were there, and you may be assured that I was glad when meeting was over....

"June 11th. Nauvoo was a scene of excitement last night. Some hundreds of the brethren turned out and burned the press of the opposite party. This was done by order of the city council. They had only published one paper (*Nauvoo Expositor*) which is considered a public nuisance. They have sworn vengeance and no doubt they will have it.

"June 24th. Since I commenced this letter, varied and exciting indeed have been the scenes in this city. I would have sent this to you before this time, but I have been thrown into such confusion I know not what to write. Nor is this all: the mails do not come regularly, having been stopped by high water, or the flood of mobocracy which pervades the country. I have received no letter by mail from you since you left.

"Nothing is to be heard of but mobs collecting on every side. The Laws and Fosters and most of the dissenting party, with their families, left here a day or two since. They are sworn to have Joseph and the city council, or to exterminate us all. Between three and four thousand brethren have been under arms here the past week, expecting every day the mob would come [351] upon us. The brethren from the country are coming in to aid in the defense of the city. Brother Joseph sent a message to the Governor, signifying, if he and his staff would come into the city he would abide their decision; but instead of the Governor coming here he went to Carthage, and there walked arm and arm with Law and Foster, until we have reason to fear he has caught their spirit. He sent thirty men from there day before yesterday to arrest Brother Joseph, with an abusive letter, saying, if thirty men cannot do the business thousands can, ordering the brethren who had been ordered out to defend the city against the mob to deliver up their arms to their men and then disperse.

"Yesterday morning (although it was Sunday) was a time of great excitement. Joseph had fled and left word for the brethren to hang on to their arms and defend themselves as best they could. Some were dreadfully tried in their faith to think Joseph should leave them in the hour of danger. Hundreds have left; the most of the merchants on the hill have gone. I have not felt frightened, neither has my heart sunk within me till yesterday, when I heard Joseph had sent word back for his family to follow him, and Brother Whitney's family were packing up, not knowing but they would have to go, as he is one of the city council. For a while I felt sad enough, but did not let anybody know it, neither did I shed any tears. I felt a confidence in the Lord that He would preserve us from the ravages of our enemies. We expected them here to-day by the thousands, but before night yesterday, things put on a different aspect—Joseph returned and gave himself up for trial. He sent a messenger to Carthage to tell the governor he would meet him and his staff at the big mound at eight o'clock this morning, with all that the writ demanded. They have just passed here to meet the Governor for that purpose. My heart said, 'Lord, bless those dear men and preserve them from those that thirst for their blood!' What will be their fate the Lord only knows, but I trust He'll spare them. The governor wrote that if they did not give themselves up, our city was sus[352]pended upon so many kegs of powder, and it needed only one spark to touch them off. If you were here you would be sure to be in their midst, which would increase my anxiety."

Now fell the thunderbolt!

On the 20th of June Joseph, feeling himself hedged around by his enemies, had written for the immediate return of the Apostles. It was his last communication to them in mortality. Seven days later, on the evening of the 27th of June, 1844,

Joseph and his brother Hyrum were assassinated in Carthage Jail.

Heber and Lyman Wight were in Salem, Massachusetts, when the dreadful news came. It struck Heber to the heart. He tried hard not to believe. Yet he, and the Apostles generally, traveling in different parts, on the night of the assassination had felt a severe mental shock, for which they could not account until the terrible news reached their ears.

Grief-stricken and almost crushed with sorrow, the Twelve turned their sad steps homeward. Heber and Lyman took the cars for Boston, where they remained during the day, and then proceeded to New York. Returning to Boston to consult with their quorum, on the 24th of July in company with President Brigham Young they set out for home. At Albany they were joined by Orson Hyde, Orson Pratt and Wilford Woodruff. They traveled night and day, and arrived at Nauvoo on the 6th of August, forty days after the martyrdom. [353]

## CHAPTER 19

CHOICE OF JOSEPH'S SUCCESSOR—A MIRACLE—THE MANTLE OF JOSEPH FALLS UPON BRIGHAM YOUNG—HEBER C. KIMBALL HIS RIGHT HAND MAN

In the death of its Prophet and Patriarch, the Church had received a stunning blow, but with superhuman vitality it revived from the shock, and rose up in God-like energy to renew its mission of salvation to mankind. Mighty men were they who had fallen, but God's work rests not upon man, and under the magic stroke of the wand of Omnipotence other great men had risen to fulfill their destiny and perpetuate the works and memories of the martyred slain.

But who was now the leader of Israel? Such was the problem presenting itself to the people. In the absence of their Prophet the Saints felt like sheep without a shepherd. He had carried the Church, as if an infant in arms, from the very hour of its birth, nursing it with the milk of revelation. It was now no longer a babe, yet still, as a little child, it had need to be led, by one in whom was the spirit and wisdom of the heavens.

A crisis had come. The First Presidency was no more. Death had dissolved that quorum. Next, stood the Twelve, an independent body, now holding the keys of the kingdom, from Joseph, its earthly founder.

But this fact, though known to the Apostles, upon whom he had rolled that burden and conferred that authority, was not so patent to the people. The order of the Priesthood was not so well known then as now. Experience had not supplemented revelation on these [354] points, and doubtless there were many Saints in Nauvoo, as there are many now, who were not informed upon things which had been plainly taught them for years.

Besides, Sidney Rigdon, one of the three first presidents, was alive, to press his claims to the leadership, and not a few of the Saints openly favored his ambitious pretensions.

Who was to decide in such a controversy, and how was the right man to be known?

God had provided the way.

Elder Rigdon, on hearing of the martyrdom, had come in haste from Pittsburgh, whither he had retired some months before from the troubles and turmoils of persecuted Saint-life in Nauvoo, to offer himself as the "guardian" and "great leader" whom he declared was necessary to save Israel. Thus, the true shepherd, having "laid down his life for the sheep," the false one returned when the wolves had fled and the danger was thought to be over, to seize the laurels which another's valor had won. And this, forsooth, was the comforting message that he bore to the affrighted people:

"The anti-Mormons have got you! You can't stay in the country! Everything is in confusion! You can do nothing! You lack a great leader! You want a head; and unless you unite upon that head you're blown to the four winds. The anti-Mormons will carry the election. A guardian must be chosen."

Such was the situation at Nauvoo when Brigham, Heber and their companions returned. Parley P. Pratt and George A. Smith had arrived some time before.

The great day came which Sidney Rigdon had set apart for the choosing of a guardian for the Church—August 8th, 1844. Sidney had spoken, urging his own claims as "the identical man whom all the prophets had [355] written and sung about" with their eyes upon that very hour and occasion; which vain-glorious remark provoked from Parley P. Pratt the humorous retort that he, himself, was "the identical man that the prophets had not sung or written one word about." Brigham Young was now addressing the vast congregation which assembled on that memorable day, in the grove where the Prophet had so often given the word of the Lord to Israel:

"If the people want Brother Rigdon to lead them, they may have him," Brigham declared. "But I say unto you, the Twelve have the keys of the kingdom of God in all the world. The Twelve are pointed out by the finger of God. Here is Brigham; have his knees ever faltered? Have his lips ever quivered? Here is Heber and the rest of the Twelve, an independent body, who have the keys of the Priesthood, the keys of the kingdom of God to deliver to all the world; this is true, so help me God! They stand next to Joseph, and are the First Presidency of the Church."

It was the voice of "one having authority." The dullest ear could detect the difference between such tones, such words, trembling with power, and the vain and empty babblings of the special pleader, Sidney. Which of these men the Spirit had chosen, was already manifest to the pure in heart among that mighty multitude.

But a still more marvelous manifestation awaited them. As Brigham proceeded his whole being became transfigured; his face shone like an angel's; his form seemed to dilate and expand, as though he were being lifted from the floor; his voice changed; his look, his very manner was that of another.

IT WAS JOSEPH, NOT BRIGHAM, WHO WAS SPEAKING!

Thousands, saw it and testified of its truth. The mantle of the dead Prophet had fallen upon the shoulders **[356]** of the living. Joseph, from behind the vail, had pointed out his own successor. God spake that day through Brigham Young, "and all the people said Amen!"

No truer friend had Brigham Young than Heber C. Kimball.[6] "Brother Brigham" had been his choice from the first, for he knew that he was the chosen of the Almighty, and as he had before stood by Joseph, he now stood firm at the side of his successor, a pillar of faith and power not to be broken.

## CHAPTER 50

THE WORK MOVES ON IN SPITE OF PERSECUTION AND APOSTASY—THE NAUVOO TEMPLE FINISHED AND DEDICATED—THE SAINTS PREPARE FOR THEIR REMOVAL TO THE ROCKY MOUNTAINS

THE work of God was only expedited by the efforts made for its overthrow. The Apostles continued to send out missonaries to the nations, and hurried on the completion of the Temple.

Elder Rigdon, after his ineffectual attempt to seize the leadership of the Church, had returned to Pittsburg, to nurse, as best he might, his wounded pride and disappointed ambition. Many, like him, were apostatizing and dividing into factions, but the main body of the Saints, "taking the Holy Spirit for their guide," stood true to Brigham and the Twelve. The Spirit was poured **[357-359]** out mightily upon the faithful, and the good work, in spite of persecution and apostasy, went rolling on.

It soon became evident to the enemy that the death of the Prophet, so far from destroying, or even impeding Mormonism, had only given it fresh impetus, an energy which they feared, if allowed to increase, might prove irresistible. They therefore renewed the attack, Brigham, Heber and the Twelve now being the especial objects of their animus.

Does not this fact, alone, tell where lay the authority?

The chief inciters of the opposition were the Laws, the Fosters, and the Higbees, apostates who had betrayed and sacrificed Joseph and Hyrum, with others who now joined them in their warfare against the Twelve. The most strenuous efforts were made, generally under cover of law, to get President Young into their power; and even his life, it is said, was attempted by the midnight assassin. Knowing their fell purpose, and remembering the fate of the martyrs, Joseph and Hyrum, who had tested the virtue of official pledges and the protecting majesty of the law in Illinois, Brigham and Heber wisely determined not to be taken.

---

[6] Heber often said that his love for Brigham exceeded his love for any member of his own family.

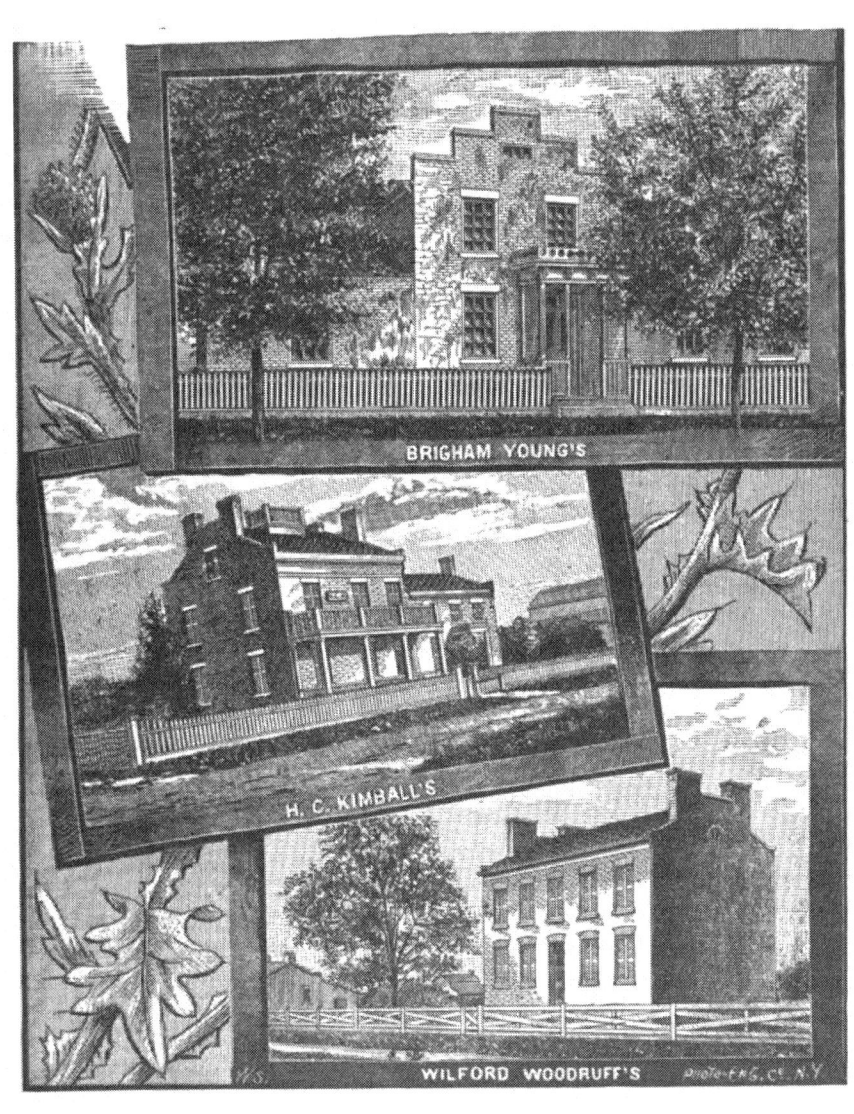

Residences of Church Leaders in Nauvoo

From their secret retreats, where they were compelled to hide, at times, from the malice of their would be destroyers, the Apostles came forth, on the morning of Saturday, the 24th of May, 1845, to lay the cap-stone on the south-east corner of the Temple. The edifice was in due time completed and dedicated, and many of the Elders and Saints received their endowments within its sacred walls.

The incident which gave rise to the story of "Bogus Brigham," with which many of our readers are no doubt familiar, happened about this time. The sheriff from Carthage, was at the door of the Temple to arrest [360] President Young, who was inside the building. Bishop William Miller, who resembled the President, throwing on Heber C. Kimball's cloak, (mistaking it for Brigham's, which was of the same size and color) sallied out and was arrested in his stead and taken to Carthage. The *ruse* worked so well that it was not discovered until after their arrival at the anti-Mormon headquarters, where "Bill Miller" was recognized, and the wrath and discomfiture of his captors knew no bounds. The real Brigham was, of course, by that time, well out of the way and laughing at the chagrin of his persecutors.

In the meantime, preparations were in progress for the exodus. The anti-Mormons were clamoring for the removal of the entire community of Latter-day Saints from the state, and they, seeing no alternative but to comply with this outrageous demand, or experience a repetition of the murderous scenes of Missouri, had resolved to again sacrifice their homes and seek a land of peace and liberty in the wilds of the savage west.

Before coming to the conclusion to thus expatriate themselves, the Saints, through their leaders, had petitioned the President of the United States, James K. Polk, and the Governors of all the states excepting Missouri and Illinois, for aid and protection from the efforts of those who were plotting their destruction. But the appeal was in vain. The Church leaders then entered into negotiations with their enemies, of the nature of which the following document will testify:

"NAUVOO, ILLINOIS, Oct. 1st, 1845.
"To Gen. J. Hardin, W. B. Warren, S. A. Douglas and J. A. McDougal:

"MESSRS:—In reply to your letter of this date, requesting us 'to submit the facts and intentions stated by us in writing, in order that you may lay them before the [361] Governor and people of the state,' we would refer you to our communication of the 24th ult. to the 'Quincy Committee,' etc., a copy of which is herewith enclosed.

"In addition to this we would say that we had commenced making arrangements to remove from the country previous to the recent disturbances; that we have four companies, of one hundred families each, and six more companies now organizing, of the same number each, preparatory to a removal.

"That one thousand families, including the Twelve, the High Council, the trustees and general authorities of the Church, are fully determined to remove in the spring, independent of the contingencies of selling our property; and that this company will comprise from five to six thousand souls.

"That the Church, as a body, desire to remove with us, and will, if sales can be effected so as to raise the necessary means.

"That the organization of the Church we represent is such that there never can exist but one head or presidency at any one time. And all good members wish to be with the organization: and all are determined to remove to some distant point where we shall neither infringe nor be infringed upon, so soon as time and means will permit.

"That we have some hundreds of farms and some two thousand houses for sale in this city and county, and we request all good citizens to assist in the disposal of our property.

"That we do not expect to find purchasers for our temple and other public buildings; but we are willing to rent them to a respectable community who may inhabit the city.

"That we wish it distinctly understood that although we may not find purchasers for our property, we will not sacrifice it, nor give it away, or suffer it illegally to be wrested from us.

"That we do not intend to sow any wheat this fall, and should we all sell, we shall not put in any more crops of any description. [362]

"That as soon as practicable, we will appoint committees for this city, La Harpe, Macedonia, Bear Creek and all necessary places in the county, to give information to purchasers.

"That if these testimonies are not sufficient to satisfy any people that we are in earnest, we will soon give them a sign that cannot be mistaken—WE WILL LEAVE THEM.

"In behalf of the Council, respectfully yours, etc.,

"BRIGHAM YOUNG, President,
"WILLARD RICHARDS, Clerk."

Agreeable to the terms of this covenant, which satisfied the commissioners named, and for a time also satisfied the anti-Mormons whom they represented, the Saints, trusting in God, and hoping little from their cruel and inhuman oppressors, were now preparing for the exodus of the Church and its pilgrimage to the Rocky Mountains—an event foreseen and predicted by the Prophet Joseph in August, 1842. [363]

---

# CHAPTER 51

THE EXODUS—HEBER'S PROPHECY FULFILLED—EVACUATION OF NAUVOO—THE CAMP OF ISRAEL ON SUGAR CREEK—BRIGHAM AND HEBER LEAD THE CHURCH WESTWARD—ARRIVAL AT THE MISSOURI RIVER

A SPECTACLE sublime. An exiled nation, going forth like Israel from Egypt, into the wilderness, there to worship, unmolested, the God of their fathers in His own appointed way; that from their loins might spring a people nursed in the spirit of prophecy, made stalwart by tribulation, that should leap from the mountains in a day to come, and roll back, an avalanche of power, to regain possession of their promised land.

Such was the meaning of that exodus. The future will justify the action of the past.

On Tuesday, February 17th, 1846, Heber C. Kimball left Nauvoo, in company with Bishop N. K. Whitney, and, crossing the Mississippi, joined the camp of Israel on Sugar Creek, with their faces toward the Rocky Mountains. Heber's prediction over the fated city, which had so alarmed Elder Rigdon seven years before, was being fulfilled; the evacuation of Nauvoo and the exodus of the Saints from Illinois had begun. President Young had left the city two days before, Heber, having sent his family away on the 16th, had tarried behind with William Clayton and Bishop Whitney, to secure and bring Church property needed for the pioneers. Sugar Creek was the starting point. Here, for nearly two weeks, some of the advance com[364]panies had been anxiously awaiting the coming of their leaders.

At half-past one, Brigham and Heber dined together in George D. Grant's tent, on bean porridge, after which frugal meal, the President, with Heber C. Kimball, Orson Hyde, Orson Pratt, John Taylor, George A. Smith and Willard Richards went up the valley east of the camp about half a mile, and held a council. A letter was read from Samuel Brannan, with a copy of an agreement between Elder Brannan and Postmaster-General Benson. The matter concerned a proposition of certain politicians at Washington and members of the government to the Mormon leaders, to take possession of California and divide the lands with them as a great "land grab" for these statesmen, in return for proffered protection to the Mormons. The proposition was at once rejected.

On the 18th, Heber accompanied President Young and several others back to Nauvoo, where many of the Saints still lingered, most of whom were getting ready to join the camp as soon as possible, while others, like those of earlier days in Kirtland and Far West, were preparing to fall away. A number of meetings, public and private, were held in the Temple, at the last one of which, on Sunday the 22nd, a panic was caused by the snapping of a piece of timber in the settling of the new floor under the weight of the multitude. Several people were seriously injured. The same afternoon, Brigham, Heber and John Taylor returned to camp.

The companies were being organized and made ready to start. They comprised about four hundred wagons, all heavily loaded, with not over half the number of teams necessary for a rapid journey. Most of the families were supplied with provisions for several [365] months; but a number, regardless of counsel, had started in a destitute condition, and some with only provisions for a few days.

Colonel Stephen Markham had about one hundred pioneers to prepare the road in advance of the main body. Colonel Hosea Stout with about one hundred men acted as police, armed with rifles. Colonel John Scott with a hundred men accompanied the artillery.

On the morning of Sunday, March 1st, the camp was notified to be ready to start at noon. At half past ten Heber went to meeting and stated that President Young was unwell, and further addressed the assembly as follows:

"It is the President's will that the camp should remove to some other location, because while we are so near Nauvoo the brethren are continually going back and neglecting their teams and families, and running to Brother Brigham about a little property they have here or there. No doubt many will be tried, but we shall see the kingdom of God established and all the kingdoms of this world become the kingdoms of our God and His Christ." He encouraged the brethren to go forward. "The grass will start before long. They were not going out of the world. If Nauvoo has been the most holy place, it will be the most wicked place." He then called upon all who meant to go ahead to say aye. The brethren responded heartily. "No doubt you mean to have President Young for your leader. We will do all that he says and everything will be right. A plague came upon Zion's Camp for disobedience when on our way to Missouri, and some of our best men fell victims, and so it would be again under like circumstances. I want no man to touch any of my things without my leave. If any man will come to me and say that he wants to steal I will give him the amount. Cease all your loud laughter and light speeches, for the Lord is displeased [366] with such things, and call upon the Lord with all your might."

Such was Heber's first pioneer address to the Camp of Israel.

All tents were now struck, and about noon the camp began to move. They traveled in a north-westerly direction about five miles, and at night camped again on Sugar Creek. The ground was covered with snow, but by dint of shoveling and scraping space was soon made for the tents, and in a short time quite a primitive little city had sprung up as if by magic from the frozen earth. Large fires were built in front of the tents and wagons, corraled in circular array according to the custom of the plains, and all were made as comfortable as possible under the circumstances.

Notwithstanding their hardships and privations, past, present and prospective, a spirit of remarkable cheerfulness reigned throughout the camp; songs were sung, jokes passed and stories told, and, in spite of the situation and forbidding surroundings, everybody seemed determined to "make the best of it" and be contented and happy. Doubtless the romance of the situation helped to season it and make it palatable; but above all was it due to the presence and sustaining power of the Holy Spirit, the peace that "passeth understanding," which rested upon the homeless pilgrims, causing them to rejoice, like the Saints of old, in suffering tribulation for the truth's sake.

At a seasonable hour the merriment was hushed. Heads were bowed in reverent prayer. The God of Israel was invoked in behalf of His cause and people; these whose home from henceforth was the houseless plain and prairie, and the remnant left behind to the mercies of the mob in the doomed city of Nauvoo. [367] Guards were then placed, the flickering firelight waned and died in the wintry stillness, and the Camp of Israel, all save the watchful sentries, slept.

Near the Chariton River, on the 27th of March, the organization of the camp was perfected. It was divided into companies of "hundreds," "fifties" and "tens," with captains appointed over each. The Apostles were placed at the heads of divisions, as presidents. Commissaries were also appointed for each company, with a Commissary General. The camp consisted of two grand divisions, presided over respectively by Brigham Young and Heber C. Kimball; the former, as President and General-in-Chief, directing the whole. Occasionally the President would return and gather a council of the captains and Apostles at Heber's encampment, and at other times Heber would go over with his captains to Brigham's camp, for the same purpose.

The law of the Lord was laid down in great strictness, honesty and morality being especially enjoined. Innocent amusement and recreation were encouraged by the leaders, in moderation, as tending to divert the people's minds from their past troubles, and lighten their present toils, but excess of mirth and loud laughter were deprecated and denounced. The Church had again been cleansed of much of its dross, by leaving it behind, and in the main it was a faithful and a pure people that journeyed westward to find another promised land.

The vanguard under Brigham and Heber reached the Missouri River about the middle of June, and received a friendly welcome from the Pottowatomie and Omaha Indians. [368]

---

## CHAPTER 52

DESTINATION OF THE SAINTS—THE CALL FOR THE MORMON BATTALION—HEROIC RESPONSE OF THE EXILES—BRIGHAM, HEBER AND WILLARD AS RECRUITING SERGEANTS—DEPARTURE OF THE BATTALION—THE CAMP OF ISRAEL GOES INTO WINTER QUARTERS—THE FALL OF NAUVOO

> Where now shall fancy's roving pinion rest?
> 'Mid barren regions of the boundless West,
> Where silvery streams through silent valleys flow
> From mountains crested with eternal snow;
> Where reigns no creed its rival creed to bind,
> Where exiled faith a resting-place shall find,
> Where builds the eagle on the beetling height
> And wings o'er freedom's hills unfearing flight.

THE point in view of the leaders of Israel was the Valley of the Great Salt Lake, a portion of Mexican territory located in the tops of the mountains, in the very heart of the American desert. Discouraging as were all reports relating to this barren and inhospitable region, a thousand miles farther on over trackless plains and bleak mountains swarming with wild beasts and savages, these intrepid men resolved to go forward, trusting in God and braving every peril. At least it was a land of liberty, uninfested by mobs and heartless priests and politicians, and with the wintry sky above, and the frozen earth beneath, or in summer the burning rocks and waterless wastes around them, they felt safer far in the society of wild Indians and savage wolves, than in the midst of the Christian civilization they had left behind. [369]

> Far from the realms where civilization reigns,
> Where Freedom's bastards bind her sons in chains,
> They sought a home within the western wild,
> And fraternized the forest's dusky child;
> No fiercer found, less savage in the test,
> Than priestly tyrants trampling the oppressed.

Journeying towards the Missouri river they founded temporary settlements, or "traveling stakes of Zion," recruiting their strength with needed rest along the way, and putting in crops for their own use or for their brethren to reap who came after them. Two of these settlements were named Garden Grove and Mt. Pisgah, the latter over a hundred miles in the rear of the vanguard now resting on the Missouri river.

It was the design of the leaders to leave the main body of the people in these places, while they, with a picked band of pioneers, hastened on to the Rocky Mountains that season. But an incident now occurred which changed their plans and delayed the departure of the pioneers until the following spring.

Word was brought to head-quarters on the Missouri, that a United States army officer with a squad of soldiers had arrived at Mt. Pisgah, with a requisition for five hundred men, to be furnished by the Mormons, to enter the army and march to California to take part in the war against Mexico,

Imagination can alone picture the surprise, almost dismay, with which this startling news was received, What! the nation whose people had thrust them from its borders, robbed them of their homes and driven them into the wilderness, where it was hoped they might perish, now calling upon them for aid? And this in full face of the fact that their own oft reiterated appeals for help had been denied? [370]

It was even so; five hundred able-bodied men, the flower of the camp, were wanted. And this in the heart of an Indian country, in the midst of an exodus unparalleled for its dangers and hardships, when every active man was needed as a bulwark of defense and a staff for the aged and feeble. For even delicate women, thus far, had in some instances been driving teams and tending stock, owing to the limited number of men available.

On the other hand, it was their country calling, and these sons and daughters of the pilgrims and patriots loved their country, loved its institutions and its laws, though the government of that country, in the hands of self-seeking demagogues and politicians, had been as a cruel step-mother rather than a tender parent to them.

What was to be done? What would the leaders decide to do? Such were the questions that flew like lightning through the camp, as these thoughts came rushing to mind. They were not left long unanswered.

## CHAPTER 52

On the 1st of July, Capt. James Allen, the recruiting officer, acting under orders of Col. S. F. Kearney at Fort Leavenworth, having arrived at "The Bluffs," went into council with Brigham Young, Heber C. Kimball, Orson Hyde, Orson Pratt, Willard Richards, George A. Smith, John Taylor, John Smith and Levi Richards. Wilford Woodruff was at Mount Pisgah, where he had received Captain Allen and his party a few days before. The brethren were assured that the offer to accept the services of a battalion of Mormon soldiers in the Mexican war, was made by the government in kindness, and meant as a means of assistance to the community, whose young and intelligent men might thus proceed, at the government's expense, to the ultimate destination [371] of their whole people, and look out the land and prepare the way for their brethren who came after them. This was the object, it was said, quite as much as to enlist their services in their country's cause.

Whether convinced or not that such was the case, the result of the council's deliberations was a resolve to raise the troops. Brigham Young, Heber C. Kimball and Willard Richards, in the role of recruiting sergeants, at once set out for Mt. Pisgah, a distance of one hundred and thirty miles, to execute the order for the Battalion. Colonel Thomas L. Kane, that noble friend of the Mormon people, who had arrived at the Bluffs, thus summarizes the result: "A central mass meeting for council, some harangues at the more remotely scattered camps, an American flag brought out from the storehouse of things rescued, and hoisted to the top of a tree-mast, and, in three days, the force was reported, mustered, organized and ready to march."

The Mormon Battalion set out for the west about the middle of July.

The project of the Pioneers, of going to the mountains that season, was now of course abandoned, and the Camp of Israel prepared to go into "Winter Quarters." This was the name given to their settlement on the Missouri, the principal part of which was on the west side of the river, five miles above Omaha of to-day. It is now known as Florence. Seven hundred houses of log, turf and other primitive materials, neatly arranged and laid out with streets and byways; well supplied with workshops, mills and factories, and with a tabernacle of worship in the midst; the whole arising from a pretty plateau overlooking the river, and well fortified with breast-work, stockade and block-houses, after the fashion of the frontier;—such was Winter Quarters, the principal one of [372] these so-called "traveling stakes of Zion." Here, in these humble, prairie settlements, surrounded by Indians, whose savage hearts God had wondrously softened into sympathy and friendship for His exiled people, the Camp of Israel, the residue of twenty thousand souls, which the Saints had numbered in Illinois, passed the winter of 1846.

Meanwhile, in September of that year, the remnant left in Nauvoo, between six and seven hundred souls, after a gallant defense of their city against the mob, which, in violation of every treaty, came upon them in overwhelming numbers, were driven from their homes at the point of the bayonet, and thrown, men, women and children, sick, dying and shelterless, upon the western shores of the Mississippi. And this—shades of the patriots!—while their brethren, the heroes of the Mormon

Battalion, were marching to fight their country's battles on the plains of Mexico! [373]

## CHAPTER 53

THE WORD AND WILL OF THE LORD CONCERNING THE CAMP OF ISRAEL—THE PIONEERS START FOR THE ROCKY MOUNTAINS—NAMES OF THE HEROES—INCIDENTS OF THE JOURNEY WEST

THE "Word and Will of the Lord concerning the Camp of Israel in their journeyings to the West," was given through President Brigham Young at Winter Quarters on the 14th of January, 1847. It was the first written revelation sent out to the Church since the death of the Prophet Joseph. Agreeable to its instructions, the Saints began to prepare for their journey to the mountains.

Early in April the pioneers started from Winter Quarters. This famous band numbered one hundred and forty-eight souls, including three women and two children. The *personnel* of the company as it left the Missouri River, was as follows:

1 Brigham Young.
2 Heber C. Kimball.
3 Orson Pratt.
4 Wilford Woodruff.
5 George A. Smith.
6 Willard Richards.
7 Amasa Lyman.
8 Ezra T. Benson.
9 John S. Fowler.
10 Jacob D. Durnham.
11 Joseph Egbert.
12 John M. Freeman.
13 Marcus B. Thorpe.
14 George Wardel.
15 Thomas Grover.
16 Barnabas L. Adams.
17 Roswell Stevens.
18 Starling Driggs.
19 Albert Carrington.
20 Thomas Bullock.
21 George Brown.
22 Jesse C. Little.
23 Phineas H. Young.
24 John Y. Greene.
25 Thomas Tanner
26 Addison Everett. [374]
27 Truman O. Angell.
28 Lorenzo D. Young.
29 Briant Stringham.
30 Albert P. Rockwood.
31 Joseph S. Schofield.
32 Luke Johnson.
33 John G. Holman.
34 Edmund Ellsworth.
35 Sidney Alvarus Hanks.
36 George R. Grant.
37 Millen Atwood.
38 Samuel Fox.
39 Tunis Reppelvee.
40 Eli Harvey Pierce.
41 William Dykes.
42 Jacob Weiler.
43 Stephen H. Goddard.
44 Tarlton Lewis.
45 Henry G. Sherwood.
46 Zebedee Coltrin.
47 Sylvester H. Earl.
48 John Dixon.
49 Samuel H. Marble.
50 George Scholes.

## CHAPTER 53

51 William Henrie.
52 William A. Empey.
53 Charles Shumway.
54 Andrew P. Shumway.
55 Thomas Woolsey.
56 Chancy Loveland.
57 Erastus Snow.
58 James Craig.
59 William Wordsworth.
60 William P. Vance.
61 Simeon Heyd.
62 Seely Owen.
63 James Case.
64 Artemas Johnson.
65 William C. A. Smoot.
66 Benjamin Franklin Dewey.
67 William Carter.
68 John G. Losee.
69 Burr Frost.
70 Datus Ensign.
71 Benjamin Franklin Stewart.
72 Horace Monroe Frink.
73 Eric Glines.
74 Ozro Eastman.
75 Seth Taft.
76 Horace M. Thornton.
77 Stephen Kelsey.
78 John S. Eldredge.
79 Charles D. Barnham.
80 Almon L. Williams.
81 Rufus Allen.
82 Robert T. Thomas.
83 James W. Stewart.
84 Elijah Newman.
85 Levi N. Kendall.
86 Francis Boggs.
87 David Grant.
88 Howard Egan.
89 William A. King.
90 Thomas P. Cloward.
91 Hosea Cushing.
92 Robert Byard.
93 George P. Billings.
94 Edson Whipple.
95 Philo Johnson.
96 Carlos Murray.
97 Appleton M. Harmon.
98 Willam Clayton.
99 Horace K. Whitney.
100 Orson K. Whitney.
101 Orrin Porter Rockwell.
102 Nathaniel Thomas Brown.
103 Jackson Reddin.
104 John Pack.
105 Francis M. Pomeroy.
106 Aaron Farr. **[375]**
107 Nathaniel Fairbanks.
108 John S. Higbee.
109 John Wheeler.
110 Solomon Chamberlin.
111 Conrad Klineman.
112 Joseph Rooker.
113 Perry Fitzgerald.
114 John H. Tippitts.
115 James Davenport.
116 Henson Walker.
117 Benjamin W. Rolfe.
118 Norton Jacobs.
119 Charles A. Harper.
120 George Woodard.
121 Stephen Markham.
122 Lewis Barney.
123 George Mills.
124 Andrew S. Gibbons.
125 Joseph Hancock.
126 John W. Norton.
127 Shadrach Roundy.
128 Hans C. Hanson.
129 Levi Jackman.
130 Lyman Curtis.
131 John Brown.
132 Matthew Ivory.
133 David Powell.
134 Hark Lark (colored).
135 Oscar Crosby (colored).
136 Joseph Matthews.

137 Gilburd Summe.
138 John Gleason.
139 Charles Burke.
140 Alexander P. Chessley.

141 Rodney Badger.
142 Norman Taylor.
143 Green Flake (colored).

The above names, with the exception of the first eight (the Apostles) are given in their order, as divided into companies of tens.

The three women who accompanied the pioneers were Ellen Sanders, one of the wives of Heber C. Kimball; Clara Decker, a wife of Brigham Young; and Harriet P. Young, her mother, wife of Lorenzo D. Young. The children were Sobieski Young, son of Lorenzo, and Perry Decker, own brother to Clara Decker Young.

President Brigham Young was the leader of the company, which, as seen, numbered among its members seven others of the Twelve. Apostles Parley P. Pratt, Orson Hyde and John Taylor were absent on missions.

The object of the pioneers, as shown, was to explore the region of the Great Salt Lake, and if possible find a home for the Saints in the midst of the Rocky Mountains. A few leaves from Heber's pioneer journal will now be interesting. He writes: **[376]**

"On the 5th day of April, 1847, I started with six of my teams and went out about four miles, where I formed an encampment with several others of my division. The same day I returned home and remained in Winter Quarters during the conference on the 6th. On the 7th and 8th I was still making preparations for my journey, and called my family together and spent some time in giving them instructions, blessing them and dedicating and consecrating them to the Most High God."

Horace K. Whitney, one of the pioneers and Heber's son-in-law, who was present at this family meeting, in his own journal says:

"Brother Kimball expressed his feelings at length. He said that any person who attempted to come into his family and sow discord among them, and promote disunion, and strive to alienate their minds from him in his absence, would be cursed. 'Don't you think so, Brother Whitney?' addressing my father. Father replied, 'Yes.' He further observed that there was not that person living in the world in whom he placed more confidence than he did in Bishop Whitney, and that there was no person in the world who would have so much influence in his (Brother K's.) absence as Bishop Whitney, and he recommended him to them as a worthy, good and exemplary man, to counsel them in his absence. He told his wife Vilate that if any person should presume to come into his house and speak against him, or any member of his family, while he was gone, to arise and command them to leave the house, *in the name of Heber C. Kimball!*"

"On the 8th," continues Heber, "Brother Parley P. Pratt arrived in Winter Quarters, having returned from his mission to England. Those of the Twelve who had departed, hearing of his arrival, returned, and in the evening we held a council at Dr. Richard's office; and it [377] was a time of rejoicing with us to behold our beloved brother and companion in tribulation. He gave us a history of his mission, and of the success, peace and prosperity of the Saints in England. They had annihilated the Joint Stock Company, cut Reuben Hedlock and Ward off from the Church, who were the instigators of it, being the men we had left to preside there, and who had called the Elders of Israel from their duties of preaching life and salvation, and set them to preaching up joint-stockism to get gain. Now things have changed, and the Elders are all preaching the everlasting Gospel, and an entire reformation has commenced, and may the Lord God of Israel roll it forth until Israel shall be saved!

"On the 9th the Twelve started again on their journey. My son William carried out President Young, Bishop Whitney (who was going with us a few miles) and myself in my carriage. The whole camp, after our arrival, started out and went to within four miles of Pappea, being about fourteen miles from Winter Quarters, and camped for the night. I lodged in the wagon with President Young, as he had fitted up a wagon for him and me to lodge together through the journey.

"In the course of the evening Bishop Whitney and myself went some distance upon the prairie, where we bowed down before the Lord and both offered up our prayers to the Most High God in behalf of the pioneers and the Twelve, that they might be protected and upheld and sustained by the Almighty; that His angels might go before them to lead them to a land which the Lord should designate to be a resting place for His people Israel; also in behalf of our families, our wives and children, and all Israel that are left behind.

"In the forenoon of Sunday, the 11th, we arrived [378] at the Elk Horn, which we crossed by means of a raft that had been constructed by some of the first pioneers that went on, at a point two and a half miles south of its junction with the Platte. Seventy-two wagons crossed the 'Horn,' three of which afterwards returned to Winter Quarters, leaving the others to go on with the pioneers. It was not our intention to have encroached on the Sabbath, but the camp were in a disordered state, some being on one side of the 'Horn,' and some on the other, and it was thought wisdom to get them together, lest they should be attacked by Indians and be unprepared for defense."

Leaving the Camp to pursue its journey towards the Platte river, the Apostles with Bishop Whitney now returned to Winter Quarters to greet Elder John Taylor, who had just arrived from Europe, bringing with him over two thousand dollars for the Church. From him they learned that Elder Orson Hyde was also on his way west. On the 15th, Heber, Brigham and others rejoined the Pioneers beyond the Elk Horn.

The camp was now organized as a military body, into companies of hundreds, fifties and tens, agreeable to "the word and will of the Lord," with the following as officers:

Brigham Young, Lieutenant-General; Stephen Markham, Colonel; John Pack and Shadrach Roundy, Majors; Captains of companies, Wilford Woodruff, Ezra T.

Benson, Phineas H. Young, Luke Johnson, Stephen H. Goddard, Charles Shumway, James Case, Seth Taft, Howard Egan, Appleton M. Harmon, John Higbee, Norton Jacobs, John Brown, and Joseph Matthews. Thomas Bullock was appointed clerk, and Thomas Tanner captain of artillery. The "artillery" consisted of one cannon mounted on a pair of wheels, and taken [379] along to frighten hostile Indians into a due regard for the rights of the pioneers, or to perform more serious execution if found necessary.

General Young instructed the camp as follows: The men were to travel in a compact body, every man to keep his loaded gun in his hand, or, if a teamster, in his wagon, ready for instant use; every man to walk by the side of his wagon unless sent by the officer in command, and the wagons to be formed two abreast, where practicable, on the march. At the call of the bugle, at five a. m., the pioneers were to arise, assemble for prayers, get breakfast, and be ready to start at the second call of the bugle at seven. At night, at half past eight, at the command from the bugle, each was to retire for prayer in his own wagon, and to bed at nine o'clock. Tents were to be pitched on Saturday nights, and the Sabbath kept.

Thus organized and equipped, the pioneers proceeded on their way, traveling up the north bank of the Platte. Towards the latter end of April they found themselves in the heart of the Pawnee Indian country.

"At one o'clock p. m. of April 21st," says Heber, "we stopped to feed beside a long narrow lake, close by the river. As soon as the wagons were formed in a semi-circle on the banks of the lake, a guard was placed to watch the Indians and take care of our teams. Many of the Indians had forded the river and followed us to where we stopped, among the number the grand chief of the Pawnee nation, 'Shefmolun.' He presented several certificates signed by travelers who had previously passed through the Pawnee country, all setting forth that the Pawnee chief was friendly and that they had made him presents of a little flour, powder, lead, etc. His object appeared to be to obtain some [380] thing from the camp. I made him a present of some salt, some tobacco, etc, and President Young also gave him some powder, lead, salt and other articles. Many of the brethren also contributed a little flour, etc. But with all this the old chief did not appear satisfied. He seemed to intimate that he expected larger presents from such a large company, and also said he did not like us to travel through their country, he was afraid we would kill their buffalo and drive them off. This was interpreted by a young man of the tribe who could talk a little English. There was not the least appearance of hostility, but, on the contrary, all who came appeared friendly and pleased to shake hands with us. Brother Shumway says there are about twelve thousand of the Pawnees in this neighborhood, and it is reported there are as many as five thousand warriors among them. We have no fears, however, because their only object appears to be to plunder, and it is the calculation of the brethren to be on the alert and well prepared by night and by day.

"We continued our journey till half past five, and then formed the encampment on the banks of the Loup Fork of the Platte river. The brethren were called together and addressed by President Young in reference to what passed at the Pawnee village, their apparent dissatisfaction, etc., and he recommended that we have a strong guard over our horses and around the camp through the night. He then called for volunteers to stand guard, and about one hundred responded, and in the number nearly all the Twelve. President Young and myself both volunteered and stood the first part of the night, till one o'clock. It was very cold indeed, and about the middle of the night it rained again.

"Thursday, 22nd. Morning fine but cool. We [381] have not been troubled by the Indians, and all is peace and quiet around the camp. The cannon was unlimbered last night and placed outside the wagons, ready for action in case of necessity. There were some merry jokes passed this morning on account of two of the picket guard losing their guns, and Colonel Markham losing his hat, during the night. It is reported that they were found asleep on their posts, and those who found them took their guns, etc., to stir up their minds by way of remembrance and to show what the Indians might do while they were sleeping on guard. It is easy to suppose that after the brethren have traveled twenty miles in the day, taken care of their teams, made fires and cooked their victuals, and stood guard night after night, that it will require some energy to keep themselves awake."

The Loup Fork was crossed with difficulty and considerable danger, owing to the quicksands. Heber and others leaped into the stream, at one time, to prevent some of the wagons being overturned. A couple of rafts were built, and the sands packing down more firmly as the horses continued fording, the passage was finally effected without accident or loss. During the next few days, however, several valuable horses were lost, two of them being killed by the accidental discharge of guns, and the others stolen by Indians.

Several of the brethren were shot at by Indians, while out hunting for the stolen animals.

The camp was quite complete in its equipment, industrial, military, literary and otherwise. Ever and anon, as often as the wagons needed repairs, Burr Frost the blacksmith and his assistants would put up their portable forge and reset the tires of wheels, etc. William Clayton and Willard Richards, scribes and historians, [382] invented a machine to measure the distance. This was done by driving a nail into one of the spokes of a wagon wheel, which at every revolution was made to strike upon a saw projecting from the wagon. The circumference of the wheel being known, the number of its revolutions indicated the distance.

The country through which they were passing is thus described: "The country is beautiful and pleasing to the eye of the traveler, notwithstanding there is only the same kind of scenery from day to day, namely, on the left the majestic Platte, with its muddy waters rolling over the universal beds of quicksands, the river frequently hid from view by the many handsome cottonwood groves; before and behind, on the right and left, a vast level prairie, and on the right at a distance the continued range of majestic bluffs. There is a loveliness and beauty connected with the scenery from day to day, but the country is not at all calculated for farming purposes, not only on account of the scarcity of timber, but also on account of the sandy nature of the whole surface of land." [383]

## CHAPTER 54

ARRIVAL AT GRAND ISLAND—THE PIONEER BUFFALO HUNT—HEBER KILLS HIS FIRST BISON—THE SPIRIT OF LEVITY REBUKED—THE PIONEERS REACH FORT LARAMIE

ABOUT the 1st of May the Pioneers reached Grand Island. Here the prairies swarmed with buffalo, in herds of tens of thousands. A grand hunt was indulged in by the brethren, most of whom had never seen a buffalo before, and after much exciting sport, ten of the animals were killed and brought to camp. The following sketch, descriptive of this, the first buffalo hunt of the Pioneers, is from the graphic pen of Horace K. Whitney:

"Sometime before we arrived here, we saw through a spy-glass three buffalo grazing on the top of the bluff to our right, some five or six miles. Two or three footmen went out in pursuit, also three horsemen, viz., Porter Rockwell, Thomas Brown and Luke Johnson. Just before we arrived here we saw a large herd some distance in advance of us, also about five or six miles to our right. Brother O. Pratt counted seventy-four by the aid of his spy-glass. They are now quite visible from our present stopping place. It is about fifty yards across the channel to Grand Island at this place. We traveled about four miles and crossed a slough or pond, which 'puts up' from the river, about noon. Soon after, Porter, T. Brown and Luke Johnson returned. They had wounded, as they supposed mortally, two buffaloes, which, however, managed to get away from them. About one o'clock p. m., we descried, at the distance of five or six miles to our right, on the side of the hill or bluff, two or three herds of buffalo grazing. An immediate halt was made. A band of ten or twelve horsemen (hunters) [384] speedily collected and made arrangements for the chase. They soon got ready and started. Brother Heber soon followed. The wagons traveled along slowly, being in full view of the chase. The horsemen took a circuitous route, in order to head the herd, but were prevented from doing so immediately by an unforeseen occurrence. An antelope passing by near us was shot at by one of the brethren (a footman) but the shot did not take effect. Directly the animal made towards the bluff, seeing which, two dogs went off in full chase. The three went right among the buffaloes which, alarmed at the appearance of the dogs, began to move off. Soon after, the horsemen made their appearance upon the brow of the hill.

"Now commenced a scene which defies all description. Every spyglass that could be found in the camp was put into immediate requisition, and the scene became one of intense interest to us all, as spectators. As soon as the buffaloes discovered the approach of the hunters, they increased their speed (which before had been slow) to a full gallop, and, passing along the side of the hill were followed by the hunters in quick and hot pursuit, leaving a cloud of dust in their rear. Most of the hunters, by riding in among them, succeeded in getting a fair shot, although they did not all prove fatal, a number of the herd making their escape that were shot through the body. Brother Heber rode in among them, made a shot at one and brought him down. His horse, partly alarmed at the discharge of the gun, and partly at the sight of the animals, suddenly started and came very near throwing him. Porter rode up to one (by way of experiment) and shot him full in the forehead, but without making the least impression, the hide of the skull-piece being an inch thick, besides being covered with a large mass of coarse matted hair, as we discovered after the animals were brought in. The chase ceased about 4 p. m. and the hunters came up to us about 5 p. m. The fruits of the day's work were as follows: one bull, three cows, and six calves, making ten buffaloes. Five wagons were immediately unloaded to bring in the game. A little after dark they returned, and the meat was dis[385]tributed, one quarter of an animal being given to each ten."

After this day's sport, President Young cautioned the brethren not to kill game wantonly, as it was displeasing to the Lord. Said he: "If we slay when we have no need, we will need when we cannot slay."

The advice was timely. A spirit of excessive levity had crept into the camp, dancing, card-playing and other games, some of them vain and foolish in the extreme, occupying most of the time of the brethren when they had stopped for rest.

Heber, noticing this tendency, reproved them and warned them of the evil results to which such things would lead. Next day, Saturday, May 28th, President Young addressed the camp in relation to the same subject. He sharply rebuked the offenders, and declared that he would not go one step farther in company with such a spirit as they then possessed. He appealed to them as men of God, to bear in mind their high and holy calling and the noble purpose of their mission. Apostle Orson Pratt and others also spoke, counseling the brethren to use their spare time in reading, and storing their minds with useful knowledge; to cease their profanity, loud laughter and excess of mirth, and fast and pray more, that the spirit of their mission might rest upon them.

A general reformation was the result. The brethren repented, and, confessing their faults, resolved to eschew the evils complained of. They faithfully kept their word, and a better feeling prevailed in the camp from that hour.

On the second of June the Pioneers arrived opposite Fort Laramie, 543 miles from Winter Quarters, which distance they had traveled in about seven weeks. [386] Here they were joined by a small company of Saints from Mississippi, who had spent the winter in Pueblo. The first half of their journey to the mountains was now over.

# CHAPTER 55

THE PIONEERS CROSS THE PLATTE—GOVERNOR BOGGS AND THE MISSOURIANS—COL. BRIDGER "A THOUSAND DOLLARS FOR A BUSHEL OF WHEAT"—THE PIONEERS' FIRST GLIMPSE OF THE VALLEY OF THE GREAT SALT LAKE

THE pioneers now crossed the Platte, hiring a flatboat for that purpose from Mr. Bordeaux, a Frenchman, the principal man at the fort. From him they learned that their old enemy, Governor Boggs, of Missouri, had recently passed over with two companies, on their way to California. True to his instincts and traditions, Governor Boggs had maligned the characters of the Mormons to Mr. Bordeaux, who answered that the Mormons could not be any worse than his party, who were quarreling and stealing all along the way.

Prior to crossing the river the pioneers had broken a new road over the plains for several hundred miles, along which tens of thousands of the Saints subsequently traveled. It was known for many years as the "old Mormon road," until the railroad came to cover it up and obliterate almost from recollection the toils and trials of [387] the ox-team journeys of early days. But now the brethren were in the wake of the Missouri companies, traveling towards the land of gold.

At the Black Hills they were seven days in crossing the river. Having there overtaken the Missourians, they ferried them over, also, at the rate of $1.50 for each wagon and load, taking their pay in flour, meal and bacon at Missouri prices. By this time their stock of provisions was well-nigh exhausted. To have it thus replenished in the Black Hills, and at the hands of their old enemies, the Missourians, they regarded as little less than a miracle.

In this locality Heber discovered a fine spring of clear, cold water, which he named for himself, "Kimball's Spring."

The Missourians, who traveled on Sundays, while the pioneers rested and kept the holy day, were quarreling among themselves continually, and, not satisfied with this, began to insult and annoy their Mormon neighbors. One evening, as Heber and Ezra T. Benson were riding ahead of their company to look out a camping ground, six men, dressed as Indians, being clothed in white and blue blankets, suddenly sprang up from the grass, about half a mile to the left of the road, and mounting their horses started on. Seeing that the sight of their blankets failed to terrify the Mormon scouts, who continued leisurely on their way, one of the party left his companions and retracing a few steps, motioned with his hand for the brethren to go back. They kept on, however, and the pseudo savage and his comrades then scampered off and disappeared behind a ridge some distance ahead.

Heber and his companion rode on, and having gained the summit, were just in time to see the six Missourians, for such they were, ride into camp, no doubt to [388] relate how badly they had scared the two "Mormons." The brethren treated the matter with silent contempt, though naturally a little indignant at the gratuitous insult offered them.

Independence Rock on the 21st of June; South Pass on the 26th. Two days later Colonel Bridger came into camp. In council with the Mormon leaders, he gave them some information, mostly of a discouraging character, in regard to the region towards which they were traveling, and in conclusion said that he would give a thousand dollars for the first bushel of wheat raised in Salt Lake Valley.

On went the heroic band, nothing daunted, wading rivers, crossing deserts and climbing mountains; trusting in God and their great destiny. It did not desert them. On the afternoon of Saturday, July 24th, 1847, their dust-covered wagons emerged from the mouth of the ravine now known as Emigration Canyon, and the Valley of the Great Salt Lake burst like a vision of glory upon their enraptured view.

> Ah! marvel nothing if the eye may trace
> The care-lines on each toil-worn hero's face,
> Nor yet, if down his cheek in silent show,
> The trickling tides of tender feeling flow;
> Tears not of weakness, nor of sorrow's mood,
> As when o'er vanished joys sad memories brood,
> Far richer fount those fearless eyes bedewed,
> They wept the golden drops of gratitude.
>
> Wherefore! Ask of the bleak and biting wind,
> The rivers, rocks and deserts left behind,
> The rolling prairie's waste of moveless waves,
> A path of pain, a trail of nameless graves;
> The city fair where widowed loneliness
> Weeps her lost children in the wilderness; [389]
>
> The river broad along whose icy bridge
> Their bleeding feet red-hued each frozen ridge;
> The Christian world that drove them forth to die
> On barren wilds beneath a wintry sky.
>
> Would e'en the coldest heart forbear to say
> Good cause had gratitude to weep that day?
> Or censure for a flow of manly tears
> That brave-souled band, immortal Pioneers?

## CHAPTER 56

THE PIONEERS ENTER THE VALLEY—EXPLORING AND COLONIZING—A RENEWAL OF COVENANTS—SELECTION OF INHERITANCES—RETURN OF THE LEADERS TO WINTER QUARTERS

Heber and Brigham entered the Valley together, on the ever memorable "Twenty-fourth," the day chosen by the Pioneers to celebrate their advent into the chambers of the mountains. As a matter of fact, however, Apostle Orson Pratt with Elder Erastus Snow and others, sent on from Bear River ahead of the main company to break a road over the mountains and through the canyons, had penetrated to and partly explored the Valley three days before. Heber remained behind with the President, who was ill, having contracted the mountain fever.

Arriving at the camp of Elder Pratt, they found that the brethren had pitched their tents beside two small streams of pure water, and were already engaged in [390] ploughing and putting in crops. A shower of rain fell that afternoon.

The next day being the Sabbath, the usual services were held and the sacrament administered to the congregation. The speakers of the day were George A. Smith, Heber C. Kimball, Ezra T. Benson, Wilford Woodruff, Orson Pratt and Willard Richards. The main theme of the discourses, naturally enough, was the "land of promise" in the "mountains of Israel," unto which the God of Jacob had led the vanguard of His covenant people.

The several days ensuing were passed in exploring the land and planning future prospects.

"Monday July 26th," says Heber, "I rode out in company with President Young and the Twelve, to visit some of the high hills which lie a little north of here. We went on a high peak which President Young named 'Ensign Peak,' and from thence had a very pleasing view of the Valley, and a great portion of the Salt Lake. On returning, Elders Richards, Benson and myself bathed in the Warm Springs. We found it very pleasant and refreshing. Brother Mathews and John Brown have been across the Valley to the mountain west, and say it is about sixteen miles to the mountain, but there is no fresh water after leaving the outlet."

Next day, Tuesday the 27th, Elder Amasa Lyman, who with others had left the pioneer camp at Fort Laramie, to meet a detachment of the Battalion at Pueblo and lead them on to the Valley, arrived in advance of his company with Elders Rodney Badger, Roswell Stevens and Samuel Brannan, the last named from California. Says Heber; "I rode out again with President Young and some others to visit the Hot Springs, and counsel on the matter of some of the [391] soldiers of the Battalion accompanying Brother Brannan to San Francisco. Some of the Utah Indians visited the camp during the day and the brethren traded with them. They appeared poor and barely clad. Some of the brethren have been to the mountains to get a log for a skiff.

"Wednesday 28th: Yesterday after riding around a little, we started for the Salt Lake and arrived in sufficient time to bathe in it. The water is much Salter than sea water, and it is supposed it would yield 35 per cent, of pure salt. This morning we started back to camp and at 8 o'clock in the evening I attended a general meeting, when the brethren were addressed by President Young on various subjects. We have selected a place for a city about half a mile north of here, and calculated to lay it off in ten-acre lots, each block to be divided into 8 lots of 1 1/4 acres each, exclusive of the streets.

"Thursday 29th. This morning I went in company with President Young to meet the soldiers and the Pueblo company. We met them in the canyon. The brethren seemed highly pleased to see us. We got back to camp about five o'clock.

"Friday 30th. This morning the Twelve met in council with the officers of the Battalion. In the evening the soldiers were called together and addressed by President Young. The meeting was opened by 'Hosannas,' and closed by requesting the brethren to build a bowery to hold our meetings under.

"Sunday, August 1st, Brother Markham says that there are already about fifty-three acres of land plowed and most of it planted with corn, beans, garden seeds, etc. There have been thirteen plows and three drags at work nearly all the week. At ten o'clock we assembled for meeting in the bowery. It was decided to build [392] a stockade of adobies, and adobie houses, and a number of men were selected to commence making adobies to-morrow.

"We also took a vote to have all the wagons move up and form one camp at the east end of the city."

The foregoing excerpts from Heber's journal will suffice to show the nature of the initial labors of the pioneers in preparing a home for themselves and their brethren and sisters who were to follow them.

A renewal of covenants now took place, the leaders setting the example by being rebaptized. President Young baptized his brethren of the Twelve who were present, confirmed them, and sealed upon them anew their Apostleship. Heber C. Kimball then baptized and confirmed President Young. This event took place on the sixth of August.

In the afternoon of the day following the Apostles selected their inheritances, Heber C. Kimball taking a block north of the Temple, President Young a block east and running south-east, Orson Pratt a block south, Wilford Woodruff a block cornering the Temple block and adjoining Elder Pratt's, George A. Smith a block on the west, and the others lots in the near vicinity.

The same evening Heber baptized fifty-five members of the camp, in City Creek, for the remission of their sins; and the next day, August 8th, the remainder of the camp renewed their covenants by baptism.

At a special conference on the 22nd of August, a stake of Zion was organized, with Father John Smith as President. It was resolved that the city then being built should be called the City of the Great Salt Lake. The various creeks and canyons surrounding were also christened, and, on motion of Heber C. Kimball, the [393] river to the west of the settlement was named the Western Jordan.

In the course of his remarks at this conference. Heber used the following prophetic language: "Brother Brigham is going to be greater than he was; he will be greater in strength, in beauty, and in glory. Call upon God and we shall increase here. Away with the spirit of alienation, and let us be united. This is a paradise to me. It is one of the most lovely places I ever beheld."

Having now established their feet, spiritually and temporally, upon this chosen land, the leaders and pioneers, with most of the returning members of the Battalion, harnessed their teams, and bidding farewell to their brethren and sisters who were to tarry, set out upon the return journey to Winter Quarters.

Several companies were now upon the road under the captaincy of such men as Parley P. Pratt, John Taylor, Edward Hunter, Daniel Spencer and Jedediah M. Grant. On the 4th of September, President Young and his company met Apostle P. P. Pratt and Captain Sessions, with their divisions, on the Little Sandy. Here the quorum of the Twelve held a council, and the President was under the necessity of rebuking two of the Apostles "for undoing what the majority of the quorum had done in the organization of the camps for traveling." Says President Woodruff in his journal: "President Young said he felt eternity resting upon him, and was weighed down to the earth with this work; and that Brother Kimball felt it also, more than any other man except himself. He should chastise any one of the quorum when out of the way. He had done it for our good, and had been constrained to it by the power of God. [394]

"Brother Kimball then addressed President Young: 'I want you, Brother Brigham,' he said, 'to save yourself, for you are wearing down. I feel tender towards you, to live, and if I and my brethren do wrong, tell us of it, and we will repent.'"

On the Sweetwater, they met Apostle Taylor and his company, and were treated by them to a rich feast, prepared as a surprise to the returning pioneers.

The Indians had now commenced to be troublesome, prowling around the camps, stealing horses and cattle, and committing other petty depredations. An exciting though bloodless affray took place between them and the pioneers on the morning of the 21st of September. The brethren were just getting ready to start, when the alarm was given by the men who had been sent out to gather up the horses, that the Indians were "rushing" them—driving them off. The camp flew to arms, just in time to received the onslaught of the savages, who, emerging from the timbers and firing their guns, charged upon them at full speed. There were at least two hundred mounted warriors. A return volley from the pioneers broke the Indian charge, and the brethren then gave chase, Heber C. Kimball and Wilford Woodruff leading the counter charge with impetuous zeal. Dashing almost alone at the swarming savages, the sight of their daring courage spread consternation among their foes, who broke and fled incontinently.

The old chief who had directed the attack now shouted to his band and proclaimed peace to the pioneers, telling them that he and his warriors were good Sioux, and had mistaken them for Crows or Snakes, with whom they were at war. The brethren thought it good policy to accept the excuse, transparent though it was, and to appear satisfied with the explanation. The [395] chief proposed the smoking of the pipe of peace with them, and wanted the "big chief of his Mormon brothers" to go to his camp. This, however, was not deemed prudent, but Heber, Col. Markham and Apostle Woodruff went instead, hoping thus to recover their horses, eleven of which had been stolen that day, besides many others on the Sweetwater.

Heber and his companions were kindly received by the Indians, who were camped about five miles away, and smoked the pipe of peace with their leading men. Seeing some of the stolen animals in camp, Heber walked deliberately up to them, took their ropes out of the hands of the astonished savages, and coolly returned with them, amid the grunts and approving nods of his swarthy admirers. They named him "the bald-headed chief." Says he:

"I saw quite a number of horses that were stolen from us on the Sweetwater, but President Young suggested that we say nothing about these for the present; but when we should get to Fort Laramie to offer Mr. Bordeaux $100 to procure them for us; inasmuch as it was deemed inexpedient to take them by force, numbering as they did some eight hundred men, and their camp comprising upwards of one hundred lodges. It was chiefly through my own exertions that we recovered the most of the horses, and I verily believe that if I had had a few more men with me of sufficient energy and resolution, while at their camp, I could have secured all of the stolen horses."

It was President Young's wise policy to placate the Indians and win their friendship, for the sake of future emigrations.

At Fort Laramie, President Young, Apostle Kimball and others of the Twelve dined with Commodore Stock[396]ton, from the Bay of San Francisco, who was eastward bound.

Continuing on their way, the pioneers and Battalion "boys" arrived in safety at Winter Quarters on the 31st of October. Upon the joy of their meeting with their families and with the Saints, we need not dwell. They found that during their absence peace and prosperity had generally prevailed.

## CHAPTER 57

THE FIRST PRESIDENCY REORGANIZED—HEBER ATTAINS TO "THE HONOR OF THE THREE"—SECOND JOURNEY TO THE MOUNTAINS—SICKNESS AND DISTRESS—HEBER'S CHARACTER AS A COLONIZER

Another notable change in the eventful career of Heber C. Kimball. The quorum of the First Presidency, which had remained vacant since the death of Joseph, was now reorganized. Brigham Young, the chief Apostle of the Twelve, was chosen President of the Church of Jesus Christ of Latter-day Saints in all the world, with Heber C. Kimball and Willard Richards as his counselors.

The subject of the reorganization had been considered by the leaders soon after their return to Winter Quarters from the Valley, but it was not until the fifth of December that the matter assumed definite shape. At a feast and council held on that day at the house of Elder Orson Hyde, who had presided at Winter Quarters [397] during the absence of the pioneers, the question was presented to the Apostles by President Young. Those present were then called upon, in their order, to express their views in relation to the subject, when Heber C. Kimball, Orson Pratt, Wilford Woodruff. Willard Richards, George A. Smith, Amasa Lyman, and Ezra T. Benson spoke to the question. President Young closed.

Orson Hyde then moved that Brigham Young be President of the Church of Jesus Christ of Latter-day Saints, and that he nominate his two counselors to form the First Presidency. Wilford Woodruff seconded the motion, and it was carried unanimously.

President Young then nominated Heber C. Kimball as his first counselor, and Willard Richards as his second counselor, and the nominations were unanimously sustained.

This action of the Apostles in their council was sustained by the Saints in general conference assembled, on the 27th of December, 1847. The conference lasted four days and was attended by at least one thousand people. It was held in the new log tabernacle at Winter Quarters, a building erected especially for the purpose. The reorganization of the Presidency was confirmed at the October conference of the following year, in Great Salt Lake City.

Apropos of this event:—In a patriarchal blessing upon the head of Heber C. Kimball, given by the Patriarch Hyrum Smith, at Nauvoo, on the 9th of March, 1842, the following language occurs: "You shall be blest with a fulness and shall be not one whit behind the chiefest; as an Apostle you shall stand in the presence of God to judge the people; and as a Prophet you shall attain to THE HONOR OF THE THREE!" [398]

On the 24th of May, 1848, the First Presidency organized the main body of the Saints on the Elk Horn, preparatory to the second journey to the Rocky Mountains. The camp consisted of six hundred wagons, the largest pioneer company that had yet set out to cross the plains. Under Brigham and Heber they were led in safety to Zion's mountain retreat, arriving in Salt Lake Valley in September, 1848.

The journey, however, was one of severe trial to President Kimball and his family. His daughter Helen, who had married Horace K. Whitney, eldest son of Bishop Whitney, had lost by death her first babe, a daughter, in the Spring of '47, while her husband was absent with the pioneers; and in the journey of '48, she lost her second born, a son, whom she considered as a little martyr. So great was the sorrow of the poor mother over this second calamity, that she was not only brought to death's door, but her reason was for a time overthrown. Vilate herself was prostrated by her daughter's deep distress, and it was only by dint of Heber's mighty faith and powerful will, that either of them were kept alive. Again and again he administered to the sufferers, praying that God would spare their lives, and declaring in prophetic words to them and the whole camp that they "should not die." Thus it was, throughout the entire journey to the mountains. That season of dire trouble Heber and his family ever after looked back upon as one of the extraordinary trials of his life.

But it also brought out the noble qualities of Vilate's sister wives, who daily administered strength and succor to the family. For Heber, prior to this, and even before leaving Nauvoo, had taken many wives, and like Abraham and Jacob of old, had become the head of a patriarchal house-hold. His family, at this time, including his [399] adopted children and those dependent upon him for support, numbered over one hundred souls.

The residue of Heber C. Kimball's history is confined to the land which his wives and children now inhabit, and where much of it that may never be written by mortal pen is cherished as precious memories in the hearts of tens of thousands. From here on, we are more than ever compelled to cull from a superabundant variety of incidents the leading events of a life which now saw some of its best and busiest days.

During the remaining two decades of his mortal existence, his history, so inseparably interwoven with that of the great work to which he had given all his energy and heart's devotion, is largely the history, for the same period, of the development of this inter-mountain region. Though leaning in his temperament to the spiritual, he was also by nature a colonizer, with the elements of a great leader in his composition. Next to those of Brigham Young, will the name and fame of Heber C. Kimball live in the hearts of God's people and forever shine in the annals of Latter-day Israel as one of the foremost of that hardy and heroic band, who, under God, redeemed and beautified this barren waste, "making its wilderness like Eden, and its desert like the garden of the Lord." [400]

## CHAPTER 58

THE CRICKET PLAGUE—SAVED BY THE GULLS—HEBER'S FAMOUS PROPHECY "STATES GOODS" SOLD IN GREAT SALT LAKE CITY CHEAPER THAN IN NEW YORK

Now came a series of trials differing from anything the Saints had yet experienced. Indeed, it seemed as if they were fated to literally "endure all things," and like the Master they served, the great Captain of salvation, be "made perfect through suffering." Hitherto they had been warred against by the powers of evil and their fellow-men. Now their opponents were the blind forces of nature, and creatures of another class.

The year 1848 was the year of the cricket plague. Myriads of these destructive pests, an army of famine and despair, rolled in black legions down the mountain sides and attacked the growing fields of grain. The tender crops fell an easy prey to their fierce voracity. They literally swept everything before them. Starvation with all its terrors seemed staring the poor settlers in the face.

They were saved by a miracle. In the midst of the work of destruction, when it seemed as if nothing could stay the devastation, great flocks of gulls suddenly appeared filling the air with their white wings and plaintive cries, and settled down upon the half ruined fields. At first it seemed as though they came but to destroy what the crickets had left. But their true purpose was soon apparent. They came to prey upon the destroyers. All day long they gorged themselves, and, when full, disgorged and feasted again; the white gulls upon the [401] black crickets, like hosts of heaven and hell contending, until the pests were vanquished and the people were

Brigham Young

saved. The heaven-sent birds then returned to the lake islands whence they came, leaving the grateful people to shed tears of joy at the wonderful deliverance wrought out for them.

Still there was a season of scarcity. The surplus of the first harvests in the Valley had barely been sufficient to meet the wants of the emigration, which had commenced pouring in from the frontiers and from Europe; and now that the crickets had played such havoc with the crops, there was danger, in spite of the interposition of the gulls, of some suffering from hunger. This was only averted by the exercise of the highest wisdom and broadest charity, and the partial observance of the principle of the United Order, which the Saints had before sought to introduce, and still have it in their mission to establish. The people were put upon rations, all sharing the same, like members of one great family. Many, however, in order to swell their scanty store, went out and dug roots with the Indians, or cooked and ate the hides of animals with which they had covered the roofs of their houses.

It was during this time of famine, when the half starved, half-clad settlers scarcely knew where to look for the next crust of bread or for rags to hide their nakedness—for clothing had become almost as scarce with them as bread-stuffs—that Heber C. Kimball, filled with the spirit of prophecy, in a public meeting declared to the astonished congregation that, within a short time, "States goods" would be sold in the streets of Great Salt Lake City cheaper than in New York and that the people should be abundantly supplied with food and clothing.
[402]
"I don't believe a word of it," said Charles C. Rich; and he but voiced the sentiment of nine-tenths of those who had heard the astounding declaration.

Heber himself was startled at his own words, as soon as the Spirit's force had abated and the "natural man" had reasserted himself. On resuming his seat, he remarked to the brethren that he was "afraid he had missed it this time." But they were not his own words, and He who had inspired them knew how to fulfill.

The occasion for the fulfillment of this remarkable prediction was the unexpected advent of the gold-hunters, on their way to California. The discovery of gold in that land had set on fire, as it were, the civilized world, and hundreds of richly laden trains now began pouring across the continent on their way to the new El dorado. Salt Lake Valley became the resting-place, or "half-way house" of the nation, and before the Saints had had time to recover from their surprise at Heber's temerity in making such a prophecy, the still more wonderful fulfillment was brought to their very doors. The gold-hunters were actuated by but one desire; to reach the Pacific Coast; the thirst for mammon having absorbed for the time all other sentiments and desires. Impatient at their slow progress, in order to lighten their loads, they threw away or "sold for a song" the valuable merchandise with which they had stored their wagons to cross the Plains. Their choice, blooded, though now jaded stock, they eagerly exchanged for the fresh mules and horses of the pioneers, and bartered off, at almost any sacrifice, dry goods, groceries, provisions, tools, clothing, etc., for the most primitive out-fits, with barely enough provisions to enable them to reach their journey's end. Thus, as the Prophet Heber had predicted, **[403]** "States goods" were actually sold in the streets of Great Salt Lake City cheaper than they could have been purchased in the City of New York.

Referring to this incident, in a sermon, a few years later, Heber says:

"The Spirit of prophecy foresees future events. God does not bring to pass a thing because you say it shall be so, but because He designed it should be so, and it is the future purposes of the Almighty that the Prophet foresees. That is the way I prophesy, but I have predicted things I did not foresee, and did not believe anybody else did, but I have said it, and it came to pass even more abundantly than I predicted; and that was with regard to the future situation of the people who first came into this valley. Nearly every man was dressed in skins, and we were all poor, destitute, and distressed, yet we all felt well. I said, 'it will be but a little while, brethren, before you shall have food and raiment in abundance, and shall buy it cheaper than it can be bought in the cities of the United States.' I did not know there were any Gentiles coming here, I never thought of such a thing; but after I spoke it I thought I must be mistaken this time. Brother Rich remarked at the time, 'I do not believe a word of it.' And neither did I; but, to the astonishment and joy of the Saints, it came to pass just as I had spoken it, only more abundantly. The Lord led me right, but I did not know it.

"I have heard Joseph say many times, that he was much tempted about the revelations the Lord gave through him—it seemed to be so impossible for them to be fulfilled. I do not profess to be a Prophet; but I know that every man and woman can be, if they live for it." **[404]**

Though Heber did not "profess to be a Prophet," he was one nevertheless, and manifested the gift of prophecy, as is generally admitted, to a greater extent than any other man in the Church, excepting the Prophet Joseph Smith.

Brigham was in the habit of saying: "Heber is my Prophet." In a conversation with Col. Thomas L. Kane on the occasion of the visit of the latter to the Territory, at the time of the settlement of the "Utah War" troubles, President Young said: "Brother Kimball said in Nauvoo, 'If we have to leave our houses we will go to the mountains, and in a few years we will have a better city than we have here.' This is fulfilled. He also said, 'we shall have gold, and coin twenty-dollar gold pieces.' We came here, founded a city, and coined the first twenty-dollar gold pieces in the United States.[7] Seeing the brethren poorly clad, soon after we came here, he said, 'it will not be three years before we can buy clothing cheaper in Salt Lake Valley than in the States.' Before the time was out, the gold-diggers brought loads of clothing, and sold them in our city at a wanton price." **[405]**

---

[7] Heber was one of the principal movers in procuring the stamp with which these gold pieces were coined.

# CHAPTER 59

HEBER C. KIMBALL CHIEF JUSTICE AND LIEUTENANT GOVERNOR OF DESERET—IN THE LEGISLATURE—LAYING THE CORNER STONES OF THE SALT LAKE TEMPLE—HEBER'S CONSECRATION PRAYER—HIS PROPHECY IN RELATION TO THE TEMPLE—HE PREDICTS ANOTHER FAMINE

PRESIDENT Kimball's experience was now more than ever of a mixed and varied character; a natural concomitant of his position as a leader in the settlement of a new country. As first counselor to his chief, and only second to him in influence among the people, we find him taking part and helping to direct in all the important movements affecting the growth and prosperity of Zion.

In March, 1849, the Provisional Government of the State of Deseret was organized, pending the action of Congress on a petition for a Territorial Government. The election, held on the twelfth of that month, resulted in the unanimous choice of the following officers. Brigham Young, Governor; Willard Richards, Secretary; Newel K. Whitney, Treasurer; Heber C. Kimball, Chief Justice; John Taylor and N. K. Whitney, Associate Justices; Daniel H. Wells, Attorney-General; Horace S. Eldredge, Marshal; Albert Carrington, Assessor and Collector of taxes; Joseph L. Heywood, Surveyor of highways; and the Bishops of the several wards as magistrates.

Heber was also Lieutenant-Governor of the Provisional State of Deseret.

At the October conference of 1849, his voice is **[406]** heard introducing the subject of the Perpetual Emigration Fund, for the benefit of the poor Saints who were unable to gather to Zion. The sum of $5,000 was raised that season by voluntary donations, and Bishop Edward Hunter despatched to the frontier as general agent of the Church, to superintend the emigration.

At the session of the Legislature of Deseret, held in March, 1851, Heber C. Kimball was President of the Council branch of the Assembly, and, in September of the same year, a member of the Council of the first session of the Legislative Assembly of the Territory of Utah.

The corner stones of the Salt Lake Temple were laid on the sixth of April, 1853, the south-east corner stone being laid by the First Presidency, Brigham Young, Heber C. Kimball and Willard Richards, assisted by Patriarch John Smith. President Young delivered the oration and President Kimball offered the consecration prayer. This prayer is worth preserving in his history. It was as follows:

"O God, the Eternal Father, in the name of Thy Son Jesus Christ of Nazareth, we ask Thee to look upon us at this time in Thy tender mercy. Thou beholdest that Thy servants, Brigham and his council, have laid the corner stone of a holy house, which we are about to erect unto Thy name. We desire to do it with clean hands and pure hearts before Thee, and before Thine holy angels.

"We thank Thee that we are permitted to live in the flesh, and have a place upon Thy footstool, and partake daily of the bounties Thy hand bestows, for Thou art our father, and Jesus Christ is our elder brother.

"Inasmuch, O Lord, as we desire to erect a house to Thy name, and if it seemeth Thee good to come and **[407]** take up Thine abode on the earth, that Thou mayest have a place to lay Thy head, we pray Thee to assist us to erect it in purity before Thee, and the heavenly hosts.

"We ask Thee to help us so to conduct ourselves, that all the holy Prophets, the angels of heaven, with Thee and Thy son, may be engaged continually for our welfare, in the work of salvation and eternal lives. Bless us in this attempt to glorify Thee. Bless this portion of the earth we dwell upon—even these valleys of the mountains, which we have consecrated unto Thee. Cause them to bring forth the productions of the soil in rich abundance. Bless the seeds that are placed therein by Thy servants and handmaidens. And inasmuch as they are disposed to do Thy work, and erect a temple to Thy name, which is their fixed purpose and determination, let the heavens be gentle over them. May the earth be sanctified for their good, and the seeds they throw into it yield to them an hundred fold in return. We pray Thee to bless such men and women—may the blessings of the Almighty richly attend them—and multiply them in their families, in their herds and flocks, in strength and in health, in salvation and in eternal lives.

"We also pray for those who do not feel favorably disposed to Thy work—may Thy blessings not attend them, but may they go backward and not forward, may they wither and not increase, and may the strength that they might have received, through their faithfulness to Thy work be multiplied and divided amongst these Thy servants who are determined to keep Thy commandments, and sanctify their affections unto Thee.

"Look upon Thy servant Brigham, O Lord, and let Thy Holy Spirit rest mightily upon him this day, and from henceforth. May he live to dictate the erection **[408]** of Thy house, see the top stone brought on with rejoicing, and administer the keys of salvation and eternal life unto his brethren therein. Bless his council in common with him, may they live to a good old age, and glorify God in all their days; may they never want for food and raiment, for fathers and mothers, for wives and children, and for the power of Thy Spirit to inspire them, and those Thou hast given them.

"Pour out Thy Spirit upon Thy servants, the Twelve Apostles; may Thy power abide upon them, to qualify them for the responsible calling unto which Thou hast called them. Also, in connection with them, let Thy Spirit rest upon the Quorums of the Seventies, the High Priests, the Bishops, the High Council, the Elders, Priests, Teachers, and Deacons; and upon every faithful member of Thy church in these valleys of the mountains, and in all the world.

"Now, O God, we dedicate this stone to Thee. May this spot be holy, and all that pertaineth to it. And inasmuch as there shall be an enemy, or a person that are evil-disposed towards Thy house, and they shall endeavor to lay snares for the feet of Thy people, may they be caught in their own net, be overwhelmed in their own dilemma, and have no power nor influence in the least to hurt Thy saints from this time henceforth forever. May the power of the Mighty God of Jacob fortify Thy servants, enabling them to execute righteousness before Thee the Lord our God.

"Hear us, O Lord, for we dedicate this, the southeast corner stone unto Thee, praying that it may sleep in peace, be preserved from decay, for it is the chief corner-stone of the house we shall rear to Thy name. May the same blessings attend the other three cornerstones, and all the works Thy servants shall set [409] their hands to do, from this time henceforth and for ever.

"Bless the architect, the superintendent, the foremen of the various departments, and all the laborers that shall raise a hand, or move a thing for the erection and perfection of this Thine house; and provide for them, their wives, their children, and all that pertains unto them, that they may want for no good or necessary thing, while they are engaged in Thy service, and from this time henceforth and forever.

"We dedicate ourselves unto Thee, with our wives, our children, our flocks, and our herds, with all the settlements and possessions that pertain to Thy people in these valleys of the mountains. And all the praise and glory we will ascribe to the Father, Son, and Holy Ghost. Amen."

In after years, President Kimball predicted, in relation to this temple, that when its walls reached the square the powers of evil would rage and the Saints would suffer persecution. The walls of the Salt Lake Temple "reached the square" in November, 1882, eight months after the passage by Congress of the celebrated "Edmunds law." One year later, in November, 1883, occurred the trial of Rudger Clawson for polygamy under the provisions of that law, in the Third District Court of Utah Territory. This, the first gun of the campaign, was the signal for the inauguration of an anti-Mormon crusade, which, for bitterness and cruelty, takes rank in the history of religious persecution with the deeds of the dark ages. Thus was fulfilled another prediction of the prophet Heber, fifteen years after his mortal eyes were closed in death.

The character of those early times, the condition of the people, and the part played by President Kimball as [410] a public teacher, are further shown in the following selections from his sermons, in which he deals more or less with the temporal situation:

In August, 1853, we find him addressing the Saints in the Tabernacle as follows:

"I know you will prosper and live in peace in the mountains of the Great Salt Lake, and be perfectly independent. You will have food and raiment, houses and lands, flocks and herds, and everything your hearts can desire, that there is in heaven and on earth, *if you but do as you are told.* You will live in peace and God will be your defence.[8] ... I have said often, you may write blessings for yourselves, and insert every good thing you can think of, and it will all come to pass on your

---

[8] In the same spirit, a few years later, Aug, 30. 1857, Heber used this stirring prophecy: "Wake up, ye Saints of the Most High, and prepare for any emergency that the Lord our God may have pleasure in bringing forth! We never shall leave these valleys—till we get ready; no, never: no, never! We will live here till we go back to Jackson County, Missouri. I prophesy that, in the name of Israel's God." The congregation shouted "Amen," and President Young said, "It is true."

heads, IF YOU DO RIGHT...."

"The Lord can turn the nations as I can an obedient horse. They are governed and controlled by the Almighty as much as we are. What can they do against us? Why, nothing whatever, but if we do not do right they will be a scourge in the hands of God to scourge us, just as the Indians are at this time.... There never would have been a disturbance if this people had done as they were told. There is not a settlement in these mountains but were instructed by Brother Brigham to build good forts and live in them. Have any of them built forts?... The Indians are now upon us, and our brethren are scattered off, three, four and five families in a place, exposed to the Lamanites.... **[411]**

"There are a few things I wanted to say. One is, TAKE CARE OF YOUR GRAIN; for it is of more worth to you than gold and silver. I know you will see harder times before another harvest than you have seen this season. There is enough, and we need never want bread, but if we do not take the right course we are *sure to see sorrow,* and THE GREATEST YOU HAVE EVER SEEN."

Mark the stress laid upon the subject of storing up grain for a day of famine. This theme forms almost the staple of President Kimball's sermons for the next three years. With the eye of faith he saw the famine afar off, and strove with all the power of his earnest and prophetic nature to impress this fact upon the minds of his hearers, that they might be prepared for the gaunt spectre's coming. But they heeded him not, to any general extent, and in due time suffered the consequences of their neglect.

A year later he touched on the subject of home manufactures:

"Will the time ever be that we can make our clothing? We nearly can at this time. I would like to see the people take a course to make their own clothing, make their own machinery, their own knives and their own forks, and everything else we need, for the day will come when we will be under the necessity of doing it, for trouble and perplexity, war and famine, bloodshed and fire, and thunder and lightning will roll upon the nations of the earth, insomuch that we cannot get to them, nor they to us."

The next is a retrospective glimpse:

"I was one of the first, in connection with President Young, who came to this valley when it was a desolate region, and we could not even get a chart from Fremont nor from any other man, from which to learn the course **[412]** to this place. I was one who helped to pick out the road. When we got to the upper ferry of Platte River, half of our company had not a mouthful of bread. I recollect one day, I believe it was on the Platte, Brother Brigham said to me, 'Brother Heber, what do you think about it, do you think we shall go any further?' I knew he asked this question to try me. I replied, I wanted to go the whole journey and find some white sandstone and see what there was in the earth. There never was a day when I would not go with him until we found a location. I knew there was a place somewhere, though at times the prospect appeared dreary. But here it was on high. It is the best country I ever saw."

By this time the approach of the famine was beginning to be felt. In the course of some remarks at a special conference in Provo, July 13th, 1855, President Kimball said:

"Perhaps many feel a little sober because our bread is cut off, but I am glad of it, because it will be a warning to us, and teach us to lay it up in future, as we have been told. How many times have you been told to store up your wheat against the hard times that are coming upon the nations of the earth? When we first came into these valleys our President told us to lay up stores of all kinds of grain that the earth might rest once in seven years. The earth is determined to rest, and it is right that it should. It only requires a few grasshoppers to make the earth rest, they can soon clear it. This is the seventh year; did you ever think of it?"

Then came the famine, the second one in the history of the Saints, in fulfillment of the warning words of their prophets and seers. It was the famine of 1856. [413]

## CHAPTER 60

THE FAMINE OF '56—HEBER A SECOND JOSEPH—A SAVIOR TO HIS PEOPLE—VILATE A MINISTERING ANGEL—A STRANGE PIECE OF COUNSEL—PRESIDENT KIMBALL'S LETTERS, DESCRIPTIVE OF THE FAMINE, TO HIS SON WILLIAM, IN ENGLAND

IN this famine, which was likened unto the famine of Egypt, Heber C. Kimball played a part like unto that of Joseph of old; feeding from his own bins and storehouses, filled by his providence and foresight in anticipation of the straitness of the times, the hungry multitude—kindred, strangers and all—who looked to him for succor. His own family were put upon short rations, to enable him to minister more effectually to the wants of others.

He had taken his own counsel, and stored up grain for the famine he had predicted, and when the time of scarcity came he had on hand thousands of bushels of wheat, with bran and shorts, corn and barley in abundance; all of which, however, was used before the next harvest-time.

Several hundred bushels of wheat he lent to President Young, to help feed those who were dependent on the President, while he himself personally undertook to relieve hundreds of the poor of Salt Lake City.

The following letter from Bishop John B. Maiben forms an interesting link in the historic chain of that period: [414]

"MANTI, SANPETE CO.,
"January 16th, 1877.

"S. F. Kimball,
  "Salt Lake City,

"DEAR BROTHER:—In answer to your enquiries in relation to the flour I distributed for your father, I will say:

"That during the early part of the year 1856, in what is known as the "time of the famine," when a great many persons who in other respects were esteemed well to do, were under the necessity of eating thistle roots, sego roots and other wild plants for sustenance of themselves and families, owing to the extreme scarcity of breadstuff, there being none in the market at any price; at this critical juncture President Heber C. Kimball, who had by wise economy and prescient forethought garnered up a quantity of surplus grain, requested my assistance to distribute flour to the families of the Saints in small quantities adapted to their number and necessity, charging them only $6.00 per 100 lbs, then the standard Tithing Office price. Although there was no flour in the market, still some individuals were selling at $25. to $30. per 100 lbs. To the best of my recollection some 20,000 to 30,000 lbs. of flour were thus distributed in various amounts, varying from five to fifty lbs., according to the size of the family.

"This act of generosity and fatherly care on the part of the late Heber C. Kimball was only in keeping with his general character as a man of sterling integrity and a faithful steward before the Lord to his fellow-men, and thus his memory is justly enshrined in the hearts of the Saints, who fondly cherish the hope to enjoy his society after a glorious resurrection.

"Yours Very Truly,
"J. B. Maiben."

Many are the acts of mercy and charity related of President Kimball and his family, especially his noble and unselfish partner, Vilate, during this time of sore [415] distress. They kept an open house, and fed from twenty-five to one hundred poor people at their table, daily, besides making presents innumerable of bread, flour and other necessaries, which were then literally worth their weight in gold.[9]

It was Vilate's chief delight to sally forth with a basket on her arm, filled with nicely cooked edibles and little domestic comforts, and seek out some poor, obscure person, in need of help, though perhaps too proud or timid to make it known. She would often go to the houses of such persons, on finding that they were away from home, and provide for their needs in their absence, in order that they might meet a glad surprise on their return, without knowing the good angel who had visited them.

It is related that, during this famine, a brother, sorely in need of bread, came to President Kimball for counsel how to procure it.

"Go and marry a wife," was Heber's terse reply, after relieving the immediate wants of the applicant.

Thunderstruck at receiving such an answer at such a time, when he could hardly provide food for himself, the man went his way, dazed and bewildered, thinking that President Kimball must be out of his mind. But the more he thought of the prophetic character and calling of the one who had given him this strange

---

[9] While thus feeding the poor on the best that her larder afforded, Vilate would send her own children into the fields to dig roots (artichokes) which she would cook for them. This, with coarse corn bread, while her guests were served with wheaten bread, potatoes and boiled beef, was the frequent diet of the Kimball family during the famine of "fifty-six."

advice, the less he felt like ignoring it. Finally he resolved to obey counsel, let the consequences be what they might. But where was the woman who would marry him? was the next problem. Bethinking himself of a widow with **[416]** several children, who he thought might be induced to share her lot with him, he mustered up courage, proposed and was accepted.

In that widow's house was laid up a six months' store of provisions!

Meeting President Kimball shortly afterwards, the now prosperous man of family exclaimed:

"Well, Brother Heber, I followed your advice—"

"Yes," said the man of God, "and you found bread."

President Kimball's letters to his son William, who was then in England, will fully tell the story of the famine, and also many of the current events of that period:

"Great Salt Lake City,
"February 29, 1856.

"To My Dear Son William, and to all whom it may concern:

"My family, with yours, are all in good health and spirits. I have been under the necessity of rationing my family, and also yours, to two-thirds of a pound of breadstuff per day each; as the last week is up to-day, we shall commence on half a pound each—at the same time they all begin to look better and fatter, and more ruddy, like the English. This I am under the necessity of doing. Brother Brigham told me to-day that he had put his family on half a pound each, for there is scarcely any grain in the country, and there are thousands that have none at all scarcely. We do this for the purpose of feeding hundreds that have none.

"My family at this time consists of about one hundred souls, and I suppose that I feed about as many as one hundred besides.

"My mill has not brought me in, for the last seven months, over one bushel of toll per day, in consequence **[417]** of the dry weather, and the water being frozen up—which would not pay my miller. When this drought came on, I had about seven hundred bushels of wheat, and it is now reduced to about one hundred and twenty-five bushels, and I have only about twenty-five bushels of corn, which will not provide for my own family until harvest. Heber has been to the mill to-day, and has brought down some unbolted flour, and we shall be under the necessity of eating the bran along with the flour, and shall think ourselves doing well with half a pound a day at that.... We have some meat and perhaps about seventy bushels of potatoes, also a very few beets and carrots; so you can judge whether or not we can get through until harvest without digging roots; still we are altogether better off than the most of the people in these valleys of the mountains. There are several wards in this city who have not over two weeks' provisions on hand.

"I went into the tithing office with Brother Hill and examined it from top to bottom, and, taking all the wheat, corn, buckwheat and oats, there were not to exceed five hundred bushels, which is all the public works have, or expect to have, and the works are pretty much abandoned, the men having been all turned off, except about fifteen who are at work on Brother Brigham's house and making some seed drills for grain, as we will be obliged to put in our grain by drilling, on account of the scarcity, which probably will not take over one-third of the grain it would to sow broadcast.

"We shall probably not do anything on the public works until another harvest. The mechanics of every class have all been counseled to abandon their pursuits and go to raising grain. This we are literally compelled to do, out of necessity. Moreover, there is not a settlement in the Territory but is also in the same fix that we are. Some settlements can go two months, some three, some can, probably, at the rate of half a pound per day, till harvest. Hon. A. W. Babbitt even went to Brother Hyde's provision store the other day, and begged to get twenty or twenty-five pounds of flour, but could not. **[418]** This I was told by William Price who is the salesman of the store. Money will not buy flour or meal, only at a few places, and but very little at that. I can assure you that I am harrassed constantly; I sell none for money but let it go where people are truly destitute. Dollars and cents do not count now, in these times, for they are the tightest that I have ever seen in the Territory of Utah. You and your brethren can judge a little by this. As one of the old Prophets said, anciently, 'as with the people so with the Priest,' we all take it together.

"Some of the people drop many big tears, but if they cannot learn wisdom by precept, nor by example, they must learn it by what they suffer.

"Now is the time for us to be like unto Joseph of old—lay up stores for ourselves, and our children; and thousands, and hundreds of thousands from the old world, the United States, and North and South America will flee to this place to get down by the side of Joseph's cribs, and granaries, and storehouses, to get that which will sustain life from "these poor deluded creatures" that they drove from the United States, and were not willing that they should have shelter in the land of their birth, and the privilege of worshiping our God and our Father who organized and prepared this earth for His children, and those who would keep His commandments; and killed our Prophet, our Patriarch, and Apostles, and hundreds of others and thousands of men, women, and children, the widows and fatherless, who died on the plains in consequence of their oppression. Will they receive the rod in consequence of this? Yes, I can say in truth, in the name of Israel's God, they shall receive fourfold pressed down. I can say in my heart, I wish to God this people would all listen to counsel, and do at the start as they are told, and move as one man, and be one. If this were the case, our enemies would never have any more power over us, our granaries never would be empty, nor would we see sorrow. There is not a good, wise, humble Saint that is filled with the elements of eternal lives, but what knows that this is true as well as myself.... **[419]**

"Now, as to my own stock—cattle, horses and sheep. My sheep are on Antelope Island. Peter Hanson is with them, and Joseph Toronto is with Brother Brigham's, five miles beyond. Some portions of the Island are covered with snow nearly three feet deep. The sheep range on the tops of the mountains where the wind has blown off the snow, and they do first rate. My cattle, sixty head of them, were put in

Cache valley with the church cattle, and those of other individuals, numbering about two thousand five hundred head, with some forty or fifty horses, some six or eight of which were mine. When the snow fell in that valley about ten inches deep, the fatter portion of the cattle broke and came over into Box Elder and Weber valleys, and scattered hither and thither. It is supposed that one-half of those two thousand five hundred head are dead. Whether mine are all dead I know not. My John horse fled out of that valley down on the Weber and died. Old Jim, Elk, Kit and Kurley remained in Cache valley, and they were with about forty head of other horses when last seen, but they have not been heard of for a considerable time, and whether living or dead we know not. The snow is about waist deep in that valley. Week before last, Heber and some other boys started to go there, but when they got to the divide between that valley and Box Elder, the snow was about twelve feet deep, and they were obliged to return. Heber found the Lize mare and your two mules on the Weber, and brought them home. They were so poor that they almost staggered.

"The Carr boys have lost most all of their cattle, as they were in Cache valley. Old Daddy Stump went there also, and most of his died. Brother Shurtliff had some ninety cows of Brother Brigham's, and he says that they are all dead except ten or a dozen. Brothers Hooper and Williams told me that they had lost about seven hundred head. Mr. Kerr, a Gentile, told me that he had six or seven hundred head, and they were all dead. Messrs. Gilbert and Gerrish had about as many, and they are all dead, as are also Livingston and [420] Bell's, and, from the accounts from all the brethren north of this place, we learn that they have lost half of their stock, and this destruction seems to be more or less throughout the Territory, and many cattle and horses are dying in the city There may be more or less of these cattle living, but they are scattered from the Malad to this place. There are some forty head of cattle on the Island, probably living.

"Some of the Indians have killed some cattle in Utah Valley. Judge Drummond, being there, issued a writ for them. T—— J—— had the writ, and summoned a posse, without consulting Brother Brigham, and, anxious to obtain a few dimes from Uncle Sam, went over to Cedar Valley, and came to the lodge where the Indians were. Battest drew his rifle upon George Parish, who warded it off on firing, and one of the brethren drew a revolver, and shot Battest through the head, and he fell dead. In a very short time after this three of our brethren were found dead; one of their names was Carson. They were herd boys. Brother Hunsaker's son has never been found yet—supposed to be dead. Last evening we received news that two more of the brethren were dead, and one mortally wounded, and that the horses were taken from the company who were going to get back some of the cattle from the Indians. It happened in the cedars, between Rush and Cedar valleys, the brethren not expecting any Indians were anywhere about.

"The more reckless portion of the Indians have gathered together, and taken something over one hundred head of cattle and horses, and the last we heard, they were making their way toward the Sevier, taking the west side of the mountains, on the borders of the desert. General Wells has issued orders to Gen. Cownover to raise men and pursue them, and take away the cattle from them. We have received no news as yet from this company. This difficulty has arisen from our Judges, Kinney and Drummond, and some of our foolish brethren who are ready to run at their nod.

"There have been courts in session here for weeks **[421]** and weeks, and I suppose that one hundred and fifty or two hundred of the brethren have been hanging around, with the council house filled to the brim. This scenery continuing for a long time, one day Brother Brigham sent Thomas Bullock to take their names, for the purpose of giving them missions, if they had not anything to do of any more importance. So Brother Brigham counseled me to make a selection—for Los Vegas some thirty, who are ordered to sell their possessions and go with their families as soon as the weather will permit, for the purpose of going down on to the Rio Virgin to raise cotton; Another company of forty-eight to go to Green River to strengthen up that settlement, make farms, build mills, etc., and some thirty-five or forty to go north to Salmon River, where Thomas J. Smith is, to strengthen up that post; some thirty to go to Carson Valley to strengthen that post; some thirty to go into the lead business near the Los Vegas; and eight to go to the East Indies. There are eighteen called to Europe, and seven to Australia.

"We left Fillmore on the day of the adjournment of the Legislature, which took place at five o'clock A. M. We got home in about four days.

"The Deseret Dramatic Association are now performing on the evenings of Wednesdays and Saturdays; 'She stoops to Conquer' comes off for the second time to-morrow night. A benefit to Bernard Snow is to be given on Monday night, when will be played, 'Virginius.'

"Brother Smoot has made a selection of one hundred men, principally young men, to go back with ox teams to fetch on the Church goods that lie in Missouri and St. Louis, if there are cattle enough left alive to do so. Your brother David, Brigham Young, Jr., and George Grant's son George, will go with them.

"Heber and Phoebe are living with Ruth and Christeen. Heber is a very steady, good boy, and takes a great burden from my shoulders, by waiting on the family and seeing to things.

"You can say to the brethren that I see their wives **[422]** occasionally at the public places. They are all well so far as I know; I have all I can do and no time to visit. Say to all the brethren that they are most kindly remembered by me. I would be glad to write to them all.

"This letter is for the benefit of all, as it gives the general news. We shall expect to see you home next season, as Brother Brigham has sent word, which you will get before you get this.

"God bless Brother Franklin, Brother Spencer, yourself, with all the rest of the brethren. Your dear mother is sitting beside me and wishes to be remembered kindly to her son William.

"Brother Brigham and all the brethren are well and would say, if they were present, Amen.

"From your father in the gospel of your Lord and Savior Jesus Christ, to his son, William H. Kimball.

"Heber C. Kimball."

The story is continued in his letter of a later date, as follows:

"Great Salt Lake City,
"April 13th, 1856.

"My Son William:

"We have not received a line from you or Daniel since August 19th, and all the news that we have received was from a business letter that came from Franklin, by the last southern mail....

"As to matters at home, things are going on in peace, with the exception of the disturbances with some of the Utes. They have killed eight of our brethren in Utah, and drove away many cattle and horses.

"The times are said to be more close this season than they have ever been in the valleys; and this is universal through all the settlements. There are not more than one-half of the people that have bread, and they have not more than one-half or one-quarter of a pound a day to a person. A great portion of the people are digging roots, and hundreds and thousands, their teams being dead, are under the necessity of spading their ground to [423] put in their grain. There is a pretty universal break with our merchants, as there is no one to buy their goods, and their stock are mostly dead. My family, with yours, have only one-half a pound of bread-stuff to a person, a day. We have vegetables and a little meat. We are doing first rate, and have no cause but to be very thankful; still I feed hundreds of others, a little, or they must suffer. Brother Brigham, myself, and others have been crying unto this people for more than three years, to lay up their grain for a time when they would have much need of it. My family, with yours, I can say with propriety, look more healthy, and fair, and rugged, and athletic, than they did when they had plenty to eat....

"I shall be very glad when you return home to take a little of my burden off my shoulders, for it has been extremely hard for me and your mother to calculate, devise and administer to near one hundred that are dependent on us, besides hundreds of others that are teasing us constantly for something to eat; still your father has got a spirit in him that is like an old lion, that endures by the help of the Almighty; but your mother is very sympathetic, and it gives her much sorrow, not because your children and mine cry for bread, but because of others. There was no need of my rationing my family, but I did it for the sake of keeping hundreds of others alive. I foresaw these times more than three years ago, and prepared myself, more or less, for it....

"This people have been told to build forts around their cities, and gather up together and be one, and to build store-houses and lay up grain to last seven years, and hundreds of other things. Have they done it? No. What is the consequence? Eight more of our brethren slain! No bread! No clothing except what we buy of the ungodly, when they are universally taught to make their clothing, so that we may be independent of any of the nations; for the connection between us and the world will be closed, in a measure. This you and your brethren in the old world can see through a glass clearly, not darkly. War, death, desolation of nations, famine [424] and desolating sickness, are becoming prevalent throughout the old world, and in the United States it will be more so, and that soon, and they (the United States) will have all they can do to attend to their own concerns at home, without troubling themselves about the Mormons.

"At our April conference there were about three hundred missionaries selected for different missions; some thirty or forty to go to Europe and the United States, and about one hundred to Carson Valley, to try to sustain that place; a large company to Green River, another to Los Vegas and another to Salmon River. All business is given up for the present on the public works. Not much of any building is going on in the city, as all mechanics are advised to go to tilling the earth. The majority of the people feel well; your mother's health is rather poor, still she is about. I see Mary and Melissa and the children every day. Helen, your sister, has just come in with the little Vilate—well, Heber, David and all the boys, with all the family, are well, and say, 'Give my kind love to brother William, and all the faithful Elders.' I am still continuing my own improvements, making good rock fence and setting out many fruit trees.

"Now I will come to a close by saying, God bless you and Franklin, Daniel and all in that land, and all that believe on your words. Even so, amen.

"HEBER C. KIMBALL."

And thus did this father in Israel not only give to the people the word of the Lord in time for a general provision against the day of famine, but when it came, his patriarchal care and benevolence were the means of preserving many from absolute want, and some perhaps from starvation. [425]

## CHAPTER 61

THE HAND-CART EMIGRATION—PERISHING IN THE SNOW—HEROIC CONDUCT OF WILLIAM H. AND DAVID P. KIMBALL—PRESIDENT KIMBALL'S PLEA AND EXERTIONS IN BEHALF OF THE SUFFERERS—THE UTAH WAR—THE GREAT REBELLION

THE year 1856 witnessed another calamity, upon the harrowing details of which it would indeed be painful to dwell. It was the year of the famous hand-cart emigration, in which several hundred souls, overtaken by winter on the plains, perished in the snows and from starvation.

On hearing of the situation of these poor emigrants, the most strenuous efforts were made by the authorities and the people in the Valley to rescue them from their terrible fate. Presidents Young, Kimball and others despatched all their teams, loaded with bedding and provisions, to the relief of the sufferers, and prayers in public and in private were offered up throughout the entire Territory for the deliverance of the unfortunate companies from the destruction impending over them.

Among those sent out to meet the hand-carts, were two of the sons of President Kimball, William H. and David P., the former of whom had just arrived home from England; also Joseph A. Young, George W. Grant and others. These brave men by their heroism—for it was at the peril of their own lives that they thus braved the wintry storms on the plains—immortalized themselves, and won the undying gratitude of hundreds [426] who were undoubtedly saved by their timely action from perishing.

David P. Kimball, George W. Grant and C. Allen Huntington carried upwards of five hundred of these emigrants on their backs across the Sweetwater, breaking the thin ice of the frozen river before them, as they waded from shore to shore. The effects of the severe colds then contracted by these brethren, remained with them, and finally conduced to the death of the two former, while the survivor, Brother Huntington, is a sufferer from the same cause to this day.

The situation and sufferings of the emigrants were the main theme of the Tabernacle discourses at the time. President Kimball thus refers to them on the 2nd of November of that fatal year:

"Some find fault with and blame Brother Brigham and his council, because of the sufferings they have heard that our brethren are enduring on the plains.... But let me tell you most emphatically that if all who were entrusted with the care and management of this year's immigration had done as they were counseled and dictated by the First Presidency of this Church, the sufferings and hardships now endured by the companies on their way here would have been avoided. Why? Because they would have left the Missouri river in season, and not have been hindered until into September.... Our brethren and sisters on the plains are in my mind all the time, and Brother Brigham has given, to those who wish it, the privilege of going back to help bring them in. If I do not go myself I will send a team, though I have already sent back nearly all my teams, and so has Brother Brigham. Those who have gone back never will be sorry for or regret having done so. If brothers Joseph A. Young, my son William H., [427] George D. Grant, and my son David P. had not gone to the assistance of those now on the plains I should always have regretted it. If they die during the trip, they will die while endeavoring to save their brethren; and who has greater love than he that lays down his life for his friends?"

"Were I in the situation of some of you, I would not sleep another night before starting to the assistance of the people that are now struggling through the snow.... As Brother Brigham has said, I would rather be helping in those on the plains than be here, if circumstances and duty would permit. We offered our offering and started to go but the Lord ordered it otherwise and we came home. But we have done a better work than if we had gone.... There would have been no general stir in behalf of our brethren on the plains; but scores and hundreds have now gone to meet them, and they have had good weather so far, have they not?"

The last of the hand-cart companies, the fifth one of the season, commanded by Edward Martin, arrived in Salt Lake City about the 1st of December. They had numbered nearly six hundred souls at starting, but lost over one-fourth of their number by death.

Let the curtain fall over the tragic scene.

During the exciting period of the "Utah War," the subject of which, treated at length, would cover the four years from 1857 to 1861, the time of the sojourn of "Johnston's army" in the valley, Heber was one with Brigham in the bold yet patriotic stand taken by Zion's leader in repelling the hostile invasion. We need not dwell upon the oft-told tale. President Kimball was a man of peace, and not of war, and, though not lacking in courage, preferred to battle with error and the powers of evil, than with his fellow-men. [428]

In the spring of 1858, when the Saints, to the number of 30,000, abandoned their homes at the approach of the army, President Kimball accompanied the exodus of his people south as far as Provo, whence he returned, after peace was assured, to his home in Salt Lake City early in July. The soldiers had marched quietly through the deserted city, crossed the Jordan, and camped at Cedar Valley, forty miles south-west, opposite the town of Lehi, where they founded Camp Floyd, afterwards renamed Fort Crittenden, and occupied it until the autumn of 1861, when the troops were withdrawn to take part in the war of the Great Rebellion.[10]

Apropos of the war:—In an old memorandum book belonging to President Kimball, in which he sometimes noted down his thoughts, appears the following:

"GREAT SALT LAKE CITY,
"March 27th, 1859.

"The word of the Lord to me, Heber C. Kimball. At 9 o'clock in the evening the Lord said to me that division would take place between the north and south within six years, and much blood would be spilt, and I should live to see it." [429]

---

## CHAPTER 62

SOME OF HEBER'S FAMILY HISTORY—A PATRIARCHAL HOUSEHOLD—NAMES OF HIS WIVES AND CHILDREN—EPISODE OF ABRAM A. KIMBALL—PETER, THE CHILD OF PROMISE—HEBER AT FAMILY PRAYERS—DAVID H. KIMBALL'S STORY—HEBER P. AND SOLOMON F. KIMBALL IN THE BLACK HAWK WAR

A FEW leaves from President Kimball's domestic life will now be in order. His was one of the most interesting, as likewise one of the most numerous families in the Church. Like the patriarchs and prophets of old, whose example he religiously

---

[10] General A. S. Johnston, who led this army to Utah, fell at the battle of Shiloh, April 6th, 1862, fighting on the side of the Confederacy. He was a brave and brilliant soldier, and one of the recognized great generals of the war.

followed, he was the husband of many wives and the head of a multitudinous posterity.

Moreover, it is safe to say that no family in Israel, in its domestic relations, better exemplified the true nature and purpose of the polygamic principle, than the family of Heber C. Kimball.

That much of this was due to his wise government and upright example, none who knew him will doubt, but that it was also largely the result of the nobility of character displayed by the true and faithful women who honored him as husband, father and friend, there is as little room for question. We can only regret that circumstances uncontrollable prevent our dwelling in detail upon their heroic lives and virtues. Only here and there an incident, by modesty reluctantly supplied, has been furnished in response to solicitation for the purposes of this work. **[430]**

We are enabled, however, to present in this chapter a complete list of the members of Heber's family, the names of the wives and children which God had given him, with whatever incidents relating to them that have come into the author's possession.

Reference has already been made to the fact that, before leaving Nauvoo, Heber, like many of his brethren, had entered upon his career as a polygamic patriarch. The story of Sarah Noon, his second wife, has been partly told in a former chapter. The other wives we cannot name in their order, but will speak of them in proceeding as the course of our narrative suggests.

VILATE MURRAY,*[11] Heber's first wife, was the mother of ten children. Their names are as follows:

Judith Marvin,*
William Henry,
Helen Mar,
Roswell Heber,*
Heber Parley,*
David Patten,*
Charles Spaulding,
Brigham Willard,*
Solomon Farnham,
Murray Gould.*

Heber's children by Sarah Noon were:
Adelbert Henry,*
Sarah Helen,*
Heber.*

Sarah, it will be remembered, was a widow with two little daughters when he married her. The names of these children were Betsy and Harriet Noon.

After the death of the Prophet Joseph, who had also **[431]** taken many wives, most of his widows were married, for time, to Brigham, Heber and others of the

---

[11] The star attached to names in this chapter signifies deceased.

martyr's brethren. The wives of the Prophet who wedded Heber C. Kimball were Sarah Ann Whitney,* eldest daughter of Bishop N. K. Whitney; Lucy Walker, Prescindia Huntington, Sarah Lawrence, Mary Houston, Martha McBride.†[12] Sylvia P. Sessions,* Nancy Maria Smith, and Sarah Scott.†

The children of the first-named are as follows:

David,*
David O.,*  } died in infancy
David Heber,
Newel Whitney,
Horace Heber,
Maria,
Joshua.

Newel has fulfilled a mission to the Southern States, and is now an acting Bishop of the Church in Logan, Cache County, Utah.

Heber's wife Lucy bore to him:—
Rachel Sylvia,*
John H.,
Willard H.,*
Lydia H.,
Anna S.,
Eliza,
Washington,
Franklin H.*

It is related that during the illness of the boy Willard, who died in infancy, his father and another Elder were administering to him, when the latter began to promise life, a speedy recovery, etc., to the little sufferer. [432] In the midst of it Heber, seized with a sudden inspiration, cried: "Hold!" The Elder paused, they took their hands from off the child's head, and he died in a few minutes.

"AUNT PRESCINDIA," who is a notable woman in Israel, with an unwritten history of great interest, is the mother of two children by Heber, namely:

Prescindia Celestia,*
Joseph.

The latter is the Bishop of Meadowville, Rich County, Utah, and has been a member of the Territorial Legislature.

The other widows of the Prophet who married Heber, had no children by him.

Among his wives when he came out of Nauvoo, were Clarissa and Emily Cutler, sisters, both the daughters of Alpheus Cutler, who left the Church while at Winter Quarters. When the Saints removed to the Rocky Mountains, Clarissa and Emily remained with their father, each with an infant son in arms. Clarissa's child was named Abram A., and Emily's, Isaac A. Feeling impressed that their mothers

---

[12] Names marked thus, whether living or dead, unknown.

would never come to the mountains, Heber, on leaving them to go west with the pioneers, blessed his little sons and, while his hands were upon Abram's head, prophesied that he would some day come to the home of his people, and would afterwards return for his brother Isaac.

There was a fatality in his father's words, as usual.

Fifteen years later, the mothers of both boys being dead, Abram came to Utah and joined the Church. He was baptized by Enoch Reese, under his father's direction. On returning to the house after his baptism, his father confirmed him, ordained him an Elder and set him apart for a mission to the states, to go and bring his [433] brother to Utah, thus resealing the blessing bestowed upon him in his childhood. Abram fulfilled his misson and returned, bringing his brother with him. Isaac also was baptized, and he and Abram afterwards went upon missions to Great Britain. The latter is now Bishop of Kanosh, Millard County, Utah.

Another incident of a prophetic nature may here be noted. One of Heber's wives, Mary Ellen Abel, or "Aunt Mary Ellen" as she is familiarly known, had lived with him for fourteen years and no child had blessed their union. Her husband prophesied that she should bear a son, and his name should be Peter. In due time the son was born and named, but was not destined to live to grow to manhood. This was her only child.

RUTH REESE, another of Heber's wives, was the mother of:—
Susannah R.,*
Jacob R.,*
Enoch H.*

In memory we yet can hear the well-known voice of Grandfather Kimball, calling to his sons in stentorian tones: "Abraham! Isaac! Jacob! Come in to prayers!" For these names, with many others of Scriptural origin, were all included in his family nomenclature.

CHRISTEEN GOLDEN, who, with many others, was married to him in Nauvoo, was the mother of:—
Cornelia C.,*
Jonathan Golden,
Elias Smith,
May Margaret.

Jonathan and Elias both have been on missions to the Southern States. The former is president of the Young Men's Mutual Improvement Associations of [434] Bear Lake Stake. Elias was a member of the house branch of the Utah Legislature during its twenty-eighth session, January, 1888.

The Gheen sisters, Anna* and Amanda were likewise among his "honorable women." The issue of the first marriage was as follows:—
Samuel H.,
Daniel H,,

Andrew H., } twins
Alice,
Sarah.

Andrew fulfilled a long and faithful mission to the Indian Territory in 1885-6-7, and is still recognized as the president of that mission. He is the present administrator of the Kimball estate.

AMANDA'S children are:
William G.,
Albert H.,
Jeremiah,*
Moroni.

"Jerry" was accidentally killed by falling from a railway train, between Fort Scott and Camas, Kansas, on the night of May 25th, 1887, while on his way to Europe to fulfill a mission.

The sisters Harriet and Ellen Sanders next occur to mind. The latter has already been mentioned as one of the three women who accompanied the pioneers from Winter Quarters to the Rocky Mountains in 1847.

HARRIET'S offspring:—
Harriet,*
Hyrum H.,
Eugene.
(Hyrum fulfilled an honorable mission to the Southern States.) **[435]**

ELLEN'S:—
Samuel,*
Joseph S,* } twins
Augusta,*
Jedediah,
Rosalia.

FRANCES SWAN,* one of Heber's wives who left him, was the mother of one child, a daughter named for herself.

Heber also married Martha Knight,† by whom he had one child, a son; name unknown.

One of his last wives was Mary Smithies,* the same whom, in her infancy, in a far-off land, he had blessed and promised that she should live to become "a mother in Israel." Her children are:—

Melvina,
James,*
Wilford,
Lorenzo,
Abbie.

In the foregoing lists we have classed together the wives who were the mothers of his children. Besides these there were many others, most of them aged ladies and widows whom he merely supported, without living with them. Following is a list of their names:—

Mary Fielding Smith,*[13]
Margaret McMinn,*
Hannah Moon,*
Dorothy Moon,
Adelia Wilcox,
Huldah Barnes,
Eliza Cravath, **[436]**
Mary Ann Shefflin,*
Charlotte Chase,
Theresa Morley,*
Ruth L. Pierce,
Maria Winchester,*
Laura Pitkin,*
Abigail Pitkin,*
Ruth Wellington,*
Abigail Buchanan,*
Sophronia Harmon,*
Sarah Stiles.†
Elizabeth Hereford,†
Rebecca Williams,†
Sarah Buckwater.†
Mary Dull.†

Thus it will be seen that Heber C. Kimball was the husband of forty-five wives.[14] and the father of sixty-five children. Truly a patriarchal household.

It may well be surmised that the government and support of a family of such dimensions were no small tax upon the wisdom, patience and provident care of even the wisest and most opulent. Forever banished be the thought—aspersion upon reason and consistency as it is—that self-seeking, ease-desiring human nature would take upon itself such burdens and responsibilities from any motive less honorable and pure than that which Mormonism maintains is the true one. Luxury and lust go frequently hand in hand; licentiousness and honest toil but rarely.

Heber C. Kimball was a man of industry, a man of virtue, of self-denial, who would sooner have thought of **[437]** severing his right hand from his body, than to have cherished an unchaste sentiment, or sacrificed a principle to sin or selfish ease. He was often heard to declare that the plural order of marriage, with its manifold cares and perplexities, had cost him "bushels of tears."

---

[13] Widow of Hyrum Smith, sealed to Heber for time.

[14] At the funeral of his wife Vilate, Heber, pointing to the coffin, said: "There lies a woman who has given me forty-four wives."

Yet his was an exemplary family—as much so as any in all Israel, polygamous or otherwise. His wives loved each other as sisters, and dwelt together in peace and unity; while his children, especially the males, sons of various mothers, clung together with an affection all but clannish in its intensity. Woe betide the luckless wight, who, even in childhood's days, imposed upon a "Kimball boy." The whole family of urchins would resent the insult, and that, too, with pluckiness surpassing even their numbers.

Family prayer was an institution in the Kimball household. Morning and evening the members were called in to surround the family altar and offer up praise and petitions to the Throne of Grace. It is a common remark to this day that such prayers are seldom heard as were wont to issue from the heart and lips of Heber C. Kimball. Reverence for Deity was one of the cardinal qualities of his nature. Nevertheless, it was noticeable that the God to whom he prayed was a being "near at hand and not afar off." He worshiped not as "a worm of the dust," hypocritically meek and lowly, or as one conscious of naught but the meanness of his nature, and the absence of merit in his cause. But in a spirit truly humble, confessing his sins, yet knowing something of the nobility of his soul, he talked with God "as one man talketh with another;" and often with the ease and familiarity of an old-time friend.

On one occasion, while offering up an earnest appeal in behalf of certain of his fellow-creatures, he [438] startled the kneeling circle by bursting into a loud laugh in the very midst of his prayer. Quickly regaining his composure and solemn address, he remarked, apologetically: "Lord, it makes me laugh to pray about some people."

Heber loved his children, and was justly proud of his numerous and noble posterity. If at times he appeared stern, and was severe in his correction, it was not that he loved them less, but their welfare and salvation more. He made no compromise with sin, but nipped it in the bud, though the soil wherein it grew were the hearts of his dearest friends and relations. His greatest desire for his family was that they should be humble, virtuous and God-fearing. The riches, fashions, and even culture of the world were as nothing in his eyes, compared with honesty, morality and the treasures of eternal truth.

Nor was he morose and sullen, because thus sober-minded and religious. Mingling with his deeply earnest, profoundly solemn nature was a keen sense of humor, a continuous play of mirth, like sunlight gilding the edges of a cloud.

One day (it was July 23rd, 1864, and a grand celebration of Pioneer day was on the tapis) he drove down to the shop of James Lawson the blacksmith, to have some repairing done to his carriage, a long vehicle with seats on either side. He had about fifteen of his boys in the carriage, all urchins ranging from ten to thirteen years.

"James," said he, with a merry twinkle in his eye, "I have no shoes for these boys, and I'm going to have them out in the procession to-morrow in this carriage, so that their feet can't be seen."

Then, with a proud glance at his youthful progeny, [439] he added: "There is a load of Elders; I have ordained them all myself."

He often took his children into his confidence, giving them practical lessons in the virtues he desired them to cultivate. His son David H. relates the following:

"One day President Young made a call upon father for $1,000., for some public purpose, and not having the ready cash, he was at a loss to know where to get it. At his suggestion we went down in the garden and bowed ourselves in prayer, father calling upon the Lord to direct him in the matter. We then arose and started down the street, and he remarked that the Lord would answer our prayer and direct him aright. When even with Godbe's corner, William Godbe came out of his store and told him that, in looking through his safe, he had come across about $1,000 in gold-dust, belonging to him, which his son Heber P. had left there for him some time before, though father until then knew nothing about it."

In the Spring of 1866 his son, Col. H. P. Kimball, was called into southern Utah at the head of a company of minute men, to aid in subduing the Indians in the Black Hawk War. His son David P. was also called, but having just returned from a mission to England, with his brother Charles, he was honorably released, and his younger brother, Solomon, sent in his stead. The evening before they started, Heber called their mother, Vilate, and her children into his room, and spent several hours with them, giving them much good counsel and explaining to them the relationship of the Lamanites, as a branch of the house of Israel, with the latter-day work, and the important part they were destined to play in this dispensation. He then blessed Heber and Solomon, and **[440]** promised them in the name of the Lord that they should not see an Indian while they were gone.

This promise, though meant for their welfare, and, it may be added, for the welfare of the Lamanites as well, was quite a disappointment to the two brothers, who were anxious, not only to see the Indians, but to have a "brush" with them. Solomon had often heard of a fight which his brother William and others had had with the red men in Battle Creek Canyon, some years before, in which William had the horn of his saddle punctured by a bullet while ascending the ravine, thus narrowly escaping being wounded or killed. Solomon had seen the saddle, which had a romantic charm for him, and he now wanted to see the Indians. The remainder of the story we will give in his own words:

"We were gone ninety days and rode hundreds of miles, following the tracks of different bands of hostile Indians, and were close upon them a great many times. They were attacking settlements all around us, killing the settlers and driving off stock. At one time, after the Indians had made a raid on Round Valley (Scipio) killing one man and running off five hundred head of stock, Col. Kimball left a part of his command at Thistle Valley to hold the fort at that place, while he went to intercept the Indians on the Sevier River. We had gone but a few hours, when the Indians made a raid on the fort at Thistle Valley, running off all their horses, killing one of the party and wounding another.

"After our company returned home we were drawn up in line in front of the Court House, where President Young, my father, and others came down to see us.

Father, looking at Heber and myself, whose clothing and countenances showed hard service, asked us if we had seen an Indian while we were gone. Our humilia[441]ting reply was, 'No.' He laughed and said, 'Did'nt I tell you so?' and then added: 'I would rather have them kill you, than to have one of my sons shed their blood.'"

But a volume might be filled with incidents of like character in his experience, and then the half remain untold. Suffice this, at present, for his inner life and private family history.

Preaching, colonizing, traveling through the settlements, encouraging the Saints in their toils and sacrifices; sitting in council among the leaders of Israel; ministering in sacred and holy places, and otherwise laboring for and blessing the Lord's people:—so wore away the remaining years of Heber C. Kimball on this planet. His name was literally "a household word" in Israel. "Brother Heber" was everywhere honored and beloved. Even the Gentiles esteemed him, admiring his honesty and outspoken candor, let him lash as he might with the whip of his tongue, the wrong-doer outside, or the hypocrite inside the Church. Loved and honored as are few men in this life, he returned in measure full to overflowing the affection of the hearts which God had given him. [442]

## CHAPTER 63

ANECDOTES AND REMINISCENCES OF HEBER C. KIMBALL—THE MAN AS OTHERS KNEW HIM—GOLDEN GRAINS FROM THE SANDS OF MEMORY

AT this point in our history we deem it proper to introduce a series of anecdotes and reminiscences relating to President Kimball, nearly all of which were contributed, at the author's invitation, especially for this work. These flowers of incident culled from the gardens of recollection, cannot fail to interest the reader, while they illustrate, as nothing else could, the character and conduct of this remarkable man.

The first is from BROTHER N. B. BALDWIN, of Fillmore, who writes as follows:
"My first acquaintance with Elder Kimball was in Zion's Camp, in the Spring and Summer of 1834. The following winter the young and middle-aged Elders, all who conveniently could, were called in to attend school in Kirtland, Ohio. William E. McLellin was the teacher of the grammar classes, grammar being then taught on the Kirkham plan, by lecture and repetition. Our class consisted of Joseph Smith (who, in the absence of the teacher at other duties, took charge of the class), David W. Patten, Heber C. Kimball, Benjamin Winchester, Nathan B. Baldwin and others that I do not now recollect.

"It seemed to be very hard for Brother Kimball to memorize sentences by hearing them repeated. One time when he was thus at fault, Joseph, in a jocular mood, said to him; 'Repeat that correctly, or I will take a stick and whip you as I would a little child.' **[443]**

"With his model meekness, Brother Kimball smilingly said; 'Well, you may whip me.'

"'Yes,' said Joseph, 'it would be just about like whipping a little child. YOU ARE JUST AS INNOCENT AS A LITTLE CHILD.'"

This simple anecdote furnishes not only a key to the character of Heber C. Kimball, showing his native meekness and veneration, but also an evidence of the estimation in which he was held by the Prophet, even at that early day. Jesus said that "except ye become as little children ye shall not enter into the kingdom of heaven."

ELDER WILLIAM B. BARTON contributes the following:

"It was my happy privilege, while filling a mission to England in 1874-5-6 to receive my appointment to labor in the Liverpool Conference. This conference included, among others, a few branches that were left of the once flourishing conferences of Clithero and Preston. I realized that I was traveling on historic ground. I found some few Saints still in that land, who were personally acquainted with the early Elders and Apostles who first preached and established the gospel in Preston; and I found that while all were kindly remembered, none had made as indelible and lasting an impression on their minds as Brother Heber C. Kimball. They pointed out with pleasure and reverence the places where he and others had stood forth proclaiming the restored gospel. Among these were the Market-place, the Cock Pit, and the Rev. James Fielding's Chapel. I was fortunate in securing a photograph of this chapel, but had no idea at the time that it would ever be used to illustrate a history of the founder of the British mission.

"This Mr. Fielding and a Mr. Aitken were two of **[444]** twelve men who had united together and made a vow that they would neither eat nor drink until the Lord revealed to them whether he would raise up His Church in their day. The Lord did make known to them that he had already established His Church on the earth, and in due time His servants would be sent with authority to preach and baptize. Brother Kimball visited Mr. Aitken and bore a powerful testimony of the truth, and prophesied to him that if he rejected the message of salvation, he would lose his influence, his flock would leave him, and he would go down; all of which was fulfilled to the very letter, with regard to him and Mr. Fielding also. Mr. Fielding had commenced to build a more commodious church, but he never finished it, and he himself was for a long time an inmate of Grosvenor hospital; a place were unfortunate and aged clergymen spent their declining years."

"Among the early converts of Apostle Kimball in that land were the sisters Mary Ann and Margaret Heaton Topping, whose parents were opposed to and never joined the Church. Brother Kimball counseled them to obey their parents, and told them that the time would come when they would cease to object to their attending the meetings of the Saints. Said he: 'When I say come, come, and all will be well,' which promise was literally fulfilled. He warned one of these sisters not to marry a young man she was engaged to, as he would apostatize and leave the Church, and told her that her future husband was not then in the Church, but would come in and remain faithful; and, said he, 'You shall see the man you are going to marry at the conference that I will notify you to attend.' These remarkable promises were all fulfilled, and Sister Topping is alive to-day to bear witness of their truth." **[445]**

BROTHER CHARLES HUBBARD, an old friend of Heber's, whom he mentions repeatedly in his history, relates this incident:

"As is well known, President Brigham Young, when he crossed the Mississippi River from Montrose, in September, 1839, and started on his mission to England, was very sick. He was brought to the house of Heber C. Kimball, in Nauvoo. Brother Kimball was also sick with the same disease (ague) but after the fever went off he climbed upon his house and was trying to finish the roof, when his brother missionary (Brigham) came out to walk a little to try his strength. In the effort he fainted and fell to the ground. Brother Kimball, not having strength to lift him, called to me, just across the river, to come and help assist Brother Brigham into the house, where, after placing him upon the bed, we administered to him and he recovered consciousness. When I left, Brother Heber followed me to the door and said:

"'Charley, I doubt very much if Brigham ever rises from that bed.'"

"But he had no sooner uttered the words, than he spoke up, as with another voice, and said, 'He shall live, and shall start upon this mission with me to-morrow morning.' And they did start the very next morning, on their mission to England.'"

ELDER JACOB HAMBLIN leaves the following on record: "At the April conference I, with others, was called on a mission to the Indians in Southern Utah, in 1854. We commenced our labors at a place we called Harmony.

"About the end of May of that year, President B. Young, Heber C. Kimball, P. P. Pratt and others, to the number of twenty persons, came to visit us. Presi**[446]**dent Young gave much instruction, etc. Brother Kimball prophesied that if the brethren were united they would be prospered and blessed, but if they permitted the spirit of strife and contention to come into their midst, the place would come to an end in a scene of bloodshed.

"Previous to this meeting, President Young asked some brethren who had been into the country south of Harmony, if they thought a wagon road could be made down to the Rio Virgin. Their replies were very discouraging, but in the face of this report Brother Kimball prophesied in this meeting that a road would be made from Harmony over the Black Ridge, and a Temple would be built on the Rio Virgin, and the Lamanites would come from the east side of the Colorado River and get their endowments in it. All these prophecies have been fulfilled."

One of the Elders laboring in the Manti Temple writes:

"In an early day when President Young and party were making the location of a settlement here, President Heber C. Kimball prophesied that the day would come when a temple would be built on this hill. Some disbelieved and doubted the possibility of even making a settlement here. Brother Kimball said, 'Well, it will be so, and more than that, the rock will be quarried from that hill to build it with, and some of the stone from that quarry will be taken to help complete the Salt Lake Temple.' On July 28th, 1878, two large stones, weighing respectively 5,600 and 5,020 pounds, were taken from the Manti stone quarry, hauled by team to York, the U. C. R. R. terminus then, and shipped to Salt Lake City to be used for the tablets in the east and west ends of the Salt Lake City Temple. **[447]**

"At a conference held in Ephraim, Sanpete County, June 25th, 1875, nearly all the speakers expressed their feelings to have a temple built in Sanpete County, and gave their views as to what point and where to build it, and to show the union that existed, Elder Daniel H. Wells said 'Manti,' George Q. Cannon, Brigham Young, Jr., John Taylor, Orson Hyde, Erastus Snow, Franklin D. Richards, Lorenzo Young, and A. M. Musser said 'Manti stone quarry.' I have given the names in the order in which they spoke. At 4 p. m. that day President Brigham Young said: 'The Temple should be built on Manti stone quarry.' Early on the morning of April 25th, 1877, President Brigham Young asked Brother Warren S. Snow to go with him to the Temple hill. Brother Snow says; 'We two were alone: President Young took me to the spot where the Temple was to stand; we went to the southeast corner, and President Young said; 'Here is the spot where the prophet Moroni stood and dedicated this piece of land for a Temple site, and that is the reason why the location is made here, and we can't move it from this spot; and if you and I are the only persons that come here at high noon to-day, we will dedicate this ground."

The late GEORGE NEBEKER said that President Kimball told him, many years ago, that he would live to see the kings and great ones of the earth pass by his door. Brother Nebeker resided in the nineteenth ward. The railway at that time was not thought of in Utah. But the iron horse now rushes along the street immediately in front of Brother Nebeker's family residence, and he himself lived to see such celebrities as President Grant, the Emperor of Brazil and other royal and great ones literally pass by his door. **[448]**

MRS. MAMIE HOOPER JENNINGS, daughter of the late Captain Hooper, relates:
"Brother Kimball gave my father a half dollar, telling him that as long as he kept it he should never want for money. Father placed faith in the promise, and testified often that he had realized its truth; he had never wanted for money, in any sum, from that time."

A FRIEND:
"He said to me one day, taking up a small stick from the ground, 'You see this stick. If it had remained down there you never would have noticed that there was any dirt clinging to it. But now that I hold it up you observe it is covered with dirt. It is just so when a man is put into office. He may be just as clean before he gets there as those around him, but his being lifted up above them makes his faults more manifest, and he is far more apt to be criticised than before.'"

The veteran Bishop, A. H. RALEIGH, speaks thus from his exile:

"Having fortunately been privileged with a personal acquaintance with the late Heber C. Kimball, from the early days of Nauvoo to the time of his decease, a period of about twenty-five years, I venture confidently to submit that no stronger or more forcible illustration of the peculiarity of his character can be presented than the notable eccentricity manifested in the subdivisions of plat E. Salt Lake City, which he fashioned by personally directing city surveyor J. W. Fox, Sen., in laying out and platting, and myself in naming the streets, while drafting the resolution which, when passed by the City Council, made it a legal survey. Though it has undergone some slight changes in the remodeling of a few lots, as also a few streets, and changing a few of these names, with **[449]** a small addition to the plat, far the most of the original remains to be a lasting monument to his memory. The great variety of form and size of lots, involving corners, angles, widths and lengths of streets, together with their peculiar names, almost exhausting the names of the fruit and vegetable kingdom, are all characteristic of the man, familiarly called 'Brother Heber,' ever evincing a strong desire to imitate nature in its eternal variety and beauty; the same in his plain, easy, natural demeanor in his daily intercourse with his fellows, either in public or private life, giving evidence of the presence of one of nature's noblemen, one of the noblest works of God,—an honest man."

FATHER J. L. HEYWOOD writes from Panguitch:
"Brother Kimball was naturally of a jovial turn of mind. When working at the pottery business he would sometimes use a chip to turn his crocks, remarking that he 'did not care who stole his trade, as long as they did not steal his tools.'

"In relation to some protuberances on his forehead he remarked that they were the 'horns of Joseph' with which to push the people together, referring to his labors as an Apostle.

"President B. Young once said that Brother Kimball could go to the city of Washington, D.C., and build up a church, and the way he would do it was by beginning so small."

ELDER JUNIUS F. WELLS:
"One day he entered the Union Academy, taught by Dr. Doremus, and taking off his high-crowned straw hat that he used so much to wear, made a profound bow to the school, without saying a word. Then, while the students were gazing at him with fixed eyes and open **[450]** mouths, he said solemnly: 'Boys; never call your father *the old man!* With another polite bow, and without saying another word, he turned and left the hall. The impression made by his presence and laconic speech was most profound."

ELDER CHARLES W. STAYNER:
"President Kimball's hat blew off on Main Street, one day, and as he was pursuing it, one of a party of men with whom he had been conversing on the corner, laughed at him. Stopping in his chase, he turned around and addressing that person said: 'Never mind; your hat will blow off some day, but your head will be in it.' The man to whom he spoke afterwards apostatized."

SOLOMON F. KIMBALL:

"I heard father prophecy that a certain Elder would lose all his means and die a poor man, because he neglected his spiritual duties to attend to his temporal affairs. I have seen that prophecy fulfilled."

JAMES LAWSON'S narrative:

"In 1855, Heber C. Kimball sent for me (I had just been married thirteen days) and said, 'Brother James' I want you to give your wife Betsy a divorce,' I said, 'Brother Kimball what is the matter? There is nothing wrong with us, and we think everything of each other?' He said, 'Nothing is the matter, but here is the divorce and I want you to sign it.' I signed it and he told me to send her home to her mother (Sarah Noon[15]) which I did. At the same time I asked her if she had been making any complaints to Bro. Kimball against me. She said, 'Never, to anybody.' I did not sleep a wink that night, and no one knows what I suffered in my feelings. **[451]** I prayed frequently to the Lord and enquired of Him what all this meant. Towards morning I received an answer to my prayers. The Spirit said unto me, 'Be comforted, my servant James, all will come out right.' Soon after this Brother Kimball went to the Legislature, which was held at Fillmore, and was absent from home about two months. When he returned he gave me a mission to Carson Valley and told me to get Betsy and bring her to the Endowment House with me. I did so and he sealed us for time and all eternity.

"After this took place I said, 'Brother Kimball what did you do that for?' He said, 'Brother James, I did it to try you as I was tried. I will tell you. After I had returned from my second mission to England in 1841, the Prophet Joseph came to me one evening and said, 'Brother Heber, I want you to give Vilate to me to be my wife,' saying that the Lord desired this at my hands.' Heber said that in all his life before he had never had anything take hold of him like that. He was dumbfounded. He went home, and did not eat a mouthful of anything, nor even touch a drop of water to his lips, nor sleep, for three days and nights. He was almost continually offering up his prayers to God and asking him for comfort. On the evening of the third day he said, 'Vilate, let's go down to the Prophet's' and they went down and met him in a private room. Heber said, 'Brother Joseph, here is Vilate.' The Prophet wept like a child, said Heber, and after he had cleared the tears away, he took us and sealed us for time and all eternity, and said, 'Brother Heber, take her, and the Lord will give you a hundred fold."

COL. ROBERT SMITH, a veteran friend of President Kimball's, and for many years almost like a member of his family, says: **[452]**

"In 1857, I was working for Brother Heber and asked him for some goods, which he refused to let me have. Feeling bad over it, I went home and laid the matter before the Lord. The next morning when I came to work, Brother Heber called me into his room and said, 'Robert, what have you been complaining to the Lord for, about his servant Heber? Here are the things you asked me for, and after

---

[15] Heber's final plural wife.

this don't go to the Lord about every little thing that happens."

"In the year 1855, he was moving a herd of sheep on to the Church Island, with a flat boat; the water was very shallow in some places and the boat got fastened on a sand-bar, and we could not get it off. There were about six of us in all. After working for some time and accomplishing nothing, Brother Heber returned to the shore, which was but a short distance, and getting behind some grease-wood he bowed down in prayer. Then coming back to the boat, he said, 'come boys, let's give her another trial, she'll move now.' All took hold and pushed and it went off the bar all right, and we arrived at the Island that night."

"At one time, putting his hand on his heart, he remarked that unless a man knew that Jesus was the Christ, he could not stand in this Church.

"He said that the Lord would allow all manner of abominations to come to Zion, in order to purify His people. This was in 1856.

"He saw in vision a U. S. Marshal in pursuit of one of his daughters, who had a small babe in her arms.[16]

"He said that this government would dissolve pretty much all the laws passed by our legislature, and that **[453]** the time would come when the government would stop the Saints from holding meetings. When this was done the Lord would pour out His judgments."

"At family prayers, just a little while before his death, he remarked that the angel Moroni had visited him the night before and informed him that his work on this earth was finished, and he would soon be taken."

FATHER O. N. LLILJENQUIST once said to the author: "My first impression of President Kimball was far from favorable. He was preaching in the Tabernacle, and belaboring a certain man very severely, and I did not like his harshness. The next time I met him was in the Endowment House, and if ever I saw a man look like a God, and act as humble as a little child, that man was Heber C. Kimball. All my prejudice vanished in a moment."

BISHOP JAMES WATSON:

"In 1864, soon after my arrival in Utah, I went with my brother Joseph to see President Kimball about a lot I desired to purchase. We found him at his mill on City Creek, superintending some workmen. Being introduced to him, I said: 'President Kimball, I wish to buy a lot which I am informed belongs to you.'

"Eyeing me in a very searching manner, he said: 'I have sold many lots and never received the pay for them,' and then turned away and resumed his directions to the workmen.

"I was very much hurt at his abrupt manner, especially as his words seemed to intimate that I was one who would not pay my debts, a reputation I had not earned. "Have you any further business with me?' he asked, turning towards me again, after the lapse of a few moments. 'No sir,' said I sternly, and walked away. **[454]**

---

[16] The heroine of this episode, which actually occurred, was Mrs. Melvina Kimball Driggs, wife of Bishop Apollos Driggs, one of the victims of the anti-polygamy crusade under the "Edmunds Law."

"Some time elapsed, and we did not meet, for I avoided him whenever I saw him coming. One day, however, we met face to face, he on his way to the Endowment House, and I near the Temple Block, where I was then working. Smiling amiably and reminding me that I had avoided him several times, he asked: 'Have you got a lot yet?' 'No sir,' I answered, coolly, although my blood was warmed by the recollection which his words called up. 'Well, you'll get one,' said he, 'and you'll get it of me, too.' (I inwardly resolved that I never would.) 'Yes, you'll come and get it of me,' he repeated, and we separated.

"Being determined that his words should not come to pass, (for I was not at all won over by his change of manner) I went and purchased a lot from a sister in the Church, paid her for it, and put up a house on the land. I then asked her for the deed, but she told me she did not have one.

"'Well, who holds the title to the land, then?' I asked.

"'Heber C. Kimball, she replied.

"I was dumb-founded. 'Well, I shall not buy it of him,' I said to myself, but I resolved to go and get the deed for her. Brother Kimball received me very kindly, and my feelings were somewhat softened towards him. Almost the first question he asked was: 'Have you got a lot yet?' 'Yes, sir," I replied, and then told him I had come to get sister ——'s deed. 'Why, I cannot give her a deed,' said he, 'for she has never paid me for that lot.' I then told him what I had done, and he said with a smile, 'I told you you would have to come to me for a lot. Wait here a moment,' he added, and went into his office. Returning presently, he handed me a deed for the land, made out in my name, and said: 'There, I'll make you a present of that deed, and you've already **[455]** paid for the land; God bless you,' and we parted friends.

"Another incident I will relate:

"On the morning of the 15th day of April, 1865, my wife and I were going through the Temple block towards the Endowment House, as we had been previously requested by our Bishop to go and get our endowments. I was in a very thoughtful mood and prayed silently in my own mind that the Lord would give me grace to always adhere to the truth and have my mind quickened by the Holy Ghost, so that I might always be able to decide between truth and error and to have courage to defend the principles of the Gospel of our Lord and Savior Jesus Christ.

"We overtook President H. C. Kimball and were walking leisurely along, when Willard G. Smith overtook us and said to President Kimball, 'Have you heard the news? President Lincoln was assassinated last night while at the theatre in Washington. See the flags are at half mast.' After some little conversation we entered the Endowment House. The thought of the sad death of President Lincoln weighed heavily on my mind, and made a deep impression on me. In going through the House Brother Kimball gave us a very impressive lecture. Fixing his eyes on me, he said:

"'Do you know that you will yet be called upon to stand in front of the enemy?' Then he paused for a reply.

"After studying a few seconds, I answered, 'No, sir.'

"Giving me a piercing look, he said: 'Don't you believe it.' I answered 'No, sir.'

"Gazing at me intently he said, 'Don't you believe what I say?' I answered 'How can I believe, when I have no evidence or knowledge of it?' 'You foolish [456] man,' he said, 'If you had a knowledge you would not require any belief.'

"Pointing to me again, he said: 'You will yet be called upon to stand in front of the enemy, while bullets will fly around as thick as hail. Yet not a hair of your head shall be hurt. Do you believe that?'

"After a little study I answered, *'No, sir.'* He seemed a little perplexed at my obstinacy and asked, 'Why don't you believe it?' I said, 'Because I have been in a hail-storm, and I know that it is impossible to be in a hail-storm without being hit, and if the bullets are to fly around me as thick as hail, I am sure I will be hit.' He said 'Don't you think if you saw them coming you could *juke* them?' I said I thought I could. 'But,' said he, 'they come so quick you cannot do it.'

"Then fixing his eyes upon me, he said: 'The day will come when you will stand in the front rank in face of the enemy, while the bullets will fly around you like a hail-storm, but if you will live pure and keep your garments clean, not one hair of your head will be hurt. *Do you believe that?*

"I said: 'Brother Kimball, I believe what you say.'"

ELDER EDWARD STEVENSON:

"I cheerfully contribute the following, concerning one of the greatest prophets of the nineteenth century—Heber C. Kimball: In 1856 a little group of friends, convened in the House of the Lord, were engaged in pleasant conversation on the isolated condition of the Latter-day Saints.

"'Yes,' said Brother Heber (by which name he was so familiarly known), 'we think we are secure here in the chambers of the everlasting hills, where we can close those few doors of the canyons against mobs and [457] persecutors, the wicked and the vile, who have always beset us with violence and robbery, but I want to say to you, my brethren, the time is coming when we will be mixed up in these now peaceful valleys to that extent that it will be difficult to tell the face of a Saint from the face of an enemy to the people of God. Then, brethren, look out for the great sieve, for there will be a great sifting time, and many will fall; for I say unto you there is a *test*, a TEST, a TEST coming, and who will be able to stand?'

"The emphasis with which those words were spoken I shall never forget.

"I was with Brother Heber on the occasion of his last meeting at Bountiful, Davis County, Utah, just previous to his death. He seemed full to overflowing; for over two hours he held the audience; that meeting and the deep instructions will endure in the hearts of true Saints while eternities roll on.

"While working with him in the House of the Lord in 1856-7, how often I have heard him speak against pride and covetousness and the fear of riches, being fearful of the Lord's displeasure and consequent judgments. Said he: 'If the Saints will repent, the Lord's wrath will be turned away, but they will not repent until it is too late.'"

PRESIDENT A. O. SMOOT:

"A short time before Brother Heber was taken ill with his last sickness, I drove through with him from Provo to Salt Lake. He was unusually free in his conversation, it being almost a ceaseless flow of prophecies in relation to individuals in and out of the Church. He foretold, with what I have since realized to be the greatest accuracy, what would befall certain men. Some of those of whom he prophesied are still in good standing, but [458] many who were in good standing then, have fallen, as he said they would."

PRESIDENT A. F. MCDONALD:

"My first intimate acquaintance with President Kimball occurred in 1868, I being then in charge of the Tithing Office at Provo. He often called into the office to do business. His public discourses about this time were the most earnest and impressive that I had ever heard; and on several occasions in the Provo meeting house, he clearly foreshadowed the time of trial the Saints are now passing through, and to a period still before us. He often used the language. 'A test, a test is coming.'

"On one occasion, when he was stopping with us during a two days' conference, he came into the Tithing Yard where I was busy putting up hay, and called me towards him and said: 'Do you want me at your house, or would you rather not have us there?' I answered that it was a pleasure and honor to have him there. Looking intently at me, he said: 'I want to say to you that you have seen your worst days; you have had some hard times and trials in the past, but from this time it will be better for you. In whatever you are called to do, or whatever you put your hands to accomplish, you will be prospered and prevail.' This is true so far in my experience.

"On another occasion in 1863, during a two days' meeting in Provo, I invited several brethren to dinner. Brother Kimball was present. During the chat at the table, conversation turned on the number of children I then had, being at that time six boys; hearing this reply he said: 'Yes, and the next, the seventh, will be a boy also, and he will be the noblest, the most talented, and the greatest you have had.' Brother R. L. Campbell, who [459] I remember was present, said in a free and jocular way: 'If it should come a girl, what then?' Upon which Brother Kimball observed; 'It will not come a girl, but a boy, and you will see it.' One year and four days after, a boy was born, and Brother Kimball, again attending a two days' meeting at Provo, called to see him and directed that he be blessed and given the name of 'Heber,' by which name he is known in our family and has grown to manhood, as we believe to fulfill the words spoken of him.

"On the night of Brother Kimball's accident at Provo, a short time before his death, I was with him. I took a silk handkerchief from my pocket and tied it over his head, and then suggested that I go and call on President B. Young, then at the house of Bishop Wm. Miller, to come and administer to him; but he said: 'I command you to administer to me and anoint me with oil in the name of the Lord; do not be in the least afraid; you hold the same Priesthood and authority from God as President Young or myself, and God hears and answers the prayers of His humblest servants and people.' I administered to him accordingly, and he soon revived, becoming quite free and jocular with us, and about two o'clock in the morning at his suggestion I went home. On the following day, myself and wife called to see him. He was much improved and quite sociable, his conversation being original, incisive, and a continual feast of inspiration. As we were leaving he asked his wife (Lucy W.) to get my handkerchief that I had put on his head the previous night, and addressing my wife he said: 'Here, Betty, take this handkerchief, and be sure that you never wash it, but keep it as it is, and when you have sickness in your family, exercise the prayer of faith, and it will prove a blessing, and will be a bond between [460] you and me for ever!' My wife has sacredly kept that handkerchief."

ELDER JOHN NICHOLSON gives a valued contribution in the following:

"In accordance with your request I furnish you with a brief outline of a discourse delivered by your grandfather, the late Heber C. Kimball, in 1867. The occasion was the usual afternoon service. Whether it was held in the Bowery or the old Tabernacle, I do not distinctly recollect, but think it was the latter. My memory is, however, quite distinct in relation to the subject of the discourse; especially the prophetic part of it, with which I was specially impressed.

"President Kimball opened by stating that there were many within hearing who had often wished that they had been associated with the Prophet Joseph. 'You imagine,' said he, 'that you would have stood by him when persecution raged and he was assailed by foes within and without. You would have defended him and been true to him in the midst of every trial. You think you would have been delighted to have shown your integrity in the days of mobs and traitors.

"'Let me say to you, that many of you will see the time when you will have all the trouble, trial and persecution that you can stand, and plenty of opportunities to show that you are true to God and his work. This Church has before it many close places through which it will have to pass before the work of God is crowned with victory. To meet the difficulties that are coming, it will be necessary for you to have a knowledge of the truth of this work for yourselves. The difficulties will be of such a character that the man or woman who does not possess this personal knowledge or witness will fall. If you have not got the testimony, live right and call [461] upon the Lord and cease not till you obtain it. If you do not you will not stand.

"'Remember these sayings, for many of you will live to see them fulfilled. The time will come when no man nor woman will be able to endure on borrowed light. Each will have to be guided by the light within himself. If you do not have it, how can you stand? Do you believe it?

"'How is it now? You have the First Presidency, from whom you can get counsel to guide you, and you rely on them. The time will come when they will not be with you. Why? Because they will have to flee and hide up to keep out of the hands of their enemies. You have the Twelve now. You will not always have them, for they too will be hunted and will have to keep out of the way of their enemies. You have other men to whom you look for counsel and advice. Many of them will not be amongst you, for the same reason. You will be left to the light within yourselves. If you don't have it you will not stand; therefore seek for the testimony of Jesus and cleave to it, that when the trying time comes you may not stumble and fall.'

"The main object of the discourse was to impress the people with the importance of having light and knowledge direct from God within themselves. The prophetic part was given as the leading reason why they should be in possession of an individual testimony, as it defined to some extent the character of the trials to which the Saints would be subjected. That Brother Kimball's predictions have been, in part, at least, already fulfilled, must be clear to all who are familiar with the events of the last few years. In the course of his remarks on the occasion in point he several times said: 'You will have all the persecution you want and more [462] too, and all the opportunity to show your integrity to God and truth that you could desire.'

"The foregoing statement is probably not as absolutely correct as could have been given immediately after the delivery of the discourse, but it is so in substance. Probably there are many others who heard it who will remember it when it is brought to their recollection."

ELDER HENRY W. NAISBITT adds this endorsement:

"I was present on the occasion when President Heber C. Kimball delivered the discourse described in the foregoing communication, and the statement as therein given is correct, as I remember it."

WM. H. BEARD, ESQ. sends the following from his home in Spiceland, Indiana:

"In the spring of 1884, I called at the home of your father, the late lamented H. K. Whitney, and while there had the pleasure of viewing a fairly executed portrait of the deceased President Kimball, and having previously read something of him as viewed by Gentile historians, I conceived the idea of learning from his own people, those who had known him long and well, his religious and social standing, during some of the most eventful periods of his life. I conversed with quite a number of persons who claimed to have known him, and the universal expression was 'he was a true, noble and worthy man.' In glancing over the musty pages of a reporter's book used on that occasion I find an account of the following interview with an old-time friend of the deceased, written with an unsteady hand, but still legible, and marked with conspicuous head lines. I give the report just as it appears, thinking, perhaps, you may find in it a few facts worthy of remembrance. [463]

"The gentleman who favored me with this interview, was bending beneath the weight of accumulated years, but he seemed to possess an extraordinarily brilliant mind, coupled with a remarkable gift of memory. After extending the usual courtesies due a stranger, I ventured to ask: 'Will you please tell me what you know of the late Heber C. Kimball?' A pleasant smile lit up his face, and in a calm, steady voice he proceeded in substance as follows. 'I have known President Kimball for more than half a century. I knew him in his youth, through all the changing developments of his early manhood, and when his hair was whitened, and his cheeks furrowed by the approach of age. He was a brave, noble and dignified man, possessing more true virtues than the world will ever know. He was an affectionate husband, a devoted father and a kind and generous friend. He always had consolation for the despondent, a helping hand for the needy, and a tear for the sorrowing and afflicted. In oratory he was not eloquent, but his thoughts were always expressed in such a calm, pleasing and effective manner as to deeply impress his hearers. He was strong in his religious convictions, thoroughly familiar with every tenet of the Mormon faith, and a fervent advocate of the right. He admired true manliness in every relation of life, and was always found on the side of justice and truth. He firmly believed in the ultimate triumph of the church, and often spoke of the wrongs endured by the Latter-day Saints in their continuous struggles for religious freedom. He was a leading light for his oppressed people, and no one ever knew him unfaithful to his trust, or unduly exacting in his official life. He loved to share our sorrows, and enjoy our happiness, for he had a warm and generous heart. His mind was broad and searching, and had he **[464]** possessed a penchant for military renown, he could have succeeded admirably as a commander of armies. As a statesman he could have been an honor to the republic, and had it not been for his unpopular faith he could have filled almost any position in life to which humanity aspires. In the death of this great man the Church has lost one of its most valued members; but our society through all the coming years, will remember him in their prayers, and continue to contribute sacred tears to his memory and great moral worth.'"

As an appropriate ending for this chapter, we append a truthful tribute from the pen of President GEORGE Q. CANNON:
"Heber Chase Kimball was one of the greatest men of this age. There was a certain nobility about his appearance as well as his disposition that would have made him conspicuous in any community, and the Church of Jesus Christ afforded ample scope for the exercise of his ability, and the trying scenes through which he passed called into play his best powers.
"He was a man of commanding presence, with eyes so keen as to almost pierce one through, and before which the guilty involuntarily quailed. He was fearless and powerful in rebuking the wrong-doer, but kind, benevolent and fatherly to the deserving. He possessed such wonderful control over the passions of men, combined with such wisdom and diplomacy, that the Prophet Joseph Smith called him 'the peace-maker.' His great faith, zeal, earnestness, devotion to principle, cheerfulness under the most trying circumstances, energy, perseverance and honest simplicity marked him as no ordinary man. He possessed great natural force and strong will power, yet in his submission to the Priesthood and obedience to the laws of God he set a pattern to the **[465]** whole Church. His example throughout life was one of which his posterity may ever think with pride, and which the Saints generally will do well to follow.
"No man, perhaps, Joseph Smith excepted, who has belonged to the Church

in this generation, ever possessed the gift of prophecy to a greater degree than Brother Kimball. Although not at all pretentious, he was somewhat celebrated among his acquaintances for his prophetic inspiration. Scores of predictions were made by him and literally fulfilled.

"Brother Kimball was the only one of his father's family who embraced the gospel, but now his is one of the most numerous families in the Church. At the time of his death, he was the father of sixty-five children, of whom thirty males and eleven females were then living. His direct descendants now number nearly two hundred souls." **[466]**

## CHAPTER 64

GEMS FROM THE WORDS OF HEBER—SPIRIT RAPPINGS—ADDRESS AT THE FUNERAL OF MARY FIELDING SMITH—LOVE, UNITY AND THE COURAGE OF THE RIGHTEOUS—JOSEPH AND THE KEYS OF THE KINGDOM—CULTIVATION OF SPIRITS—HEAVEN AND HELL—ADMINISTRATION OF ANGELS AND THE SPIRITS OF THE ANCIENTS—THE RESURRECTION—THE SPIRIT WORLD—THE CLAY AND THE POTTER—A CAUSE OF APOSTASY—A MIRACULOUS CANE—THE CHURCH IN HEAVEN

BEFORE closing the record of his eventful career, we propose to present here some gems from the public sayings of President Kimball, as serving to show still further the spirit and character of the man, his views of life and death, time and eternity, and likewise forming links in the chain of his history that might otherwise be lacking. In the hurry of his later years he kept no regular journal, as in the earlier part of his life, thus leaving his biographer to gather information from whatever sources were available.

These selections cover a period of years, from 1852 down to the time of his death.

His first sermon published in the Journal of Discourses, happens to touch on modern spiritualism. He says:

"The invisible world are in trouble; they are knocking, and rapping, and muttering; and the people are inquiring of them to know concerning the things of God, and there is not a soul of them can tell them anything about the end of the world. They are in a dreadful **[467]** situation; and in the city of Rochester, near where I used to live, the last information I received from there, there were one hundred and thirty-five spiritual writers in that city. I have a brother-in-law there, who is a Presbyterian priest; he couldn't enquire of God about future things, so he enquired of the spirits; but they could not tell him anything about the dead nor the living. They are just about as intelligent in their revelations as this world are in theirs. They are all in commotion—what is going to be done? I will tell you—God is going to make a short work upon the earth, and the invisible world are troubled about it."

His second published discourse was a funeral address in memory of Mary

Fielding Smith, the wife of Hyrum Smith, who died at his house September 22nd, 1852. Here is his tribute to that estimable woman:

"As regards Sister Mary Smith's situation and circumstances, I have no trouble at all, for if any person has lived the life of a Saint, she has. If any person has acted the part of a mother, she has. I may say she has acted the part of a mother, and a father, and a bishop. She has had a large family, and several old people to take care of, and which she has maintained for years by her economy and industry.

"One thing I am glad of, and I feel to rejoice in the providence of God that things have been as they have. She came here sick on the Sabbath, eight weeks ago last Sunday, for me to lay hands upon her. She was laid prostrate upon her bed, and was not able to recover afterwards. I felt as though it was a providential circumstance that it so happened. She always expressed that she knew the thing was dictated by the Lord that she should be placed in my house, though accidentally. She probably would not have lived so long, had she been [468] where she could not have had the same care. On Tuesday evening, eight weeks and two days since, she came here sick; from that time until her death she was prayerful and humble. I have never seen a person in my life that had a greater desire to live than she had, and there was only one thing she desired to live for, and that was to see to her family; it distressed her to think that she could not see to them; she wept about it. She experienced this anxiety for a month previous to her death.... I am glad I did right to Sister Mary, and took care of her, and that my family had the pleasure of nourishing her; the satisfaction that this gives me is worth more to me than a hundred thousand dollars. Do I believe they know it in heaven? Yes, as much as you do. I want to live all the time in righteousness, as I know that God sees me and all the works of His hands."

A lesson on love and unity is here given: "The Gospel and plan of salvation that I have embraced, is music to me; it is sweet to my body, and congenial to my spirit; and it is more lovely than anything else I have ever seen since I have been in the world. I love it, and that is why I love this people better than any other people on God's earth, because there was never a better people; that is, I am speaking of the majority of them.

"The world considers it to be quite ridiculous for us to be of one heart and of one mind. It is this union among those who are faithful 'Mormons,' that makes the world afraid of us.... Jesus says, *Except ye are one, ye are not mine!* There is more oneness in this people than in any other people that ever lived upon the earth. There was not that oneness in the days of Jesus, and I suppose there never has been since the [469] days of Enoch. Because there was such a oneness among the people of Enoch, and they could not continue to be one and live with the people in the same world, God took them and their city with a part of the earth to Himself, and they sailed away like one ship at sea separating from another."

The power of unity and the courage of the righteous are thus portrayed:
"When Brother Brigham and myself and others left Kirtland to go to Missouri

with Joseph Smith, was there any fear in us? No. It never entered into our hearts from the day we started to the time we returned. I had a spirit on me as much superior to this earth, as the earth is superior to the degraded spirits of the wicked that dwell on its face. It was the Spirit of the Lord that stood by me, and diffused strength into my body, and into my limbs, until the very hair of my head felt all alive. Did they fear us in that upper country? Yes, they ran as though they were never going to stop in the world. We felt perfectly able to clear out that country to Nova Scotia, and we could have done it, with two hundred and five men, if the Lord had commanded us, as the Gideonites in days of old. Yes; two hundred and five men, with the Spirit and power of God upon them and their faces shining like the sun, it cannot be told what they could accomplish, neither can we form any conception of it."

Here is a testimony that Joseph gave the keys of the Kingdom to the Twelve:
"Since Brother Joseph stepped behind the vail, Brother Brigham is his lawful successor. I bear testimony of what Brother Joseph said on the stand at Nauvoo, and I presume hundreds here can bear witness of the same. Said he, 'these men that are set here **[470]** behind me on this stand, I have conferred upon them all the power, Priesthood, and authority that God ever conferred upon me.' There are hundreds present this day who heard him utter words to that effect more than once. The Twelve had then received their endowments. Brother Joseph gave them the endowments, and keys and power were placed upon them by him, even as they were placed upon him by Peter, James and John, who ordained him. That is true, gentlemen, because they held the Apostleship last, and had the authority to confer it upon him, or any whom the Father had chosen. Brother Joseph called and ordained the twelve Apostles of the last days, and placed that power upon them."

Relative to the cultivation of spirits he says:
"If you do not cultivate yourselves, and cultivate your spirits in this state of existence, it is just as true as there is a God that liveth, you will have to go into another state of existence, and bring your spirits into subjection there. Now you may reflect upon it, you never will obtain your resurrected bodies, until you bring your spirits into subjection. I am not talking to this earthly house of mine, neither am I talking to your bodies, but I am speaking to your spirits. I am not talking as to people who are not in the house. Are not your spirits in the house? Are not your bodies your houses, your tabernacles or temples, and places for your spirits? Look at it; reflect upon it. If you keep your spirits trained according to the wisdom and fear of God, you will attain to the salvation of both body and spirit. I ask, then, if it is your spirits that must be brought into subjection? It is; and if you do not do that in those bodies, you will have to go into another estate to do it. You have got to train yourselves according to the law of God, or you will never obtain your resurrected bodies." **[471]**

Here is a view of the location of heaven and hell:
"You are talking about heaven and about earth, and about hell, etc.; but let me

tell you, you are in hell now, and you have got to qualify yourselves here in hell to become subjects for heaven: and even when you have got into heaven, you will find it right here where you are on this earth. When we escape from this earth, we suppose we are going to heaven. Do you suppose you are going to the earth that Adam came from? That Eloheim came from? Where Jehovah the Lord came from? No. When you have learned to become obedient to the father that dwells upon this earth, to the Father and God of this earth, and obedient to the messengers He sends—when you have done all that, remember you are not going to leave this earth. You will never leave it until you become qualified, and capable, and capacitated to become a father of an earth yourselves. Not one soul of you ever will leave this earth, for if you go to hell, it is on this earth; and if you go to heaven, it is on this earth; and you will not find it anywhere else."

It was the view of President Kimball that the angels are daily around us. Says he:

"I am now in my fifty-fourth year; I am a Latter-day Saint, full in the faith, and not only in the faith, but I have a knowledge of the truth of this work. I know that God lives and dwells in the heavens; for I have asked Him scores of times, and hundreds of times, for things, and have received them. Is not that a pretty good proof that He hears me, when I ask him for things and get them; and is not that a proof that He lives, and dwells in the heavens? I think it is. I suppose He dwells there. He could not dwell anywhere else, but in what particular portion He dwells, I do not precisely **[472]** know, though He is not so far off as many imagine. He is near by, His angels are our associates, they are with us and around about us, and watch over us, and take care of us, and lead us, and guide us, and administer to our wants in their ministry and in their holy calling unto which they are appointed. We are told in the Bible that angels are ministering spirits to minister to those who shall become heirs of salvation."

We have the spirits of the ancients, also, administering to the Saints:

"Who have you now in your midst? Have you Abraham and Isaac and the Apostles Peter, James and John? Yes, you have them right in your midst—they are talking to you all the time...."

"Who are you to be subject to? You say you are willing to be subject to God—to Jesus Christ. You are willing if Peter came along, to listen to him. Well, Peter is here, John is here, Elias is here, Elijah is here, Jesus is here, and the Father is here. What! in person? If not in person, their authority is here, with all the power that ever was or ever will be, to seal men and women up to everlasting."

Of the imperishable part of man and of the resurrection, he says:

"So far as we are concerned, we were taken from the earth, and we may expect to return to it again; and that portion of me which is pure, after the dross of this mortality is separated from it, I expect will be Brother Heber. It is that which will be resurrected; but all that is not pure will remain; that is it will not go back into my body again; and if there are ten parts out of the hundred which are dross and corruption they will remain in the earth; I do not expect to take that up again, but I expect **[473]** to take up the purified element that will endure forever; still the dross is beneficial in its place...."

"Now, will you go and pollute yourselves, and lose the right and title to a resurrection, to dwell with the Saints, and with God the Father, and His Son Jesus Christ, who is my brother?"

Of the departed Willard Richards and the labors of the Elders of Israel in the spirit world, he gives quite a broad glimpse:

"He (Willard) has gone; and it will not be long before Brother Brigham and Brother Heber follow after. He has gone to the world of spirits to engage in a work he could not do if he had remained in the flesh. I do not believe he could have done as much work for the general good of the cause of God, had he remained in the flesh, as he can accomplish now in the spirit; for there is a work to do there—the Gospel to preach, Israel to gather, that they may purify themselves, and become united in one heart and mind.

"What! in the spirit world? Have I not told you often that the separation of body and spirit makes no difference in the moral and intellectual condition of the spirit? When a person, who has always been good and faithful to his God, lays down his body in the dust, his spirit will remain the same in the spirit world. It is not the body that has control of the spirit, as to its disposition, but it is the spirit that controls the body. When the spirit leaves the body the body becomes lifeless. The spirit has not changed one single particle of itself by leaving the body. Were I to fall into a mud-hole I should strive to extricate myself; but I do not suppose I should be any better, any more righteous, any more just and holy when I got out of it than when I was in it. **[474]**

"Our spirits are entangled in these bodies—held captive as it were for a season. They are like the poor Saints, who are for a time obliged to dwell in miserable mud shanties that are mouldering away, and require much patching and care to keep them from mingling with mother earth before the time. They feel miserable in these old decaying tabernacles, and long for the day when they can leave them to fall and take possession of a good new house.

"It seems natural for me to desire to be clothed upon with immortality and eternal life, and leave this mortal flesh; but I desire to stick to it as long as I can be a comfort to my sisters, brethren, wives and children. Independent of this consideration I would not turn my hand over to live five minutes. What else could give birth to a single desire to live in this tabernacle, which is more or less shattered by the merciless storms which have beat upon it, to say nothing of the ravages made upon it by the tooth of time? While I cling to it I must of necessity suffer many pains, rheumatism, head-ache, jaw-ache and heart-ache; sometimes in one part of my body and sometimes in another. It is all right; it is so ordained that we may not cling with too great a tenacity to mortal flesh, but be willing to pass through the vail and meet with Joseph, and Hyrum, and Willard, and Bishop Whitney and thousands of others in the world of spirits.

"Are they all together as we are to-day? I believe all Israel have to be gathered; and to accomplish this the Elders, both in this and the world of spirits, will go forth to preach to the spirits in prison. Where? Down in hell. I appeal to the Elders who have been from this place to preach the Gospel to the world, if it was not like going from heaven to hell. It is a world of sorrow, [475] pain, death and misery, and you cannot make anything else of it."

Here is something on death and the after life:

"As for death, I do not trouble myself much about it. When the time comes for me to depart from this life and go into what we call eternity, to pass through the vail, it is simply to leave the body to rest awhile, and blessed are the dead who die in the Lord, for their sleep shall be sweet unto them. Death is merely a sleep of the body, and all the fear I have concerning it is what arises from my conditions. I was taught in my youth that after death I had to go directly into the bowels of hell, and go down, down, down, because there was no bottom to it. I am not troubled about any such thing as that, for I never expect to see any worse hell than I have seen in this world. And those who do not the works of righteousness, and are not worthy to be gathered with the spirits of the Saints, will go into precisely such society, in the world of spirits, as they are now in.

"The spirits of the Saints will be gathered in one, that is, of all who are worthy; and those who are not just, will be left where they will be scourged, tormented and afflicted, until they can bring their spirits into subjection and be like clay in the hands of the potter, that the potter may have power to mould and fashion them into any kind of vessel, as he is directed by the Master Potter."

In another sermon, he thus enlarges upon his favorite theme of "the clay in the hands of the potter:"[17]

"The potter tried to bring a lump of clay into subjection, and he worked and tugged at it, but the clay was [476] rebellious and would not submit to the will of the potter, and marred in his hands. Then of course he had to cut it from the wheel and throw it into the mill to be ground over, in order that it might become passive; after which he takes it again and makes of it a vessel unto honor, out of the same lump that was dishonored.... There may ten thousand millions of men go to hell, because they dishonor themselves and will not be subject, and after that they will be taken and made vessels unto honor, if they will become obedient.... Can you find any fault with that?"

He gives the following wise hint on one of the causes of apostasy:

"I will give you a key which Brother Joseph Smith used to give in Nauvoo. He said that the very step of apostasy commenced with losing confidence in the leaders of this Church and kingdom, and that whenever you discerned that spirit, you might know that it would lead the possessor of it on the road to apostasy....

"No man or woman can have the spirit of prophecy and at the same time do

---

[17] Heber's exposition of this theme was highly approved by the Prophet Joseph, who declared it to be the true interpretation.

evil and speak against their brethren; and you will find that man or that woman barren and unfruitful in the knowledge of God, and filled with disputations."

Next come some reminiscent allusions, coupled with a prophecy:

"How much would you give for even a cane that Father Abraham had used, or a coat or ring that the Savior had worn? The rough oak boxes in which the bodies of Joseph and Hyrum were brought from Carthage, were made into canes and other articles. I have a cane made from the plank of one of those boxes, so has Brother Brigham and a great many others, and we **[477]** prize them highly and esteem them a great blessing. I want to carefully preserve my cane, and when I am done with it here I shall hand it down to my heir, with instructions to him to do the same.[18] And the day will come when there will be multitudes who will be healed and blessed through the instrumentality of those canes, and the devil cannot overcome those who have them, in consequence of their faith and confidence in the virtues connected with them....

"If I had those relics of Abraham and the Savior which I have mentioned, I would give a great deal for them. In England when not in a situation to go, I have blessed my handkerchief and asked God to sanctify it and fill it with life and power, and sent it to the sick; and hundreds have been healed by it; in like manner I have sent my cane. Dr. Richards used to lay his old black cane on a person's head and that person has been healed through its instrumentality, by the power of God. I have known Joseph hundreds of times to send his handkerchief to the sick, and they have been healed. There are persons in this congregation who have been healed by throwing my old cloak on their beds."

This of the Church organization in heaven:

"When you go into heaven, into the celestial world, you will see the Church organized just as it is here, and you will find all the officers down to the Deacon. Our Church organization is a manifestation of things as they are in heaven, and you are all the time praying that the Church here may be brought into union and set in order as it is in heaven." **[478]**

## CHAPTER 65

GEMS FROM HEBER'S WORDS CONTINUED—HIS STRIKING VIEW OF TIME AND ETERNITY—HIS WORDS AND WORKS AT THE LAST CONFERENCE PRECEDING HIS DEATH—HIS LAST SERMON

As President Kimball advanced in years the tone of his mind seemed to deepen, and often was displayed not only that quaint originality which made him a marked individual throughout his life, but he frequently flashed out thoughts at once

---

[18] This cane is now in the possession of Bishop Abram A. Kimball, who testifies that healing virtues attach to it.

brilliant and profound. Here, for instance, is a philosophical spark on "Time and Eternity," struck from his mind at the age of sixty:

"People talk much about time and eternity, and they say they do not care so much for eternity as they do for time. And again, others say they do not care so much about time as they do about eternity. They do not think for a moment what they are talking about. What is time? (striking the pulpit.) That is all there is about it. That little circumstance of my striking the pulpit is in eternity. It is eternity on the right and on the left, behind and before, and the time being, as it appears to us, is the centre of it. So we pass on from time to eternity every day we live. We are in eternity. Civilized nations have divided a portion of eternity into seconds, minutes, hours, days, months and years for their own convenience, to mark their passage through time.

"The uncivilized or savage tribes of men, the American Indians, for instance, have no other calendar than incidents in nature, such as the rising and setting of the **[479]** sun, hence they count by so many sleeps; the full and dark of the moon, hence they count by so many moons. In short, the only idea we have of time is gathered from natural phenomena in eternity. We might introduce here a comparison of a ship in the middle of the Atlantic. Is it not a pathless waste of waters all around to the passengers on board, except on the frail timbers where they stand? So it is with eternity, with this difference, eternity is shoreless.

"Let the brethren and sisters come to the conclusion that now is the time to set out anew, and then continue from this time henceforth and forever in doing right. If any of you have been in the practice of drinking spirituous liquors to excess, cease at once the wicked and destructive practice. If such a practice is committed, it has its time, and makes its mark on the broad face of eternity; if you cease the practice no time is given to it, and it cannot leave its trace on eternity from that instant until you again commit the same wrong. This reasoning will apply to every other wrong committed by the children of men.

"Let us spend time in doing right, and we shall receive in the Lord's time right for right, grace for grace. If we do not associate with the wicked world any more than is unavoidably necessary for the time being, do you think they will have anything in common with us in eternity?—or we with them? No."

The thought that the present moment is the centre of all eternity is worthy of a philosopher and a poet. So also is the idea that our evil deeds, performed in time, make their mark "on the broad face of eternity." His figure of the ship in mid-ocean with "the pathless waste of waters all around," is decidedly beautiful. In fact, these passages, with many others that might be **[480]** quoted from his sermons and sayings, show how largely Heber C. Kimball was endowed with those qualities of mind known as causality and comparison. Who can doubt that, had he been classically educated, he would have taken high rank among profound and learned men?

The thirty-eighth annual conference of the Church of Jesus Christ of Latter-day Saints was the last conference he attended. He there spoke several times. Of his first address the reporter says:

"President H. C. Kimball reasoned on the principle of unity, its growth among the Saints, and the course to be pursued by them—the obedience, faithfulness and diligence necessary to reach that condition of unity required of us. We look forward with anticipation to building up the centre stake of Zion; and many are anxious for it and will expect to be included among those called to go to Jackson county, who realize but little of the progress they have to make before they are prepared to do so. We have to become much more united, to put away evil from us, to shun evil speaking, and realize the full meaning of the injunction, 'touch not Mine anointed, and do My Prophets no harm.' If we do wrong we must make restitution, cease all wickedness, shun iniquity of every kind, and live to so possess the Spirit of God that it will guide and direct us. The angels and holy beings in the eternal worlds are interested in the work of God in which we are engaged; they watch its progress; and they exercise care over those who are laboring to spread truth and righteousness."

Of his address to the Saints at a succeeding meeting of the conference, the Church reporter continues:

"President H. C. Kimball said if anybody wished [481] to see a miracle they had only to look upon the congregation before him, and look back over the growth of the Church from the time when the entire members of it could be seated in a small room; and we are increasing rapidly. He urged the exercise of increasing watchcare over our growing sons and daughters. They should all attend meetings regularly, learn the principles of truth and grow up to be more useful. He was in favor of ordaining the boys to the Priesthood, and watching and training them with great care, that they might learn of the power and importance of the blessing thus bestowed upon them. The spirit and sealing power of Elias are with President Young, to seal together the fathers and the children, that they may be one and that the whole people may be united in working out salvation. We should all take a course to save our offspring; and the man who cannot save his children—his family, cannot save himself."

The following is the notice of his last public speaking, which occurred on the 7th of June, just previous to his death:

"President H. C. Kimball spoke at some length on the power and order of the Priesthood, instructing the congregation upon various things connected therewith. He pointed out the blessings flowing from obedience to the authority which the Lord has conferred upon His servants on the earth; and the evil results which follow disobedience and rebellion; for the Lord governs and rules in all worlds, and we cannot, if we would, get to any place where His power is not."

His closing words at this time were almost a prophecy of his approaching end; being upon the subject of family training, during which he quoted from the revelation wherein the Lord commands His servants to set their houses in order. [482]

# CHAPTER 66

DEATH OF VILATE, THE WIFE OF HEBER'S YOUTH—PRESIDENT BRIGHAM YOUNG PREACHES HER FUNERAL SERMON—HIS FEELING TRIBUTE TO HER MEMORY—HEBER PROPHESIES OF HIS OWN DEATH

On the 22nd of October, 1867, there was gloom in the household of Heber C. Kimball. On that day died Vilate, the partner of his youth, the noble and unselfish sharer of his life's joys and sorrows. In the sixty-second year of her age, after an almost unexampled life of toil, heroism and self-sacrifice, God called her home to a glorious rest.

One of the immediate causes which led to her death—though for months she had been a sufferer, and the sun of her life was visibly setting—was the untimely end of her son, Brigham Willard Kimball, who died on the plains while returning from a mission to England. Vilate took the death of her son very much to heart, and her grief over the event is supposed to have hastened the termination of her own life.

Her loss was a heavy blow to her sorrowing husband. Heber's struggle, in faith and prayer, to hold her to earth, was almost as great as that of death to take her away. He related that when she first fell sick, on going into her room to administer to her, he saw, standing at the head of her bed, an evil spirit, a female. Kneeling down he prayed, and then rebuked the apparition in the name of Jesus. It disappeared, but soon returned with a host of fallen beings.

He then called in several other Elders, and unitedly **[483]** they rebuked the evil spirits, when they departed, and he saw them no more at that time.

Thus he struggled on, hoping and praying to the end that she might be spared. Sometimes, in his yearning for the continuance of their companionship here a while longer, it seemed as though he would prevail with the Lord. But the last hope of this at length faded, the end came, and he bowed in resignation to the inevitable.

"I shall not be long after her," was the sad prophecy that fell from his quivering lips, as he followed the remains of his beloved partner to the tomb.

The thread of Vilate's life has been fully traced in that of her noble husband, at whose side she stood as a helpmeet and a heroine for five and forty years. But the record has only been traced, not told, and angel tongues must take up the theme which mortal pen were powerless to unfold.

Her pure spirit took its heavenward flight at about three o'clock in the afternoon. The funeral services over her remains were held on Wednesday the 24th of October, at her residence in Salt Lake City. There were present on the occasion to pay their last respects to her sainted memory, President Brigham Young, Elders Orson Pratt, John Taylor, Wilford Woodruff, Geo. A. Smith, Geo. Q. Cannon, Joseph F. Smith, of the Twelve Apostles; Patriarchs John Smith, John Young; President Joseph Young; Bishops P. H. Young, Lorenzo Dow Young, John Sharp, E. F. Sheets; many principal citizens and a vast concourse of friends.

After appropriate singing, and a prayer by Elder Joseph Young, President

Brigham Young pronounced the funeral address. He said that he had not come to weep because the body of Sister Kimball was laid in the coffin; if he wept it was because he saw his friends **[484]** weeping around him, but there was no cause for weeping, and he would say, let us dry up our tears. He was reminded of the time when the deceased and Brother Kimball stood by him when his first wife was taken from him. He felt then to rejoice in the glorious hopes which the gospel had revealed to them, and he could say of those who had died that there was no period known to them in which they could experience so much joy as when they had passed through the portals of death and entered upon the glorious change into the spirit world. He had known intimately Sister Kimball for nearly forty years, and from that time to this, if any person ever found fault with her, it was more than he knew. Her life, conversation, feelings, kindness to her family and to her neighbors seemed all to come before him, and he could say of a truth that a better woman never lived—according to her knowledge. She was ever disposed to do good and to meet every obligation that devolved upon her. He had been cherished and comforted by her in hours of affliction, and knew her kindness of heart. Since he had heard of her death, he had experienced none but joyful feelings—for she had lived the life of a Saint—till he had come to sit beside her bier. It did not belong to the manhood which God had given them to mourn on such occasions, but it was through the weakness of their fallen nature that they were overcome. Her spirit had now passed into the spirit world, to wait with the spirits of the just the morning of the resurrection. She had kept the faith, and with all who had partaken of the holy Priesthood, was beyond the powers of death, and can no more be afflicted. It was his faith that Joseph the Prophet would be the first resurrected of the last dispensation, and that to him would be committed the keys of the resurrection, and through him would the **[485]** powers of the resurrection be extended to others till all who had been faithful would be resurrected in glory. He concluded with kindly words of the deceased, reiterating affectionate sentiments, and assuring the afflicted family and friends that her life had been as honorable as any woman who had ever lived, and that she had secured her resurrection with the just.

President Young was followed by others, including President Kimball, who spake most touchingly of the virtues of his faithful wife.

Her remains were laid in the family burial ground.

So closed the mortal career of one of the noblest of women, the purity and loftiness of whose character will loom as a monument through coming ages, while the memory of her good deeds will shine forever like the pathway of the just.

# CHAPTER 67

DEATH OF APOSTLE KIMBALL—ALL ISRAEL MOURNS—EXPRESSIONS IN HONOR OF THE ILLUSTRIOUS DEAD

THE words of Heber were indeed prophetic, that he should not be long on earth after the departure of the beloved wife of his youth. The event for which both had earnestly prayed, that they might live and die, and rise and reign together, was destined by the heavens to be.

On the morning of the 22nd of June, 1868,—eight months later to a day—death again entered the household, [486] leveling his fatal shaft at the mighty heart of its patriarchal head. At the age of sixty-seven years, his mind yet unimpaired, his iron frame unbent by age, but with health shattered by toil and trial in the service of his Maker, Heber C. Kimball, the Apostle of Jesus Christ, the tried and trusted friend of God, passed peacefully from earth away.

His death was superinduced by a severe fall, sustained by him several weeks before. He had driven from Salt Lake City to Provo, alone, arriving there in the night. While nearing his residence in that city, where lived his wife Lucy and her family, the wheels of his buggy went suddenly into a ditch, throwing him over the forward wheels violently upon the ground. After lying for some time stunned and helpless, and chilled by the night air, he was finally discovered and assisted into the house by his friend, Bishop A. F. Macdonald.

This accident, though he partly recovered from its effects, was the immediate fore-runner of his fatal sickness.

The *Deseret Evening News* of Monday, June 22nd, 1868, in an extended editorial thus announced his death:

"A prince and a great man has this day passed from among us! President Heber Chase Kimball, who was born June 14th, 1801, fell asleep at 20 minutes to 11 o'clock this morning, June 22nd, after a pilgrimage on the earth of sixty-seven years and eight days. Many of the residents of this city will be prepared to hear this sad news; but upon the Saints throughout this Territory and in foreign lands, it will fall unexpectedly and heavily. Two weeks ago yesterday he preached in the new tabernacle, and those who listened to him on that occasion could not have imagined from his appearance that in so brief a period as has since elapsed we should only have his lifeless remains to gaze upon. Since he was thrown from his buggy last spring in Provo, his family and inti[487]mate associates have noticed that his health was not so good as it had been; but a casual observer would not have perceived any change; he moved around and attended to his duties with his accustomed diligence and vigor. On the 10th instant, at the mass meeting in the new tabernacle, it was remarked that his face was very much flushed. He complained that day of dizziness, and torpidity of his right side; he attributed the feeling to rheumatism, with which he was sometimes affected. The next day, Thursday, the 11th, he went down town twice; but his family and others noticed that in walking, he did not use his right leg with his usual freedom. On Friday, the 12th, he arose in the morning and dressed himself; but was compelled to return to bed. His son Heber called upon him, and he conversed quite freely with him about his affairs. This was the last conversation of any length that he had with any person. It was soon plainly apparent that he was attacked with paralysis of the right side, and from this time until his death, he was only able to utter a sentence occasionally, though most of the time he appeared to be fully conscious of everything transpiring around him. When his particular friends called upon him, especially Presidents Young and Wells, he seemed to arouse himself to speak, and by the pressure of their hands and the beaming of his countenance, would signify his pleasure at seeing them. Until Saturday last it was hoped that he would recover and be himself again. Every indication of a change for the better was eagerly noted. Every one was reluctant to admit that Brother Heber would not recover. If such a thought presented itself it was immediately repelled. But on Saturday evening it was visible to all that he was changing for the worse. Yesterday he failed rapidly. From early in the morning until afternoon his body suffered, though he himself seemed unconscious of it. He was administered to by President Young and the Twelve, and he was much relieved. Towards evening he rallied, opened his eyes and for some time was conscious, and appeared to recognize those who stood around him. This was the last awakening of the faculties prior to [488] death.[19] He relapsed into unconsciousness, and gradually passed away without a contortion of countenance or the slightest movement of a limb.... His family and many of his friends were in the room where he lay, and so peacefully did life leave his body, that some five minutes had elapsed before those who were watching his countenance were satisfied that his spirit had fled. Like a babe falling into a gentle slumber, he passed away. It was a frequent remark of his that he should not die. Those who stood around his bedside were reminded of it by President Young—who saw his beloved and faithful friend and fellow-laborer breathe his last—quoting the remark, and adding that Brother Heber was not dead, he had gone to sleep. Gloom and death were not there. None experienced those undefinable feelings of dread which sometimes prevail on such occasions. Sadness there was; but it was not mingled with doubt; it was for the loss of the society of the loving husband, the tender father, the steadfast friend, the wise counselor and the undaunted leader. Yet this grief was not the only feeling. If there can be any pleasure in contemplating the separation of the body and spirit under any circumstances, then that chamber in which the earthly remains of Heber C. Kimball lay this morning was a place of joy. It was a scene of victory and triumph. A faithful, unflinching servant of God, one who had passed through the most severe ordeals with unyielding integrity, had met man's great enemy, and through the atonement of the Savior and the previous promises which he had given, had come off conqueror. What a host of faithful ones have awaited his arrival in the spirit world! Recall the names, beginning with Joseph, the head of the dispensation, and what a glorious list is presented to the mind! With what ineffable gladness will they

---

[19] His last words, uttered distinctly the evening before his death, were: "Truth, eternal Truth."

meet and welcome him to that happy land! Will it not be home to him when he meets those bright ones with whom he has labored so long and so familiarly, and who know his **[489]** guileless simplicity, his truthfulness, his unshrinking faith, his integrity and worth?

"As this news is flashed with lightning speed from one end of the Territory to the other, profound grief will fill every heart. The love of the Saints for Brother Heber is deep-rooted and universal. A great people will this day mourn in learning of his departure, and how deep will be the sorrow also of his brethren and sisters in foreign lands! Yet it is not for him we should mourn. He is ransomed and free. We yet remain in thralldom. The course of those who live is not finished, the battle is not won. The supreme wish of every heart who witnessed his departure doubtless was that their end might be like his."

On the same day the Mayor of the City issued the following:

"To the Citizens of Salt Lake City.—

"As a token of respect to the memory of our esteemed friend and fellow-citizen, the late Hon. Heber C. Kimball, whose demise took place at his residence in this city, at 10:40 this a. m., it is hereby requested, that all unite throughout the city in closing their respective houses of business on Wednesday the 24th inst, being the day appointed for the funeral obsequies of deceased.

"Daniel H. Wells, Mayor.

"Mayor's Office, Salt Lake City,
    "June 22d, 1868."

The following telegrams, sent from different parts of the Territory, will show how universal was the respect paid to the honored dead:

"Logan, 22nd.

"President B. Young:

"We feel very sorry, but not without hope, respecting President Kimball's death.

"Peter Maughan." **[490]**

"Springtown, 23d.

"To the Bishops of Sanpete Co.:

"A great and worthy man in Israel is fallen—President Heber C. Kimball—not by transgression, but by the providence of God. The distance is too great for us to attend his funeral to-morrow. This, therefore, is to request your congregations, to meet to-morrow at two o'clock p. m., and offer up their prayers and condolence in behalf of the bereaved family, as a tribute of respect to the memory of the illustrious dead, thereby respecting ourselves.

"Orson Hyde."

"St. George, 24th.

"President B. Young:

"The Saints of the south, assembled in the St George Bowery, mingle their tears with yours in the funeral obsequies of our lamented brother, President Heber C. Kimball. With his bereaved family we deeply sympathize; with all Israel we mourn his loss, and with him we rejoice that he has entered into his glory.

"Erastus Snow."

Here is the City's tribute to his memory:

"At a regular meeting of the City Council of this city, on Tuesday evening last, the 23rd inst, his Honor the Mayor, announced the death of the Honorable Heber C. Kimball, and, on his suggestion, a committee was appointed to draft resolutions expressive of the feeling of the council on the occasion.

"Councilor Burton, on behalf of the committee, presented the following preamble and resolution, which were read and unanimously adopted:

"*Whereas*, It has pleased the Almighty, in the dispensations of His Providence, to remove from our midst by the hand of death our esteemed fellow citizen and much beloved President, Heber C. Kimball, who, with unwavering integrity and untiring zeal, has ever been a faithful laborer in the cause of truth and an earnest advocate of civil and religious liberty, and of every principle calculated to ennoble and elevate humanity; therefore, be it [491]

"*Resolved*, That while we recognize the hand of the Lord in all things, we deeply feel the loss which the community has sustained in his death, and in common with the citizens of this city and Territory, and the Latter-day Saints throughout the world, we most sincerely sympathize with his family and friends in this their sad bereavement.

"The Council adjourned without the transaction of further business.

"Daniel H. Wells, Mayor.
"Robert Campbell, Recorder.

"Council Chamber,
    "June 23rd, 1868."

A full account of the funeral of President Kimball is reserved for the next and final chapter.

---

## CHAPTER 68

OBSEQUIES OF PRESIDENT KIMBALL—TRIBUTES AND TESTIMONIES OF HIS BROTHER APOSTLES—"HE WAS A MAN OF AS MUCH INTEGRITY AS ANY MAN WHO EVER LIVED"—EARTH RETURNS TO EARTH AND THE SPIRIT UNTO GOD WHO GAVE IT

The day set for the funeral of President Kimball was Wednesday, the 24th of June. The place, the large Tabernacle, Salt Lake City. His own desire, expressed many times before his death, was that it should be held at his private residence, and with as little display as possible; but out of deference to public sentiment, and to accommodate the great multitude of his friends who **[492]** desired to be present, it was found necessary to hold the services in the Tabernacle.

Throughout the city on that day, all ordinary business was suspended, and draped flags, at half mast, swung to the breeze from the tops of public and private buildings. It was a general time of mourning. The very heavens seemed weeping in unison with the earth. The skies were hung with black clouds, the solemn thunders roared, the wind sighed and moaned, and the rain fell heavily.

Long before the hour for the commencement of the services, thousands were on their way to the Tabernacle to pay the last tribute of respect to the memory of the mighty dead; one whom all Israel revered and mourned as a father and a friend. Notwithstanding the pouring rain, fully eight thousand people assembled within the vast auditorium. Many of the settlements and counties throughout the Territory were represented by their leading men.

While the masses congregated at the Tabernacle, Presidents Brigham Young and Daniel H. Wells, with the Apostles and many others, representing general and local authorities in the Priesthood, repaired to the late residence of President Kimball, where the funeral procession formed under the personal supervision of President Young.

The procession moved from the residence at 2 o'clock p. m., in the following order:

1st. Croxall's brass band, consisting of Messrs. M. Croxall, C. Evans, R. Golightly, T. McIntyre, W. D. Williams, J. Croxall, T. Croxall, T. Griggs, J. Cartwright, J. Currie, W. Foster, C. Sansom, B. Eardley, H. Sadler, J. Wakeham, W. Adkins, G. Wareing, D. Evans, H. Sperry and W. Lloyd. **[493]**

2nd. Of the High Council, Elders W. Eddington, J. L. Blythe, C. V. Spencer, W. H. Folsom, T. E. Jeremy, J. Squires, P. Nebeker and G. W. Thatcher.

3rd. Of the Presidency of the Salt Lake Stake of Zion, Elders D. Spencer and G. B. Wallace.

4th. Of the Presidency of the Seventies, Elders Joseph Young, L. W. Hancock, A. P. Rockwood, H. S. Eldredge and J. Van Cott.

5th. The Presidency of the High Priests, Elders John Young, S. W. Richards and E. D. Woolley.

6th. Presiding Bishop E. Hunter and his Counselors, L. W. Hardy and J. C. Little.

7th. Of the Twelve Apostles, Elders Orson Pratt, John Taylor, Wilford Woodruff, Geo. A. Smith, Ezra T. Benson, Lorenzo Snow, Geo. Q. Cannon and Joseph F. Smith.

8th. President Brigham Young and Counselor Daniel H. Wells.

9th. The corpse, in a neat coffin wrapped in black broadcloth and deeply fringed with white cashmere and black lace, borne by twelve pall-bearers, namely, Elders R. T. Burton, T. McKean, G. W. Grant, L. S. Hills, B. Y. Hampton, W. Calder, H. Heath, A. Dewey, H. S. Beatie, H. P. Richards, H. Dinwoodey, and John T. Caine.

Immediately following the remains walked the three eldest sons of President Kimball, namely, William H., Heber P., and David P., succeeded by his wives, the elder sons and daughters, the younger sons and daughters, and many other relatives in the rear. The families of Presidents Young and Wells in carriages, and a number of the most prominent citizens on foot, terminated the procession.

To the solemn strains of the "Dead March in Saul," **[494]** from Captain Croxall's band, the cortege, passing down East, North and West Temple Streets, successively, to the west gate of Temple Block, entered the Tabernacle at door No. 32, north side, and occupied reserved seats in front of the stand. The casket with the remains was deposited on a draped bier raised from the middle aisle. Seven elegant vases of roses and other beautiful flowers were placed upon the coffin. During the services a bird flew into the building and, alighting on the coffin, remained for several minutes.

In consonance with the solemnity of the scene, the interior of the Tabernacle was draped in mourning.

The assemblage was called to order by President Brigham Young.

The choir then sang the following hymn, composed for the occasion by Sister Eliza R. Snow:

> Be cheer'd, O Zion—cease to weep:
>   Heber we deeply loved:
> He is not dead—he does not sleep—
>   He lives with those above.
>
> His flesh was weary; let it rest
>   Entombed in mother Earth,
> Till Jesus comes—when all the bless'd,
>   To life will be brought forth.
>
> His mighty spirit, pure and free
>   From every bond of Earth,
> In realms of immortality,
>   Is crowned with spotless worth.
>
> He lives for Zion:—he has gone
>   To plead her righteous cause,
> Before the High and Holy One—
>   Let all the Saints rejoice. **[495]**
>
> Let wives and children humbly kiss
>   The deep-afflicting rod:
> A father to the fatherless,
>   God is the widow's God.

Elder George Q. Cannon offered the opening prayer.

The choir sang "Farewell all earthly honors," with the chorus "There is sweet rest in heaven," and remarks were then made as follows, by the speakers named:

### ELDER JOHN TAYLOR.

"Were I to give way to my feelings at the present time I should not be able to address this congregation. I feel as, I suppose, most of you feel—sympathy with the family of the deceased who now lies before us. When I speak of this as being my feeling, I am aware that I express the feeling of the generality of this people. In this bereavement that has afflicted us, we all participate. A wave of sorrow has rolled throughout the Territory, and feelings of sympathy and sorrow gush up from the fountains of every heart. We have met at this time to pay the last tribute of respect to no ordinary personage, but to a good man who was called and chosen, and faithful; who has spent a lifetime in the cause of God, in the establishment of the principles of truth and in trying to upbuild the Church and Kingdom of God on the earth; who has endeared himself by his acts of kindness, affection, integrity, truthfulness and probity to the hearts of thousands of Latter-day Saints, who feel to mourn at this time with no ordinary sorrow.

"That he is esteemed and venerated by this people as a friend, a counselor and a father, this immense congregation, who have met on this inauspicious occasion, is abundant testimony and proof, if any is wanting. But his life, his acts, his services, his self-abnegation, his devotion to the cause of truth, his perseverance in the ways of righteousness for so many years have left a testimony in the minds, feelings and hearts of all who feel to mourn his departure from our midst. But we **[496]** meet not at the present time particularly to eulogize the acts of Brother Kimball, who is one of the First Presidency, and who stands, or who has stood as one of the three prominent men that live on the face of the earth at the present time.

"We do not mourn over him as over an individual in a private capacity; neither, when we reflect on the circumstances with which we are surrounded, and the gospel we believe in, do we mourn that he lies there as he is. For although to us he is absent and lifeless and inanimate, yet his spirit soars above clothed upon with immortality and eternal life. And as he has been in possession of the principles of eternal truth, by and bye, when the time shall roll around, that gospel and the principles of truth that he has so valiantly proclaimed for so many years, will resurrect that inanimate clay, and He who, on the earth proclaimed "I am the resurrection and the life," will cause him again to be resuscitated, reanimated, revivified and glorified, and he will rejoice among the Saints of God worlds without end.

"It is not then an ordinary occasion upon which we have met at the present time. It is not to talk particularly about our individual feelings and bereavement, although they are keen, poignant and afflictive; but we meet at the present time to perform a ceremony and to pay our last respects to the departed great one who lies before us. We do not mourn as those who have no hope; we do not sympathise with any foolish sympathy. We believe in those principles, that he, for so many years, has so strenuously advocated, and believing in them, we know that he has simply passed from one state of existence to another. It is customary for men to say "how have the great fallen!" But he has not fallen. It is true that he has gone to sleep for a little while. He sleeps in peace. He is resting from his labors and is no more beset with those afflictions with which human nature always has to contend: he has passed from this stage of action, he has got through with the toils, perplexities, cares and anxieties in regard to himself, his family, and in regard to the Church with which he was [497] associated; and in regard to all sublunary things, and while mortals mourn "a man is dead," the angels proclaim "a child is born."

"We believe in another state of existence besides this; and it is not only a belief, but it is a fixed fact, and hence for a man of God to bid adieu to the things of this world is a matter of comparatively very small importance. When a man has fought the good fight; when he has finished his course; when he has been faithful, lived his religion and died as a man of God, what is there to mourn for? Why should we indeed be sorrowful? There is a church here on earth; there is a church also in the heavens. He has migrated from one, and has passed into the other.

"We have had leave us before, Joseph, Hyrum, David Patten, Willard, Jedediah, and a mighty host of good, virtuous, pure, holy and honorable men. Some have died, as it were, naturally; others have been violently put to death. But no matter, they are each of them moving in his own sphere. Brother Kimball has left us for a short time that he may unite with them. And whilst we are engaged carrying on the work of God, and advancing and maintaining those principles which he so diligently propagated and maintained while he was on the earth, he is gone to officiate in the heavens with Jesus, with Joseph and others for us. We are seeking to carry out his will, the will of our President and the will of our Heavenly Father, that we may be found fit to associate with the just who are made perfect, and be prepared to join with the Church triumphant in the heavens. It is this that our religion points us to all the time.

"We embraced the Gospel of Jesus Christ, and he who now lies before us was one of the first to proclaim it to thousands that are here. And what did that teach us? To repent of our sins, and, having faith in the Lord Jesus Christ, to be baptized for the remission of our sins, to have hands laid upon us for the reception of the Holy Ghost and to gather together to Zion that we might be instructed in the ways of life; that we might know how to save ourselves—how to save the living and [498] how to redeem the dead; that we might not only possess a hope that blooms with immortality and eternal life; but that we might have a certainty, an evidence, a confidence that was beyond doubt or peradventure, that we were preparing ourselves for a celestial inheritance in the kingdom of our God. And when a man goes to sleep as Brother Kimball has done, no matter how, he lays aside the cares of this world; the weary wheels of life stand still, the pulse ceases to beat, the body becomes cold, lifeless and inanimate; yet at the same time the spirit still exists, has gone to join those who have lived before; who now live and will live for evermore. He has trod the path that we have all to follow, for it is appointed to man once to die, and after that, we are told, the judgment. We have all to pass through the dark valley of the shadow of death, and as I said before, it matters little which way this occurs; but it does matter a great deal to us whether we are prepared to meet it or not; whether we have lived the life of the righteous; whether we have honored our profession; whether we have been faithful to our trust; whether we are prepared to associate with the spirits of the just made perfect, and whether when He, who has said "I am the resurrection and the life" shall sound the trump we shall be prepared to come forth in the morning of the first resurrection.

"Joseph Smith stands at the head of this dispensation. His brother Hyrum Smith was associated with him. They were both assassinated. No matter; they are gone. Brother Heber is now gone, and whilst we mourn the loss they rejoice at meeting one with whom they were associated before; for he was the friend of Joseph and Hyrum Smith, and he was the friend of God, and God is his friend, and they are his friends. And as they associated together in time so they will in eternity. It behooves us then not to think so much about dying, but about our living, and to live in such a way that when we shall fall asleep, no matter when, or how it may transpire, that our hearts may be pure before God. When I look upon a man like Brother Kimball, I feel like saying let my **[499]** last end be like his. Let my life be as spotless, as holy and as pure, that I may stand accepted before God and the holy angels. Our ambition ought to be to live our religion, to keep the commandments of God, to obey the counsel that those lips now silent and cold have so often given to us; to honor our calling and profession, that we may be prepared to inherit eternal lives in the celestial kingdom of our God. May God help us to do so, in the name of Jesus, Amen.

### ELDER GEORGE A. SMITH.

"The occasion which has called us together is truly one of mourning; but our mourning is not as the mourning of those who have no hope. Our father, our brother, our President, has fallen asleep. He has fallen asleep according to the promise that those who die unto the Lord should not die, but should fall asleep. Still, the circumstances with which we are surrounded cause us to feel keenly, deeply this bereavement of his company, of his counsel, of his support, of his society, and the benefit of that wisdom which ever flowed from his lips. Short is the journey from the cradle to the grave, and all of us are marching rapidly in that direction; and the present occasion is certainly calculated to inspire in our minds a desire that in all our lives and actions we may be prepared for that coming event, that we may be prepared to rest in peace, and in the morning of the first resurrection to inherit eternal life and celestial exaltation. The association which we have had with President Kimball has been of long standing. He entered the church early after its organization. In 1832, with President Brigham Young, he visited Kirtland, and made himself personally acquainted with the Prophet Joseph, whose bosom friend he was from the time of their first acquaintance until the day of his death. President Kimball was a man that seemed embarrassed when called upon to speak in public in the early part of his ministry. My first acquaintance with him was in 1833, **[500]** when in company with President Young he moved his family to Kirtland. The Saints were then building the Kirtland Temple. He had but little means, but he subscribed two hundred dollars and paid over the money. Efforts were being made to build another house, for school and other purposes, and he subscribed one hundred dollars for that also, to buy the nails and glass. That was the first public meeting at which I ever saw Heber C. Kimball. When he was chosen one of the Twelve Apostles, and they were called into the stand to bear their first testimony as Apostles to the Saints, there was an embarrassment and a timidity about his appearance that was truly humble. And when he went abroad to preach, many felt almost afraid to have Brother Kimball preach because he had not as great a flow of language as some others. But it turned out, I am sorry to say, that some of those who were the most eloquent seemed to be those who fell off by the wayside. It was a dark hour around the Prophet in Kirtland, many having apostatized, and some of them prominent Elders, when Brother Kimball and some others were called upon to take a mission to England. He went abroad when some of the first Elders were covered with darkness, and apostasy ran rampant through the Church. He started almost penniless, made the trip across the ocean, introduced the gospel to England, and laid the foundation for the great work that has since been accomplished there, accompanied by Orson Hyde, Willard Richards and Joseph Fielding. Brothers Kimball and Hyde remained in England about one year, and in that time 1,500 were baptized there. It was strange, the power and influence which he had over persons whom he had never before seen. On one occasion he went out five days to some town which he had never visited before, and among people whom he had never seen and who had never seen him, yet in those five days he baptized eighty-three persons. It seemed that there were a power and influence with him beyond that which almost any other Elder possessed. He returned home just in time to find the Saints in their troubles in Missouri. He **[501]** had hardly got home until the clouds of mobocracy intensified by apostasy again gathered around the Prophet. In a short time after, Joseph was in prison and his counselors were in prison and all were closely guarded.

"During this time President Kimball visited the prison, the Judges and the governor, and exerted himself to relieve the prisoners; and he had a peculiar influence with him, so that he could pass among our enemies unharmed, when others were in danger.

"When the Saints were driven from Missouri, as soon as their feet were planted in Nauvoo, he built with his own hands a log cabin for his family, and started again to renew his mission to Great Britain, with President Young and others of his quorum. It is not my intention to trace his history, but I have culled out these few circumstances to show you his integrity, his faithfulness, and his untiring labors to benefit mankind.

"We are called now to mourn; but we do not mourn as those who have no hope. Brother Kimball was a man who was the son of nature. The literature he loved was the word of God. He was not a man to read novels. He studied the revelations of Jesus. His heart was filled with benevolence. His soul was filled with love; and he was always ready to give counsel to the weakest child that came in his way. Thousands and thousands will remember him with pleasure.

"As we follow him to his last resting place, we must recollect that those men who stood side by side with Joseph Smith the Prophet, who bore with him his burdens, and shared his troubles; who stood shoulder to shoulder with President Young while he faced the storm of apostasy, mob power and organized priestcraft, are rapidly passing away. Brother Kimball was foremost among them. Joseph loved him, and truly it may be said that Brother Kimball was a Herald of Grace. May we all so live that with our brother we may inherit the blessings of celestial grace, is my prayer in the name of Jesus, Amen. **[502]**

## ELDER GEORGE Q. CANNON.

"The scene in which we are participating this day reminds us more strongly than any language can do, how frail is mortal existence, and how slight a tenure we all have upon this life. Two weeks ago, to-day, he, whose lifeless remains we now surround, was moving among us in this Tabernacle; if not in the enjoyment of perfect health, yet in the enjoyment of such a degree of health as not to inspire us with any apprehensions as to his life. If we had been asked, How long is Brother Heber likely to live? the probable answer would have been, he is as likely to live ten or twenty years as any other period. But since then, two weeks, two brief, short weeks, have gone, and we have assembled ourselves together to pay our last respects to his memory. It seemed to me when I entered the building, and sat down and looked upon the congregation, that the greatest eloquence I could indulge in would be silence. Yet it is due to him that our voices should be heard in instruction to those who remain, and in testimony of his great worth; and if possible to spread before them, the great and glorious example which he has set for us, and which if we will but emulate and follow, will result in the attainment of the most glorious blessings of which mortal heart can conceive.

"I have known Brother Heber from my childhood. To me he has been a father. I never was with him but what he had good counsel to give me. And when I speak this I speak what every one who was acquainted with him might say. He was full of counsel, full of instruction, and he was always pointed in conveying his counsel in plainness to those to whom he imparted it.

"Have we any cause, in reality, to mourn to-day? Have we any cause for grief and sorrow? When I stood by his bedside and saw his spirit take its departure there was no death there; there was no gloom. I had seen but two persons die before, and they died by violence; but when I watched Brother Heber I asked myself, Is this death? Is this that which men represent **[503]** as a monster, and from which they shrink with affright? It seemed to me that Brother Heber was not dead, but that he had merely gone to sleep. He passed away as quietly and as gently as an infant falling asleep on its mother's lap; not a movement of a limb; not a contortion of his countenance; and scarcely a sigh. The words of Jesus, through Joseph, were forcibly brought to my mind,—"they that die in me, their death shall be sweet unto them." It was sweet with him. There was nothing repulsive, nothing dreadful or terrible in it, but on the contrary it was calm, peaceful and sweet. There were heavenly influences there, as though angels were there, and no doubt they were, prepared to escort him hence to the society of those whom he loved and who loved him dearly. I thought of the joy there would be in the spirit land, when Joseph, and Hyrum, and David, and Willard, and Jedediah, and Parley would welcome him to their midst, and the thousands of others who have gone before, and like them have been faithful. What a welcome to their midst will Brother Heber receive! to labor and toil with them in the spirit world in the great work in which we are engaged.

"It is now twenty-four years lacking three days, since Joseph and Hyrum were taken away from us. Twenty-four years so fruitful in labor, so abundant in toil, so rich in experience! During that period Brother Heber has never wavered, never trembled. It may be said of him with as much truthfulness to-day, as was said by Brother Brigham on one occasion in Nauvoo, 'his knees never trembled, his hands never shook.' He has been faithful to God; he has been true to his brethren; he has kept his covenants; he has died in the triumphs of the faith; and as the Savior has said, 'that which is governed by law is preserved by law and perfected and sanctified by the same;' so will it be with him. He has gone to the paradise of God, there to await the time when this corruption shall put on incorruption, when this mortality shall put on immortality.

"My brethren and sisters, here is an incentive to us to be faithful. Contrast the death of this man with the [504] death of the apostate—the traitor. Contrast the future—as it is revealed to us in the revelations of Jesus Christ—of this man, with the future of the renegade from the truth, and the wicked and those who love not God and who keep not His commandments. Are there any incentives presented to us this day to be faithful? They are too numerous for me to dwell upon or mention. There is every reason why we should be faithful. It is easier to keep the commandments of God than it is to break them. It is easier to walk in the path of righteousness than it is to deviate from it. It is easier and more pleasant to love God than it is to break His commandments.

"Then let us be true to God. Let us walk each day so that we may be worthy, when our life is ended, to associate with him whose spirit inhabited this tabernacle that lies here, and with others who have gone before, and with those who remain, that we may dwell together with them eternally in the heavens; which may God grant, for Christ's sake, Amen."

## PRESIDENT D. H. WELLS.

"It is a great calamity to humanity when a great and good man falls. Earth needs their services. Good men are too scarce. The loss is not so much to them as it is to us who remain—as it is to humanity who are still left to wield an influence against the wickedness which is on the earth, and to sustain holy and righteous principles which the Lord has revealed from the heavens for the guidance of man. Herein is the loss which we feel when such men as Bro. Kimball are taken away, He has made his mark. He has earned imperishable fame, and he will live in the hearts of the good, the true and the faithful—in the hearts of the just; and he will be remembered by the wicked, for he has often invaded the realms of darkness and sustained holy and righteous principles with all his might, power and influence, all the days of his life. It is true, for him we need not mourn, because [505] he has passed to that home where Satan has no power. He has secured to himself a crown of eternal glory and righteousness in the celestial kingdom of our God. Not that he will come immediately unto this exaltation. The Savior of the world, himself, did not enter into His glory on the dissolution of His spirit and body; He went first to minister to the spirits in prison, being clothed with the holy Priesthood. So with our brother and beloved friend, for he is still our friend, and, as has been remarked, he was the friend of God and of all good men. He is not lost. He has only gone to perform another portion of the mission which he has been engaged in all his life, to labor in another sphere for the good of mankind, for the welfare of the souls of men. But he has laid for himself a foundation that is imperishable, on which a superstructure of glory and exaltation will grow and increase throughout all eternity.

"I do not stand here to eulogize our friend and brother to-day, but to satisfy my own feelings and pay a tribute of respect to his memory, for I loved him and he loved me, and he loved this people. He has friends also where he is gone. Who can answer the question whether they are more numerous than those who have assembled together to-day and those throughout this Territory? Who can say that they are not more numerous on yonder shore? Yet it matters not. Those who are faithful will yet be gathered with him and others, and come with him to a celestial glory, and with him dwell where there is no sorrow nor affliction. He rests from his labor, from the toil which surrounded him on the earth. This is, to-day, a source of consolation to his family and friends, to those who were intimately connected with him. They may be assured that he rests in peace. Let his example be followed; let his teachings be remembered; let us all live so that we may have a reasonable hope of meeting with him and being associated with him in a never ending future.

"May God help us to be faithful unto the end, as he has been; to fight the good fight and keep the faith, that at last, with him and those who have gone before, we [506] may be found worthy to walk the golden streets of that eternal city, whose builder and maker is God: Amen.

## PRESIDENT BRIGHAM YOUNG.

"I wish the people to be as still as possible and not to whisper. I do not know that I can speak so that you can hear me; but if I can I have a few reflections to lay before you. We are called here on this very important occasion, and we can say truly that the day of this man's death was far better to him than the day of his birth. I will relate to you my feelings concerning the departure of Brother Kimball.

"HE WAS A MAN OF AS MUCH INTEGRITY, I PRESUME, AS ANY MAN WHO EVER LIVED ON THE EARTH.

"I have been personally acquainted with him forty-three years and I can testify that he has been a man of truth, a man of benevolence, a man that was to be trusted. Now he has gone and left us. I will say to his wives and his children, that I have not felt one particle of death in his house nor about it, and through this scene we are now passing I have not felt one particle of the spirit of death. He has fallen asleep for a certain purpose,—to be prepared for a glorious resurrection; and the same Heber C. Kimball, every component particle of his body, from the crown of his head to the soles of his feet, will be resurrected, and he, in the flesh, will see God and converse with Him; and see his brethren and associate with them and they will enjoy a happy eternity together.

"Brother Kimball has had the privilege of living and dying in his own house in peace; and has not been followed up by mobs and massacred. I consider this a great consolation to his family and friends; and it is a great comfort to me to think that Brother Heber C. Kimball had the privilege of dying in peace. It is not a matter of regret; it is nothing that we should mourn for. It is a great cause of joy and rejoicing and comfort to his friends to know that a person has passed away in peace **[507]** from this life, and has secured to himself a glorious resurrection. The earth and the fullness of the earth and all that pertains to this earth in an earthly capacity, is no comparison with the glory, joy and peace and happiness of the soul that departs in peace. You may think I have reason to mourn. Brother Heber C. Kimball has been my first counselor for almost twenty-four years. I am happy to state, it is a matter of great joy to me; this is the third counselor that has fallen asleep since I have stood to counsel this people—and they have died in the faith, full of hope; their lives were filled up with good works, full of faith, comfort, peace and joy to their brethren. I have looked over this matter. In the fourteen years that Brother Joseph presided over the Church, three of the prominent counselors he had apostatized. This was a matter of regret. Sidney Rigdon, F. G. Williams and William Law, whom many of this congregation knew in Nauvoo, apostatized and left Brother Joseph. I have not been under the necessity of mourning and lamenting over the apostasy of any one of my counselors, and I hope I shall never have this to regret. I had rather bury them by the score than see one of them apostatize.

"A great deal could be said concerning Brother Kimball, whose remains are here. He is not dead. His earthly tabernacle has fallen asleep to be prepared for this glorious resurrection that you and I live for. What can we say to one another? Live as he has lived; be as faithful as he has been; be as full of good works as his life has manifested to us. If we do so, our end will be peace and joy, and we will fall asleep as peacefully. I held my watch with one hand and fanned him with the other, while he breathed his last.

"For this family to mourn is perhaps natural; but they have not really the first cause to do so. How would you feel if you had a husband or a father that would lead you from the truth? I would to God that we would all follow him in his example in our faithfulness, and be as faithful as he was in his life. To his wives, his children, his friends, his brethren and sisters, to this family whom God **[508]** has selected from the human family to be his sons and daughters, I say let us follow his example. He has gone to rest. We can say of him all that can be said of any good man. The Lord selected him and he has been faithful and this has made him a great man; just as you and I can become if we will live faithful to our God and our religion. There is no man but what can do good if he chooses; and if he be disposed to choose the good and refuse the evil. If any man choose the evil he will dwindle, especially if he has been called to the holy Priesthood of the Son of God. Such a man will dwindle and falter, stumble and fall; and instead of becoming great and good, he will be lost in forgetfulness.

"We pay our last respects unto Brother Kimball, I can say to the congregation, we thank you for your attention. We are happy to see you here. It would be a pleasure to us if it would be prudent, and we had time, for you to see the corpse; but it would not be prudent and we have not the time. This, perhaps, will be a matter of regret to many of you; but you must put up with it. I want to say to every one who wishes to see Brother Heber again, live so that you will secure to yourselves a part in the first resurrection, and I promise you that you will meet him and shake hands with him. But if you do not live so, I can give you no such promise.

"Now, my friends, I feel to bless you; and the family, the wives and the children of Brother Heber C. Kimball. I bless you in the name of Jesus Christ. Will you receive the blessings which a father and husband has placed upon your heads? If you live for them you will enjoy them. I think he has never cursed one of his family; but his heart was full of blessings for them. He has blessed his brethren and sisters and neighbors and friends. His heart was full of blessings; but he was a scourge to the wicked and they feared him. Now, my friends, I cannot talk to you, my sore throat will not let me. But I feel to thank you for your kind attention here to-day, in paying our respects to the remains of Brother Kimball, and may God bless you. Amen." **[509]**

At the close of the President's remarks, the choir sang: "O my Father, Thou that dwellest," and Bishop Edwin D. Woolley pronounced the benediction.

The procession then returned, proceeding to the spot selected by President Kimball as the final resting place of his mortal remains. Here, beside the grave of his beloved Vilate, his body was entombed.

And now occurred a remarkable, though purely natural phenomenon. As the first clods of earth fell upon the coffin, the setting sun burst forth from his cloudy covering, shedding a golden halo of glory upon the scene, while instantaneously in the eastern horizon appeared a rainbow, the bright and beauteous token of promise, directly spanning the grave. It was no illusion; and as the last particles of mother earth were gathered above the still bosom that slept below, the rainbow dissolved.

---

So passed from earth the immortal part of him whom men named Heber C. Kimball; one of God's "noble and great ones," recalled with honor from the toils of time to share with Him the triumphs of eternity. Freed from his mortal prison-house of sorrow and of pain, his mission in this life completed, he sought once more the scenes and society of Home, in the realms of eternal rest.

> Past angels, Gods and sentinels, who guard
> The gates celestial, challengeless and free,
> That sovereign spirit soared unto its own;

By shouting millions welcomed back again,
With all his new-won laurels on his brow—
The meed of valor and of victory—
To exaltations endless as THE LIVES. **[510-11]**

# APPENDIX

A GLIMPSE OF THE GREAT BEYOND—THRILLING EXPERIENCE OF DAVID PATTEN KIMBALL LOST IN THE DESERT—COMMUNING WITH THE SPIRITS OF THE DEPARTED—DAVID PREDICTS HIS OWN DEATH AND THE DEATH OF FOUR OTHERS—THE FULFILLMENT

THE following narrative, under the caption of "A Terrible Ordeal," was originally published in a little volume called "Helpful Visions," the fourteenth book of the Faith-Promoting Series, issued from the office of the *Juvenile Instructor*, in 1887. It was edited then, as now, by the author of this work. Its relevancy to the present volume will be apparent as we proceed.

On the 22nd of November, 1883, David Patten Kimball, fourth son of Heber Chase and Vilate Murray Kimball, departed this life. Nearly two years before his death, he wrote to his sister Helen, in Salt Lake City, the letter from which the appended extract is taken. This letter was dated January 8th, 1882. David was then a resident of Jonesville, or Lehi, Arizona, three miles from Mesa, where the letter was written.

The experience related was of so remarkable a character as to meet with dubiety on the part of some, especially those inclined to be skeptical regarding spiritual manifestations. Some went so far as to ascribe the sights and scenes through which the narrator claimed to have passed, to the fevered fancy of a mind disordered by strong drink. Nor is this surprising, when it is remembered that even the Apostles of Jesus, on the day of Pentecost, were accused of being "drunken with new wine," when the power of the Spirit fell upon them and they "spake with tongues and prophesied." Skepticism is the same in all ages. What is here presented is the plain and simple testimony of an honest man, who firmly adhered to it till the day of his death, which occurred in literal fulfillment of things told him "while in the spirit."

Here is the excerpt from David's letter. The events described took place while he was returning home from a trip to Prescott, the capital of Arizona, in the early part of November, 1881:

"On the 4th of November, I took a very severe cold in a snow storm at Prescott, being clad in light clothing, which brought on pneumonia or lung fever. I resorted to Jamaica ginger and pepper [512] tea to obtain relief and keep up my strength till I could reach home and receive proper care. On the 13th I camped in a canyon ten miles west of Prescott, my son Patten being with me. We had a team of eight horses and two wagons. That night I suffered more than death. The next night we camped at Mr. McIntyre's, about twenty miles farther on. I stopped there two nights and one day, during which time I took nothing to drink but pepper tea. On the 16th we drove to Black's ranch, twenty-eight miles nearer home, and were very comfortably located in Mr. Black's house.

"About 11 p. m. I awoke and to my surprise saw some six or eight men standing around my bed. I had no dread of them but felt that they were my friends. At the same time I heard a voice which seemed to come from an eight square (octagon) clock on the opposite side of the house. It commenced talking and blackguarding, which drew my attention, when I was told to pay no attention to it. At this point I heard the most beautiful singing I ever listened to in all my life. These were the words, repeated three times by a choir: 'God bless Brother David Kimball.' I at once distinguished among them the voice of my second wife, Julia Merrill, who in life was a good singer. This, of course, astonished me. Just then my father commenced talking to me, the voice seeming to come from a long distance. He commenced by telling me of his associations with President Young, the Prophet Joseph and others in the spirit world, then inquired about his children, and seemed to regret that his family were so scattered, and said there would be a great reformation in his family inside of two years. He also told me where I should live, also yourself and others, and a great many other things. I conversed freely with father, and my words were repeated three times by as many different persons, exactly as I spoke them, until they reached him, and then his words to me were handed down in a like manner.

"After all this I gave way to doubt, thinking it might be only a dream, and to convince myself that I was awake, I got up and walked out-doors into the open air.

"I returned and still the spirit of doubt was upon me. To test it further I asked my wife Julia to sing me a verse of one of her old songs. At that, the choir, which had continued singing, stopped and she sang the song through, every word being distinct and beautiful. The name of the song was, 'Does He Ever Think of Me.'

"My eyes were now turned toward the south, and there, as in a large parquette, I beheld hundreds, even thousands, of friends and relatives. I was then given the privilege of asking questions and did so. This lasted for some time, after which the singing commenced again, directly above me. I now wrapped myself in a pair of blankets and went out-doors, determined to see the singers, but could see nothing, though I could hear the voices just the same. I returned to my couch and the singing, which was all communicative and instructive, continued until the day dawned. All this time the clock I have mentioned continued its cursing and blackguarding.

"Mr. and Mrs. Black were up in due time and got breakfast. I **[513]** arose and made my toilet, plain as it was, and took breakfast with my host and hostess. When my boy got ready to start, I went to pay my bill, and to my surprise heard a voice say or communicate: 'David Kimball has paid his bill.' When I got into the wagon, my guards, or those who were around my bed during the night, were still with me. My father had told me that he and President Young and others would visit me the next night.

"We drove on until about 11 a. m., when a host of evil spirits made their appearance. They were determined to destroy me, but I had power of mind to pay no attention to them, and let them curse all day without heeding them any more than possible. Five times they made a rush *en masse* to come into the wagon, the last one, where I was, but were kept off by my friends (spiritual). About 2 p. m. I told my boy to stop and we would water our horses. We used for this purpose barrels that we had along with us. After this I walked to the west side of my wagons, and looking to the east, I saw and heard the evil spirits floating in the air and chanting curses upon Brigham Young. I saw two other groups of the same kind, but did not hear them. Then I looked to the south, and the whole atmosphere was crowded with fallen spirits, or those who had not obtained bodies. Others who tried to torment me were spirits who had lived upon the earth. Having seen so many and being complimented by my guard for seeing so well, I became a little timid and asked my spiritual friends if they had any help. The answer was, 'Yes, plenty.' I now told my boy to drive on—he was entirely oblivious of all that was taking place with me—and soon after I was so exhausted that I fell into a troubled sleep and must have slept quite a little while.

"After I awoke I seemed to be left alone, and was lying on my back, when, all at once, I saw an old man and two young girls. This vision coming on me so suddenly, I was startled, and finding my guard gone, I jumped out of the wagon and got up on the spring seat beside my boy. But I could not get away from them. I was told in a coarse, gruff voice that the devil was going to kill me, and that he would follow me night and day until he destroyed me. I remembered the promise father had made me the night before—that he intended to visit me the next evening—and I nerved up and tried to pay no attention to my persecutors, but I must confess I was frightened.

"We arrived at Wickenburg just at sundown. The old man and the girls were tormenting and tantalizing me all the way, but never coming very near to me. We got supper and I took a room at Peeple's hotel and retired about 10 p. m. When everything was quiet my spirit friends, eight in number, returned and my tormentors were required to leave. Soon after, a glorious vision burst upon me. There were thousands of the Saints presented to me, many who had died at Nauvoo, in Winter Quarters, on the plains and in Utah.

"I saw Brother Pugmire and many others whom I did not know were dead. When my mother came to me it was so real and I was so overjoyed that I exclaimed aloud. So powerful was this vision that I **[514]** asked President Young, who seemed to be directing matters, three times to relieve me, or I would faint. A great many others passed in regular order; and I recognized nearly all of them, and was told the names of all I did not know. My father sat in a chair with his legs crossed and his hands clasped together, as we have often seen him. Those who passed along had hidden him from my view till then.

"This scene vanished, and I was then taken in the vision into a vast building, which was built on the plan of the Order of Zion. I entered through a south door and found myself in a part of the building which was unfinished, though a great many workmen were busy upon it. My guide showed me all through this half of the house, and then took me through the other half, which was finished. The richness, grandeur and beauty of it defied description. There were many apartments in the house, which was very spacious, and they differed in size and the fineness of the workmanship, according to the merits on earth of those who were to occupy them. I felt most at home in the unfinished part, among the workmen. The upper part of the house was filled with Saints, but I could not see them, though some of them conversed with me, my father and mother, Uncle Joseph Young and others.

"My father told me many things, and I received many reproofs for my wrong-doings. Yet he was loth to have me leave, and seemed to feel very badly when the time came for me to go. He told me I could remain there if I chose to do so, but I plead with him that I might stay with my family long enough to make them comfortable, to repent of my sins, and more fully prepare myself for the change. Had it not been for this, I never should have returned home, except as a corpse. Father finally told me I could remain two years, and to do all the good I could during that time, after which he would come for me; he mentioned four others that he would come for also, though he did not say it would be at the same time.

"On the 18th of November, about noon, we left Wickenburg (which is twenty-two miles from Black's Ranch where we stopped the previous night) on our journey home. I was exhausted from what I had experienced, and could feel my mind fast giving away, but I had confidence that I would reach home alive. There were no Elders to administer to me and no kind friends to look after my wants except my son, who had all he could do in looking after eight horses and two wagons. As my mind wandered and grew weaker, I was troubled and led by influences over which I had no power, and my friends, the good spirits, had all left me.

"We drove about twenty miles that afternoon, camping about eight miles from water, on the Salt River desert, which is about fifty miles across. During the fore part of the night I heard the horses running as though they were frightened. My son was asleep, but I got up and put my overcoat across my shoulders and went out where they were and got them quieted down. I was about to return to the wagon, when the same old man with gray whiskers, who had tormented me before, stepped between me and the wagons. He had a **[515]** long knife in his hand. I was frightened and fled, he pursuing me and telling me he was going to kill me. What I passed through I cannot describe, and no mortal tongue could tell. I wandered two days and three nights in the Salt River desert, undergoing the torments of the damned, most of the time, which was beyond anything that mortal could imagine.

"When my mind was restored, and the fever which had raged within me had abated, I found myself lying on a bleak hill-top, lost in the desert, chilled, hungered, thirsty and feeble. I had scarcely any clothing on, was barefooted, and my body full of cactus from head to foot. My hands were a perfect mat of thorns and briars. This, with the knowledge that no one was near me, made me realize the awful condition I was in. I could not walk. I thought I would take my life, but had no knife or any thing to do it with. I tried to cut an artery in my arm with a sharp rock I had picked up, hoping I might bleed to death, but even this was denied me. The wolves and ravens were hovering around me, anxiously awaiting my death. I had a long stick and I thought I would dig a deep hole and cover myself up the best I could, so the wolves would not devour my body until I could be found by my friends.

"On the night of the 21st, I could see a fire about twenty-five miles to the south, and felt satisfied that it was my friends coming after me. I knew the country where I was; I was about eight miles from houses where I could have got plenty of water and something to eat, but my strength was gone and my feet were so sore I could not stand up. Another long and dreary day passed, but I could see nothing but wolves and ravens and a barren desert covered with cactus, and had about made up my mind that the promise of two years' life, made by my father, was not to be realized. While in this terrible plight, and when I had just about given up all hope, my father and mother appeared to me and gave me a drink of water and comforted me, telling me I would be found by my friends who were out searching for me and that I should live two years longer as I had been promised. When night came I saw another fire a few hundred yards from me and could see my friends around it, but I was so hoarse I could not make them hear. By this time my body was almost lifeless and I could hardly move, but my mind was in a perfect condition and I could realize everything that happened around me.

"On the morning of the 23rd, at daylight, here they came, about twenty in all, two of my own sons, my nephew William, Bishop E. Pomeroy, John Lewis, John Blackburn, Wiley Jones and others, all friends and relatives from the Mesa, who had tracked me between seventy-five and one hundred miles. I shook hands with them, and they were all overjoyed to see me alive, although in such a pitiable plight. My own feelings I shall not undertake to describe. I told them to be very careful how they let me have water, at first. They rolled me up in some blankets and put me on a buck-board and appointed John Lewis to look after me as doctor and nurse. After I had taken a few swallows of water, I was almost frantic for more, but **[516]** they wisely refused to let me have it except in small doses every half hour.

"I had about seventy-five miles to ride home. We arrived at my place in Jonesville on the afternoon of the 24th of November, when my wife and family took charge of me and I was tenderly and carefully nourished. In a few days I was around again. I told my experience to President McDonald, Bishop Pomeroy, C. I. Robson and others, and most of them believed me, but my word was doubted by some. The report had gone out that I had been drinking and was under the influence of liquor. This was an utterly false report. I told them I had just two years to live, so they could tell whether it was a true manifestation or not.

"Now, Sister Helen, during the last twelve years I have had doubts about the truth of 'Mormonism,' because I did not take a course to keep my testimony alive within me. And the letter I wrote you last August, I suppose caused you to feel sorrowful, and you prayed for me and God heard your prayers. And our father and mother plead with the Lord in my behalf, to whom I will give the credit of this terrible but useful ordeal through which I have passed and only in part described, an ordeal which but few men have ever been able to endure and relate what I have seen and heard.

"Now, my dear sister, you have a little of your brother David's experience, and let who will think that I have been drinking. I know these things were shown to me for my own good, and it was no dream but a glorious and awful reality. My story is believed by my brethren who have respect for me. I will console myself with the knowledge I have obtained. Let the world wag on, and let hell and the devil keep up their warfare against the Saints of God—I know for myself that 'Mormonism' is true. With God's help, while I live I shall strive to do good, and I will see you before long and tell you all, as it never will be blotted out of my memory.

"With kind regards, in which my wife and children join, I remain, as ever,
"Your affectionate brother,
"DAVID P. KIMBALL."

ACCOUNT OF PATTEN KIMBALL AND OTHERS, REGARDING THE SEARCH FOR AND FINDING OF HIS FATHER.

THE following is an account furnished by Solomon F. Kimball, brother of David, who was in Mesa at the time of the occurrences described, and thoroughly conversant with the facts:

"On the morning of November 19th when Patten arose and missed his father, he thought probably he had gone out to hunt for the horses, and felt no uneasiness concerning him. He made a fire, prepared breakfast and waited some time, but could not see or hear him [517] anywhere. The horses came strolling into camp and were tied up, fed and watered. Patten then ate his meal, saddled a horse and rode back towards Wickenburg, until he came to a small place called Seymour on the Hassayampa, but could find out nothing of his father's whereabouts. He went back to the wagon and hunted the country close around camp but found nothing but his father's overcoat, which was a few hundred yards from the wagon. It being an old camp-ground, it was impossible to find his tracks. He finally came to the conclusion that he had gone towards home, so he hitched up his team and drove homeward until he came to Mr. Calderwood's at Agua Fria (Cold Water). At this place there was a well dug on the desert about twenty miles from Salt River. Patten had traveled about twenty-two miles before reaching this point, but was disappointed in not hearing anything of his father. He had traveled all night and Mr. Calderwood was up and around when he arrived. He related his story to him and was advised by him to leave his team there and take the best pair of horses, and hitch them to his buckboard and go on to the Mesa. Here he could get help to come and hunt for the missing man. The distance was forty miles, which would take all the rest of the day (the 20th). He acted on the advice, however, and arrived at his destination at 9 p. m. The news was circulated, and in less than two hours, twenty of the best and most experienced men at Mesa and Jonesville were on the road, taking Patten back with them. They also took a wagon to carry water and provisions, but most of them were on the best of horses. They had sixty miles to ride before beginning the search, which was accomplished by daylight next morning. After feeding their horses and eating a lunch they held a consultation and agreed to abide by the following rule. If any one of the party found his tracks he was to make a smoke and this would call the others in that direction. They then started out in different directions. They scoured the country until about noon, when Sern Sorenson and Charles Rogers found his tracks. They supposed they were about twelve miles from where he was lost, and about ten miles from Agua Fria, close to the main road on the south side. They soon gathered some brush and started a fire, putting on plenty of green weeds, etc., to cause a smoke, and soon attracted the attention of their comrades. His tracks were followed. They wound round and round, going in no particular direction. Some places he would cross his tracks eight or ten times in going one hundred yards, which made it quite difficult to follow.

"After spending a part of the afternoon in trailing him up, the tracks finally took a direct course leading to the north. By this time all the searching party were together.

"Another meeting was held and the plan adopted was for eight horsemen, four on each side of his tracks, to ride at a considerable distance apart, so as to cut off the track if it turned to the right or left, and two or three of the best trailers to keep on the tracks, while the buckboard and wagon followed up. These were out of sight most of the time, as very good time was made by the trailers after this plan was adopted. The ground was quite soft, and those on the trail would **[518]** gallop their horses for miles, but darkness soon put an end to their work for this day, a good thing for both men and animals.

"They had traveled upwards of one hundred miles in about twenty hours. They were working men and had plenty of strength to carry them through under all circumstances. They camped on the highest ground that could be found close by, and made a large fire which was kept up all night by those on guard.

"As soon as it was light enough to see the tracks, every man was at his place moving as fast as he could under the circumstances.

"This was the morning of the 22nd. One great drawback they met with that day was that when they would come to a deep ravine where water had run during rainy weather, the tracks would follow up sometimes for miles and then continue in the former direction. Places would frequently be found in the sand where the lost one had dug down for water with his hands. Now and then they would find a piece of his clothing and see places where he had run into the fox-tail cactus, cat's-claw and other thorny bushes. One place was found where he had broken off the limb of a tree for a walking stick. The party followed his tracks all day without stopping, only as they were obliged to, on account of losing the trail or from some other cause.

"Darkness overtook them again, but nothing could be seen or heard of the missing man. They slept on his tracks, keeping up a fire all night as before. His sons and others could not rest, and followed his tracks after dark by striking matches and putting them close to the ground to see if they might possibly find him. Some thought they could hear a sound, but it was so indistinct they could not discern the direction from which it came. It was indeed he who called, for they were then only a few hundred yards from him, but he was too hoarse to make them hear. On the morning of the 23rd at daylight his anxious friends were on his tracks, and had gone but a short distance when Charles Peterson saw him. He had a long staff in his hand, and had raised up as high as he could get, being on one knee and the other foot on the ground, and was stretching himself as far as he could and looking eagerly for their arrival. The crowd made a rush, and in a few seconds were with him, Bishop E. Pomeroy being the first. He was in his right mind and knew all present, and was glad to shake them by the hand, calling each by name. He was in good spirits and joked the boys frequently and gave them instructions to be careful in giving him water, etc. There was no water except in a canteen that had been reserved for his especial use. The company suffered themselves for want of water. They had traveled upwards of one hundred and fifty miles in less than forty-eight hours.

"David had dug a deep hole with his stick and had used his hands to move the dirt. He said he was digging his own grave. He was rolled in blankets and put on the buck board. All drove to the nearest houses, seven or eight miles distant, on the Hassayampa, where they refreshed themselves with water and something to eat. Soon they were on the road homeward. They drove to Mr. Calderwood's, which was about thirty miles, and stayed all night. He was very kind [519] to them and told them to help themselves to anything he had, such as hay, grain and food. He acted the man in every respect. A large number of men had also left Phoenix in search of David, among them being the U. S. Marshal, and others. White men and Indians were riding over the desert in every direction. Next morning the company" drove to Jonesville, forty miles distant, where they arrived about 3 p. m.

"David was carried into his house where he was surrounded by his loving wife and children.

"When he recounted his experience, he said that one thing that kept him from choking to death for want of water, was the damp pebbles which he dug from low ravines and held in his mouth. The Indians said that no human being could walk as far as he did and go without water four days and five nights and live. The party that found him said he must have walked at least seventy-five miles, some said one hundred.

"He testified that on the afternoon of the 22nd, his father and mother came and gave him water and told him that his friends would find him. His clothing was all gone except his under garments, which were badly torn.

"Before leaving home on his trip to Prescott, David had worked several days fixing up his books and accounts and burning up all useless papers, after which he told his wife that he felt different in starting on this trip from anything that he had ever felt before. He said it seemed to him that he should never return. He told her that if this proved to be the case, he had fixed his business up in such a shape that she would have no trouble, and would know as much about it as himself. She frequently spoke of these curious remarks, and felt considerably worried. When the news came that he was lost, all was plain to her, and she never expected to see him come home alive. Nothing could comfort her, and she watched night and day until he was brought home."

In the fall of 1883, David came to Salt Lake City on a visit to his sister Helen and others, to whom he confirmed with his own lips all that his letter contained, and told other things in relation to his marvelous experience. He declared solemnly that he was perfectly sober when he passed through the trying ordeal related, and bore a powerful testimony to the truth of "Mormonism." He seemed a little reticent to most of his relatives, and talked but little of his strange experience, feeling pained that so many doubted his word, and being unwilling to make himself obstrusive. When he bade his friends farewell before returning south, there was something in his manner which seemed to say that he was taking leave of them for all time. This visit was no doubt made with that prospect in view, for it was almost two years from the time he was lost on the desert. He [520] returned home to St. David, Cochise County, Arizona, and almost the next news that came from there was the tidings of his death.

A letter from his nephew, Charles S. Whitney, who was then living with him, written home on the 22nd of November, 1883, contained this:

"Uncle David died this morning at half-past six, easily, and apparently without a bit of pain. Shortly before he died, he looked up and called, 'Father, father!' All night long he had called for Uncle Heber. You remember hearing him tell how Grand-pa came to him when he was lost on the desert, and how he plead for two years more and was given that much longer to stay. Last Saturday, the day he was so bad, was just two years from the day he was lost, and to-day is just two years from the day his father and mother came to him and gave him a drink of water, and told him that his friends would find him and he should live two years longer. He knew that he was going to die, and bade Aunt Caroline good-bye day before yesterday."

During the last two years of his life David revealed to three of his personal friends the names of the four persons whom his father had told him in vision that he should come for, at or near the time when he would return for him. He exacted the promise from these friends (who, it seems, had some doubt regarding the divine nature of his vision, which doubt he was anxious to dispel) that they would not divulge the names of these individuals until after their death. The names, with respective dates of decease, are as follows:

William H. Hooper; died December 30th, 1882.
Horace K. Whitney; died November 22nd, 1884.
Heber P. Kimball; died February 8th, 1885.
William Jennings; died January 15th, 1886.

As will be seen, the longest interval given from the death of David P. Kimball is two years, one month and twenty-three days. William H. Hooper, who was the first of the four to go, preceded David by about eleven months, while Horace K. Whitney, the second to depart, followed him one year later to a day.

# INDEX

ADAM
    altar where, offered sacrifice after he was cast out of Eden, 132

ADAM-ONDI-AHMAN, 129, 130
    altar where Adam offered sacrifice, 132
    laid out a city at, 131, 132
    Saints flee to, for safety, 131
    temple block dedicated, 131, 132

AGENCY, 91, 92
    a third of the hosts of heaven followed Lucifer because of their, 91, 92
    destoying human, is Satan's peculiar mission, 91, 92

AITKEN, ROBERT, 99, 100
    Apostles visit, 179
    gives speech in "Zion's Chapel", 175
    Heber's prophecy to, 259
    prayed to know if the Lord would raise up his church in his day, 259

ALBION, JAMES
    baptized, 184, 185
    converted, 184
    daughters baptized, 184, 185
    Elders preach in his chapel, 184

ALCOHOL
    antagonistic to the spirit of the Lord, 101
    no public house or grocery keeps, in Nauvoo, 190, 191

AMERICA
    is the old world, not the new, 130

ANGELS, 274

APOSTASY
    the first step of, 276, 277

APOSTLES
    Brigham Young sustained as president of the Twelve, 149
    BY and HCK never lifted up their heels againt the Prophet, 204
    called to stand in their place next to the First Presidency, 192
    charges brought against, 64, 65
    desiring to bring wives on mission and HCK's advice against it, 102
    every individual who used an influence against the, apostatized, 65
    felt a severe mental shock on night of the martyrdom, 207
    general epistle to Saints in England, Scotland, Ireland, Wales, 189
    have all the power, priesthood, and authority that Joseph had, 273
    Joseph advises, to move to Commerce, 158
    Joseph and Hyrum teach the, 159, 160
    Joseph Smith commands, to go forth without purse or script, 164
    leave for America, 189
    meet in Manchester before leaving for America, 187-189
    Oliver Cowdery's "Charge to the Twelve", 57-60
    renewal of covenants by baptism, 229
    return home upon hearing of the death of the Prophet, 207
    sail for England, 169
    seeing the success in England, desire to thrust in their sickle, 102
    select inheritances in the Salt Lake Valley, 229
    stand in their place next to the First Presidency, 192
    take leave of Far West as appointed by revelation, 156
    the calling of the Twelve, 56-61
    the Lord calls men to fill the place of those who fell away, 119
    their first mission, 61-64
    three, are rejected and cut off and later reinstated, 117, 118
    to present JS as a candidate for presidency of the United States, 204
    vision of the Prophet concerning the Twelve, 68, 69

ATHEISM
    and being on the ocean, 79, 80

BENNETT, JOHN C.
    apostatized and excommunicated, 199
    he at once began to slander the Saints, 199
    missionaries sent to refute slanderous charges of, and others, 199, 200
    wormed himself into the good graces of the Saints, 199

BIRMINGHAM
    conference in, organized, 187

BLACK HAWK WAR, THE
    prophecy of Heber concerning Heber P. and Solomon F. Kimball in, 257, 258
BODY, THE, 275, 276
BRANNAN, SAMUEL, 213
BRIDGER, COLONEL
    would give a thousand dollars for first bushel of wheat, 226, 227
CAMP OF ISRAEL, THE, 212-215
    "traveling stakes of Zion", 216
    arrive at Fort Laramie, 225
    arrive at the valley of the Great Salt Lake, 227
    at the Black Hills, 226
    begins to move, 214
    Brigham Young's instructions to, 222
    cross the Platte river, 226
    destination of, 215, 216
    goes into Winter Quarters, 217
    Governor Boggs attempts to malign the character of the Mormons, 226
    Heber discovers a spring of clear water, 226
    Heber General-in-Chief, 215
    Heber's first address to, 214
    innocent amusement and recreation were encouraged, 215
    invention to measure distance, 223
    it was a faithful and pure people that journeyed westward, 215
    leaves Winter Quarters, 218
    notwithstanding their hardship a spirit of cheerfulness reigned, 214
    organization of camp perfected, 215
    organized as a military body agreeable to the will of the Lord, 221, 222
    provisions replenished by old enemies, 226
    reaches Grand Island, 224
    renewal of covenants by baptism, 229
    Saints reorganized preparatory to second journey to Salt Lake, 232
    six Missourians dress as Indians, 226
    some incidents of the journey west, 221-224
    the grand buffalo hunt, 224, 225
    the law of the Lord laid down in great strictness, 215
    the spirit of levity rebuked, 225
    the word and will of the Lord concerning, 218
CANNON, GEORGE Q.
    easier and more pleasant to love God than to break commandments, 293
    father introduced to the gospel, 170
    remarks made by, at the funeral of Heber C. Kimball, 292, 293
CHATBURN, 110-112
    "holy ground" where prophets had traveled to and dedicated, 120
    an occurence while passing through, 111, 112
    brethren endeavor to persuade HCK not to go to, 110
    considered a very wicked place, 110
    Heber preaches the first principles, 111
    Heber's farewell in, 120
    Heber's farewell letter to the Saints in, and Downham, 124, 125
    many converted, 111
CHURCH, THE
    a line of demarcation being drawn, 118
    God's work does not rest upon man, 207
    martyrdom did not destroy, but gave it fresh impetus, 209
    never imperilled half as much as when members sought for mammon, 116, 117
    never in a better state, 153
    renewal of covenants by baptism, 229
    Saints prepare for their removal to the Rocky Mountains, 211, 212
    the fierce flames of affliction, 132, 133
    the main body of, stood true after martyrdom, 209
    those who deny the faith and the progress of, 182
CIVIL WAR, THE
    Heber's prediction of, 250
CLARK, GENERAL
    speech of, at Far West, 137, 138
CLERGY
    afraid to meet missionaries face to face, 108
    most active in publishing falsehoods, 108
COWDERY, OLIVER
    excommunicated, 118
    his "Charge to the Twelve", 57-60
    sustained as assistant counselor, 117
CROOKED RIVER, THE BATTLE OF, 133, 134
DANIEL, THE PROPHET, 130

# INDEX

DAVIESS COUNTY, 131

DEATH, 276
life is short, and all are marching rapidly in the direction of, 290
makes no difference in the disposition of the spirit, 275

DESERET
Brigham Young elected Governor, 237
Heber gives some counsel to the Saints, 239, 240
Heber is Treasurer and Lieutenant-Governor of, 237
provisional government of the State of, organized, 237
the famine of 1856, 241-248

DEVILS
scene of, in Preston, 89, 90
why the Elders saw the, 90, 91

DISPENSATION, THE LAST
opening of, 19

DOWNHAM, 110-112
an occurence on the way to, 111, 112
brethren endeavor to persuade HCK not to go to, 110
considered a very wicked place, 110
Heber's farewell letter to the Saints in, and Chatburn, 124, 125
many converted, 111

ELIAS, 97-100
God had prepared the way for the advent of the Gospel, 98
the mantle of, falls on many shoulders, 97, 98
work both spiritual and temporal, 98

ELLSWORTH, DAVID, 61, 62

ELMER, JOHN, 62

ENGLAND
Apostles leave, early because of possible war between, and US, 186, 187
conference of the Church in, 122, 123
Elders see the Queen of, Heber blesses her, 185, 186
emigration of the Saints to America commenced, 180
harvest plenteous, but the laborers were few, 120-122
opposition great in some parts, 183
saints in, did not escape persecution, 170
the first opening made for the preaching of the Gospel in, 84, 85, 87

ENOCH, THE ORDER OF
a system of divine economy whereby the ancients were sanctified, 38
is the order of the celestial worlds, 53

EXODUS, THE, 212, 213

FAITH
of a little child, 55

FAITHFULNESS
will make any man a great man, 295, 296

FAMILY
a man who cannot save his, cannot save himself, 279
Heber urged increased watchcare over sons and daughters, 279

FAMINE OF '56, THE, 241-248
Heber is able to feed others from his own storehouses, 241, 242
Heber predicts, 239, 240
Heber takes his own counsel, 241
Heber's letters to son William descriptive of the famine, 243-248
Heber's strange piece of counsel to a man in need, 242, 243
Vilate a ministering angel, 242

FAR WEST
all taken prisoners by militia, 135
apostates point out men of influence to the mob, 136
Apostles take leave of, as appointed by revelation, 156
atrocities of the mob, 138, 139
Brigham and Heber set in order the Church in, 147
HCK and Brigham Young appointed captains of fifty, 135
HCK obliged to abandon new home and possessions to the mob, 130, 131
Heber forced to hide during the day, 154
Heber's denunciation of William McLellin and Heber's testimony, 136
Heber's prophecy of retribution, 139
Joseph Smith gives himself up, 135
mob again threatens the Saints in, 154
mob plunders, 135
more actions of the mob, 154, 155
origin of, persecution same as that of Jackson County troubles, 131
professed brethren who piloted mob in, 135, 136
recommenced laying the foundation of

Temple in, 156
Saints bore misfortunes cheerfully, 136, 137
Saints sign over property, 136, 137
speech of General Clark, 137, 138
the fall of, 135-139
the Priesthood was reorganized and the Church set in order, 117, 118

FIELDING, JAMES, 84, 85, 87, 99
Heber's prophecy with regard to, 259
prayed to know if the Lord would raise up his church in his day, 259
tells his congregation to pray to the Lord to send his servants, 85
turns against the Elders, 87-89

FIELDING, JOSEPH
called to preside over the Church in England, 122

FIELDING, MARY, 84
Heber's funeral address, 271, 272

FIRST PRESIDENCY, THE
Heber called to, as predicted by Hyrum Smith, 232
letter of, from Liberty jail, 147-149
reorganized, 231, 232
the Twelve stand in their place next to, 192

FORT LARAMIE, 225

FREE MASONRY, 25
Heber's rebuke of, 25

GATHERING
the noble and great ones gather in Ohio, 36, 37
the purpose of, 36, 37

GOD
not as far off as many imagine, 274
only, knows the why and the wherefore, 151

GOODSON, JOHN
burns Books of Mormon and Doctrine and Covenants and apostatizes, 102, 103

GOSPEL, THE
God had prepared the way for the advent of, 98
man demanding some evidence of the truth of, 172, 173
milk before meat, 106, 107
preaching, never depended upon man's learning or oratory, 113, 114
was chiefly to the poor and humble, 114

GRAND ISLAND, 224

GREAT SALT LAKE, THE, 215, 216
Brigham and Heber enter the valley of, 227, 228
exploring the valley, 228
Saints arrive at the valley of, 227

GREENE, JOHN P.
a vision of the warfare between the powers of good and evil, 27, 28

HAND-CART EMIGRATION, THE, 248-250
carrying the emigrants across the Sweetwater, 249
discourse by Heber on situation and suffering of emigrants, 249, 250
several hundred souls overtaken by winter, 248

HEAVEN, 273, 274

HELL, 273, 274, 276

HILL CUMORAH, THE, 33

HUMILITY
another name for strength, 114
learning is the parent of, 114
next to virtue, is the one grand requisite of a servant of God, 114

HYDE, ORSON
answers arguments advanced by a learned minister, 94
description of scene with the evil spirits, 90
gives farewell address to the Saints in England, 123
Heber and Hyrum Smith his mediators, 151, 152
his repentance and return to the Church, 151, 152
meets with Apostles on the way to Jerusalem, 187
preaches to passengers, 81
suspended from exercising the functions of his office, 157

INDIANS, THE
commenced to be troublesome, 230, 231
President Young's policy to win the friendship of, 231

JESUS CHRIST
the voice of the Shepherd, 110-112

KIMBALL, CHARLES S
regarding the experience of David

# INDEX

Patten Kimball, 306

KIMBALL, DAVID H.
  experience of, with his father, 257

KIMBALL, DAVID PATTEN
  account of Solomon F. Kimball regarding the experience of, 303-306
  birth of, 164
  Charles S. Whitney regarding the experience of, 306
  experience of, 298-306

KIMBALL, HEBER C.
  "the bald-headed chief", 230, 231
  a diamond in the rough, 26, 27
  a Free Mason, 25
  a great storm at sea, 127
  a man of as much integrity as any man who lived on earth, 294
  a soldier, 25
  a strange piece of counsel to a man in need, 242, 243
  a test is coming, 266
  a time of sickness and distress in the family of, 232, 233
  a vision of the warfare between the powers of good and evil, 27, 28
  always had good counsel to give, 292
  and Brigham Young sick at the start of their mission to England, 164-166
  and others see vision of gathering of the saints & other events, 29, 30
  and the gift of prophecy, 236
  and the study of grammar, 55, 56
  another encounter with evil spirits, 158, 159
  arrives back home in Kirtland from mission to England, 128
  attacked with cholera, 51
  attempts to cheer up members in Kirtland, 128, 129
  attempts to visit Parley P. Pratt and others in jail, 155, 156
  baptism of, 30, 31
  baptizes first persons into Church in a foreign land, 92
  beginning of friendship with Brigham Young, 28, 29
  birth of, 19, 20
  birth place of, 19, 20
  blessing and prophecy given to Parley P. Pratt and fulfilment, 84, 85
  by nature a colonizer with the elements of a great leader, 233
  call to preside over the mission in England, 73-76
  called as an Apostle, 56, 57
  called on mission to refute slanderous reports of John Bennett, 199, 200
  called to the First Presidency as predicted by Hyrum Smith, 232
  commanded to take Sarah Noon as a plural wife, 197
  continually engaged in the work of the ministry, 115
  conversion of, 29, 30
  daughter Helen Mar given to the Prophet as a plural wife, 198
  death of, 282-285
  death of Heber's parents, 26
  death of Vilate, 280, 281
  departure for Liverpool, 123, 124
  departure for mission to England, 76-78
  digest of letters of, and Lyman Wight to the Prophet, 204, 205
  discourse on situation and suffering of hand-cart emigrants, 249, 250
  discovers a spring of clear water, 226
  dream in England of swimming in a great water, 83
  dream of John F. Boynton and the panther, 73
  dream of Joseph while crossing the ocean, 80
  dream of man lending Heber a lot of land, 95, 96
  dream of the field of grain and the large bull, 109, 110
  early hardships, 22
  early incidents in the life of, 20-22
  everywhere honored and beloved, 258
  exhortations to the youth, 201, 202
  expressions in honor of, at his passing, 284, 285
  faithful but fruitless attempts to get brethren released, 149, 150
  family, of makes it safely to Illinois and is taken care of, 156, 157
  farewell letter to the Saints in Chatburn and Downham, 124, 125
  feelings while crossing the ocean, 79, 80
  feels his weakness at hearing of mission call to England, 74
  first address to the Camp of Israel, 214
  first child blessed in Great Britain, 103
  funeral address and tribute to Mary Fielding Smith, 271, 272
  funeral of, 285-297

# INDEX

gains favor with the captain and passengers, 127
gems from the teachings of, 271-279
General-in-Chief of the Camp of Israel, 215
given the gift of tongues in order to preach to Swiss emigrants, 70
gives description of the "Cock Pit", 101
gives famous "clay in the hands of the potter" sermon, 200
gives farewell address to the Saints in England, 123
gives history of mission to the Saints at Adam-Ondi-Ahman, 129
gives report of branches raised up during his former mission, 172-174
has dream that he needs to go back to Preston, 96
HCK with others attacked by evil spirits, 89, 90
healed by the Prophet, 75
heals a dying child, 81
hears of Joseph and the brethren had escaped, 155
Heber's "baptism of fire", 31
Heber's attempt to wash his clothes, 45
Heber's denunciation of William McLellin and Heber's testimony, 136
Heber's farewell in Chatburn, 120
Heber's only source of consolation during Kirtland difficulties, 72, 73
Heber's rebuke of Masons, 25
Heber's search for God, 27-30
Heber's temperament, 26
helped carry the Prophet's burdens, 292
hireling priests find fault and threaten missionaries, 103
his character and appearance, 23, 25
his lone mission, 69-71
his was the Savior's lineage, 112
how others remembered him, 269-271
in danger of being tarred and feathered, 155, 156
in Liverpool sees wide distinction between rich and poor, 82
instructions to his family before he left Winter Quarters, 220
kills a buffalo, 224, 225
Kimball family moves to Ohio, 34, 35
leaps onto shore, 82
learns of the birth of Heber P., 62
leaves for home at end of mission, 189
letter to the Millennial Star, 189-192
letter to wife about Apostles's desire to bring wives on mission, 102
letter to wife from London, 181, 182, 184
letter to Willard Richards in Bedford, 104, 105
letters to son William descriptive of the famine of '56, 243-248
Lord speaks to the mind of, in Far West, 150
made a chaplain of the Nauvoo Legion, 192
many sorrow in learning of the death of, 284, 285
marries Vilate, 22, 23
meeting the Prophet and the Saints at Nauvoo, 190
meets Joseph Smith, 34
meets Vilate, 22, 23
miraculously supplied with money, 167, 168
motive to leave on his mission to England, 79
moves from Kirtland to Missouri, 129
names of his wives and children, 251-255
never wavered, 293
no gloom in the death of, just calm, peaceful and sweet, 282, 284, 292, 293
no truer friend had Brigham Young than, 209
obliged to abandon new home and possessions to the mob, 130, 131
obtains license to preach, 105, 106
on "Time and Eternity", 277, 278
on the cultivation of our spirit, 273
on the importance of having light and knowledge direct from God, 268, 269
on the location of heaven and hell, 273, 274
one of the foremost who redeemed and beautified the barren waste, 233
ordained an Elder, 32
parentage of, 20
performs a task never before done in that country, 69, 70
phrenological chart of, 192-194
poisoned by doctor and life preserved by Brigham Young, 166, 167
power as a speaker well recognized, 200
prayer and, 256
prays for and blesses family before departing on mission, 76, 77
preach the first principles, 104, 105
prediction concerning Nauvoo, 158

# INDEX

prediction concerning Thomas Webster and its fulfillment, 125, 126
predicts his mission to Europe with Willard Richards, 75, 76
predicts the Garrick will arrive at New York first, 127, 128
prophecies that Moon family will receive Gospel, 107
prophecy about Willard Richards' wife and fulfilment, 96, 97
prophecy and counsel to Mary Ann and Margaret Heaton Topping, 259, 260
prophecy concerning Abram A. and Isaac A. Kimball, 252, 253
prophecy concerning Mr. Fielding and Mr. Aitken, 259
prophecy concerning Peter, the child of promise, 253
prophecy concerning recovery of Brigham Young, 260
prophecy concerning the Salt Lake Temple and persecution, 239
prophecy of own death, 280
prophecy of retribution, 139
prophecy of, concerning Heber P. and Solomon F. Kimball, 257, 258
prophecy that "States goods" will be sold cheaper in Salt Lake, 235, 236
purchases land in Commerce and begins to build a house, 160
receives patriarchal blessing, 70
reflections on the poor of England, 121
reminiscences of, as told by others, 258-271
requested to tarry and help families out of Missouri, 149
sees and blesses the Queen of England, 185, 186
some counsel to the Saints in the early times of Utah, 239, 240
son David Patten is born, 164
stricken with cholera in London, 179
tested by the Prophet, 196
tests James Lawson, 263
thanks the Lord for a safe trip to England, 82
the "horns of Joseph", 262
the "peace-maker", 138, 139
the famine of 1856, 239-248
the mob and the Abolitionist, 63
the prayer of his heart, 112
the ship which lost its reckoning, 80, 81
Treasurer and Lieutenant-Governor of Deseret, 237
visits branch in Walkerfold, 101, 102
visits his native state, 62
visits the birth place of his mother, 63, 64
visits the brethren in Liberty jail often, 149
when a man is put into office, 261
why he did not fear, 272, 273
with Brigham sets in order the Church at Far West, 147
writes to the Church in England, 152, 153
Zion's camp a trial of faith to prove worthiness of, 37

KIMBALL, HEBER P.
Heber learns of the birth of, 62

KIMBALL, SOLOMON F.
account of, regarding the experience of David Patten Kimball, 303-306

KIMBALL, VILATE
a few gems by, 202, 203
a ministering angel during the famine of '56, 242
a time of sickness and distress in the family of, 232, 233
baptism of, 31
daughter Helen Mar given to the Prophet as a plural wife, 198
death of, 280, 281
funeral of, 280, 281
letter to HCK describing the scenes taking place in Nauvoo, 205, 206
marries Heber, 22, 23
meets Heber, 22, 23

KIMBALL, WILLIAM H.
Heber's letters to, descriptive of the famine of '56, 243-248

KINGDOM OF GOD, THE
no man can build up, except God be with him, 113, 114

KIRTLAND, 33, 34
Brigham Young had to flee, because of enemies, 118
condition of the Church in, 169
financial crash of 1837, 72
HCK and company arrive in, 34
Heber attempts to cheer up members in, 128, 129
members left in, were weak in faith, 128, 129
no longer a fit abiding place for the

Saints, 118
no quorum in the Church exempt from influence of apostasy, 73, 74
one's life was in danger if he spoke in defense of Joseph Smith, 72, 73
persecution and mobocracy in, 35, 36
spirit of speculation becomes prevalent in the Church, 71-73
the Prophet and Sidney Rigdon forced to flee, 118
the Prophet blamed for financial catastrophe, 72, 73

KIRTLAND SAFETY SOCIETY, THE, 72
why the Kirtland Bank failed, 72

KIRTLAND TEMPLE, THE
building of, 54, 55
dedication of, 66, 67
Heber's description of, 65-67
John the beloved seen, 67
spirit of prophecy poured out, 67-69
the Prophet commands the saints to prepare themselves, 67
the solemn assembly, 67
the whole church united in the building of, 54, 55

LAW OF CONSECRATION, THE
a system of divine economy whereby the ancients were sanctified, 38

LAWSON, JAMES
tested by Heber as Heber was tested by the Prophet, 263

LEVITY
the spirit of, rebuked, 225

LIBERTY
several in, friendly to the brethren and revolted at the mob, 154

LIBERTY JAIL
Heber requested to assist the brethren in jail, 149
Heber's faithful but fruitless attempts to get brethren released, 149, 150
letter of First Presidency from, 147-149

LONDON
first baptism in, 178
first, conference was organized, 186, 187
metropolis of the world and depot of wickedness, 185
Satan doing all he could in opposition, 185
second convert in, 178, 179
the Elders hold open-air meetings in Tabernacle Square, 176-178
the first convert, 176

LONGTON
ten baptized in a village near, 114, 115

LYMAN, AMASA
called on mission to refute slanderous reports of John Bennett, 199, 200

MACKLESFIELD, 183

MAMMON
Church never imperilled half as much as when members sought for, 116, 117

MANCHESTER
became headquarters of the British Mission, 169, 170
branch grew rapidly, 169, 170
first general conference at, 174, 175
second general conference at, 180

MANTI TEMPLE, THE
Brigham Young shows the spot where Moroni dedicated the land, 261
Heber prophecies that a Temple would be built and where, 260, 261

MARRIAGE, PLURAL
a prime cause of troubles culminating in the Prophet's martyrdom, 199
angel with a flaming sword commanded Joseph to establish, 194
how Vilate was converted to the doctrine of, 196-198
no family in Israel better exemplified the nature and purpose of, 250, 251, 255, 256
Prophet first reveals, to a chosen few, 195, 196
the Prophet tests Heber, 196
to test the faith of the Saints as never before, 194-196

MARSH, THOMAS B.
becomes president of the Twelve, 61
ordained an Apostle, 57

MATTHEWS, TIMOTHY R., 99

MCDONALD, A. F.
Heber gives wife of, handkerchief and says it will be a blessing, 267, 268
Heber predicts wife's future pregnancy and the child's gender, 267

MCLELLIN, WILLIAM, 135, 136

MEMORIAL TO THE MISSOURI LEGISLATURE, 140-146

how Missouri redressed the wrongs, 146, 147
MENDON BRANCH, THE, 31
MERCY
be merciful and you shall obtain mercy, 151
MILLENNIAL STAR, THE
a monthly periodical started, 171
Heber's letter to, 189-192
MILLER, ELEAZER, 42
MISSOURI
how, redressed the wrongs, 146
memorial to, Legislature, 140-146
MOON, MATTHIAS
conversion of family of, 107, 108
HCK baptizes remainder of family, 108
HCK prophecies that Moon family will receive Gospel, 107
MORMON BATTALION, THE, 216, 217
Amasa Lyman leads a detachment of, to the Salt Lake Valley, 228
Brigham and Heber go and meet, in the pueblo valley, 228, 229
organized and set off, 217
recruiting sergeants, 217
return to Winter Quarters, 229-231
the call for five hundred able-bodied men, 216
the Twelve meet in council with the officers of, 229
NAUVOO
after martyrdom Brigham and Heber were compelled to hide, 209, 211
Apostles share details of mission to a gathering of the Saints, 191
Apostles surprised to see such improvements while away, 190
epidemic of disease in, and miraculous display of divine power, 163, 164
gathering place of the Saints, 158
Heber's prediction concerning, 158
Joseph Smith flees, 206
no public house or grocery that keeps spirits in, 190, 191
Saints coming to, from all parts of continent daily and hourly, 190
Saints gathering to, had been "baptized by fire", 158
Saints in, are generally in good health and spirits, 190
Saints left in, were driven from their homes, 217, 218
some dreadfully tried in their faith, 206
the inciters of opposition were the Laws, Fosters, and Higbees, 209
Vilate's letter to HCK describing the scenes taking place in, 205, 206
NAUVOO EXPOSITOR, THE
burning the press of, 205
NAUVOO LEGION, THE
called out to celebrate independence, 190
Heber and Brigham made chaplains in, 192
NAUVOO TEMPLE, THE
in due time completed and dedicated, 211
laying of the capstone, 211
NEW JERUSALEM, THE
capital city of the kingdom of God, 38
we will have to become much more united before building, 279
OBEDIENCE
blessings flow from, to authority and evil from disobedience, 279
easier and more pleasant to love God than to break commandments, 293
PAGE, JOHN E.
ordained an Apostle, 119
PATTEN, DAVID W.
death of, 133, 134
PAUL, 114
PAWNEE INDIANS, 222, 223
PERPETUAL EMIGRATION FUND, THE, 237
PRATT, ORSON, 128
stays in New York, 189
work firmly established in Scotland under presidency of, 179, 180
PRATT, PARLEY P., 128, 155, 156
blessing and prophecy given to, by HCK and its fulfilment, 84, 85
composes poem, 188
escapes from prison as Heber prophesied, 160
retort to Sidney Rigdon's claim, 208
returns from mission to England, 220, 221
PRESTON
a general election of parliament, 83, 84
baptized members now confirmed, 94
branch in, organized, 94

branch in, was the first branch organized in a foreign land, 94
Christmas conference, 112, 113
Church conference at, 171
Rev. Fielding turns against the Elders, but not his congregation, 87-89
Saints in, commence holding meetings in the "Cock Pit", 101
Spirit of the Lord leads Elders to, 83
the Church in, becomes numerous, 104
the first opening made for the preaching of the Gospel in Europe, 85, 87

PRIDE
is the offspring of ignorance, 114

PROPHECY, THE GIFT OF, 236

PROPHETS
the mission and destiny of ancient and modern, are the same, 19

PUNISHMENT
purpose of divine, is to purify, 39

RELICS, 277

RELIEF SOCIETY, THE
inception of, 200-202

RESURRECTION, THE, 274, 275

REVELATION
iconoclast of tradition, 195

REWARD, 126, 127

RICHARDS, JENNETTA
convinced of the truth and is baptized, 93
HCK's prophecy about, being Willard Richards wife and fulfilment, 96, 97
sorrowful at her father's refusal to let HCK preach in chapel, 96
the first confirmation in England, 93

RICHARDS, JOHN
closes the doors of his chapel to HCK, 95, 96
displays no bitterness of spirit, 95
invites Elder Kimball to preach to his congregation, 94, 95
Lord softens heart, 96
on seeing HCK in his house, orders him to leave, 172

RICHARDS, WILLARD
HCK's prophecy about future wife and fulfilment, 96, 97
letter to, from HCK while in Bedford, 104, 105
obtains license to preach, 105, 106
ordained an Apostle, 171

RIGDON, SIDNEY, 129
appointed delegate to Washington, 157
faith beginning to fail under the terrible tension of trial, 153, 154
offer's himself as the "guardian" to the Church, 207, 208
released on bail, 153, 154
response to Heber's prediction concerning Nauvoo, 158
set a day apart for choosing a guardian for the Church, 208
the Church sustains, as counselor to Joseph Smith, 117

ROCKWELL, PORTER
hunting buffalo, 224, 225

RUSSELL, ISAAC
falls away, 152
leading saints astray, 153

SALT LAKE TEMPLE, THE
corner stone laid, 237
Heber's consecration prayer at cornerstone laying of, 237-239

SCOTLAND
opened to the work, 170
work firmly established in, 179, 180

SEAGULLS, MIRACLE OF THE, 233, 235
aftermath, 235, 236

SMITH, GEORGE A.
called on mission to refute slanderous reports of John Bennett, 199, 200
ordained an Apostle, 119, 156
remarks made by, at the funeral of Heber C. Kimball, 290-292
states that Heber had a power and influence over people, 291

SMITH, HYRUM, 129
sustained as assistant counselor, 117

SMITH, JOHN
sustained as assistant counselor, 117

SMITH, JOSEPH, 90, 129
after death of, the saints felt like sheep without a shepherd, 207
angel commands, to establish plural marriage, 194, 195
assassination of, 206, 207
blamed for financial catastrophe in Kirtland, 72, 73
BY and HCK never lifted up their heels

# INDEX

against, 204
called a "fallen prophet" by men who have been his friends, 73
candidate for presidency of the United States, 204
commands the Twelve to go forth without purse or script, 164
contest with Satan and his power, 159
escapes from jail, 155
forced to flee Kirtland, 118
gives endowments to 1st Presidency, Twelve and Presiding Bishops, 67
gives himself up at Far West, 135
HCK and Brigham Young visit, in Richmond jail, 139
heals a multitude of sick, 163, 164
Heber and Vilate's daughter Helen Mar given to, as a plural wife, 198
Heber helped carry the Prophet's burdens, 292
Lord reveals to, that "something new" needed to save the church, 73, 74
martyrdom did not destroy the Church but gave it fresh impetus, 209
on teaching the mysteries of the kingdom, 195
plural marriage was a cause of troubles culminating in death of, 199
presented to the Church to see if they still sustained him, 117
tests Heber, 196
the crisis of choosing successor to, 207-209
vision of, concerning the Twelve, 68, 69

SMITH, SR., JOSEPH
gives HCK a patriarchal blessing, 70
sustained as assistant counselor, 117

SMITHIES, MARY, 103
"she shall live until she becomes a mother in Israel", 103
first child blessed in Great Britain, 103
later becomes wife of HCK, 103

SNOW, ELIZA R.
composed a hymn for the funeral of Heber C. Kimball, 287

SNOW, LORENZO
arrives in London to take charge of Church there, 186

SPIRITUALISM, 271

TAYLOR, JOHN
ordained an Apostle, 119

preaches sermon in Kirtland, 169
remarks made by, at the funeral of Heber C. Kimball, 288-290
we all have to die, but are we prepared for it, 289, 290

TEMPERANCE REFORM, THE, 101
a work preparatory to the preaching of the Gospel, 101
preaching in the "Cock Pit", 101
the Elders attend and speak at a few, meetings, 175, 176

TIME AND ETERNITY, 277, 278

TRUTH
all, is new to the ignorant, 106
human nature to oppose that which is new, 106
much that is true, is not expedient, 106, 107
must be inculcated by gradual degrees, 107

UNITY, 272, 278, 279
Lord hates false witnesses and those that sow discord, 65

UNIVERSE
one vast symbolism, 97, 98

UNRIGHTEOUS DOMINION, 91, 92

UTAH WAR, THE, 250

WALES
work in, 182

WALKERFOLD
HCK visits branch in, 101, 102

WALMESLEY, THOMAS
wife is healed, 92, 93

WEBSTER, THOMAS, 125, 126

WELLS, DANIEL H.
remarks made by, at the funeral of Heber C. Kimball, 293, 294

WHITMER, DAVID
excommunicated, 118, 119

WHITNEY, HORACE K.
account of the grand buffalo hunt, 224, 225
journal entry of Heber's instructions to his family, 220

WHITNEY, NEWEL K., 117

WIGHT, LYMAN
digest of letters of, and Heber C. Kimball to the Prophet, 204, 205

WILLIAMS, FREDERICK G.

fails to receive sustaining vote as counselor to the Prophet, 117
WINTER QUARTERS, 217
Camp of Israel leaves, 218
some Church leaders and the Mormon Battalion return to, 229-231
WOODRUFF, WILFORD
fight with the "Prince of Darkness", 180, 181
heals sick children and uses handkerchief in administration, 163, 164
marvelous success in Staffordshire and Herefordshire, 170
ordained an Apostle, 119, 156
WOOLWICH
branch organized, 186
fast developing into an important branch, 186
Heber preaches in, 185
YOUNG, BRIGHAM, 31
"Bogus Brigham" incident, 211
and Heber sick at the start of their mission to England, 164-166
beginning of friendship with HCK, 28, 29
called on mission to refute slanderous reports of John Bennett, 199, 200
cares for Heber when poisoned, 166, 167
death of wife Miriam, 32
elected Governor of Deseret, 237
feels eternity resting upon him, 230
forced to flee Kirtland, 118
gives address at Vilate Kimball's funeral, 280, 281
made a chaplain of the Nauvoo Legion, 192
mantle of Joseph falls on, 208, 209
miraculously supplied with money, 167, 168
moves to Ohio, 34, 35
no truer friend had, than Heber C. Kimball, 209
present when Heber passed away, 282, 284
remarks made by, at the funeral of Heber C. Kimball, 294-296
shows where Moroni dedicated the grounds for the Manti Temple, 261
speaks in tongues, 34
sustained as president of the Twelve, 149

transfigured in front of thousands of Saints, 208, 209
with Heber sets in order the Church at Far West, 147
Zion's camp a trial of faith to prove worthiness of, 37
YOUTH
Heber's exhortations to, 201, 202
ZELPH, 43, 44
ZION
a work of such magnitude requires preparation, 53
capital city of the kingdom of God, 38
is liberty, equality, fraternity, and righteousness, 38
Jackson County site of the city of, and the temple of God, 38
mission of the saints is to prepare the world for the return of, 38
must be built on the principles of the celestial kingdom, 52, 53
redemption of, must needs come by power, 49, 52
saints begin to gather to, 38
saints did not live up to the higher law required of them, 39
the two Zions shall be one, 38
why, was not redeemed, 52-54
ZION OF ENOCH
counterpart to modern Zion, 38
the two Zions shall be one, 38
to return as a leaven of righteousness, 38
ZION'S CAMP
a rebellious spirit in some and its consequence, 41
a trial of faith, 37
a woman warns Luke Johnson, 46
attack of cholera, 48, 50-52
baptism of Dean Gould, 46
continually harassed by spies, 41
Fishing River revelation, 48, 49
God's command, 39
Heber attacked with cholera, 51
Heber returns home, 52
Heber's attempt to wash his clothes, 45
Heber's own words of the pilgrimage, 39-52
in peril and threatened all the time, 46
Joseph predicts a scourge upon the camp because of unruly spirit, 44
Joseph shows the folly of their wickedness, 44

many attempts by people to ascertain the number of men in, 42, 43
meeting with Bishop Partridge, 45, 46
preaching on the Sabbath near Jacksonville, 42
questions put to the men by three gentlemen, 43
saved by a storm, 46, 47
sheriff Neil Gilliam, 48
the camp reorganized, 45
the change of heart of Colonel Sconce and his men, 47, 48
those willing to give their lives in, ordained to the ministry, 56
what did, accomplish?, 52, 54
Zelph, 44

Made in the USA
Monee, IL
26 May 2023